Being Maasai

EASTERN AFRICAN STUDIES

Abdul Sheriff
Slaves, Spices & Ivory in Zanzibar

Abdul Sheriff & Ed Ferguson (Editors)
Zanzibar Under Colonial Rule

Isaria N. Kimambo
Penetration & Protest in Tanzania

T.L. Maliyamkono & M.S.D. Bagachwa
The Second Economy in Tanzania

B.A. Ogot & W.R. Ochieng' (Editors)
*Decolonization & Independence in Kenya**

Tabitha Kanogo
Squatters & The Roots of Mau Mau 1905–1963

David W. Throup
Economic & Social Origins of Mau Mau 1945–1953

Frank Furedi
The Mau Mau War in Perspective

David William Cohen & E.S. Atieno Odhiambo
Siaya

Bruce Berman & John Lonsdale
Unhappy Valley

Bruce Berman
Control & Crisis in Colonial Kenya

Thomas Spear & Richard Waller (Editors)
Being Maasai

James de Vere Allen
Swahili Origins

Holger Bernt Hansen & Michael Twaddle (Editors)
Uganda Now
Changing Uganda

Michael Twaddle
Semei Kakungulu
*and the Origins of Uganda**

Bahru Zewde
A History of Modern Ethiopia
1855–1974

*forthcoming

Being Maasai

Ethnicity & Identity
in East Africa

Edited by
THOMAS SPEAR
&
RICHARD WALLER

James Currrey
LONDON

Mkuki na Nyota
DAR ES SALAAM

EAEP
NAIROBI

Ohio University Presss
ATHENS

James Currey Ltd
54b Thornhill Square, Islington
London N1 1BE, England

Mkuki na Nyota Publishers
P.O. Box 4205, Dar es Salaam

East African Educational Publishers
PO Box 45314
Nairobi, Kenya

Ohio University Press
Scott Quadrangle
Athens, Ohio 45701, USA

© James Currey Ltd 1993
First published 1993

93 94 95 96 97 5 4 3 2 1

British Library Cataloguing in Publication Data

Being Maasai : Ethnicity and Identity in
East Africa. — (Eastern African Studies Series)
I. Spear, Thomas   II. Waller, Richard   III. Series
967.6

ISBN 0-85255-215-7 (Paper)
ISBN 0-85255-216-5 (Cloth)

Library of Congress Cataloging-in-Publication Data Available

ISBN 0-8214-1045-8 (Paper)
ISBN 0-8214-1029-6 (Cloth)

Typeset in 10/11 pt Baskerville by Colset Pte Ltd, Singapore
Printed and Bound in Great Britain by Villiers Publications, London N6

Contents

I. *Introduction*

THOMAS SPEAR

II. *Becoming Maasai*

v

Contents

Maps, Figures
&
Illustrations

vii

Maps, Figures & Illustrations

Contributors

David J. Campbell is Professor of Geography and African Studies at Michigan State University. He received his doctorate from Clark University. He has written numerous papers and articles on strategies for coping with drought and food deficits and on rural development and land use in semi-arid areas of Africa.

Elliot Fratkin received his doctorate from Catholic University and teaches anthropology at Penn State University. He has written on pastoral production, prophets, and gender among the Rendille, Samburu, and Ariaal peoples of northern Kenya and is the author of *Surviving Drought and Development: Ariaal Pastoralists of Northern Kenya* (1991).

John G. Galaty received his doctorate in anthropology from the University of Chicago and is Associate Professor of Anthropology and Director of the Center for Society, Technology, and Development at McGill University. He has written extensively on Maasai culture and co-edited several volumes on pastoralism and development, including *The World of Pastoralism* (1990) and *Herders, Warriors, and Traders* (1991).

Donna Klumpp received her doctorate in anthropology from Columbia University. She has done extensive research on Maasai art and aesthetics, particularly beadwork, as well as comparative work on East African costume and ornament. She is currently Academic Director of Friends' World College in Machakos, Kenya.

Corinne A. Kratz received her doctorate in anthropology from the University of Texas at Austin and has conducted extensive fieldwork in Kenya on the Okiek. She is the author of numerous articles on Okiek identity, art, language, and history, as well as a Smithsonian Institution monograph on initiation ceremonies, and is currently researching Okiek marriage arrangements.

Contributors

John Lamphear received his doctorate in history from the School of Oriental and African Studies (SOAS) and has published on pastoralists in northern Kenya and Uganda, including *The Traditional History of the Jie of Uganda* (1976) and *The Scattering Time: Turkana Responses to the Imposition of Colonial Rule* (1991). He is currently Professor of History at the University of Texas at Austin.

Neal Sobania received his doctorate from the School of Oriental and African Studies (SOAS) and is Associate Professor of History and Director of International Education at Hope College in Michigan. He is the author of *A Background History to the Mount Kulal Region of Northern Kenya* (1979) and *Man, Millet, and Milk: Shifting Ethnicity in Pre-Colonial Kenya* (in press), and co-editor of a modern history of Kenya (in preparation).

Gabriele Sommer, M.A., is a graduate student in the African Studies Program at the University of Bayreuth, Germany. She has carried out research on Cushitic as well as minority languages and is currently conducting a project on processes of language shift among the Yei-speaking people of southern Africa. She is the author of *A Survey of Language Death in Africa* (in press).

Thomas Spear received his doctorate in history at the University of Wisconsin at Madison. He has written histories of *Zwangendaba's Ngoni*, the Mijikenda (*The Kaya Complex*), eastern and central Kenya (*Kenya's Past*), and *The Swahili* (with Derek Nurse); and is currently completing a social and economic history of the Meru and Arusha peoples of Tanzania. Formerly at La Trobe University and Williams College, he is now Professor of History at the University of Wisconsin-Madison.

Paul Spencer received his doctorate from Oxford and is Reader in African Anthropology at the School of Oriental and African Studies, London University. He is the author of *The Samburu* (1965), *Nomads in Alliance* (1973), and *The Maasai of Matapato* (1988), has edited volumes on the anthropology of dance and ageing, and is currently working on *Models of the Maasai*.

J.E.G. Sutton, FSA, took his first degrees at Oxford and his doctorate at Makerere. He is Director of the British Institute in Eastern Africa, the centre for historical and archaeological research in Nairobi. He has taught at the University of East Africa (Dar es Salaam) and was later Professor and Head of Archaeology at the University of Ghana. He is the author of numerous articles on East African agricultural and pastoral history and *Archaeology of the Western Highlands of Kenya* (1973).

Telelia Chieni was born in Matapato c. 1913 and has lived her whole life in one of the Maasai areas least affected by change. A mature and confident woman, she related to Paul Spencer in 1976 her experiences as a girl, the senior of seven wives of Masiani, the mother of two daughters and four sons, and the grandmother of thirteen grandchildren.

Contributors

Rainer Vossen lectures in the Department of African Linguistics at the University of Bayreuth, Germany, having received his doctorate from the University of Cologne and his Habilitation from Bayreuth. He has published widely on Nilotic, Maa, Khoisan, and Bantu language history, including *The Eastern Nilotes* (1982), *Towards a Comparative Study of the Maa Dialects of Kenya and Tanzania* (1988), *Patterns of Language Knowledge and Language Use in Ngamiland, Botswana* (1988), *New Perspectives on the Study of Khoisan* (1988), and *Die Khoe-Sprachen* (in press).

Richard Waller received his doctorate from Cambridge University, was Senior Lecturer in History at Chancellor College, Malawi, and is currently Assistant Professor of History and International Relations at Bucknell University, Pennsylvania. He has published extensively on Maasai history, ecology and socio-economic relations in the nineteenth and twentieth centuries and is currently working on *Studies in the History of the Maasai*.

Acknowledgements

This volume has been a group enterprise. Many of the papers were first presented at a series of panels at the African Studies Association meeting in Atlanta in 1989, and we have been sharing our work since. We were able to come together again in October 1990 to discuss and refine our work at a workshop at Bucknell University, to which we are grateful for sponsorship and support.

The authors received individual support from a number of different institutions and individuals, to which acknowledgement is made in the individual papers that follow. The editors received additional administrative support from Williams College and Bucknell University that made editorial work easier.

John Berntsen's imposing presence stands behind much of our work. John's path-breaking contributions to the field of Maasai history are manifest in all that has followed, as indicated in the continual references to his work here. Unable to participate formally because of his diplomatic duties, he has nevertheless been an active supporter and perceptive critic of our work.

James Currey has provided steadfast support from the outset and deserves special commendation for his imagination and perseverance in keeping the lines of scholarship with Africa open during these trying times.

As editors in what is usually viewed as a thankless and onerous task, we would like to thank the contributors for helping to make this an exciting and challenging experience for both of us.

Thomas Spear
Richard Waller

*Maasai Women: Popular stereoscope photographs of the early 1900s (see also p. xiv)
indicate that a standardised image of the 'the Maasai' was already being created and
presented to the public. In essentials, it has not altered much in eighty years.*

PART ONE

Introduction[1]

THOMAS SPEAR

Everyone 'knows' the Maasai. Men wearing red capes while balancing on one leg and a long spear, gazing out over the semi-arid plains stretching endlessly to the horizon, or women heavily bedecked in beads, stare out at us from countless coffee-table books and tourists' snapshots. Uncowed by their neighbours, colonial conquest, or modernization, they stand in proud mute testimony to a vanishing African world.

Or so we think. Reality is, of course, different. Long considered archetypical pastoralists, Maasai are in fact among the most recent arrivals on the East African scene; their adoption of a purely pastoral way of life is an even more recent innovation; and many people who speak Maa, the Maasai language, and call themselves Maasai are not pastoralists at all. We must re-examine carefully the myths surrounding Maasai identity and, in so doing, question our thinking regarding ethnicity generally.

The ancestors of modern Maa-speakers came from the southern Sudan sometime during the first millennium AD. Slowly moving down the Rift Valley that cuts through central Kenya and Tanzania, they eventually supplanted or absorbed most previous inhabitants of this semi-arid savannah bisecting the fertile highlands on either side. Originally agro-pastoralists, raising sorghum and millet along with their cattle and small stock, they came to specialize more and more in a pastoral way of life appropriate for the plains, leaving grain production to communities of farmers inhabiting the fertile highlands either side of the valley and hunting and gathering to specialized groups who lived in the forests bordering the highlands and plains. Over time, pastoral Maasai and others increasingly came to see this division of labour in exclusive ethnic terms as the Rift world became cognitively divided among Maa-speaking pastoralists, Bantu farmers, and Okiek hunter-gatherers.

Such a neat, tripartite division never really matched the complex realities of life in the Rift, however, where periodic droughts, diseases,

1

wars, movements of people, and innovations constantly blurred ethnic boundaries. In the northern reaches of the Rift west of Lake Turkana, Turkana drove Maa-speakers south and east of the lake where they settled as Samburu cattle herders alongside unrelated Rendille camel herders, some of the two later combining as Ariaal. Other Maasai settled in and around the swamps surrounding Lake Baringo to become Chamus irrigation farmers. Further south, pastoral Maasai, divided into a number of different sections, came to dominate the Rift as far as central Tanzania. In central Kenya, pastoral Maasai fought, traded with, and married Kikuyu farmers to the east, Kalenjin-speaking pastoralists and farmers to the west, and Southern Cushitic mixed farmers and Okiek hunter-gatherers in their midst, while further south, they displaced Maa-speaking Loogolala and Parakuyo herders from southern Maasailand and the Pangani valley and interacted with Bantu-speakers in the surrounding highlands (see Galaty, 'Maasai Expansion', this volume).

Models for the Maasai[2]

In spite of these complex realities, 'Maasai' and 'pastoralism' have become so closely linked in the historical and ethnographic literature, not to mention in the thought of Maasai pastoralists themselves, that Maasai are commonly viewed as prototypical pastoralists, secure in their own exclusive ethnicity. Yet various peoples either claiming to be Maasai or deeply influenced by Maasai culture occupy a variety of specialized economic niches in the Rift Valley and highlands of central and southern Kenya and northern Tanzania, and each exhibits its own distinctive cultural ecology and ethnicity. What is unusual about this area is the degree to which ethnic form follows economic function, with each ethnic group narrowly defined in terms of its economic specialization. Thus people normally thought of as Maasai are pastoralists living on the plains; Okiek are hunter-gatherers exploiting the forest margins; and Arusha are farmers tilling the fertile soils of Mount Meru. Yet all can also speak Maa and participate to some degree in Maasai regional social, ritual, and economic cycles. In a situation where ethnic groups are defined exclusively in economic terms and yet cultural categories are broadly inclusive, the problem becomes a dual one of how to explain high degrees of economic specialization and ethnic differentiation on the one hand, and equally high degrees of cultural homogeneity across different ethnic groups on the other.

Alan Jacobs' pioneering ethnography of pastoral Maasai encapsulated contemporary views in drawing a sharp cultural and economic boundary between pastoral 'IlMaasai' and mixed economy 'Iloikop' or 'Kwavi'. Only the former, contended Jacobs, were 'real' Maasai, pure pastoralists

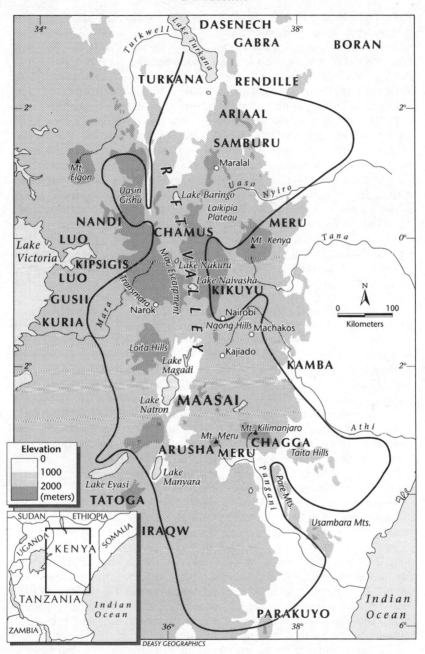

Maa-Speaking People and their Neighbours

who reflected the highest Maasai cultural ideals and practices. The others were mere pretenders to pastoral status, cultural scavengers who sought to ape the Maasai by copying them.[3] While Jacobs' view reflected the contempt of his Maasai informants for poor people without cattle (*iltorrobo*) and for farmers who worked the soil (*ilmeek*), the sharp distinction between two separate cultural–economic modes proved to be too neat, reflecting neither socio-economic nor historical reality.

Noting that neither the historical literature over the past century nor their own contemporary informants make the clear and enduring socio-economic distinction between Maasai and 'Iloikop' or 'Kwavi' claimed by Jacobs, John Berntsen and Richard Waller carefully documented how shifting definitions of the two over time reflected both a fluid, interdependent regional economy and the respective fates of different peoples in the pastoral wars for survival that raged throughout the nineteenth century. Theirs are interactive models whose roots are in the regional interdependence of local hunting and gathering, agricultural, and pastoral economies and which stress the symbiotic relations between different groups. Maasai pastoralists on the plains were at the centre of the regional economy, both because of their central location and because cattle served as a universal store of value facilitating trade and social exchange throughout the area. Given the vagaries of pastoral economy, however, pastoralists ultimately depended on hunter-gatherers and farmers to supplement their diet, to provide needed crafts and ritual services, to maintain a balanced ratio of people and stock on the plains, and to provide refuge in times of natural disasters. Such exchanges of goods, services, and people took place within established cultural modes that incorporated different peoples into common social institutions. If Okiek hunters or Arusha farmers were functionally different from pastoralists, they nevertheless were often affiliated with the same or related clans and age-sets, spoke Maa, intermarried frequently, and adopted pastoralists who had lost their cattle to disease, drought, or warfare. Different economic groups, ethnically defined, thus participated as a matter of course in a common interdependent regional economy and culture.[4]

Berntsen's and Waller's interpretations were thus much more dynamic than Jacobs', and they highlighted the shared cultural and economic frameworks that symbiotically bound different ethnic groups together. They made sense of both normative patterns of behaviour in the Rift as well as the extraordinary fluid historical situation throughout the nineteenth century, and they accorded well with the documentary record. In doing so, however, they left unanswered the question of how such ethnic boundaries had been established and maintained between such economically differentiated but interdependent, and ethnically separate but culturally integrated societies.

Two answers have been attempted to this complex analytical problem. The first de-emphasizes apparent economic and ethnic differences among pastoral, agricultural, and hunter-gatherer societies. Based on a broad definition of the mode of production, Peter Rigby and Elliot Fratkin both see agriculture, hunting and gathering, and pastoralism as merely separate means of production within a common kinship, communal, or domestic mode of production that is characterized by production for use (as opposed to exchange) and by kinship as the means of organizing and reproducing social relations and their symbolic expression. Given the different means of production — stock, land, and forest reserves, respectively — each has historically developed its own relations of production — age, descent, and flexible groups — which, as historical products, formed both infrastructure and superstructure, ensuring social reproduction of the group as well as mediating and determining future historical relations with others. Different societies possessing different means and relations of production were thus incorporated complementarily within a single larger mode of production.[5]

Pastoralists solved the manifold problems of maintaining sufficient stock and access to grazing and water in a semi-arid environment to ensure their own survival by coming together in small, mobile herding units while at the same time maintaining wide-ranging links throughout the society, based on age-sets that united all the men of a given age in a single comprehensive social institution. Economic responsibilities were divided functionally according to sex and age, with boys responsible for herding the cattle; young men for protecting them; women for milking, household labour, and reproducing the family; and older men for managing the family and its collective herds. Relations throughout pastoral society and with other societies beyond were also mediated by age, as elders sought among their age-mates for distant cattle partners to disperse their herds, marriage partners to ensure their social survival, and exchange partners to maintain access to a variety of different goods and services.

Farmers, by contrast, ensured access to their basic resources, land, and the labour to work it, through lineage structures that brought together all the descendants of those who first established claim to the land in a perpetual kinship group that ensured continued access to land and labour through the generations. Lineage elders held the land in communal trust, and they exchanged women with one another as wives to reproduce the lineage and as labour to produce for the domestic economy.

Hunter-gatherers, in turn, needed access to large reserves with varying ecological potentials to secure the variety of gathered and hunted resources on which they depended for their livelihood. Since each adult was capable of providing his or her own food requirements, however, and they faced little competition with others, individuals were able to come together periodically in flexible groups within a particular forest range to share resources with one another.

When pastoralists and farmers or hunter-gatherers came together in a single, communal mode of production, they did so on the basis of their own established systems of social relations. Pastoralists sought to maintain as wide a circle of exchange and marriage partners as possible by incorporating their agricultural, and hunting and gathering neighbours within their age-sets, while farmers married pastoral women and adopted pastoral men into their lineages. Each set of social relations was thus historically specific to a single means of production but ultimately came to embrace those with different means of production in order to mediate relations among them within a common mode of production.

As elegant as this analysis is, however, it begs the questions of precisely how such economic specialization led to ethnic differentiation among Maasai and related peoples, and of how relations have been structured between historically different peoples. Whereas most ethnic groups in Africa normally encompassed broad ranges of economic activities, how do we account for such specialization among Maa-speaking groups and their neighbours?

John Galaty has sought to approach this problem by seeing pastoralists, farmers, and hunters as symbolically opposed within a single mode of production. In a process he labels 'synthesis through exclusion', there is '. . . a triangle of productive alternatives, including pastoralism, agriculture and hunting, the autonomy of each being maintained through an "ethnic" division of subsistence activities, while . . . the limits of each subsistence form are resolved through trade of goods and exchange of persons between groups.'[6] Each group has viewed itself and others in systematically opposed ways that usually deflate the values of others while simultaneously reinforcing its own. Pastoralists thus protected their access to animals and grazing lands by viewing hunters who destroyed animals or farmers who monopolized potential grazing land as profligate consumers of valuable resources. Since such oppositions occurred within the context of a wider symbolic system in which others also had their own stereotypes, however, they had the effect not only of reinforcing ethnic differences, but also of maintaining a complementary tension between peoples which facilitated ongoing social and economic relations. Hunters thus deflected pastoralists' gibes by viewing pastoralists as needlessly wasting labour and potential food on their herds, while farmers criticized pastoralists' disdain for work, dislike of agricultural foods, and seeming lack of concern for land conservation. Opposed ethnic categories constructed in these mutually reinforcing ways transcended history. Individual peoples, languages, and cultures may have changed over time, but the fundamental 'ethnic' differences between herders, farmers, and hunters persisted, with none merging into or encompassing another. 'Synthesis through exclusion' thus established mutually exclusive symbolic identities arrayed around differential access to resources, which, at the same time, integrated them into an enduring complementary regional system of production and exchange.

Interpretations of ethnicity and identity among Maa-speaking peoples have thus changed considerably over the past twenty-five years. Partly this has simply been a matter of development, as our knowledge and sophistication has increased over time, but it has also been the result of different disciplinary approaches being applied simultaneously. Anthropologists like Jacobs, Rigby, Fratkin, and Galaty have tended to focus on normative views revealed in their own field work, while historians like Berntsen and Waller have sought to place such ethnographic materials in a more dynamic historical perspective by drawing on the extensive documentary and oral materials available to explore changes over time. As history and anthropology increasingly merge these days, however, simple disciplinary and methodological differences are no longer as revealing as they once were. Theoretical differences among historians and anthropologists alike are now emerging as more significant indices of difference. Marxist analyses employed by Rigby and Fratkin, for example, are much more historically focused than earlier functionalist approaches, but differ significantly from Galaty's semiotics orientation. At the same time, historians have become more conceptually orientated and employ an often eclectic variety of Marxist, structuralist, and symbolic approaches, as can be seen in the case studies which follow.

Some of these differences can be seen in the debate over the identity of Okiek hunter-gatherers who lived in widely scattered groups in pockets of the forest on the fringes of the plains. Since many of these groups spoke the language of their pastoral neighbours and followed some of their cultural practices, they were once depicted as a depressed caste or underclass within pastoral society, similar to *ilkunono* iron workers. Termed '*iltorrobo*' — literally poor people without cattle — by pastoral Maasai, pastoralists themselves viewed Okiek as culturally and economically deprived peoples living in the forest who provided Maasai with honey, labour for herding, ritual services viewed as polluting by Maasai, and refuge. Some analysts reflected this view in seeing Okiek as simply impoverished pastoralists living at the margins of pastoral society, differing from other pastoralists only in their different means of production, and cited in evidence the facts that pastoralists who lost their cattle often sought refuge in Okiek societies, that most Okiek spoke the language of their Maa or Kalenjin-speaking neighbours, and that Okiek were often affiliated with Maasai clans and age-sets.[7]

Two who have studied Okiek culture and history more closely, however, have decisively disproved this interpretation. Roderic Blackburn and Corinne Kratz both see Okiek as the cultural descendants of autonomous hunting populations long resident in the area. As evidence, they cite the existence of a common historical culture found among widely scattered Okiek groups, their highly specialized cultural ecology associated with honey, and archaeological and linguistic evidence of their existence in the highlands long before that of their pastoral neighbours. As small groups at the mercy of their more powerful neighbours, however, they have been able to maintain their own integrity only by accommodating economically, linguistically, and culturally to these neighbours.[8] Once linked in these ways, the symbolic oppositions between pastoralists and hunters have then served to maintain and reinforce difference.[9] Living at what pastoral Maasai consider the margin has thus become a way of life for Okiek, fully embedded in their own culture and artfully exploited for their own ends (see Klumpp and Kratz, this volume).

While there has been considerable debate on the position of hunter-gatherers within Maasai societies, there has been little discussion of that of farmers. This is surprising, since farmers are far more numerous than hunter-gatherers and play at least as important a role in pastoral economies. Pure pastoralists cannot survive in the long run without access to grains to supplement the pastoral diet, to food reserves during droughts, or to refuge in times of trouble. Social relations between pastoral and agricultural societies were thus intense, and were facilitated by shared cultural norms. Most of the farmers with whom Maasai interacted were Bantu or Kalenjin-speakers who farmed the fertile highlands surrounding the plains — Kikuyu, Chaga, Sonjo, Nandi, and others. Women conducted frequent trade between pastoral and agricultural homesteads; bilingualism and intermarriage were common; farmers were often affiliated with Maasai clans or age-sets; herding duties and stock were often reciprocated; and pastoralists frequently sought refuge among farmers when drought or disease devastated their herds. Other farmers — Arusha, Nkuruman, and Chamus — were, however, culturally Maasai, defining themselves as such, speaking Maa, participating in Maasai clans and age-sets, intermarrying with Maasai pastoralists, and conducting frequent exchanges of food, labour, and stock with them. While Kikuyu and others could cross cultural boundaries and become Maasai, only relative status separated agricultural and pastoral Maasai.

As agricultural Maasai, however, they were farmers who belonged to a culture which was fundamentally shaped by pastoral values, thus raising the question of how farmers could maintain a pastoral culture while pursuing the needs of agriculture. For there is a difference between Fratkin's and Rigby's models, positing a single mode of production in which separate societies pursue their own means and relations of production, and societies with different means of production adopting fundamentally similar relations of production. Gulliver's extensive studies of agricultural Arusha Maasai consider this question, but in positing a fundamental contradiction between pastoral and agricultural values, Gulliver concludes that the continued adherence of agricultural Arusha Maasai to pastoral Maasai cultural norms was dysfunctional to their own economic success and bound to decline.[10] The fact that Arusha today continue to disprove his prediction reveals the degree to which Gulliver neglected the crucial historical question of how and why Arusha have continued to maintain such a culture over several centuries (see Spear, 'Being Maasai', this volume).

Our view of the Maasai has thus moved far beyond a simple opposition between pure pastoralists and others to embrace a view in which
Maasai society is seen as encompassing a triangle of economic forces —
pastoralism, hunting-gathering, and agriculture — within complex
cultural structures which were both highly differentiated and complementary. These views still largely centre on pastoralism, as seen in the
relative neglect of farmers and hunter-gatherers, however, and see others
in terms of pastoral economic needs and cultural dominance. This is a
strangely static view, given that pure pastoralism was probably a relatively late arrival on the East African scene; prior to the seventeenth
century, many people appear to have followed different varieties of
agro-pastoral-hunting subsistence. The incidence of economic specialization and consequent ethnic differentiation among different societies
thus can not be taken for granted, but is what needs to be explained.
What is needed is a processual view that accounts for economic and
ethnic differentiation within broader historical and cultural frameworks
that include both the processes of economic specialization and ethnic
differentiation in the eighteenth and nineteenth centuries and the manifold social and cultural ways that economic diversity and interdependence were inextricably linked together. For, in the Maasai case, both
economy and culture transcended the economic practices of individual
societies and their claims to distinctive cultures and ethnicities.[11]

Defining 'Maasai': The Development of Pastoral Cultures

First, however, it is necessary to understand how the Maa-speaking
peoples and their cultures have come to be defined historically. The
origins of pastoralism in East Africa go back to the third millennium
BC and the adaptation of agro-pastoral Southern Cushites from Ethiopia
to the arid environment of the Lake Turkana basin, where herding
small stock and humpless long-horned cattle and fishing soon came
to dominate their economies. By the beginning of the first millennium
BC, Southern Cushites had moved south onto the fertile grasslands
of the Rift Valley and highlands of central and southern Kenya, where
they coexisted with earlier hunter-gatherer populations exploiting the
savanna-forest margins, who then began to acquire stock in trade
with the pastoralists while continuing to maintain their hunting and
gathering existence. Meanwhile, to the west of the Rift Valley, Southern
Nilotic-speakers from the Sudan were establishing a mixed economy
combining pastoralism with raising sorghum and millet and hunting.
Thus, by the beginning of the modern era, three different cultural
complexes occupied central and southern Kenya, each characterized
to various degrees by agro-pastoral-hunting economies. Over the
course of the first millennium AD, these were joined by three more
groups of people, Eastern Nilotic ancestors of the Maasai moving south
from the Sudan border and Eastern Cushitic-speaking peoples from

Ethiopia — both of whom also combined pastoralism with agriculture and hunting-gathering — together with Bantu-speaking farmers from the west and south (see Galaty, 'Maasai Expansion'; Sommer and Vossen; and Sutton, this volume).[12]

John Lamphear has characterized the history of the past 2,000 years as a period of increasing diversity and specialization throughout the area, as different peoples slowly came to occupy particular ecological niches in which they could develop more specialized economies and differentiated cultures. Agriculture came to predominate in the fertile, well-watered highlands as Bantu-speakers cleared and settled one highlands area after another; pastoralism became confined to the semi-arid plains; and hunting continued to dominate the forest fringes, thus establishing a basis for regional economic interdependence and trade as each people sought to supplement their own increasingly specialized production with products from other areas.

During that period, continual immigration accompanied by social interaction caused the creation of a diverse array of communities — each characterized by a mixed economy, extensive cultural intermixture, borrowing, and multi-lingualism — the members of which participated in wide-ranging regional exchange networks. By the seventeenth century, plains communities were more social 'phenomena' than ethnic groups. Ongamo-Maa-speakers, recently split from their Eastern Nilotic ancestors, for example, began to absorb earlier Southern Cushites and participated in a number of these communities, including Sirikwa, a mixed community of Nilotic and Cushitic-speakers who herded long-horned cattle and practised terraced and irrigated agriculture. Sirikwa was probably the last of the mixed plains communities, however, as the revolutionary development of highly specialized pastoralism swept the plains during the eighteenth and nineteenth centuries (for a different interpretation of Sirikwa, see Sutton, this volume).[13]

Turkana in the north and pastoral Maasai in the south came to exemplify the pastoral revolution, as each emerging society slowly adopted iron weapons, humped Zebu or Sanga cattle better adapted to semi-arid environments, and politico-religious functionaries able to serve as foci for group solidarity and identity. A disastrous series of droughts and famines in the eighteenth and nineteenth centuries that forced mixed farmers to abandon the plains gave the newly specialized pastoralists able to thrive in such an environment their chance, and both Maasai and Turkana expanded dramatically. Along with the new dominance of pastoralism came the development of intensely pastoral cultures that stressed the singular value of cattle and asserted pastoralists' rights to their guardianship over all others. It was, Lamphear argues, in this period that traditions of origin were developed that stressed the tripartite division of the world into pastoralists, farmers, and hunters as increasingly specialized economic groups became ethnically differentiated.

Introduction

If the early Maasai were the last of the old agro-pastoral communities, with their rainfed cereal agriculture, long-horned cattle, and mixed populations, the pastoral Maasai who came to dominate the plains in the eighteenth century soon became the epitome of the new. Prior to the seventeenth century, mixed economy Maa-speakers had infiltrated and settled with earlier peoples; by the late eighteenth century, pastoral Maasai were sweeping all others from the plains as the region became economically, politically, socially, and symbolically divided between the 'people of cattle' and those without. Hunters became an enduring symbol for the degeneracy of a life of poverty without cattle in the untamed wilderness, while pastoralists dominated the plains militarily and established their cultural hegemony. By the end of the nineteenth century, however, specialized pastoralism was itself in retreat before the disastrous series of droughts, famines, epidemics, and ultimately colonialism that swept the plains. Many Maasai and Turkana were forced back, at least temporarily, into the more secure world of a mixed economy, while mixed farmers triumphed in western Kenya.[14]

Pastoral Maasai thus established their initial dominance over the plains through economic and social reforms which ideally suited them to a transhumant pastoral existence, but they consolidated their victories by establishing the hegemony of an intensely pastoral culture in which cattle alone had value and those who pursued other livelihoods were to be despised. Cattle, unlike land, were a variable and potentially wasting resource. Successful herd management required conserving a herd large enough to produce sufficient milk and meat for its owners and to reproduce itself over time, including the ability to recover following droughts and other periods of high loss. Female milking and breeding stock were thus valued over all others, and large flocks of goats and sheep were maintained for meat and trade.

Semi-arid conditions greatly increased the risks of loss. Variable and uncertain rainfall regimes meant that water supplies and good grazing could not be taken for granted, and diseases or predators could take an unpredictable toll. The only real insurance a herder could take against the possibility of such catastrophic disasters was to participate in complex exchange networks that spread his risk by allowing him to disperse his herd among widely scattered stock partners and to maintain access to wet and dry season pastures as well as water. Since the ratio between stock and people was relatively fixed, he also had to be able to share labour. A herd that was too small could not feed those dependent on it, while one that was too large could not be managed with available family labour. Thus, as herds grew, one had to be able either to acquire additional labour outside the family to take care of them or to place excess cattle in the care of others, while, if they shrunk, either excess consumers had to be able to find work with others or one had to borrow cows from others to feed them.[15]

Pastoral Maasai accomplished these goals through social institutions that widened social relations and facilitated exchange. Descent was de-emphasized and broadened as Maasai clans extended across separate territorial sections to embrace large numbers of potential agnates. Age-sets included all Maasai men within a given age span over a large area, and the distinctive period of withdrawal from society by the *murran* developed enduring links among age-mates, a strong sense of pastoral values, and the continued cohesion of the family herding unit under the domination of the eldest male (see Spencer, 'Becoming Maasai', this volume).[16] A typical homestead was a fluid herding unit, comprised of a variable number of independent stock-owning families who cooperated with one another to manage their herds, while each stock-owner maintained extensive links with agnates, affines, and age-mates elsewhere (see Galaty, 'Maasai Expansion', this volume).

Thus Maasai pastoral ideology and social institutions both were predicated on and reinforced the distinctive needs and values of a pastoral economy, while at the same time they rejected those of others. Hunters who consumed wild animals rather than conserving domestic stock and lived in the untamed wilderness were viewed as greedy, unrestrained, and uncultured, suitable only for slaughtering cattle, circumcising youth, gathering honey, and performing other tasks pastoralists avoided as polluting. Farmers, on the other hand, destroyed grazing lands to plant crops in demeaning agricultural labour, and thus were seen as fit only for providing food, beer, and wives for pastoralists.[17]

If the ideology was highly ethnocentric and exclusionary in assigning and valuing roles, however, it was unusually accessible to anyone who wished to embrace it. Hunters and farmers were, in fact, included as separate categories within pastoral Maasai society by virtue of the critical roles they played.[18] Entry into pastoral society was open, dependent not on descent or background, but on control of resources and on participation in pastoral social relations. One could enter pastoral society along a variety of routes, from obtaining cattle to joining a Maasai age-set, speaking Maa, or affiliating with a Maasai clan (see Sobania; Spear, 'Being Maasai'; Waller, 'Acceptees and Aliens'; and Fratkin, this volume). All these institutions stretched beyond the boundaries of pastoral Maasai society to include other societies in the area, allowing one to pre-adapt to Maasai society in advance of entry while still maintaining a stake in one's own society. Bantu-speaking Sonjo farmers, for example, could gain rights to Maasai cattle through bridewealth or other exchanges and herd them with Maasai affines; become initiated within a Maasai age-set and build up extensive relations with Maasai age-mates; affiliate their own descent group with Maasai clans; or learn to speak Maa, all prior to becoming Maasai themselves. For many, becoming Maasai was a two generation process in which a father laid the essential foundations for his son's later entry into pastoralism.[19]

Countless individuals surrounding the plains maintained just such intermediary statuses, if only to avail themselves of the opportunities for social exchange that they provided. Rare was the ambitious Kikuyu or Nandi farmer without a pastoral Maasai affine, age-mate, or agnate with whom to exchange stock, foodstuffs, services, labour, or women. Conversely, survival was hardly possible within pastoral society without access to resources and to the people who controlled them outside the pastoral sphere. Okiek honey and ritual experts were prerequisites for Maasai rituals; grain was a necessity to supplement the diet, especially during hard times; and stock to rebuild drought-stricken herds could often only be obtained from outside the pastoral economy.

Pastoralist ideology, then, represented as much an ethnic claim to resources and their management as a claim to identity. The symbolic oppositions inherent in establishing Maasai cultural hegemony represented more than a simple means of identifying and reinforcing pastoral values; they also represented a way of controlling who had access to limited pastoral resources and the ability to manage them. At the same time, however, pastoral survival depended on access to resources outside pastoral society, and so it was necessary to extend pastoral institutions beyond the bounds of pastoralism and to grant access to them to others. Maasai cultural pride, arrogance, and dominance of the plains facilitated this process in the successful role model they projected to others. Cultural exclusion and social inclusion — hegemony and homogeneity — thus operated hand-in-hand; the one controlling access to resources within pastoral society and the other facilitating access to resources outside. While pastoral Maasai themselves might be reluctant to speak the languages or participate in the social institutions of others, hunters and farmers readily learned Maa and participated in pastoral social institutions, and pastoral Maasai had few reservations about their doing so. The corollary of pastoral Maasai hegemony was ethnic differentiation and the definition of others in frequently pejorative terms. But those same others could and did become pastoral Maasai by becoming 'people of cattle', while pastoral Maasai frequently became others by losing their cattle and becoming farmers or hunters. In between these two extremes, people commonly trod the cultural pathways that wove together societies with different economies and ethnic identities into a single complementary regional economy and culture.

By the end of the nineteenth century, however, the Rift world was in disarray as its societies were assaulted by a succession of droughts, diseases, and civil disorders through the 1880s and 1890s. While bovine pleuro-pneumonia and rinderpest devastated their herds, smallpox ravaged human populations and civil wars rent pastoral societies as they struggled among themselves to survive. Pastoral resources were stretched beyond their limits, and adjacent farmers and hunters were inundated with refugees. The diseases, newly introduced to East Africa along the expanding trade-routes, were soon followed by German and British troops bent on colonial conquest, now made easier by the weakened state of most local societies.

Introduction

With the very survival of the pastoral ideal at stake, Maasai found refuge wherever they could. Many sought out previous partners among their neighbours, but others made new alliances with European officials who were eager to enlist Maasai as mercenaries. In return, participating Maasai received support against their enemies and gifts of impounded stock that enabled them to rebuild their herds and return ultimately to the plains to resume their pastoral way of life.[20]

During the colonial peace that followed, pastoral Maasai gained the opportunity to regroup and recover, but only on terms dictated by their new European overlords. The terms were the establishment of exclusive African reserves, separating the various complementary elements of the wider Rift Valley economy from one another, and indirect rule, mandating the establishment of ostensibly 'traditional' patterns of governance. Maasai were quick to capitalize on these terms and were successful in resuscitating the pastoral ideal and establishing it is a colonial, as well as their own, ideology, effectively walling off the Maasai reserves from colonial and African intruders alike (see Waller, 'Acceptees and Aliens', this volume).

The pastoral ideal thus enjoyed a revival in the twentieth century after the disasters of the nineteenth, and it was soon embraced not only by Maasai but also by a variety of outsiders, ranging from district officers posted to Maasailand for long periods of time to tourists, academics, and others in search of 'Vanishing Africa'. The strategy worked for more than half a century, until Kenyan Independence brought to power less romantic politicians riding a wave of Kikuyu land hunger and intent on opening up the land to 'development'. Pastoral Maasai were again put on the defensive, as the scramble for land for farms, ranches, and game reserves threatened continued access to the necessary range of pastoral resources. While the present outlook for pastoral survival appears dim, Maasai are clearly trying to adapt through asserting collective and individual rights to land and reformulating the ideology of what it is to be Maasai. Class has clearly become an increasingly major factor in Maasai society today as control over land becomes at least as important as that over cattle; education and work elsewhere supplants the socialization of the *murran*; and farming or ranching for the market replaces subsistence herding (see Campbell and Fratkin, this volume). But ethnicity also remains a salient strategy as Maasai politicians publicly proclaim the importance of maintaining 'traditional' values, often as they pursue private accumulation themselves, and Maasai seek to mobilize a new generation of outsiders to their cause.

Ethnicity in a Wider Context

The debate over ethnicity and identity among both Maasai and outsiders reflects the wider debate on ethnicity among social scientists generally. Earlier writers assumed that ethnic groups developed as homogeneous cultural units, geographically and socially isolated from other such groups, and often.reified such groups as evolutionary stages in the development of humankind. While this view is still found distressingly often in the popular press, the academic debate has long since divided into two camps — often labelled 'instrumentalists' and 'primordialists' — focused, respectively, on the causes and effects of ethnicity.[21]

Primordialists assume ethnicity, its historical claims, its shared understandings, and its ability to govern social relations, as a historical artifact, and focus on trying to understand its demonstrated power in the modern world. That ethnic claims continue to evoke strong and often bloody responses is well attested, and primordialists seek to explain this by referring to the historical content and depth of ethnicity, focusing on the affective power of traditional symbols to evoke deep emotional responses within individuals and collectivities.[22]

Primordialists tend to take the source of those claims for granted, however, as anachronistically rooted in the past and capable of being dislodged only when socio-economic changes cause reality to become so dissonant with the symbols that people are forced by threatening crisis and anomie to abandon them for more contemporary symbols consonant with their new behaviour. Taking ethnicity for granted thus assumes an evolutionary progression from 'ethnic' to 'modern' in which ethnicity gradually disappears as a category in the face of development and nationalism. What is disarming for the 'primordialists', then, is the remarkable upsurge of ethnicity that often results from economic development and modernization.

This leads many analysts to see it as rooted not in the distant past, but in much more recent times, when colonized and modern elites have sought to mobilize values to support their own claims to restricted resources in both the traditional and the modern sectors. Ethnicity then becomes instrumental, capable of being 'invented' and manipulated in the service of one social goal or another. Ethnicity's power derives precisely from its ability to create a shared historical consciousness and to mobilize this in the service of modern aims, its ability to reflect both traditional and modern concerns, Janus-like, simultaneously.[23]

'Instrumentalists' see ethnic groups, like other categories, as social constructs formed in relation to people's own immediate needs and to their relationships with others. Barth, in his seminal collection, *Ethnic Groups and Boundaries*, puts it this way:

> First, it is clear that [ethnic] boundaries persist despite a flow of personnel across them. In other words, categorical ethnic distinctions do not depend on an absence of mobility, contact and information, but do entail social processes of exclusion and incorporation whereby discrete categories are maintained *despite* changing participation and membership in the course of individual life histories. Secondly, one finds that stable, persisting, and often vitally important social relations are maintained across such boundaries and are frequently based precisely on the dichotomized ethnic statuses. In other words, ethnic

distinctions do not depend on an absence of social interaction and acceptance, but are quite to the contrary often the very foundations on which embracing social systems are built.[24]

A shift is thus made from studies of the internal cultural content of ethnicity to the processes by which ethnic groups are generated and maintained in opposition to other such groups. For Barth and his colleagues ethnic groups are socially effective forms of social organization which mediate relations with those inside and outside the group by maintaining semi-permeable boundaries through which outsiders flow to become insiders and vice versa. Ethnic boundaries define who is playing the same game according to the same set of rules and who is not. They do this by establishing shared understandings and criteria for judgement and by utilizing the potential for social relationships established by the distinctive cultural ecology of each group and the complementarity between different groups. Ethnicity at its most basic, then, establishes and controls social access to critical resources.

Our interpretation of ethnicity historically in Maasai is similarly instrumental, stressing the ways in which ethnic ideologies effectively served to control access to pastoral, agricultural, and gatherering resources respectively, while also noting the ways in which shared cultural understandings among different groups, so defined, ensured complementarity and each's survival. We do not, however, make the mistake of ignoring the 'primordialists'' concerns by simply dismissing ethnicity as a form of 'false consciousness',[25] for, however derived, ethnicity remains a powerful ideology for identity formation and social action. That is precisely why leaders seek to invent and evoke it, and why followers are so often willing to kill and die for it. It is thus important to understand the power of the symbols embedded in myth, language, and social behaviour that sustain social identities, for it is this very power that makes ethnicity so effective once such loyalties are evoked. In fact, pastoral ideology, arising out of the needs of the eighteenth and nineteenth centuries as a means of controlling restricted resources, became so powerfully justified in myth and action that it was readily accepted not only by ordinary people but also by educated 'progressives' and by colonial officers themselves as each sought to resolve the contradictions of colonial rule in the pseudo-traditional terms of indirect rule.[26] It is, then, both the ways ethnicity functioned to mediate socio-economic relations among the peoples of central East Africa and the powers that it evoked that are the subjects of our studies here.

Notes

1. I have benefited greatly here from the suggestions of my fellow contributors, and especially from the incisive comments of Richard Waller.
2. The phrase is a play on Paul Spencer's ms. title, 'Models of the Maasai' (n.d.).

Introduction

3. Alan Jacobs, 'The Traditional Political Organization of the Pastoral Masai', D.Phil. thesis, Oxford, 1965.
4. John Berntsen, 'The Maasai and their Neighbors: Variables of Interaction', *African Economic History*, 2 (1976: 1–11); *idem*, 'The Enemy is Us: Eponymy in the Historiography of the Maasai', *History in Africa*, 7 (1980: 1–21); Richard Waller, 'Economic and Social Relations in the Central Rift Valley: The Maa-Speakers and their Neighbours in the Nineteenth Century' in B.A. Ogot (ed.), *Kenya in the Nineteenth Century* (*Hadith*, No. 8), (Nairobi, 1985: 83–151). See also Alan Jacobs, 'The Irrigation Agricultural Maasai of Pagasi: A Case Study of Maasai–Sonjo Acculturation', *MISR Social Science Research Conference Papers, C: Sociology* (1968); Paul Spencer, *Nomads in Alliance* (London, 1973).
5. Peter Rigby, *Persistent Pastoralists* (London, 1985); Elliot Fratkin, 'The Organization of Labor and Production among the Ariaal Rendille, Nomadic Pastoralists of Northern Kenya', Ph.D. thesis, Catholic University (1987: 19–27).
6. John Galaty, 'East African Hunters and Pastoralists in a Regional Perspective: An Ethnoanthropological Approach', *SUGIA, Sprache und Geschichte in Afrika*, 7/1 (1986: 110). See also *idem*, 'Being "Maasai": Being "People of Cattle"; Ethnic Shifters in East Africa', *American Ethnologist*, 9/1 (1982: 1–20); *idem*, 'Maasai Pastoral Ideology and Change' in P.C. Salzman (ed.), *Contemporary Nomadic and Pastoral Peoples: Africa and Latin America* (*Studies in Third World Societies*, No. 17) (Williamsburg, Va., 1985).
7. Roger van Zwanenberg, 'Dorobo Hunting and Gathering: A Way of Life or a Mode of Production?' *African Economic History*, 2 (1976: 12–24); Cynthia Chang, 'Nomads without Cattle: East African Foragers in Historical Perspective' in E. Leacock and R.B. Lee (eds), *Politics and History in Band Societies* (New York, 1982: 269–282).
8. Roderic Blackburn, 'The Okiek and their Neighbors: The Ecological Distinctions', African Studies Association paper, Baltimore, 1978; Corinne Kratz, 'Are the Okiek really Maasai? or Kipsigis? or Kikuyu?' *Cahiers d'études Africaines*, 79 (1980: 355–368). For a historical view, see Stanley Ambrose, 'The Introduction of Pastoral Adaptations to the Highlands of East Africa' in J.D. Clark and S. Brandt (eds), *From Hunters to Farmers* (Berkeley, 1984: 212–239).
9. Waller, 'Economic and Social Relations'; Berntsen, 'Maasai and their Neighbors'; Galaty, 'East African Hunters and Pastoralists'; Ambrose, 'Pastoral Adaptations'.
10. P.H. Gulliver, 'The Arusha: Economic and Social Change' in P. Bohannan and G. Dalton (eds), *Markets in Africa* (New York, 1965: 250–284). See also, *idem*, *Social Control in an African Society* (London, 1963).
11. Cf. Mukhisa Kituyi, *Becoming Kenyans* (Nairobi, 1990: 38–41); G. Schlee, 'Interethnic Clan Identities among Cushitic-Speaking Pastoralists', *Africa*, 55 (1985: 17–38).
12. For a comprehensive synthesis of regional archaeological sequences, together with the linguistic and ecological evidence involved, see Ambrose, 'Pastoral Adaptations'.
13. The argument here, along with a wealth of supporting historical detail, is developed by John Lamphear in 'The Persistence of Hunting and Gathering in a "Pastoral World" ', *SUGIA, Sprache und Geschichte in Afrika*, 7/2 (1986: 227–265).
14. This completes Lamphear's argument from 'Persistence of Hunting and Gathering'. See also Richard Waller, '*Emutai*: Crisis and Response in Maasailand, 1883–1902' in D. Johnson and D.M. Anderson (eds), *Ecology of Survival* (Boulder, 1988: 73–113). For a return to mixed farming today, see David Campbell, this volume; *idem*, 'Response to Drought among Farmers and Herders in Southern Kajiado District, Kenya,' *Human Ecology*, 12/1 (1984: 35–64); and Kituyi, *Becoming Kenyans*.
15. Waller, 'Economic and Social Relations': 105–106; John Galaty, 'Land and Livestock among Kenyan Maasai' in J. Galaty and P.C. Salzman (eds), *Change and Development in Nomadic and Pastoral Societies* (Leiden, 1981: 69–70).
16. M. Llewelyn-Davies, 'Women, Warriors and Patriarchs' in S. Ortner and H. Whitehead (eds), *Sexual Meanings* (Cambridge, 1981: 330–358).
17. Galaty, 'Being "Maasai" '; *idem*, 'Maasai Pastoral Ideology'.
18. Galaty, 'East African Hunters and Pastoralists'.
19. Jacobs, 'Irrigation Agricultural Maasai'.

20. Waller, *'Emutai'*.
21. G.C. Bentley, 'Ethnicity and Practice', *Comparative Studies in Society and History*, 29 (1987: 24–55).
22. See, for example, C. Geertz, 'The Integrative Revolution: Primordial Sentiments and Civil Politics in New States' in C. Geertz (ed.), *Old Societies and New States* (New York, 1963: 105–157). For African examples, see P.H. Gulliver (ed.), *Tradition and Transition in East Africa* (London, 1969); I. Hancock, 'Patriotism and Neo-Traditionalism in Buganda: the Kabaka Yekka ("The King Alone") Movement, 1961–1962', *Journal of African History*, 11 (1970: 419–434).
23. L. Vail, 'Introduction: Ethnicity in Southern African History' in L. Vail (ed.), *The Creation of Tribalism in Southern Africa* (London, 1989: 1–19).
24. F. Barth, 'Introduction' in F. Barth (ed.), *Ethnic Groups and Boundaries* (Boston, 1969: 9–10). (Itals in original)
25. A. Mafeje, 'The Ideology of Tribalism', *Journal of Modern African Studies*, 9 (1971: 253–261).
26. R. Waller, 'The Maasai and the British, 1895–1905: The Origins of an Alliance', *Journal of African History*, 17 (1976: 529–533).

PART TWO

Becoming Maasai

Introduction

We open with a series of papers that provide an overview of Maasai history — how Maasai came to be 'Maasai'. 'Becoming Maasai' was not a simple linear process, and attempts to project more recent definitions of what it is to be Maasai (i.e. definitions of 'Maasainess') backwards have only served to confuse the issue. At best, such accounts may tell us something of the history of what is now the dominant definition of 'Maasainess', but often, because they fail to comprehend the essential ambiguities of ethnicity, they substitute simple (and simplistic) assertion for complex reality. The much debated non-issue of the identity of the so-called agricultural 'Iloikop' and of their relationship to 'pure pastoral Maasai' — the 'real thing' — is a case in point (see Spear, 'Introduction'). Yet the pastoral ideal developed by the Maasai during and after the nineteenth century, and adopted by their defenders since, is a recent innovation which, as some of our contributors later argue, is now in a further process of revision. The Rift Valley and its adjacent highlands were always a far more confused and complicated place, characterized by great linguistic, social and economic diversity, in which ethnic pluralism and multi-lingualism have more commonly been the rule than the highly restrictive and prescriptive ethnicities which appear, questionably, to be the current pattern.

'Becoming Maasai' occurred in a series of stages in which definitions of what it meant to be Maasai, and therefore of who in fact *was* Maasai, changed radically in response to both internal and external pressures. We introduce the first two stages here, and foreshadow the next two. The history of early Maasai migration into the Rift would appear to be one of accommodation and adaptation, with successive groups establishing themselves beside, and intermixing with, existing populations to produce the palimpsest of pluralist communities noted in the 'Introduction'. Many were probably economically diversified, mixing herding with grain cultivation and, perhaps, hunting and gathering,

19

Becoming Maasai

as Sutton's reconstruction of Maasailand before the 'pastoral revolution' indicates.

By the eighteenth century, however, with the infusion of new weapons and breeds of cattle, together with the development of new forms of age-organization and prophetic leadership, Maasai in the central area and Turkana in the north began to develop much more highly specialized pastoral economies. Thrown out in wider transhumant 'pastoral orbits' and 'deadly jousts' among competing age-sets, in Galaty's words, these specialized pastoralists came to dominate the Rift over the course of the nineteenth century by controlling the key dry-season grazing grounds and water points which alone guaranteed pastoral subsistence. In the process they also redrew the ethnic map of the region as those groups who lost out strategically were then forced to the margins and forfeited both their stock and their former identity. Some, of course, followed their stock into the victors' camps as cattle increasingly became concentrated in the hands of the few who now determined what 'Maasai' was and shaped its identity in their own image and for their own purposes of exclusion.

By the end of the nineteenth century, however, this newly developed 'pastoral ideal' was itself in crisis, undermined by internal competition, external pressures, a series of disastrous epidemics, and, finally, colonial conquest. Colonial overrule only compounded the problem of Maasai identity because it promoted and validated a particular nineteenth-century version of 'Maasai tradition' which came increasingly to be at variance with the economic and social fact (see Waller, 'Acceptees and Aliens', this volume).

Inevitably, an identity based on a vanishing pastoral ideal was contested and these disputes have now reached a new stage as, under the aegis of development sponsored by an independent Kenya government dominated by non-pastoralists, land is supplanting cattle as the critical and valued resource in Maasailand (see Campbell, this volume). This in turn has tipped the debate in favour of a definition of Maasai to include various forms of mixed pastoralism and even cash cropping. With tragic irony, the 'true' (i.e. 'traditional') Maasai are now those who are being marginalized as a pastoral proletariat, and the future would appear to belong to those agricultural Maasai who were once pejoratively known as 'Iloikop' (Hedlund, 1979).

We will take up the later stages of this process in due course, but here we seek to focus on the first two stages of 'becoming Maasai', perhaps the most difficult period of Maasai history to reconstruct with any accuracy, and thus prone to conflicting interpretations of the limited evidence.

Comparative linguistics, surveyed here by Sommer and Vossen, provides the most integrated and coherent picture of the early Maasai past because it is able to combine all of the varieties of Maa and related languages into a single family tree and, through area analysis, to posit the geographical movements, and to some extent the historical events, necessary for the tree to develop in the ways that it did. Put simply, the earliest ancestors of the Maasai came from the southern Sudan, and their descendants then spread southwards down the Rift Valley into central Kenya where a division between northern and southern dialects took place as different groups split off from the main body and settled.

If historical linguistics stresses a coherent, abstract, and elegant linear model of 'becoming Maasai', as successive groups of people moved south, real history is seldom any of these. Sutton and Galaty ('Maasai Expansion') flesh out the linguistic framework with their interpretations of the archaeological and oral data. We still know rather little about the history of early pastoralism in Eastern Africa, although some of the most important recent work has been done in Maasailand in the Lemek Valley by Robertshaw *et al.* and in the adjacent western highlands by Sutton (see Bibliography). What is becoming clear, however, is that there are broad temporal sequences involved in the shift from earlier forms of mixed agro-pastoralism to more specialized forms of subsistence pastoralism that reached their apogee with the so-called 'pure' pastoralism practised by nineteenth-century Maasai and Turkana, but it is equally clear that the process did not involve a simple linear development of increasing specialization. Subsistence pastoralism with little or no apparent agricultural production has been found in very early contexts by both Robertshaw and Sutton, and it is far from certain that one unbroken line of succession was dominant.

A perspective stressing the development of a distinctive Maasai pastoral culture in place, as incoming Maa-speakers mixed and interacted with previous populations, is offered by Sutton. His discussion of pre-Maasai (by which he means pre-nineteenth-century *pastoral* Maasai) traditions over the past millennium reveals an array of different socio-economic groups — pastoral Sirikwa and Tatog, hunter-gatherer Okiek, plains-based irrigation farmers, and highland cultivators — who would provide the bases for the subsequent development of what came to be seen as 'Maasai'. 'Becoming Maasai' was thus less a process of conquest and displacement of prior peoples by established Maasai pastoralists or a pastoral 'revolution' than a process of socio-economic transformation and pastoral 'revival' as Sirikwa and others subsequently interacted with incoming Maa-speakers to emerge as 'modern' pastoral Maasai or Kalenjin.

Galaty then focuses on the subsequent 'pastoral revolution' and the combination of ecological ('pastoral orbits') and social processes ('deadly jousts') that drove pastoral Maasai expansion. The resulting conflicts not only redefined the plains world along new, economically-specialized, ethnic lines, but also led to endless contestations of those identities among themselves and others (a point further elaborated by Galaty, 'Inclusion'; Klumpp and Kratz; and Waller, 'Acceptees and Aliens', later).

Conflicts developed as different groups of Maa-speakers struggled for control over the central resources of pastoral economy, particularly when, late in the century, a disastrous series of droughts and diseases decimated both pastoralists and their herds, rendering life on the plains untenable for large numbers of herders. The wars occurred as pastoral Maasai occupying the central Rift and adjacent highlands successfully expanded outwards against other pastoralists and agro-pastoralists on their periphery: Parakuyo and Loogolala in the south-east, Loosekelai and Uas Nkishu in the west, and Laikipiak in the north. Those defeated suffered losses of cattle, pastures, water points, women, and frequently, the *loibons* who had provided ritual leadership to the *murran*. Unable to continue to maintain a pastoral existence, the losers either sought refuge among the ranks of the victors, hoping thereby to rebuild their own herds sufficiently to remain within the pastoral economy, or fled to agricultural or hunter-gatherer communities on the pastoral margins where they adopted other ways of life, often hopeful of being able to accumulate enough cattle to return eventually to the plains. Some were successful, but many remained and were eventually assimilated by their host communities, leaving traces of remnant pastoralists among all the surrounding peoples. Thus, while identifiable ethnic communities were defeated and 'disappeared' from history, their members usually survived by joining others in the widespread practice of social mobility and assimilation that marked the life of pastoralists and their neighbours. The process of 'becoming Maasai' thus took on additional variants in the nineteenth century, first in the consolidation of a 'pastoral ideal' among Maasai, creating a new sense of what it meant to be Maasai, and second in the ceaseless process of people 'becoming' and 'un-becoming' Maasai, depending on their ability to maintain a foothold in the pastoral economy.

Pastoral Maasai were not the only expansionary power, however. Turkana had earlier joined Maasai in the 'pastoral revolution' of the eighteenth and nineteenth centuries, establishing a strong alternative pastoral focus in the north, and, by the early nineteenth century, were themselves poised to expand at the expense of their less fortunate neighbours, with much the same effects. Lamphear's study of Turkana expansion parallels in many ways what we have seen earlier for Maasai, but his is an important corrective, offering an alternative Turkana vision of pastoral hegemony. While Turkana development often seemed to mirror Maasai in the development of more militarily effective age-sets, new iron weapons, Zebu cattle, and central ritual leadership, these were independent processes in Turkana, reflecting their own history and conditions, and offered an alternative to Maasai hegemony. That the borders between these two ethnicities were hard and engendered brutal conflict is not surprising, given their struggle to control limited pastoral resources and hence to define pastoralism, and many Maasai were among the losers.

Sobania's paper on Laikipiak is a study of one such group of Maasai

Introduction

who lost out in the struggle for pastoral survival. Sobania ponders what it meant for Laikipiak to be defeated, 'finished', become 'lost', in an analogous process to that suggested earlier by Sutton for the Sirikwa. There is no doubt that the Laikipiak ceased to exist as an identifiable ethnic unit, but small groups of Laikipiak were able to maintain independent existences as they sought to restock and re-establish themselves on the borders of Samburu and Rendille. They were eventually defeated by their neighbours and by disease, but Laikipiak remnants can be found today among all the surrounding peoples. Their struggle reveals many of the dynamics in the pastoralist quest for survival, and identity.

. Further south, Spear explores the very different fate of another defeated group. Overcome in the Parakuyo wars, Arusha Maasai sought refuge on the fertile slopes of Mount Meru. Their dramatic subsequent success as farmers reveals a number of important characteristics not normally associated with Maasai, including suppressed traditions of Maasai farming, the complementary nature of Maasai pastoralism and agriculture, and the ability of Maasai to adapt pastoral institutions and values to agricultural practice. Continued Arusha participation in Maasai age-sets and ritual with their pastoral Kisongo neighbours was not simply a cultural relic. Their successful fusion of 'being Maasai' with 'being farmers' was, in fact, crucial to their success. They were able to employ Maasai age-set organization and military tactics successfully against their highland neighbours, gaining large numbers of cattle and women to build their own economy in the process, while at the same time maintaining profitable complementary relations with pastoral Maasai on the adjacent plains. Arusha success at assimilating both Meru and Kisongo is dramatic testimony of the openness of Maasai societies and the degree to which ethnicity itself was as much a function of economic form as a birthright.

The historical picture is thus a complex one, reflecting in part countless historical eddies in the broader processual current of socio-cultural differentiation and development. But, in comparing these accounts based on different types of sources, certain caveats are also necessary. The first concerns dating. While the genetic development of a language can be dated relatively or sequentially, assigning absolute chronological dates to linguistic developments is highly problematic at best. Archaeological sites, by contrast, can be dated scientifically with some accuracy, and thus there is always a temptation to try to associate, and so tie down, linguistic developments to archaeological ones. Such cross correlation is a dubious task, however, because languages are *not* the same as either assemblages of material culture *or* peoples, since peoples can, and do, change the sites they occupy, the way they live, *and* the languages they speak. Thus, when Sommer and Vossen reconstruct Maasai development, they are reconstructing the history of the language (Maa) and its spread by whoever was speaking it at the time. We may assume, probably correctly, that those speakers were the ancestors of the present

Maasai, but we also know that Maasai assimilated large numbers of other peoples, who introduced further changes in the language while adopting it as their own, and that Maasai themselves frequently became assimilated elsewhere and adopted other languages. Or when Sutton, an archaeologist, identifies sites as pre-Maasai, he takes modern pastoral material culture as his point of reference, but he is, of course, aware that Maa-speakers existed long before the pastoral revival of the eighteenth century.

One must thus be careful to maintain clear distinctions between different categories of data. While the Maa linguistic lineage may stretch back to the southern Sudan, that for subsistence pastoralism of the Maasai type may have developed quite separately in the south. Given the paucity of data and the manifold problems in interpreting them, however, these papers help us to understand the complex cultural ecology of pastoralism, the social dynamics of the Maasai system, and the subtle ways Maasai interacted with others in the difficult and on-going process of 'becoming Maasai'.

One

Dialects, Sectiolects, or Simply Lects?

The Maa Language in Time Perspective

GABRIELE SOMMER & RAINER VOSSEN

The Maa language is spoken by Maasai in southern Kenya and north-central Tanzania as well as by Samburu (Sampur, 'Burkeneji') and Chamus (Camus, Njemps) in central Kenya. It belongs to the eastern branch of the Nilotic languages, other members of which are Bari and Lotuko in the southern Sudan, Karimojong and Teso in eastern Uganda, and Turkana in northwest Kenya. As the cradleland of early Eastern Nilotes was probably situated east of present-day Juba in the southern Sudan (Vossen, 1982: 468), the modern distribution of Maa-speakers must be seen as the result of a general north–south movement of their ancestors which commenced early in the first millennium AD. The first Maa-speaking immigrants reached the Rift Valley area by the end of the ninth century and probably the Tanzanian territories to the south by the mid-sixteenth century at the earliest.

Today the Maa language is divided into a number of more or less closely related varieties which can be grouped into two major clusters: North Maa includes the Samburu and Chamus dialects, while South Maa consists of an as yet uncertain number of variants which make up Maasai. The generally consistent picture of north–south movement of, and internal differentiation among, the Maa-speaking population is, however, upset by certain similarities between the most widely distanced dialects of Samburu and Chamus in the far north on the one hand, and Parakuyo (Baraguyu) in the far south on the other. These indicate, first, prior historical interaction between them subsequent to the split between North and South Maa, but prior to the Parakuyo move south, and second some of the complexities of subsequent interactions between and among small groups of Maa-speakers.

The structure of our presentation follows from these key features of Maa linguistic history. Thus we will first give a general overview of external as well as internal relations and then embark on a discussion of some of their 'ethno-historical' implications.

Maa External Relations

East Africa, with its diversity of geographical zones, attracted large numbers of people of varying ethno-linguistic affiliation over thousands of years. Besides Nilotes and Cushites, Bantu and Khoisan-speakers immigrated from different directions or formed part of a largely unknown autochthonous population, respectively. Interethnic contacts, often highly intensive and long enduring, thus played a prominent role in the development of external relations of East African peoples including the Maa-speaking population.

Generally speaking, external linguistic relations can be of three kinds: genetic, areal, and typological. Genetic relationships denote the common descent of languages from, ultimately, a common linguistic mother, which we usually call the 'proto-language'. Areal relationships are characterized by shared features, commonly labelled borrowings or loans, resulting from language contact. Typological relationships, finally, imply the universal tendency of languages to develop, irrespective of their genetic heritage, similar structural features. The distinct nature of each of these kinds of relationship determines the limits of their historical interpretability in such a way that, for instance, genetic linguistic relationships (as expressed in language classifications) bear witness, to a certain extent, to the *origin of the speakers* of the languages involved. In contrast to this, areal relationships can only testify for (non-genetic) *contacts between the speakers* of the languages involved, and nothing more. Historians should therefore be cautious when inferring from linguistic classifications; the usage of 'relationship' in linguistics is clearly polyvalent.

Regardless of any non-linguistic differences which may exist within the Maa-speaking community — be they economic, cultural or historical — Maasai (including Parakuyo and their kinsfolk, the Samburu and Chamus) refer to their language as a single linguistic unit by calling it *ol-máà*. The *genetic position* of Maa among the languages of Africa is fairly clear. It belongs to the Nilo-Saharan phylum (Greenberg, 1963) which is subdivided into several branches, groups and subgroups of which Nilotic — a member of Eastern Sudanic — is the most complex in terms of number of languages actually spoken. Nilotic itself consists of three primary branches: West, South and East (Köhler, 1955), each of which contains a number of individual languages and dialects. The Maa language has its place in the eastern branch whose internal classification may be diagrammed as in Fig. 1.1 (Vossen, 1981, 1982).

As the genealogical tree illustrates, the closest relative of Maa is Ongamo, a language now probably extinct, which was formerly spoken on the eastern slopes of Mount Kilimanjaro (Heine and Vossen, 1975–76). Ongamo and Maa together make up the ONGAMO–MAA group of East Nilotic whose ancestor language, Proto-Ongamo–Maa, itself forms

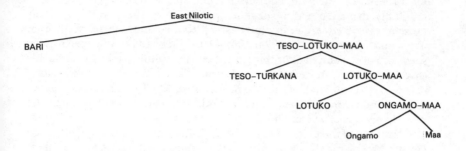

Fig. 1.1 Eastern Nilotic Languages

part of the LOTUKO–MAA group of languages now spoken largely in northern East Africa (Vossen and Heine, 1989). After their separation from the Lotuko, probably during the first half of the first millennium AD, Proto-Ongamo–Maa-speakers are likely to have gradually moved southwards as far as south-central Kenya to the plains between the Nyandarua Range (formerly Aberdare Range) and Mount Kilimanjaro. According to Ehret (1971: 53):

> A proto-Masaian [i.e. ONGAMO–MAA] homeland between the Nyandarua Range and Kilimanjaro would allow neatly for the possibility of Ongamo expansion around Kilimanjaro north and south along the plains of the neighboring rift-valley region. Early widespread Masaian settlement in the area is required in any case by the strong Masaian loanword strata in Chaga, Gweno, Taita, and Kikuyu Bantu languages spoken all about the area today.

In the course of their southward migrations the Proto-Ongamo–Maa must have encountered various peoples speaking East Cushitic and South Nilotic languages. A deep-rooted relationship between ONGAMO–MAA peoples and as yet unidentifiable Eastern Cushites must have existed for some time in northern Kenya, for considerable cultural borrowing from these Cushites is attested in a remarkable loanword set (Ehret, 1974a: 88) and one of the most striking characteristics of Maa culture, prohibition against eating wild fowls and game, may also have resulted from these contacts (Ehret, 1974a: 40).

Around the same time or slightly thereafter, the early ONGAMO–MAA peoples were also influenced strongly by Southern Nilotes who had preceded them in much of the East African Rift Valley (Ehret, 1971, *passim*). Southern Nilotes themselves had had long lasting and highly intensive inter-relations with Cushitic, particularly Eastern Cushitic, people before their expansion into Kenya from the north during the second half of the last millennium BC, thereby adopting much of what made up these Cushites' socio-political organization (e.g. the practice

27

of circumcision) (Ehret, 1974c: 157). But it was long after the split of
the Proto-Ongamo–Maa community that these Southern Nilotes were
gradually driven by Maa-speaking people from the plains into their
present restricted areas in the west of Kenya and the north-west of
Tanzania (Ehret, 1971, 1974a: 56; Ogot 1968: 131). We can merely
speculate about the date of this split, however, which, following Ehret's
chronology of Eastern Nilotic prehistory, is likely to have taken place
early in the second half of the first millennium AD. On admittedly speculative glottochronological grounds the mid-fifth century AD would be the
most likely date (Vossen, 1977: 214).

By the end of the first millennium AD, Maa-speaking people inhabited
large areas of the Kenyan Rift Valley while the Ongamo, after their
separation from the Maa-speakers more than 1,000 years ago, must have
gone straight to the Kilimanjaro region where they claim to have been
since 'times immemorial' (Dundas, 1924: 42). Ongamo display no
recollection of Maa relations prior to their arrival on Mount Kilimanjaro
nor do the Maa-speaking peoples, to the best of our knowledge, have
traditions in which the Ongamo are recalled at all.

So far we have discussed Maa external relations in the context
of genetic descent and ethno-linguistic interaction with others. What
remains to be addressed is the aspect of *linguistic-typological affiliation*.
Generally speaking, language typology is a tool less appropriate for
historical reconstruction than genetic linguistics. In Africa, however, it
has occasionally contributed remarkably to our understanding of
historical events as we shall see.

The distribution of language types, i.e. the distribution of certain
linguistic features and structures, is tied as a rule to geographically deter-
minable areas. In many cases the emergence of such areas goes back
historically to the encounter of speakers of different languages which
have mutually influenced each other. Typologically definable areas thus
represent convergence areas, the study of which may yield answers to
questions of early ethnic contacts and cultural relations.

A highly intriguing picture emerges from Heine's purely syntactical
typology of African languages based on the order of meaningful elements
(such as subject, verb, object) (Heine, 1975, 1976b), for it contains a
geographically defined area, named by Heine the *Rift Valley Convergence
Area*. All languages spoken within this area, some Eastern Sudanic
languages such as Maa included, belong to one and the same type, while
languages located outside it, among them a number of other Eastern
Sudanic idioms, do not belong to this type. The case illustrates perfectly
the ways in which genetic (Eastern Sudanic), typological (verb–subject–
object word order), and areal (Rift Valley Convergence Area) external
relations are sometimes interwoven.

In conclusion, Maa external relations can be summarized as follows.
For the most part modern Maa-speakers are clearly descendants of an
ancient community called Proto-Eastern Nilotes who were located in the

southern Sudan for centuries before the first split occurred. This split gave birth to the early Bari and Proto–Teso–Lotuko–Maa societies. During the second half of the first millennium BC, a second essential break-up took place among the early East Nilotic communities. The Proto-Teso–Lotuko–Maa speakers would seem first to have expanded slowly in two directions, while still living contiguously to one another. As time went by, however, they must at some point have separated completely to develop into two new communities, one of which is known as Proto-Lotuko–Maa. These appear to have taken possession of the lands in the south-eastern corner of Sudan. Probably during the first half of the first millennium AD Proto-Ongamo–Maa emerged from the break-up of the Proto-Lotuko–Maa. Their southward moves appear to have come to an end in south-central Kenya which later became a centre of ONGAMO–MAA dispersal.

On their migrations to the south, the Proto-Ongamo–Maa are likely to have followed a route between the Dodos escarpment in the west and Lake Turkana in the east. If so, they would surely have encountered, and possibly absorbed, a good number of Lowland Eastern Cushites, whose early presence on the western shore of Lake Turkana has been inferred by Ehret (1980) from loanword sets occurring in East and South Nilotic languages. Most of the East Cushitic loanwords in Maa, however, can be shown to have been transmitted via South Nilotic, rather than borrowed directly from East Cushitic. The Proto-Baz language, a now extinct member of Lowland East Cushitic, was found a likely donor. The borrowed vocabulary includes terms denoting initiation practices, and numerals such as 'seven', 'thirty', 'forty' and 'fifty' as well as words relating to cattle-keeping ('virgin ewe', 'cowbell') (Heine, Rottland and Vossen, 1979).

Maa Internal Relations

As has been mentioned briefly before, the Maa language is divided into a number of more or less closely related varieties. Nearly twenty such varieties have been identified, yet the actual number must be larger. The ways in which Maa varieties relate to one another can be ascertained by means of application of dialect-geographical methods (see below). According to this, dialectal relations are subject to a hierarchy expressing degrees of linguistic proximity or distance.

A clear-cut borderline can be drawn between North Maa and South Maa. While North Maa consists of Samburu and Chamus in north-central Kenya, South Maa comprises all the other varieties in southern Kenya and adjacent north-central Tanzania. To some extent, South Maa varieties are arranged in the form of a continuum, such that the nearest geographical neighbours are also the nearest linguistic neighbours. It will be noticed, however, that this is not the case throughout the Maa-speaking community.

A third branch of Maa, Central Maa, might be distinguished on the grounds of data collected from Laikipiak descendants who refer to themselves as Kore and live on Lamu Island and on the opposite mainland around Mokowe, Kenya (Heine and Vossen, 1979). On the one hand, the Kore dialect, which, according to Dimmendaal (1990), has undergone processes of considerable change in terms of reduction, shares a number of lexical and phonological features with North Maa. On the other hand, it associates with South Maa because of other, mainly lexical, correspondences. Moreover, there are particular developments separating Kore from both North and South Maa so that, all in all, there would seem to be sufficient justification to consider Kore provisionally as a Maa branch in its own right (see Fig. 1.2).

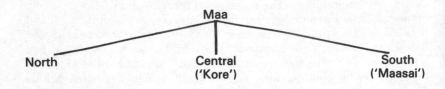

Fig. 1.2 Maa Dialects

Considering the present-day distribution of Maa-speaking peoples, one might distinguish at least twenty-two autonomous, territorially demarcated sections (see Map 1.1). The affiliation of a Maa-speaker to any one of these socio-political units depends on his willingness to participate actively in the political life of this group, through the recognition of all the claims and obligations connected therewith. The sections are as follows:

Arusha (L-Arusa)	Laitayiok (L-Aitayiok)	Purko
Chamus	Loitai (L-Oitai)	Salei
Dalalekutuk	Loitokitok (L-Aitokitok)	Samburu
Damat	Loodokilani (L-Oodokilani)	Serenget
Kaputiei	Matapato	Sikirari I (Ngong)
Keekonyokie	Moitanik	Sikirari II (Loitokitok)
Kisongo (Kisonko)	Parakuyo	Siria
		Uas Nkishu (Wuasinkishu)

The sectional boundaries which have developed and frequently changed over centuries prove to be a reasonable starting point for the investigation of Maa internal dialect variation. Synchronic linguistic

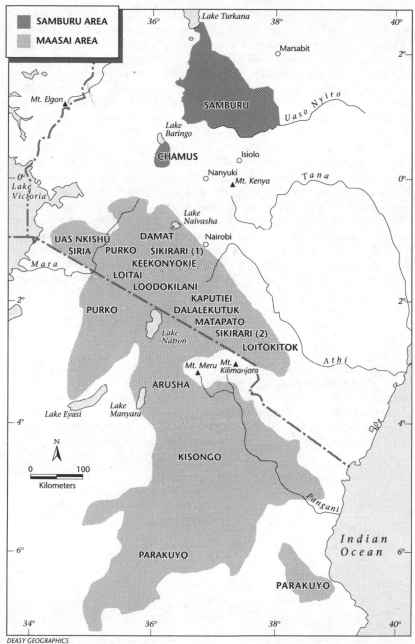

SAMBURU AREA
MAASAI AREA

Map 1.1 Maa Dialects

Becoming Maasai

evidence suggests that the differentiation of Maa varieties corresponds in some way or other to the actual territorial distribution of their speakers. That a certain conformity of territorial and linguistic, i.e. dialectal, boundaries in fact exists, was shown in a word-geographical study analysing material which was taken from various written sources as well as from field-notes collected in the 1970s (Vossen, 1988). With the help of informants from 18 out of the 22 sectional dialects, 610 wordlists were compiled which formed the data basis for our dialect-geographical investigation.[1]

The method of analysis consisted of a quantitative and a qualitative approach which sought to establish a relational system of dialectal proximity by measuring the degree of lexical identity and divergence or partial divergence.[2] As a result, a quasi-hierarchy of Maa relations was obtained from which the division into North Maa (Samburu and Chamus) and a more complex South Maa (Maasai) dialect group (see above) stands out. South Maa was further subdivided into a Tanzania (TSM) and a Kenya (KSM) branch. TSM split into Arusha/Kisongo on the one hand and Parakuyo on the other, but a comparably clear subgrouping of the more complex KSM cluster could not (yet) be set up. (The sections Laitayiok, Serenget and Salei — all located in present-day Tanzania — as well as the Moitanik section in western Kenya were not included in the analysis due to the lack of linguistic data. Their consideration, however, would possibly alter the above classificatory picture, at least with regard to the TSM branch.)

Before summing up the state of the art in Maa dialectal subclassification in a diagram (see below) it should be emphasized that, generally speaking, the members of the KSM branch show the highest rates of proximity followed by their Tanzanian counterparts among which the degree of relational proximity is less prominent. Most distantly related are, of course, the North Maa vs the South Maa varieties.

1 North Maa (NM)	2 South Maa (SM)	
1.1 Samburu	2.1 Kenya South Maa (KSM)	
1.2 Chamus	Loitokitok	Loodokilani
	Dalalekutuk	Purko
	Damat	Sikirari I
	Kaputiei	Sikirari II
	Keekonyokie	Siria
	Matapato	Uas Nkishu
	Loitai	
	2.2 Tanzania South Maa (TSM)	
	2.2.1 Arusha/Kisongo	
	2.2.2 Parakuyo	

Having outlined the major aspects of Maa internal linguistic relations, we will now look at the historical implications of this evidence. The most cogent information is contained in the fundamental division of North and South Maa. It clearly marks the beginnings of the generally southbound migrations of the main bulk of Maa-speaking groups. Given the fifteenth century as a likely date for the break-up of Maa, these migrations would seem to have taken place between the mid-sixteenth and early nineteenth centuries when the southernmost groups, the Parakuyo among them, finally reached their present homeland in central Tanzania. Unlike the majority of Maa-speakers (i.e. South Maa), early North Maa speakers gradually expanded to the north. It is not known where exactly, or for what reasons, they later split into two major divisions, Samburu and Chamus, but we might estimate this split to have occurred around the turn of the eighteenth and nineteenth centuries.[3]

The above-mentioned dates of linguistic splits — North vs South Maa and Samburu vs Chamus — are derived from glottochronological calculations. As shaky as they may be because of imponderables inherent in the method, they represent at least chronological clues. As for the linguistic diversification of South Maa, however, no such clues are available. The differences between KSM and TSM, let alone those between varieties of each of the two, are often so slight that they do not allow for glottochronological counts. This holds true especially for lexicon, which forms the basis of glottochronological dating. Hence, all that we can conclude from dialectal relations within South Maa is that varieties showing particularly high degrees of linguistic proximity are highly likely to have coexisted for a long time. In most cases such varieties are contiguous to one another as nearest neighbours geographically.

Historical Relations between Distant Groups of Maa-Speakers

While the hierarchy of dialectal relations within Maa does not give reason for far-reaching historical conclusions, the study of peculiar lexical correlations among distant groups of Maa-speakers appears to be important for the reconstruction of early Maa history.[4] The case of the Samburu and, to a lesser degree, Chamus of north-central Kenya and the Parakuyo, the southernmost Tanzania South Maa section, is particularly revealing in this context. Early contacts between the two groups are assumed to have taken place before the split of North and South Maa and date roughly to the middle of the sixteenth century.

Before we go into some of the linguistic details of the Samburu–Parakuyo case and their historical interpretability, a brief outline of the historical background seems appropriate. As early as the ninth century Maa-speaking peoples are said to have inhabited areas of the Kenyan Rift Valley (cf. Vossen, 1982: 72). However, little is known about the history of the various groups of Maa-speakers between this early date and the first appearance of orally transmitted historical accounts, which, for the last 400 years, turn out to be very useful sources in regard to historical reconstruction. They show, for instance, that this period of Maa history was characterized most strikingly by (1) a southbound expansion in which most of the Maa-speaking peoples except Samburu and Chamus, participated and (2) the fact that this migration, like Maa history in general, was accompanied by countless feuds and battles on the one side, and the establishment of intersectional alliances on the other. Warfare arose not only between Maa peoples and their non-Maa neighbours but also among Maa-speaking groups themselves. Traditions of the Bantu-speaking Luhya in western Kenya (sixteenth and seventeenth centuries) and of the Southern Nilotic Nandi on the Uasin Gishu plateau (after 1770) recall tension between the so-called traditional enemies, the Maasai and the Iloikop (cf. Vossen 1982: 73).

Samburu and Parakuyo, like most of their Maa-speaking relatives, refer to a legendary place called Kerio as their place of origin. In their oral traditions Maa-speakers in general relate that the immigration of their forefathers from the north took place in the early seventeenth century or even before. As stated earlier, glottochronological calculations date the split between North and South Maa roughly to some time between 1280 and 1580 (Vossen, 1978: 49 n18), or prior to the beginnings of the southward movement of the majority of the Maa-speaking population. Slightly preceding the southward expansion of Parakuyo (or their ancestors), toward the end of the sixteenth century, Samburu and Parakuyo seemed to have lived together in an area far north or northwest of the Laikipia plateau (K.R. Dundas, n.d.).[5] These conclusions can be drawn from a number of significant lexical correspondences shared by the two groups. Whether these correspondences hint at (a) a historical relationship (meaning that the Parakuyo were once a branch of the Samburu), or (b) a close contact situation that existed in the early stages of Maa history is not quite clear. Our data exhibit 21 fully or partially identical words[6] between Samburu and Parakuyo. Since these words, as a rule, are not found in other Maa dialects,[7] their existence in both Samburu and Parakuyo can only be explained in terms of (i) common Maa genetic heritage which the other groups subsequently lost, or (ii) the result of language contact. The latter explanation is no doubt more likely, because only two groups of speakers are involved and, a former Parakuyo presence in north-central Kenya is fairly well attested by the fact that, ultimately, all Maa-speakers came from the north. If explanation (i) were to be correct, one would have to show why only the northernmost and the southernmost Maa-speakers maintained that vocabulary while almost all other Maa-speaking groups residing between the Samburu and Parakuyo lost it.

The identical words in Samburu and Parakuyo are listed below in alphabetical order, indicating form, meaning and sectional distribution.[8] Two of them, namely 'bird' and 'nine', are of particular importance for our hypothesis. In a set of items which usually differ between

Meaning	Form	Sectional distribution
'agree'	*a-camá*	Parakuyo, Samburu (*a-camú* in Chamus)
'begin'	*a-ŋás*	Parakuyo, Samburu, Chamus
'bird'	*eŋ-kwéŋì*	Parakuyo, Samburu (Chamus *ŋ-kwèèŋi*)
'clothing'	*ɛn-áŋká*	Parakuyo, Samburu (Chamus *ŋ-aŋka*)
'daytime'	*m-parkéjì*	Parakuyo, Samburu
'to fly'	*a-ipirrí*	Parakuyo, Samburu (North, West, and Central S.), Chamus, Matapato
'hole'	*úd-ótó*	Parakuyo, Samburu, Chamus
'joy'	*ɛ-ŋídà*	Parakuyo, Samburu, Arusha, Kisongo
'to love'	*a-Cám*	Parakuyo, Samburu, Chamus
'nine'	*saal*	Parakuyo, Samburu, Chamus
'ox'	*l-mɔ́ŋɔ́*	Parakuyo, Samburu, Chamus
'rib'	*ol-máráì*	Parakuyo, Samburu, Chamus
'shoulder'	*o-sîp*	Parakuyo, Samburu
'to tear'	*a-kíj*	Parakuyo, Samburu, Chamus
'truth'	*n-adédè*	Parakuyo, Samburu
'vomit'	*a-rugɔmá*	Parakuyo, Samburu, Chamus

South and North Maa,[9] they are exceptions in so far as they occur only in Parakuyo among South Maa dialects, thereby stressing our assumption that Parakuyo and Samburu may have lived together (either as close relatives or as neighbours) before the split between North and South Maa took place. The Samburu equivalent for 'bird' seems to have been preserved in Parakuyo over a time-span of around 400 years right into the present time. One of the equivalents for 'nine' in Parakuyo, viz. *saal*, provides further evidence for the reconstruction of early Parakuyo territorial history. Since it can be shown to be a loanword from East Cushitic, and since nothing is known about a presence of Eastern Cushitic peoples in Tanzania either in the past or in the present, the Parakuyo (or their ancestors) seem to have brought the word along on their move from northern Kenya.[10]

In summary, it would appear that in the mid-sixteenth century Samburu and Parakuyo were dwelling in an area north or north-west of the Laikipia plateau. After their separation by the end of the sixteenth century, Samburu moved in a north-westerly direction and occupied an area between the Cherangany Hills and Lake Baringo. The Parakuyo, on the other hand, started a southward migration through the Rift Valley until they reached and settled in what is now Loitai region, where they coexisted with the Loitai for about 200 years.[11] By the turn of the eighteenth and the nineteenth century, however, the Parakuyo appear to have gradually been expelled from this area by Loitai. They reassembled not much later, however, and formed a new political centre in the Pangani river area, where they expanded their territory. Parakuyo settlements extended at that time from Usambara to the south of Mount Meru and Mount Kilimanjaro. Until the middle of the nineteenth century, however, the Parakuyo were more or less constantly involved in feuds with neighbouring Kisongo, who finally succeeded in defeating them. It was then, in the second half of the nineteenth century, that the Parakuyo were pushed to the periphery of the South Maa territories where they have been living in scattered groups until today.[12]

The case of Parakuyo–Samburu interaction above is the only one so far to whose clarification linguistics is able to contribute. More dialect-geographical investigation is needed to unravel inter-relations and interactions between Maa-speaking groups that are not indicated in the oral traditions. The linguistic data are there; their evaluation should not be too long in coming.

Notes

1. The questionnaires had actually been filled in by the informants themselves in a spelling which they thought was adequate.
2. For the definition of 'partial divergence', see Vossen, 1988: 19 .
3. For a less linear reconstruction of expansion, cf. J. Galaty 'Maasai Expansion' (this volume), where a concentric 'core–periphery' model, with, e.g., Damat, Keekonyokie, Matapato, and Loitai at the centre, and other groups radiating out from that, is proposed to account for the configuration of Maasai sections.
4. The linguistic evidence taken into account here derives from the so-called single-word evaluation, a procedure by which particular intersectional lexical relations that remained unrevealed in the quantitative and qualitative assessments, are interpreted historically (cf. Vossen, 1988: 23).
5. As Vossen (1978: 42) points out, there is evidence suggesting that the Parakuyo are descendants of the now partly annihilated, partly expelled Loogolala Maasai who are said to have lived on the 'Samburu-occupied' Laikipia plateau as early as the sixteenth or seventeenth century. The Samburu, on the other hand, are often mentioned in connection with Laikipiak (Vossen, 1980: 114) to whom the Samburu themselves refer as relatives. This attitude presumably points to close and long-enduring contacts between Samburu and Laikipiak, rather than genealogical affiliation.
6. Partially identical items are the following: 'dawn', 'elbow', 'roof, 'be satiated' and 'stick'. Regional variants of Samburu showing correspondences in Parakuyo are: 'darkness', 'sand', 'to shake' and 'to sleep'.
7. Some of them do indeed occur in other Maa varieties, albeit as adopted variants rather than genuine representatives of these sectional varieties.
8. As becomes clear at first sight, only three ('daytime', 'shoulder', 'truth') out of the sixteenth lexical items are, strictly speaking, shared exclusively by Samburu and Parakuyo. The Chamus equivalents for 'agree', 'bird', and 'clothing' no doubt go together with Samburu/Parakuyo as partially diverging forms. Moreover, eight equivalents ('begin', 'hole', 'to love', 'nine', 'ox', 'rib', 'to tear', 'vomit') are entirely identical between the three sectional speeches, which raises the number of lexical correspondences between Samburu, Parakuyo and Chamus, as opposed to any other Maa dialect, to a total of eleven, i.e. nearly seventy per cent. This high percentage, nonetheless, does not contradict the existence of exclusive lexical links between Samburu and Parakuyo, because Samburu and Chamus were still one people, speaking one and the same Maa variety, at the time of the linguistically inferred Samburu–Parakuyo historical relationship. In fact, oral traditions relate that Chamus origins are rooted in a community of Samburu precursors (cf. Vossen, 1980: 99).
    Furthermore, our chart illustrates that the word for 'joy' is not shared uniquely by

Samburu and Parakuyo. Its occurrence in Arusha and Kisongo, however, may be seen as a result of relatively recent contacts between Parakuyo, Arusha and Kisongo, since they all belong to TSM. The only case, then, of exceptional word-sharing by a section which might disturb the hypothesis of early Samburu–Parakuyo relations is Matapato's participation in the series of equivalents for 'to fly'.

9. These items are (besides 'bird' and 'nine'): 'bewitch', 'blood', 'day', 'egg', 'hippo', 'lake', 'ox', 'seven' and 'sorcerer'.
10. The other word for 'nine' in Parakuyo, *nt ŋ*, is confined to TSM (cf. Vossen, 1988: 95). It appears to have been adopted by Parakuyo from Kisongo and/or Arusha.
11. The living together of Parakuyo and Loitai in the vicinity of present-day Narosura (cf. Vossen, 1978: 42) is corroborated by linguistic evidence. Of all KSM dialects Loitai is closest to Parakuyo, a fact which cannot be considered to rest upon recent contacts because both groups have been territorially divided for more than 100 years.
12. See note 3, above.

Two

Becoming
Maasailand

J.E.G. SUTTON

Historians have not always appreciated the vital contributions which archaeology and linguistics have made to the study of East Africa before the nineteenth century. The history of Maasailand could not indeed be written without data provided by field archaeology, since usable oral traditions relating to the period before 1800 hardly exist. This chapter explores the history of the Rift Valley and the adjacent highland areas during the second millenium AD. It concentrates on the pre-Maasai pastoral tradition, especially that developed by the Sirikwa, who were essentially the ancestors of the modern Kalenjin groups of the Western Highlands of Kenya, and on the growth and influence of agricultural and hunting communities, including irrigation agriculture, within and to the east and west of Maasailand. It suggests an interpretation of the expansion of the Maasai as, essentially, the development of a 'Maasai' identity across the high grasslands in recent centuries — in effect, the 'Maasaiization' of Maasailand.[1]

Comparative linguistic evidence suggests an early Maasai expansion from the region near the south end of Lake Turkana, close to that occupied by the Maa-speaking Samburu in the nineteenth century (Sommer and Vossen in this volume). This is indicated by linguistic geography, by two persuasive observations in particular. First, since the Maa tongue belongs to the Plains (Eastern) division of Nilotic, and all other branches of that division lie in north-western Kenya and adjacent parts of Uganda and Sudan, the separation of the 'Maasaian' branch must have occurred somewhere in or close to the south-eastern edge of that broad zone. That could have happened up to a millennium ago.[2] Second, there is apparently more basic variety between the Maa dialects north of the Equator than between those to its south, indicating that the southward expansion is relatively recent. A fairly short span of time — perhaps two to four centuries — is also suggested for these movements by the sheer expanse of territory occupied by speakers of a single language whose dialects are mutually intelligible. This rather shallow time-span is enough to satisfy other attempts to construct a chronology for the central Maasai sections in particular, by calculating from the succession of their named age-sets or from the genealogy of their ritual leaders (*loibons*). However, as historical sources, both age-sets and genealogies have been squeezed rather too enthusiastically in the past and it is doubtful whether either can be of much effective help as a chronological guide for the period before 1800.[3]

In this view, Maasai expansion may have occurred in two stages. The first would have been at least three hundred years ago, probably considerably earlier, when early Maa-speakers in northern Kenya, having separated from other Plains Nilotes, moved southwards into lusher high equatorial grasslands as far as the elevated Nakuru stretch of the Rift Valley, thereby displacing or assimilating earlier populations. In the second stage, in the eighteenth century at the latest, Maa-speaking groups would have radiated outwards from the Nakuru–Naivasha area, south-westwards across Loita, Mara and Serengeti and south-eastwards to Ngong and across the Athi and Kaputiei plains as far as the foothills of Kilimanjaro (Map 2.1).

This second stage in a sense re-emphasized the first as it covered over many of its traces. It involved the emergence of a central Maasai confederation or alliance, comprising several sections in the high grasslands, together with a new and territorially extensive role for the *loibons*, who as individuals and families could demonstrate through heredity, charisma and wisdom their possession of the powers essential for the well-being of the Maasai community, its land and cattle (Berntsen, 1979a). These Maasai sections, sometimes regarded as the typical or 'true' Maasai, who insisted, at least in theory, on a purely pastoral diet, were probably a late internal development of the eighteenth or early nineteenth century.[4] They gained control over the Rift Valley and the adjacent plains through a series of struggles with other Maa-speakers, the so-called '*Iloikop* Wars', for strategic resources of water and pasturage. The losers were either absorbed or forced onto the margins where they had to abandon or modify their pastoral economy (see Galaty in the next chapter).

The formative period of Maasai history may therefore be read in a more dynamic and varied way. 'Movement' can be interpreted as the rapid social, institutional, and ritual development of self-conscious ethnicities as much as actual territorial expansion. It might be argued that what expanded was not a different group of people, the Maasai themselves, but a new identity, expressed in culture and language, which became 'Maasai'. There were, therefore, not two stages of physical movement but two stages of a cultural process, so that, about two hundred years ago, a heightening of the sense of 'Maasainess' and of the ideal of the pastoral life occurred which was geared to a restatement of dietary rules and to the operation and rituals of the age-organization. One might

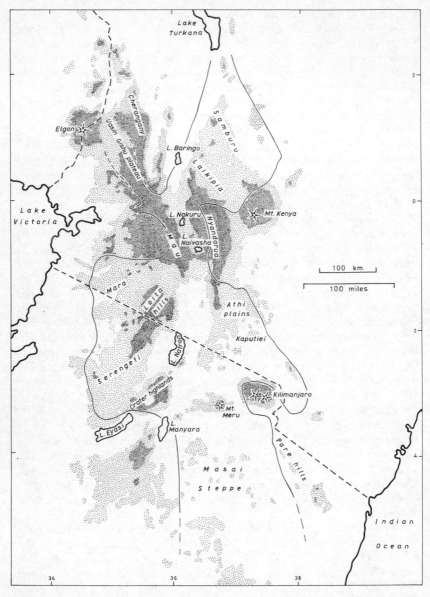

Map 2.1 Maasailand and the Surrounding Country

envisage this as a 'pastoral revival' of a sort which can probably be documented at certain other times and places in Eastern Africa's history. By this view, Maasai adaptation to the high grasslands was perfected in Laikipia, to the north of Mount Kenya and Nyandarua, some four hundred years ago. Interaction with the Sirikwa around Nakuru, who were long experienced with the highland ecology and its pastoral exploitation, was doubtless instrumental in this. The southward-pushing Maasai then revived the old pastoral ideal of the Sirikwa and, under its new Maasai identity, carried it into the southern plains on either side of the Rift in the second stage of expansion. On these plateau grasslands they could endeavour to pursue a pastoral life without reliance on cultivated foods as a matter of 'choice' — in contrast to the situation in the drier northern plains where subsistence pastoralism appeared to be the only economic alternative to a hunting-gathering existence (Jacobs, 1965). The second stage should thus be seen as a self-identification of 'real Maasainess', devised to exclude other Maa-speakers who had been pushed off the finest grasslands or who simply did not wish to compete for them.[5] Thus, one might see the unusual homogeneity of Maa dialects as partly the result of continual interaction between highly mobile and successful pastoralists who came to share a similar identity and culture.

The Maasai way of life depended on maintaining adequate military organization with suitable tactics and weapons for defence and attack alike.[6] The reasons for this were both economic and territorial. Firstly, the pastures, as well as the water-points and salt-licks for cattle, had to be defended if they were to be exploited efficiently to maintain a predominantly pastoral economy in a fashion adequate to support the community (Waller, 1979). But such defence of territory and its natural resources could not, for all its efficiency, guard against every calamity, be it an unusually severe drought or a disease reducing the numbers of livestock and the milk supplies. In order to feed the community until the

---

Map 2.1 Maasailand and the Surrounding Country

The approximate boundaries of Maasailand — defined as those regions in which the Maasai language was dominant over a hundred years ago, i.e. before the rinderpest epidemic — are indicated by the continuous line.

The names marked for various districts within Maasailand, though based in several cases on those for individual Maasai sections of the present or past, are used here essentially geographically (i.e. as toponyms rather than ethnonyms). For this reason conventional spellings are retained.

Contours, indicated by shading, are at 1,500 and 2,000 metres (approx. 5,000 and 6,500 feet). The Rift Valley is shown by the south–north line of lakes through the middle of the region, the elevated Naivasha–Nakuru stretch being commonly called the 'Central Rift'.

herds had recovered their former size, and equally to obtain suitable cows and breeding bulls for that purpose, raiding was often necessary. Otherwise the community, or a good part of it, had to adapt, at least temporarily, to a different diet and way of living, if not to break up completely. In a way then, the 'truest' Maasai are those who have come through the best and the worst of times most successfully; they are in the long run the minority which has managed, by defeating rivals and excluding them from the finest grasslands and their watering points, to maintain the pastoral life and ideal and to define proper 'Maasainess' — and a view of Maasai history — on their own terms.

This has meant giving recognition to the twin virtues of warrior prowess and the possession of fine cattle maintained through skilful herd management. The prestige and success of 'Maasai' as an ethnic affiliation, over Sirikwa among others, depended upon the military superiority of Maa-speakers, apparently from the first stage. It appears that the effectiveness of Maasai military methods was due, among other things, to larger, socketed, spear blades as opposed to the lighter, tanged, ones previously general in the East African highlands and surrounding plains. New emphasis was also placed on formalizing the theory and practice of the age system and on defining the duties of the constituent age-sets, including their regular initiation through circumcision and the details of their transition to 'power'. Maasai success thus has to be explained by the combination of novel forms of military organization and tactics with the rapid social, institutional, and ritual development of a self-conscious ethnicity in which a particular form of age-organization was central.

The Sirikwa and the Pre-Maasai Pastoral Tradition

The emergence of the Maasai, as we know them from the nineteenth-century record, may thus be as much a result of change within the 'pre-Maasai' population as a consequence of some large-scale migration. The exact balance of factors must remain conjectural, but the issues may be addressed more effectively by surveying what is known of the older populations both in and on the borders of Maasailand.

Before the era of Maasai ascendancy, the Sirikwa way of life had been dominant in the Western Highland region for several centuries. At its greatest extent, the Sirikwa territory covered the highlands from the Chepalungu and Mau forests northwards as far as the Cherangany Hills and Mount Elgon (Map 2.2). There was also a south-eastern projection, at least in the early period, into the elevated Rift grasslands of Nakuru (Sutton, 1973, 1987). Thus the areas of Sirikwa and Maasai occupation were not coterminous and it was only this outlying south-eastern area that was taken over permanently by Maasai, probably no later than the seventeenth century. Here Kalenjin place names seem to have been superseded in the main by Maasai names.[7]

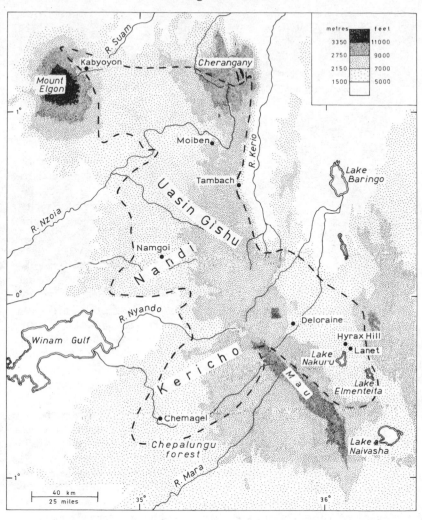

*Map 2.2 Sirikwa Territory, c. AD 1200–1700 (after **Azania, XXII**)*
   The broken line indicates the approximate limits of Sirikwa occupation as
established by archaeological survey; excavated Sirikwa 'holes' are named. The
modern district names, Nandi and Uasin Gishu, are used here for reference, not as
ethnic terms.

Photo 2.1 Sirikwa Homestead at Chemagel in Sotik during Excavation. For interpretation of details see plan opposite (Photo: J. E. G. Sutton, 1964).

Certain of the Sirikwa, at least on the western and south-western side towards the end of the period, combined grain-agriculture with their management of cattle, goats and sheep. This is demonstrated by excavations of their integrated cattle-pen and homestead complexes, normally known, albeit misleadingly, as 'Sirikwa Holes'. Some of these Sirikwa homesteads in Nandi and Sotik were still constructed with substantial round houses attached to the typical sunken stock-pen as late as the eighteenth century. The stock enclosure was heavily fenced, gated and guarded. Kitchen furniture and utensils were more abundant than one would normally expect among people depending on their animals for their entire subsistence. These late Sirikwa homesteads served as family bases. When the houses and the fences showed signs of wear after a few years, or when the dung-heaps sited to guard the entrance from view became uncomfortably large, the whole complex could be replicated a few metres away on the same hillside.

Previously it was argued that this combination of cultivation and pastoralism was the Sirikwa norm (Sutton, 1973). But it now appears that the original, perhaps the 'ideal', Sirikwa life was more uncompromisingly pastoral. This is demonstrated, at least in the Nakuru area,

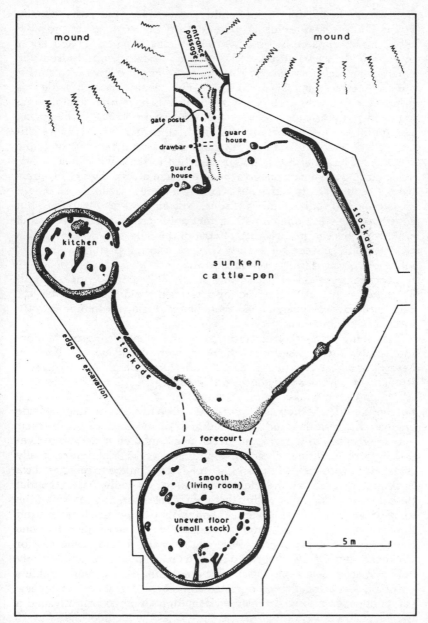

Fig. 2.1 Plan of Sirikwa Homestead and Cattle-pen as Excavated at Chemagel. This is a late example in the south-western part of the Sirikwa zone. The size of the attached houses and their domestic refuse indicate the combination of grain cultivation with stock-keeping.

from about the twelfth or thirteenth century. Here the excavations at
Hyrax Hill reveal a decidedly pastoral economy, with small, probably
zebu, cattle, apparently with a strong emphasis on milk, and flocks
of goats and sheep (Sutton, 1987).[8] Meat, deriving entirely from the
domestic animals, was largely roasted, and signs of cultivated plants or
the cooking of vegetables are lacking. The keeping of zebu cattle was
probably not new in itself, for humped breeds have been identified on
highland pastoral sites over two thousand years old.[9] But the Hyrax
Hill findings, by comparision with anything earlier, suggest more efficient use of these cattle and an emphatically pastoral exploitation of the
ecology.[10] The small flimsy houses attached to the hollowed cattle-pen
and guarding its gate do not give the impression of forming a solid family
base or centre of daily activity as occurs in a more agricultural situation,
or as indicated on later Sirikwa sites. Not only in diet, therefore, but
equally in the selection and management of livestock and of the overall
ecology of this elevated Nakuru stretch of the Rift, one may imagine a
close parallel between these early Sirikwa and the pastoral Maasai of
much more recent times. In other words, the typical Maasai economy
had been largely pioneered here long before the Maasai identity evolved.
The latter, as suggested, revived, by devising more efficient methods, the
early Sirikwa ideal, one that had been diluted during the four or five centuries of Sirikwa ascendancy.

The change in methods introduced by the Maasai consisted of more
than simply their possession of heavier, more deadly spears. Between
Maasai and Sirikwa there were more fundamental differences of
strategy, in fighting and defence and also in organization and settlement.
Although recent Maasai camps, comprising the homesteads of several
families and their central stockyard, are properly fenced, they lack the
emphatically guarded and protected look of the Sirikwa homesteads,
with their small individual family stock-pens and their fence foundations
dug into the hillside, their elaborate gateworks and sentry points
and their inward-facing houses. One might be tempted to imagine these
Sirikwa, especially as they felt competition, cattle-theft and military
threats more keenly, redoubling their defensive efforts and developing an
increasingly inward world-view. Though they could not have entirely
hidden their homesteads and cattle-pens from view, their frequent
preference for the peripheries of the plateaus and for sites concealed by
woodland, if not perfectly protected at the rear uphill side, and with the
approach from below masked behind great dung-heaps, suggests that a
premium was being placed on protection. There was, indeed, a cultural
commitment to a closed defensive system for both the community and its
livestock. As cattle-raiding increased — or as the methods and scale of
raiding were transformed during the early part of the Maasai era —
these Sirikwa defensive methods, and the settlement system and social
organization which were integrated with them, proved vulnerable. While
they would normally have been proof against individual thieves or

against small groups of rustlers hoping to succeed by stealth, they were obviously inadequate against larger long-distance raiding parties which, in rounding up cattle, did not hesitate to smash or burn down fences. These old 'Sirikwa Holes', therefore, far from being effective devices for livestock protection, became veritable traps. They and the Sirikwa way of living had to be discontinued.

In the Maasai era, guarding cattle on the plateaus has depended less on elaborate defences than on mobility and cooperation, both of these being combined with grazing and herd-management strategies. The practice of the later Kalenjin — that is, after they had abandoned the Sirikwa pattern and had ceased in effect to be Sirikwa — illustrates this change vividly. On their reduced pastures, notably on the borders of the Uasin Gishu Plateau, they would, when bodies of raiders approached, relay the alarm from ridge to ridge so that the herds could be combined and rushed to the cover of the forests. There, the approaches to the glades would be defended by concealed archers, and the advantage would be turned against the spears of the plains warriors.

The Sirikwa, then, represent both a period and people with a distinctive way of living. Though they ceased to exist as such two to three hundred years ago, they did not simply 'disappear' (see Sobania in this volume); nor did they 'flee' to the south or, alternatively, to the north as is sometimes averred. Some Sirikwa, especially in the southeast around Nakuru, were 'Maasai-ized', their cultural and ecological experience proving instrumental to Maasai pastoralism as it established itself in the fine high grasslands and then radiated southwards. The main body of the Sirikwa, however, remained in the Western Highlands where they reacculturated to form the new Kalenjin communities all around the Uasin Gishu Plateau and further south. This is, in the first place, no more than a simple geographical deduction; but it receives strong support from the Kalenjin traditions and the strength of memory of the Sirikwa there. Moreover, any alternative historical reconstruction has to face the virtually insuperable problem of explaining where the Kalenjin have 'come from'.

Certain Sirikwa elements or splinters did move further afield. Southwards, some appear to have been assimilated into Maasai sections in the Loita–Mara region and others into Tatog.[11] Equally large, or larger, numbers helped to form the Kuria and related peoples between the Mara and Lake Victoria where they adopted a Bantu language but retained the form and nomenclature of certain Sirikwa–Kalenjin social institutions. Further north, between the Winam Gulf and Mount Elgon, other Bantu-speaking Luyia groups betray the assimilation of similar elements in some of their clan and age-set names (Sutton, 1973, 1976). Northward again, beyond Elgon and Cherangany, more has been recorded about likely Sirikwa elements in the drier hills and plains, now essentially assimilated within Pokot, Karimojong and other peoples. Sometimes, they are linked to 'Oropom' memories in the region. The names 'Siger' and 'Sangwir', used both of places and people, have been considered semantically, if not etymologically, cognate with 'Sirikwa' (see Lamphear in this volume).[12] But, essentially, the Sirikwa — though not by that name — remained where they always had been, in the highland mass sloping away westwards from the Mau, Kerio and Cherangany Escarpments comprising the Kalenjin homelands. Territorially it was only the Nakuru area (and, less definitively, part of the Uasin Gishu Plateau) which passed from Sirikwa into Maasai control. Here the Sirikwa were pushed westward to help form the new Kalenjin groups or, alternatively, remained to be assimilated into the expanding and successful Maasai ethnicity.

Other Pastoralists of Pre-Maasailand

Although the Sirikwa represented perhaps the main pastoral tradition from which the Maasai borrowed in the high grasslands, they were not the only early pastoralists in the Rift Valley region. To the south-west, on the Loita–Mara plains and across Serengeti to the Crater Highlands, were Tatog-speaking peoples with a predominantly pastoral economy. Knowledge of their life and herding methods in the high plains is both imprecise and indirect, being derived from observations of the modern Tatog, who exploit very different terrain further south, and also from oral information about their former occupancy of Ngorongoro and areas beyond, which is corroborated in the vaguest of ways by Maasai memories of *Il Tatua*.[13] The survival on the northern side of the Mara of bands of Omotik 'Dorobo' with a language of the Tatog division confirms that the latter once, before the Maasai expansion here, adjoined the southern boundary of the Sirikwa/Kalenjin.[14]

It is possible that some Tatog-speaking groups extended into the lower parts of the Rift, and were in contact with the irrigation-agriculturalists along the escarpment foot at Nkuruman, Sonjo, Engaruka, Manyara and Eyasi. Similarly, on the far sides of Mara and Serengeti, they would have touched the territories of various Bantu cultivators. The option of obtaining food by exchange with such neighbours was essential for survival in times of crisis. Even so, the extent of their territory, falling away westwards from high mountains and forest edges above the Rift escarpment to the open plains, ensured a degree of versatility, provided that competition was not too severe and that these cattle-keepers were free to exploit the seasonal pastures and water-points as circumstances varied from year to year. Like the Sirikwa, these Tatog-speaking groups also 'disappeared' from many of their former areas of occupation. Some have undoubtedly been assimilated into Maasai sections, but others have retained their Tatog identity by shifting southwards to exploit poorer grasslands around Hanang and elsewhere.

The best pastures to the east of the Rift, south of the Nakuru–Naivasha 'bottleneck', those of Athi, Kaputiei and Amboseli, and the foothills of Kilimanjaro and Mount Meru, were probably outside the limits of earlier Tatog territory. But the linguistic distributions and loanword patterns may yet allow a case for early Tatog or other Highland Nilotic speakers there (Ehret, 1971). Archaeologically, the Iron Age of the plains on this side of the Rift is poorly known. It is possible, largely on negative information, that this region was previously occupied by an earlier 'Maasaian' division, before the late expansion of the existing pastoral sections.[15] Alternatively, Cushitic-speaking groups, the linguistic descendants of the early highland pastoralists of both sides of the Rift in the first millennium BC, may have been dominant here until quite recently. There is no need for a simple or single explanation.

At this point it is necessary to turn to the broader regional context of pastoralism, and to look at the interaction of pastoral pursuits with agriculture and forest activities. Although the grasslands of Kenya and northern Tanzania are generally well watered — except for much of the northern plains and the more arid sections of the Rift floor lying both south and north of the Nakuru–Naivasha elevated stretch — the continuity of pastoralism has been dependent on the natural versatility of the region and its rainfall, and on the propinquity of forested hills to most parts of the grasslands. Much of the forest margin and of the medium-altitude fertile lands has been settled by agricultural peoples. Some of these agriculturalists have kept small numbers of cattle as well as goats; others have relied on exchange with nearby Maasai for cattle products. Such cooperation has been essential for certain peripheral non-cultivating Maasai sections in the south-east, as it was presumably for other pastoralists in earlier times. More generally, the continuity of the pastoral life in the best of the high grasslands over the last thousand years — that is, in both Maasai and pre-Maasai times — has doubtless benefited from the possibility of falling back in times of crisis on the agricultural and forest resources of the region. The 'pure pastoral' ideal and its historical propaganda may deny this, and may particularly abhor any suggestion of reliance at times on vegetables or game meat; but, in the long run, it seems probable that a markedly pastoral economy on the scale of the Sirikwa or Maasai required the existence of equally well-established complementary economies and contrasting ways of life within the region as a whole (Lamprey and Waller, 1990).

The Forests and the 'Dorobo' Factor

Before the Iron Age there were, it seems, no formally settled agricultural peoples at this latitude. It is possible, though inadequately demonstrated, that the early pastoralists of the highlands in the first millennium BC undertook some cultivation alongside their cattle-keeping or had in places an agricultural option to fall back on.[16] There was also the hunting option, although some of those who specialized in stock-rearing at this time may have already normally eschewed wild meat. Nevertheless there was space then as later for groups specializing in hunting, both on the grassland plateaus and their margins and in the dense high forests. In recent times, and apparently throughout the last two if not three millennia, forest people have fulfilled a special role in relation to the plains pastoralists, in supplying forest products, honey in particular. If these commodities have not been strictly vital to the pastoralists nutritionally, the symbiosis has nevertheless fulfilled an essential supportive and cultural role in the history of highland pastoralism.

Such forest-dwellers, hunters and honey-collectors are commonly known to Maasai as 'Dorobo': the word properly means 'poor' — by inference, those without cattle. While few of these people call themselves by that name, there are Maa-speaking clans or families in Samburu who do. These may simply be groups of poor Samburu who have been recently forced to survive by exploiting and exchanging forest resources and by providing essential services for cattle-keepers (including the herding of stock which is not their own property). But, at the same time, these Samburu Dorobo seem to be heirs to a long technical and cultural tradition.[17] This view is encouraged by the example of various groups to the south and west whom Maasai again call Dorobo, but who know themselves by other names and speak older languages (though being bilingual for purposes of interaction). In particular there are Okiek, most of whom have been living in the high forests of Lembus, Tinderet and Mau above and behind the edges of what was until recently Maasai territory. These scattered Okiek groups speak a distinct Kalenjin tongue, yet most of them have found themselves in recent centuries outside the south-eastern bounds of normal Kalenjin activity and speech, and have been dealing more frequently with Maasai (see Klumpp and Kratz in this volume). The obvious explanation of this linguistic anachronism is that the Okiek represent a tradition descending from the era of the Sirikwa, when the latter extended from the Western Highlands across these forests into the Nakuru section of the Rift. This is not to present the Okiek simply as a Sirikwa survival; they are, rather, a relic of one aspect of that age, and a clear indication that the special ecological role of forest-dwellers alongside pastoralists has a long history in the highlands, a history much older than that of the Maasai as such.[18]

The existence of other, non-Okiek, Dorobo communities confirms that this phenomenon is both extensive and ancient; and that, although pastoral languages and identities may change, forest bands have proved more robust and conservative as cultural units and have succeeded in asserting their own individuality in this way as hunter-gatherers. The Omotik in northern Mara and the Loita hills, for example, constitute two or three pockets of hill forest-dwellers who retained a Tatog-type dialect, long after Tatog pastoralism in this area was superseded by that of Maasai. In Serengeti the persistence of a few Southern Cushitic-speaking hunter-gatherers called Asa must represent a much older relic from at least a thousand years ago, which has survived two linguistic changes among their pastoral clients, firstly to Tatog and later to Maa.

The remarkable strength of the internal cultural traditions of various Dorobo groups is also exhibited by their ability to relocate themselves geographically and still to preserve their identity and language. Thus certain Okiek bands have for some time lived in high forests east of the Rift, both on Mount Kenya and at Kinare south of Kinangop, far from other Kalenjin-speakers. Such moves must have been responses to opportunities to exploit an untapped forest niche and also a pastoralist demand in the plains below. One Okiek ('Akie') group has migrated much further afield, to the southern extremity of the Maasai Steppe, and has preserved its identity and language there, apparently unaware now of the existence of other Kalenjin or indeed of other Okiek far to the north. Possibly, its movement occurred in company with a section of the Kisongo Maasai, or conceivably of the Parakuyo, as they expanded southward, say up to two hundred years ago.

Agricultural Populations East and West of the Rift Valley

Cultivators have, like forest-dwellers, also played an essential supportive role in the maintenance of pastoralism over time. East of the Rift, most of the cultivating peoples on the south-eastern slopes of Nyandarua and Mount Kenya and further east, as well as around the base of Kilimanjaro and other mountains to the south-east, speak Bantu languages. Although their numbers seem to have increased remarkably in quite recent times, especially through cutting upwards into the most fertile soils of the montane forest edges, settlement in these locations stretches back many centuries, at least to the middle part of the Iron Age. In most, though not in the highest, forest clearings, earlier Bantu settlement of the first millennium AD is attested.[19]

This highland Bantu agricultural tradition has constantly interacted with the pastoral presence in the region at large, in some districts in a very intimate way, just as it has adapted to ecological intricacies and changing opportunities in the region. All the Highland Bantu possess some vocabulary of Cushitic derivation. This does not necessarily mean that a Cushitic agricultural tradition has at some point, a thousand years or more ago, been simply Bantuized. The Cushitic element may have been as much pastoral as agricultural in the surrounding plains, and have been absorbed into the expanding Bantu agricultural tradition. Similarly the existence now, west of the Rift in north-central Tanzania, of Southern Cushitic-speaking cultivators with cattle (Iraqw, etc.) should not be seen as a simple relic of the situation before the expansion of both Nilotes and Bantu. Although the ancient linguistic dominance of Southern Cushitic in the whole highland region, perhaps back to 1000 BC, is undeniable, the emergence of the Iraqw as such and their successful agricultural adaptation to the hills of Mbulu district are very recent developments.

Several instances can be detected of westward colonization by Bantu groups from the east moving into the Rift or right across it to reach the far escarpments and to find new agricultural land surrounded by, or adjacent to, the grasslands. One such group seems to have crossed the generally rather dry Maasai Steppe from the Pare hills to the slight western escarpment of Irangi two or more centuries ago. The existence there of an isolated area of Bantu speech may not derive entirely from such late movement; nevertheless the Rangi tongue was doubtless reinvigorated by this late element from the east. From vocabulary hints, it consisted of smiths as well as farmers. Further clues to this movement can be seen in the abandoned agricultural settlements, some combining iron-working, in the more elevated western parts of the Steppe.[20] These settlements obviously succeeded for a while and doubtless provided services for local pastoralists, but in the long run the situation probably proved too marginal.

More substantial — or at least more influential — has been east–west crossing of the Rift further north, from Kikuyuland south of Mount Kenya and the Nyandarua range to the south-western Mau and Kisii district. It is attested very clearly in the languages of Gusii, Kuria and Logoli, which betray a Bantu ancestry from two sides, i.e. the Eastern Highlands as well as Lake Victoria (Sutton, 1973). Very little is known about this movement in detail, yet one can well see how the lush terrain of the Mau slopes and Kisii would have appealed to cultivators of Mount Kenya extraction. One such group, cultivating the forest margins of the Mau in Kericho district, preserved a Bantu dialect until being assimilated into the Kipsikis division of the Kalenjin early in the present century. Similar memories are recorded elsewhere in that district; but, since no oral traditions of the actual cross-Rift movement seem to survive, it probably occurred before the main southward expansion of Maasai around the Mau and into Mara. The pioneers of this westward Bantu colonization would have crossed between the Sirikwa and Tatog zones. It is not necessary to assume a vacant corridor there, however, since neither pastoral group would have had any obvious reason to obstruct an agricultural development of this sort.

A separate movement from the Mount Kenya region across the Rift, or perhaps merely an offshoot of the same westward colonization, is evident in Sonjo, in the dry broken country between the upper and lower escarpments overlooking Lake Natron. On the modern map, the Sonjo villages form an agricultural island in the midst of Maasailand. Each village has maintained itself by being sited close to a spring or a minor but reliable river, from which narrow canals, carefully constructed and maintained, are led to irrigate extensive field basins. Not all of the food is produced in the irrigated fields, for in most years a fair proportion can be grown on rainfall alone. But irrigation has always been essential to the whole agricultural system and thus to the survival of the Sonjo people; for, without that annual supplement and the ability to increase reliance on it in poor years, the settlement would not be sustainable in this relatively arid situation.

The antiquity of the Sonjo as such is probably quite three centuries, maybe rather more. On linguistic evidence they appear to have had some contact with Tatog-speakers, indicating that the Sonjo settlement in the region, if not necessarily on their present village sites, occurred before the displacement of Tatog by Maasai in Loliondo, Sale and Serengeti. A more important contact, however, probably amounting to substantial assimilation, occurred with a Southern Cushitic-speaking community already resident in this area, and very likely cultivating with irrigation on certain of what are now Sonjo sites (Sutton, 1986, 1990). This observation is highly pertinent to the question, examined below, of the connection between Sonjo and the now deserted irrigation-agricultural villages at Engaruka and further south.

There was certainly considerable interaction between some of these westward colonizing Bantu and Highland Nilotic-speakers in the region beyond the Mau and the western edges of the Mara and Serengeti Plains. Among the Bantu communities there, the Kuria on what is now the Tanzania–Kenya border and others to their south have preserved cycling systems of age-sets, most of the names being obviously Kalenjin and the rest shared with Kalenjin. Certain of them are shared again with the Kikuyu and Embu of Mount Kenya, thus recalling, if in an inscrutable way, the cross-Rift link.[21] Between Kuria and southern Kalenjin several elements in the age-organization are so similiar as to indicate close contact and a degree of common ancestry in recent centuries which, as suggested, has probably to be placed in the period of the Sirikwa break-up and of the formation of the new southern Kalenjin communities (that is Nandi and especially Kipsigis with Sot) in or about the eighteenth century. The Kuria, it appears, emerged through the local Bantuization of some of the most southerly Kalenjin in this transitional period. The point is demonstrated by the Kuria homesteads, consisting of a ring of houses around a central fenced cattle-pen (Sutton, 1973). Although the latter is not hollowed, the overall design is based very clearly on the Sirikwa one, especially the large and late Sirikwa 'Holes' of the nearby Sotik area. Arguably therefore, these most southerly of the Sirikwa, with substantial agricultural homesteads combined with stock-pens, were modernizing in other ways in the eighteenth century by simultaneously adopting a Bantu tongue and a reformed Kalenjin age-organization.

Irrigation Cultivators of the Rift Wall

The interaction between herders on the plains and irrigation cultivators in small oases close to the walls of the Rift has long been a feature of the region and doubtless pre-dates the Maasai. Irrigation settlements have acted as refuges and suppliers for pastoralists and also, in some cases, as centres of acculturation through which individuals and families could learn to become Maasai. The best known and the most challenging of these settlements have been those of the 'Engaruka complex', dating to pre-Maasai times, of which the early Sonjo settlements described above would have been a northern outpost or outposts.

Compact villages thrived by irrigated agriculture between six and three centuries ago, at Engaruka itself, halfway between Lakes Natron and Manyara, and at lesser sites both along the foot of that escarpment and by Lake Eyasi (Map 2.3). This is one of the driest parts of the Rift floor. Invariably, therefore, these settlements were situated by permanent rivers descending from the wetter highlands, or in minor cases by springs issuing at the base. The several villages at Engaruka itself were compact and substantial, and closely reminiscent of those of recent Sonjo. The arrangement of the irrigated fields, however, was a little different in detail from Sonjo, not because of any real distinction in method and technology, but merely to cope with the different configuration and terrain of the irrigable areas — Engaruka's fields being extensive, but much more dusty and stony than those of the Sonjo villages. Thus, at Engaruka itself, the remains of two thousand hectares of an ancient field system remain visible because of the stonework which lined the main canals, their branches and the lesser feeders among the fields, and the dividing and levelling of the fields with stone lines and terraces.

In the midst of this arid region the Engaruka community intensively farmed as much land as could be reached by these exquisitely engineered gravity-fed canals and also reared some small cattle as well as goats and/or sheep. The cattle were, it appears, kept in stone-walled pens, which are visible among the fields; and, owing to the lack of spare land for grazing, they would have been stall-fed. The manure which they yielded would have been put to use on the fields. Such a well-integrated agricultural system was obviously a reaction to a severely circumscribed situation, of splendid potential up to a point but with no room for expansion beyond the limits (and levels) of the land which could be reached by channelling the flow of water in the escarpment streams. In time it felt strains, as the population, having grown on the success of the system, reached the maximum size which the fields could feed. With declining stream-flows and soil fertility, it would have been a losing battle despite, or perhaps because of, all the technical ingenuity and agricultural intensification. Engaruka and the smaller related communities to its south broke up therefore in the seventeenth century, or at the latest the early eighteenth, very probably before the Kisongo Maasai established themselves in the adjacent plains. The population would have dispersed, but part of it, probably one already established in the north, survived as Sonjo. The latter succeeded in this by assimilating small numbers of incoming Bantu from the Eastern Highlands and making mutual arrangements for land-use and other services with pastoral Maasai as the

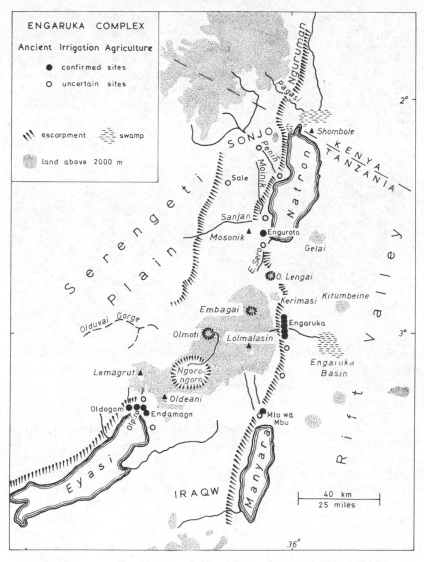

Map 2.3 Engaruka and Related Settlements, c. AD 1500-1700 — and Sonjo (after Azania XXI: copyright British Institute in Eastern Africa)

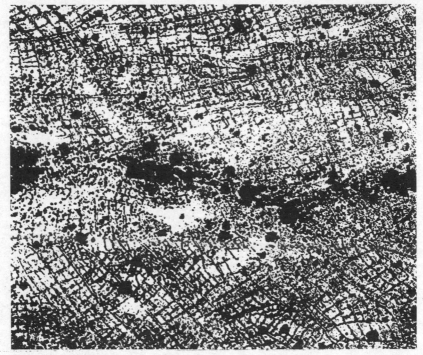

Photo 2.2 Engaruka: Aerial photograph of part of the ancient irrigation system at the escarpment foot, showing grid of stone-divided fields and double-line feeder channels (courtesy of Tanzania Surveys and Mapping).

latter were establishing themselves both on the plateau above and in the Rift below.[22]

The observation that the people of the Engaruka complex, including early Sonjo, probably spoke a language of the Southern Cushitic group, related to that of the present Iraqw a little further south, would, if confirmed, assist further steps towards reconstructing the cultural and economic history of the region. It is important, however, to limit speculation in this area and to avoid a simplistic ethnohistorical argument. Although Cushitic languages would have been spoken from about 1000 BC in what became Maasailand, most of the specific features of agriculture and building in stone, which have been claimed as part of a Cushitic cultural package diffusing from Ethiopia, developed later and separately in East Africa. The existing example of Konso, a Cushitic-speaking people in southern Ethiopia with impressively terraced hillsides, walled villages, stall-fed cattle and the use of their manure on the intensively cultivated fields, does not constitute evidence of an actual connection with the East African Rift, not even of an indirect one drawing on an ancient Cushitic cultural substratum, as some scholars used to suppose.[23] It is relevant nonetheless in another, more subtle way, in particular in suggesting interpretations for various features in the archaeology of Engaruka.

Connections do become apparent, however, within more restricted regions or when considering specific cultural details and recent language relationships, as between Engaruka and Sonjo (the latter now Bantu). A more difficult case is posed further north along this Rift wall, on the Kerio Escarpment in Marakwet and adjacent parts of Pokot and Elgeyo. Here the existing irrigated agriculture, relying on canals led off the escarpment streams, especially those below Cherangany, though not a replica of Engaruka's ultra-intensive system, displays several similarities in principle. These cultivators are now Kalenjin-speaking; but this linguistic situation is likely to be quite recent, of the post-Sirikwa era of the last two centuries or so. Of all the main existing Kalenjin territories, the Kerio Valley and the Tugen Hills beyond are the only areas falling outside the former Sirikwa range. Conjecturally therefore, when the Sirikwa way of life was breaking up around the Uasin Gishu plateau two to three centuries ago, and the new Kalenjin communities were forming, some of these ex-Sirikwa elements moved down the escarpment and merged into the irrigation cultivators. The result, rather as in Sonjo, was linguistic change among the specialist cultivators, but with the difference here that the new language was not so culturally and geographically specific; it was part of the regional Kalenjin continuum, both along the valley and in the highlands above the escarpment.

Alternatively, rejecting the speculative connection during the Sirikwa era between the agriculture of the Engaruka, Sonjo and Nkuruman escarpment and that of the Kerio, it might be argued that the latter has been culturally related to the Pokot, who constitute linguistically another branch of Highland Nilotic. Pokot is in fact often regarded as part of Kalenjin, but there is an obvious linguistic distance between it and the rest of the Kalenjin which, though not so deep perhaps as that between Tatog and Kalenjin, must go back well into the Sirikwa era, possibly before it. In other words, then, the argument for essential transformation of the former Sirikwa into later Kalenjin, right through the highlands west of the Rift and north of the Mau specifically excludes the Pokot. From that there might be grounds for positing the earlier Pokot as agricultural specialists to the north-east of the Sirikwa, exploiting the favourable basins below the Kerio Escarpment and the Siger massif. The present extent of pastoral Pokot to both east and west would then have been a relatively late expansion from the largely agricultural core, in that there would have been room for some of the Sirikwa splinters and refugees who moved northward off the plateau in the eighteenth century to be eventually assimilated. The Pokot expansion and competition for pastures were felt by the northern Maasai in the nineteenth century, particularly in the Rift north of Lake Baringo and on the Leroghi plateau (Sobania, 1980).[24]

Lake Baringo itself, in particular the flats at its southern end which were cultivated by irrigation in the nineteenth century by the Chamus section of northern Maasai, reinforced by Laikipiak and Samburu elements, might, by the same argument, have been previously a Pokot settlement. The early history of Chamus is very complex with several levels of incorporation, marked by the stylized clan 'histories' and several economic and cultural traditions interacting in a small area. The present, Maa-speaking, population incorporated at various times substantial non-Maa elements who, according to tradition, represent earlier inhabitants of the lakeshore area and who are thought of as 'Dorobo' rather than irrigation agriculturalists. Moreover, it now seems certain that the irrigation system at Baringo was elaborated in the nineteenth century.[25] But there is no a priori reason why irrigation cultivators at Baringo should have conformed linguistically, even in earlier times, to those in Marakwet or, further afield, at Nkuruman or Engaruka. It should also be noted that the irrigation technology beside Lake Baringo is rather different from that of these other places, each situated at the foot of an escarpment where gorge openings and waterfalls provide more frequent opportunities for taking off levelled canals.

Economic and Cultural Versatility in Historical Perspective

Whether the above reconstruction is entirely correct or not, the Pokot provide an instance of economic versatility notwithstanding their strong sense of cultural identity. Indeed, this has long been true of the whole of what has recently constituted Maasailand and its fringes. Specific identities may have had their own particular cultural orientations; but in practice, if not necessarily by their own admission, most have been modified over time, whether through internal compromises with the environment and economic opportunities, or through the transformation of communities and their identities. Becoming Maasai was one of these processes. Ceasing to be Sirikwa, as all Sirikwa — whether they used that name for themselves or not — did sooner or later, was for some the reverse side of that coin. For most Sirikwa it meant becoming Nandi, Keiyo, Marakwet, Sebei or some other (modern) Kalenjin section.

Some identities survived by radically redefining themselves. The case of Arusha is discussed by Spear elsewhere in this volume. This group maintained the Maasai language as it settled below Mount Meru and depended heavily on the produce of the fields. The yield round the year was increased by leading irrigation canals off the mountain streams, similar to those of neighbouring Meru cultivators, and, on the other side of the Sanye plain, of the Chagga of Kilimanjaro. At Taveta, up to a point, as at Nkuruman and Baringo, smaller groups of Maasai specialized in cultivating, again frequently with irrigation techniques, and identified themselves with that place and specialization. They could assist other, more pastoral, Maasai, especially in years when food was short or when some of the cattle had to be kept nearer to water or on the restricted permanent pastures of a mountain such as Meru. Having few cattle themselves did not render these cultivators poorer by any objective standard, or necessarily less Maasai; rather, they could exploit 'Maasainess' in language and in clan and age relationships. The history of Maasailand therefore, both during the recent Maasai era and before it, may be seen as one of versatility and adaptation, as a constant balance between opportunity and identity, with periodically the need for communities to redefine themselves or to revive the pastoral ideal. The latter undercurrent, supported by a fair measure of cultural and genetic continuity transcending the linguistic changes of the present and preceding millennia, has ensured a historical thread and tradition for the high equatorial grasslands.

Notes

1. The approach of this chapter, based on linguistic, archaeological and other considerations, expands that adopted in Sutton (1973). The present version has been reduced by the editors and I am grateful for their judicious efforts and provision of cross-referencing. For a survey of the linguistic relationships, see Sommer and Vossen in this volume.
2. See Ehret (1971) although his preference is for constructing longer chronologies. Also Ambrose (1982).
3. Fosbrooke (1956) and Jacobs (1968a). It is necessary to understand better how time and generational succession have been conceived before such information can be put to chronological use. It is often assumed, moreover, that the length of age-sets has been constant. Because of the centrality of their succession to Maasai culture and society, it is not surprising that this impression has pervaded oral testimonies as well as anthropological thinking until recently. The supposition that, before recent disruptions and disasters, 'normality' had prevailed, and that the institutions had worked regularly, looks grossly unhistorical. For one thing Maasai social institutions, like any others, were designed to deal with stress as much as with normality, and they would, therefore, have adapted and evolved as the surrounding circumstances changed. The information derived from the central pastoral sections, those which, it is argued here, formed relatively recently, most probably does not apply in detail to other Maasai sections, either central or peripheral, before the nineteenth century. For discussions of the use of age-set chronologies, see Berntsen (1979a) and Baxter and Almagor (1978), Introduction.
4. This is based largely on Jacobs (1965) but not necessarily on the historical conclusions he draws. For other interpretations, see Sutton (1973) and Lamprey and Waller (1990).
5. The claim, recorded in, for example, Merker (1910: 7–15), that there had occurred an aboriginal division, between the 'true' Maasai and the rest of the speakers of the language who happened to live at both the southern and northern peripheries, tends to confirm the opposite historical reconstruction.
6. The simplistic image of Maasai as a 'warrior nation' has been substantially revised; see, for example, Jacobs (1979).
7. Certain Maa-speaking groups, notably Loosekelai (known as *Sigilai* to the Kalenjin) and Uas Nkishu (who gave their name to the Uasin Gishu Plateau), did penetrate further west into the Sirikwa heartlands in the eighteenth and nineteenth centuries. It seems, however, that Maasai occupation of the Upper Nyando Valley and the Uasin Gishu Plateau was intermittent and probably contested, and the scarcity of Maasai

place-names there, in contrast with those of Kalenjin derivation (many probably current from Sirikwa times), tends to confirm this.

8. A contrast is apparent between Sirikwa and earlier Iron Age pastoralists in this region, as revealed at the Deloraine site at Rongai. Culturally, the pre-Sirikwa occupants of Deloraine, dated to about the end of the first millenium AD, seem closer to those of much older, pre-Iron Age times.

9. See, especially, F. Marshall (1990).

10. It is important to notice how the keeping of livestock in the high grasslands over a period of some three thousand years has, to a degree, created its own ecology. The balance of cattle and small stock, grazing strategies and the use of controlled burning have all had a lasting impact, in particular on the availability of short grass and the delimitation of forest margins. Hunters and honey-collectors as well as pastoralists and also cultivators on the fringes of the highlands have adapted to these ecological developments. So have game animals. Several species of short-grass, open-plain herbivores are probably more numerous now than they were before cattle herds and herders first pioneered this region, helping to turn bush and rank grass into desirable open pasture. The restriction of bush on the lower margins of the grasslands has had the further effect of keeping tsetse fly at bay; see Sutton (1973); Lamprey and Waller (1990).

11. According to an earlier account, one Tatog section was known as Sirikwajek; see Wilson (1952: 40).

12. The Sirikwa of Nakuru early in this millennium do not appear to have been 'old-style' pastoralists, either in their breed of cattle or in their way of managing them; see Lamphear (1986).

13. For Tatog, see Tomikawa (1979).

14. F. Rottland, personal communication, and in Heine *et al.* (1981: 270–273).

15. The position of Ngassa or Ongamo on the east side of Kilimanjaro perhaps supports this. Ngassa falls into the same 'Maasaian' branch of Plains Nilotic but is usually regarded as a language separate from Maa itself. Its existence might suggest a broad spectrum of 'Maasaian' peoples round the north-eastern periphery of the highlands stretching from Turkana to Kilimanjaro early in the present millennium; see Sommer and Vossen in this volume.

16. Discussed in Robertshaw (1990), especially chapters 3 and 14.

17. Spencer (1973), Appendix; Sobania in this volume. For discussions of interpretations of 'Dorobo' origins, see Kratz (1980) and Waller (1985b).

18. Blackburn (1976); Kratz (1980). Blackburn's map misleadingly labels as Okiek many other 'Dorobo' bands in both Kalenjin and non-Kalenjin areas. Among these are the Omotik and Samburu Dorobo bands. It is possible, however, that certain of these were previously Okiek who have lost the language and identity after long separation.

19. See *Azania*, 6 (1971), a special volume on the Iron Age in Eastern Africa, especially the contributions by Soper, Odner and Siiriainen; also Phillipson (1977), chapter 6.

20. Information from T. Peterson. Some of these sites are mentioned in H.A. Fosbrooke, 'Early Iron Age Sites in Tanganyika Relative to Traditional History' in J.D. Clark (ed.), *Third Pan-African Congress on Prehistory* (London, 1957: 319).

21. O. Bischoffsburger, *The Generation Classes of the Zanaki* (Fribourg, 1972); H.E. Lambert, *Kikuyu Social and Political Institutions* (London, 1956); M.J. Ruel, 'Kuria Generation Classes', *Africa*, 32 (1962: 14–36).

22. For description and discussion of Engaruka and related irrigation settlements, see Sassoon (1966); Sutton (1978, 1986, 1989). See also Robertshaw (1986). A more general and comparative discussion is attempted in Sutton (1984).

23. See, for example, Murdock (1959), especially chapter 25. For a recent study of Konso, see H. Amborn, 'Agricultural Intensification in the Burji–Konso Cluster of Southwestern Ethiopia', *Azania*, 24 (1989: 71–83) and Sutton (1989).

24. I am grateful to Michael Bollig for discussing his unpublished research on Pokot history.

25. This is based largely on David Anderson's research which could not, unfortunately, be included in the present volume. But see Anderson (1988, 1989).

Three

Maasai Expansion & the New East African Pastoralism*

JOHN G. GALATY

In debates over the role of the Maasai in the history of East African pastoralism several questions recur that are central to our understanding of how economies and societies of the region emerged and were transformed. First, when and in what way did the practice of specialized pastoralism first arise in East Africa and become consolidated as an organized system of production? Second, when and how did communities of Maa-speakers expand and move southward to occupy much of the East African Rift Valley region, and how was this expansion related to their specialized pastoral organization and technology? And, thirdly, when and by what process did Maasai territorial units coalesce and a distinctive Maasai identity or ethnic consciousness emerge? Much of the evidence bearing on these questions is fragmentary, coming as it does from the diverse disciplines of historical and comparative linguistics, archaeology, oral history and anthropology, whose methods and assumptions do not always mesh.

This chapter will deal not only with what is known about the history of specialized pastoralism and Maasai expansion but also with the debates about how current knowledge should be construed and interpreted. For instance, it is evident from the cultural geography of the recent past that, by the mid-nineteenth century, Maa-speaking peoples inhabited a vast area stretching from north of Lake Turkana in what is now southern Ethiopia through Kenya to central Tanzania. The Rift Valley itself provided a north–south axis of Maasai occupation and a corridor for their expansion. The Rift Valley region, however, comprises a more diverse economic geography. It is transected by the actual semi-arid valley but includes highland forests and plateaus, and it is integrated into a single system through mobile resource use or trade (Waller, 1985b). But does the current Maasai distribution represent the outcome of an expansionary intrusion throughout the Rift Valley region of a discrete people over a relatively short period of time or a more diffuse and osmotic process whereby a language and a culture spread through previously existing communities, with the emergent societies assuming different forms depending on the social and linguistic fabric of those assimilated? And did Maa-speakers develop highly specialized pastoralism and then introduce it into East Africa through their expansion, or did they merely adopt and refine the specialized pastoral practices of their predecessors?

In addressing these questions, this chapter will consider how Maasai expansion involved an evolution in Rift Valley regional economy and polity, with the emergence of the Maasai pastoral economy and society as a system of specialized resource use and labour allocation, as an encompassing pattern of economic value and cultural ideology based on livestock, and as a structure of social organization and identity within a wider regional socio-economic system which also included foraging, hunting, agro-pastoralism and both irrigation and rain-fed cultivation. From this point of view, the development of pastoralism, through what Sutton called 'the Maasai Revolution' (1990: 52), may have represented only one part of a wider economic refiguration within the Rift Valley region towards more productive and specialized pursuits, the proponents of which were linked through trade, social ties and reciprocal cultural interactions.

The Origins of Specialized Pastoralism: A Leitmotif In East African Historiography

The Maasai represent the southernmost extension and the highest degree of pastoral specialization among Eastern Sudanic-speaking peoples. A history (or prehistory) of the community, and of the system of specialized pastoralism in East Africa which they exemplify, must consider first the differentiation and southward movement of those Eastern Nilotes who developed into the Maa-speakers; and second the social and economic evolution of the Rift Valley region of Kenya and Tanzania where the Maasai emerged as a synthesis of diverse influences and peoples. Given the unique status of Maasai pastoral specialization, a key question which recurs for each historical stage of pastoral evolution is whether animal husbandry was, or was not, combined with cultivation. At stake is the underlying issue of whether specialized pastoralism has a long and enduring history in the region, inherited by Maasai from others who originated the adaptation, or whether in fact diversified forms of agro-pastoral or even agro-pastoro-foraging subsistence were the norm, with specialized pastoralism an occasional and perhaps a very late evolution.

Ehret (1982: 391) suggests on linguistic grounds that 'the productive advantage of the shift to livestock raising' may have stimulated the emergence from around the fifth millennium BC of Eastern Sudanic-speaking peoples, for whom there is no linguistic or archaeological evidence of cultivation. During their expansion, they developed an intensive form of cattle pastoralism involving the milking and bleeding of animals, and originated several cultural traits that still characterize their Maa-speaking descendants, including age-organization and the extraction of lower incisors (Ehret, 1974a: ii,49,56).

The first pastoralists in East Africa were very likely Southern Cushitic-speakers, associated between 3300 and 1300 BP with intensive cattle pastoralism and plains hunting in a region from the Kenyan Highlands through northern Tanzania (Ambrose, 1984: 227–230). Robertshaw and Collett (1983a) consider that, despite the absence of direct archaeological evidence, the practice of cultivation by Southern Cushites can be inferred from their occupation of areas in the Kenya Rift Valley where cultivation has since been proven theoretically possible, and this presumption is echoed by Ehret, who suggests that Southern Cushites knew grain culti-vation (principally sorgum) as well as stock raising (Ehret, 1974a: 7–8). Ambrose is of the opinion, however, that agriculture would have proven as unreliable in the distant past as it is in the present, and he points out that, since contemporary Southern Cushitic farmers in Northern Tanzania cultivate the caudatum sorghum associated with Sudanic-speakers (which was introduced into the region by Southern Nilotic-speakers at a later date) rather than the durra sorghum used by virtually all other Afroasiatic-speakers in Ethiopia, Southern Cushites probably did not cultivate during the Neolithic period (Ambrose, 1984: 236).

The presence of pastoralists in the Lemek Valley of south-western Kenya from the mid-first millennium BC is attested by the archaeological remains of several communities, most notably those associated with the Elmenteitan tradition, specializing in caprine and cattle husbandry, who occupied the region from 400 BC to AD 600, and perhaps longer (Robertshaw, 1990: 294–295). Ambrose (1984: 87) proposes that the Elmenteitans were Southern Nilotic-speakers, who may have coexisted with, and later displaced, earlier Southern Cushitic groups in the region. On the question of whether Elmenteitan communities in the Loita–Mara combined animal husbandry with agriculture, Robertshaw maintains, despite the absence of carbonized seeds or grinding stones, that, since the soils and rainfall were suitable, cultivation, albeit unreliable, was prob-ably practised (Robertshaw, 1990: 296). Marshall, however, arguing from the relatively large and diversified herds managed, their structure and age at slaughter, their use for both milk and meat, the intensive form of animal processing, the relative lack of wild faunal remains or evidence for agriculture, and also from current Maasai pastoral practice in the region, suggests that the Elmenteitan communities of the Loita–Mara region were specialized pastoralists, although they may have gained grain through trade (Marshall, 1990: 242–243). Regardless of whether limited grain production was already practised by Southern Cushitic or Southern Nilotic populations, Bantu-speaking highland farmers, who arrived in East Africa around two thousand years ago, would have served as reliable partners in the livestock–grain trade and may thus have facilitated the practice of more specialized animal husbandry by freeing pastoralists from the need to cultivate or forage for their necessary food supplements (Robertshaw and Collett, 1983a, 1983b.)

The differences of opinion just reviewed over what degree of pastoral specialization can be inferred from archaeological evidence reflect in part the ephemeral nature of most agricultural remains. But these opinions also reflect convictions, partially derived from theory, about whether specialized pastoralism could have developed in the absence of grains (whether gained through cultivation or trade) to supplement pastoral subsistence in times of stress, whether the ecological and technological possibility of cultivation by itself constitutes sufficient evidence from which to infer its practice (given the convenience of a diversified economy) or, alternatively, whether the relatively low and unreliable yields of semi-arid land with rain-fed cultivation would prove insufficiently rewarding in the face of the relatively high productivity of specialized pastoral labour. The question of whether or not the Maasai experience of specialization in animal husbandry is unique and whether it does offer a valid model for earlier pastoral adaptations brings us to the issue of Maasai origins and migration into East Africa.

The Early Maa-Speakers and the Old Pastoralism

It appears that the early Pastoral Iron Age in East Africa (around fourteen hundred years ago in the central Rift Valley) may have been associated with Nilotic expansion and the development of more intensive and highly specialized forms of pastoralism (Robertshaw and Collett, 1983b: 74; Bower and Nelson, 1978: 564).[1] Lamphear has described as 'old pastoralism' the system of East African animal husbandry practised during this era. He suggests that this system was more sedentary and less specialized than would later be the case, and involved less extensive pasture use and more varied mixes of animal and crop husbandry and foraging, with species of less efficient non-humped pre-zebu bovines (Lamphear, 1986). Presumably, 'old pastoralism' would also have involved less sharp ideological distinctions, in particular between hunting, cultivation and animal husbandry, than would be the case following the arrival of the Maa-speakers (Galaty, 1982a). If, in Lamphear's view, the Maasai were associated with the development of the 'new pastoralism', more specialized and efficient than the old, what would have been the status of Early Maa-speakers during the era of 'old pastoralism'?

There is very little about 'origins' in Maasai oral tradition, except a firm but ritualized conviction of their northern origins and the routine assertion by all Maa-speakers that their history began when they ascended *endigir e kerio*, the [Kerio?] Escarpment.[2] It is most frequently suggested, based on the linguistic divergence of existing Maa dialects, that Maa-speakers arrived in the Rift Valley around AD 1600 (Lamprey and Waller, 1990: 19), but an even shallower time depth is proposed by

Sutton, who states that the main expansion of the Maasai from the north into the Rift Valley would have begun only 'two hundred years ago or slightly earlier', that is, in the seventeenth or eighteenth century (Sutton, in this volume). Given the lack of a clear tradition of migration, Lamprey and Waller suggest that there might perhaps have been several Maasai migrations into the Rift Valley, the ancestors of the modern Maasai being only the last, or that the Maasai 'emerged as a community with a distinct identity only in Maasailand itself' (Lamprey and Waller, 1990: 19).

These options are not, however, mutually exclusive, as the following discussion will indicate. In fact, there is reason to believe, on the linguistic evidence, that there was an early Maasaian presence further south in Kenya, where, by AD 500, intense interaction occurred with Southern Nilotic communities (Vossen, 1982: 71; Ehret, 1971: 53). Ehret suggests there must have been 'early, widespread Maasaian settlement' by AD 1000 in the plains country between the Nyandarua Range and Kilimanjaro, at a time when most of the cultural attributes associated with Maasai social and economic organization must have already been acquired (Ehret, 1971: 54). In direct contrast to the 'old pastoral' image, Vossen observes that, under the influence of Southern Nilotes, whose presence is attested by Ehret, the early Maa-speaking population perfected their nomadic and purely pastoral way of life after splitting from the Ongamo (Vossen, 1982: 71; Ehret, 1971: 43). However, Sutton holds that Southern Nilotic (Sirikwa) settlement in the Western Highlands of Kenya goes back only somewhat more than a thousand years and argues that, although previous pastoralists had occupied these fine grasslands for two thousand years before them, it was the Sirikwa who were the first to perfect a specialized form of dairy pastoralism, combining milk cattle with goats and sheep for meat, even though many Sirikwa also cultivated (Sutton, in this volume).

In Lamphear's view, the 'old pastoralists' included or were the Sirikwa, a 'phenomenon' rather than a single people, who may have included both Kalenjin and early Maa-speakers (wrongly associated with the *Iloikop*) who participated in a highland-based mixed economy (Lamphear, 1986).[3] Ehret notes evidence (for a later date than that adduced above) for the dominant influence of other early Maa-speakers in the Rift Valley, who also preceded, and spoke a different dialect from, modern Maasai. The 'early Maasai' who, reconstructed vocabulary suggests, may have practised both pastoralism and cultivation were 'hardly identifiable with modern pastoral Maasai who eschew all cultivation' (Ehret, 1971: 73,75,178).

In fact, there does exist a Maasai tradition of the 'earliest inhabitants' of Maasailand, who 'looked just like Masai but cultivated', and who were referred to by the term *Ilumbwa* (Hollis, 1905: 280–281). Interestingly, Maasai sometimes used the same term for the Southern Nilotic Kalenjiin-speaking Kipsigis. If the term *Ilumbwa* signified early agro-pastoral Maasai, it may be of note that some variant of *Lumbwa* has also been used to refer to Maasai in general (including the Maa-speaking Parakuyo) by their southern neighbours in Tanzania, and that Maasai often refer to the Parakuyo by the same name. It may also be reasonable to hold that there was a second 'early Maasai' presence in the southern Rift Valley prior to the later Maasai expansion, living in close proximity to earlier Southern Cushites and Southern Nilotes, and that all these peoples were associated with 'old pastoral' practices.

Maasailand in the nineteenth century was, and still is today, socially and economically complex. Although specialized pastoralism and pastoralists predominated, many other economic varieties were and are practised by Maa-speakers. There is no reason to believe that early Maasailand should have been any less complex, or that the development of 'purely pastoral' society, in Vossen's terms, and of mixed pastoralism and cultivation, could not have been pursued by various groups of early Maa-speakers, who influenced or came under the influence of different sets of neighbours, including Southern Cushitic, Southern Nilotic or Southern Kalenjin-speakers, in turn. Moreover, given the semi-arid nature of the Rift Valley savanna, its occupation would have required the sort of intensification of mobile pastoral production identified with Maasai today. Thus there may have been a continuous process of striving towards greater pastoral specialization, wherever and whenever possible, rather than a particular moment in history when 'pure pastoralism' was definitively achieved. It may be too simple, then, to posit a historical progression from diversified to specialized pastoralism and then to ask when it occurred. In East Africa, it has always been occurring, even before the 'new pastoralism'.

The Maasai Revolution and the New Pastoralism

Lamphear has suggested that the 'new pastoralism', perfected around five hundred years ago, involved the refinement of Late Iron Age technology, the acquisition and spread of more efficient, heat-resistant breeds of East African humped zebu cattle, and, perhaps, new forms of social organization and religious leadership (Lamphear, 1986). Yet we now have zooarchaeological and linguistic evidence that the zebu was widespread in East Africa fifteen hundred years before that time and well-grounded convictions that specialized pastoralism may have been practised even earlier (Marshall, 1990). Comparative ethnological and linguistic studies also suggest that the institutions of age-organization and prophetic leadership must have been part of the very early fabric of East African and especially Cushitic-ized Nilotic culture. Nevertheless, there still appears to have been a cultural 'rupture', which led to the emergence of the modern Maasai, 'expanding and erupting across the fine plateau grasslands of Kenya and northern Tanzania' (Sutton, 1970: 24). After reviewing the history of this expansion, we will return to the question of how cultural innovation may have precipitated, or at least made possible, a 'Maasai Revolution'.

Lamphear, following Jacobs' account of the split between Maasai and *Iloikop*, has proposed that the 'new pastoral' Maasai struggled with, and gained ascendancy over, the 'old pastoral' *Iloikop*. The *Iloikop* hypothesis holds that there was a division between the 'purely pastoral Ilmaasai and the semi-pastoral or agricultural Wakwavi (Iloikop)', the latter identified as including the present-day Parakuyo, Arusha, Chamus, and Samburu, as well as the now extinct Loogolala, Loosekelai and Laikipiak (Jacobs, 1965: 112). However, while the Arusha and Chamus do indeed cultivate, there is no evidence that the other groups were less pastoral than Maasai or that they reconized greater affinity with one another as *Iloikop* than they did with Maasai. The persistence of this incorrect hypothesis has tended to distort Maasai history by presenting it as a simple struggle between different economic forms, rather than a conflict over pastoral resources, and as involving only two sides rather than complex and shifting alliances.[4]

However, notwithstanding the fact that neither an 'ethnic duality' nor a systematic difference in pastoral practice or commitment actually existed, the terms *Iloikop* and/or *Kwavi* did have a certain past currency, and, if Ehret's linguistic inferences are correct, there were at the time of the Later Maasai expansion at least two types of Early Maa-speakers inhabiting Maasailand, one of which may be identified with the *Lumbwa* who, according to some traditions, once occupied the Maasai Steppe in Tanzania. We may also be able to infer from the distribution of certain clans and sub-clans (e.g. Laitayok-Siria) across Maasai sections the existence of at least one other and probably more Early Maa-speaking entities. But from where did Maasai expansion begin, or, more fundamentally, where and how did the Later Maasai community develop before its expansion and differentiation?

If we assume that the Later Maasai were different from Early Maa-speakers, whom they encountered and assimilated rather than simply evolved from, then either they must represent another expansionary wave into the Rift Valley region from an area of pastoral genesis in northern Kenya, or they were already occupants of a nuclear region stretching from Lake Baringo in the north to perhaps Lake Natron in the south, from which they spread in virtually every direction. The latter solution may appear to contravene the tradition of northern origin, but that deep-seated belief may refer to an earlier period, with the lake basin of the Rift Valley serving as a later and secondary point of differentiation and dispersion. Certainly, if principles of linguistic geography were applied to the distribution of Maasai dialects in the mid-nineteenth century, the Nakuru-Naivasha lake region might well represent the theoretical Maa nucleus, a point either within or close to the area of Sirikwa tradition.

Maa Expansion and the Evolution of Specialized Pastoralism

On one level, Maasai history, as conveyed by tradition, is a chronicle of conflict and violence, of groups victorious and groups annihilated, dispersed and assimilated. However, most migration processes are far less dramatic. Although the widespread distribution of closely related Maa dialects suggests that relatively rapid and decisive movements occurred, most instances of actual expansion were preceded by movements within or through territory used by other communities and periods of coexistence often preceded and succeeded periods of open conflict.[5]

Maasai expansion out of the central Rift Valley homeland occurred in three stages: frontier expansion, internal segmentation and external amalgamation.[6] The first stage involved the creation, over a period of several hundred years, of northern, western and south-eastern frontiers through a centrifugal movement of groups who practised a 'new', more specialized, form of pastoralism and who have come to be known collectively as *Iloikop*. In fact, these groups probably had a closer sense of genealogical and cultural affinity with core Maasai than with one another, given the 'spiral' nature of their divergence. The degree of current linguistic differentiation between frontier and core, together with oral tradition, offers good evidence for the time and order in which they diverged.

On the northern frontier, the initial expansion of those Maa-speakers who were known as *Kore* to their non-Maasai neighbours followed the split of the 'northern Maa' Samburu–Chamus from the Maa nucleus by the end of the sixteenth century. The Samburu subsequently expanded north and east of the Cherangany Hills, while the Chamus inhabited the shores of Lake Baringo (Vossen, 1977: 214; 1982: 74).[7] By the early nineteenth century, however, the Chamus had separated linguistically from the Samburu. The Samburu, who were expelled with their camel-keeping Rendille allies from west of Lake Turkana and successively defeated by Loosekelai Maasai and Turkana, left the area altogether and moved to the El Barta Plains and the region north of Leroghi, where they reportedly had to dislodge the Boran before coming to dominate this 'heartland' (Anderson, 1981: 5; Sobania, 1980: 82–83, 88–89).

The Laikipiak, forming a branch of 'Central Maa' (Heine and Vossen, 1979), were the next Maa-speakers to differentiate from the Maa nucleus. A loose federation of groups, perhaps a residue of 'old pastoralists', rather than a single entity, they came to dominate the Laikipia Plateau and the surrounding areas (Waller, 1979: 148–150).

In western Kenya, local traditions of Maa-speaking *Kwabuk* (probably Uas Nkishu, Loosekelai and Siria Maasai) assert that they were instrumental in the defeat and dispersal of the Sirikwa of the Uasin Gishu Plateau and in blocking the expansion of the Nandi until the nineteenth century (Sutton, 1973 and in this volume).[8] Maa-speakers were settled in South Nyanza when the Luo moved southward in the seventeenth century and in the Nyando Valley near the Gusii at the end of the eighteenth century (Ogot, 1967: 189; Ochieng, 1975: 94). Other widespread traditions of Maasai and *Kwavi* raiding in the west during the seventeenth and eighteenth centuries doubtless refer to the same Maa-speaking groups.

The fourth great divergence from the Maa nucleus was that of Loogolala, who inhabited much of the southern Rift Valley and surrounding plateaus from the seventeenth century (Fosbrooke, 1948: 5; Jacobs, 1972: 83). It would appear that the southern frontier was constituted by social elements identified by four names: Loogolala, Lumbwa, Parakuyo, and *Enkang Lema*, the latter associated with the area just north of Kilimanjaro and near Moshi (Krapf, 1854: 5). Although Parakuyo and Samburu–Chamus are widely separated and differentiated, geographically and linguistically, they share a unique set of key terms. This suggests that they were probably associated in northern Kenya prior to Loogolala–Parakuyo migration southwards (Sommer and Vossen, in this volume).[9] Similarly, shared vocabulary between Parakuyo and Loitai suggests that Loogolala communities once lived in the Loita area, perhaps in Narosura. Since Parakuyo were and are called both *Ilumbwa* and *Iloogolala*, it is likely that progressive and relatively peaceful amalgamation of these diverse groups occurred during their southward movement and in response to pressure from the expanding Maasai.

. No clear-cut linguistic duality underlies the differentiation of 'core' and 'peripheral' Maasai peoples. Indeed, it is not clear that frontier Maasai would have seen themselves as 'peripheral', for their centrifugal movements were so successful that they may not have regarded 'proto-Maasai' as their point of origin. However, to outside eyes and in the long run, the process did involve outward migrations by practitioners of a 'new' and more specialized form of pastoralism who formed a spiral galaxy of sections north, west and south-east of the core lands. These frontier groups did not share any affinity, since each was closer to central Maasai than to any of the others, but they did come to occupy a common position *vis-à-vis* the nuclear groups, as culturally and politically 'other' to those who through a subsequent process of fission and expansion would become the central Maasai sections.

The frontier groups evolved through expansion and the term *Loikop* may represent a 'sign' of their common experience.[10] They assimilated, and accommodated to, their predecessors and neighbours and they developed pastoral techniques and forms of social life which distinguished them from those who subsequently came to be the central Maasai sections. Using grazing lands on either side of the narrowly delimited Rift Valley, they tended to expand laterally, occupying relatively greater areas than did the central Maasai sections. Also, they were characterized by more intimate forms of contact with non-Maasai groups. The close relation between Samburu and Rendille, for example, led to the emergence of the interstitial and bilingual Ariaal, who practise a dual camel/cattle economy (Spencer, 1973; Fratkin, in this volume). Uas Nkishu developed close relations with Bantu-speaking groups in western Kenya, who welcomed many as refugees after their defeat by the Purko (Waller, 1984). Parakuyo, widely dispersed on the plains of east-central Tanzania, live in an almost symbiotic relation to upland cultivators with whom they engage in a regional division of labour and trade. Indeed, many Parakuyo, though themselves still specializing in animal husbandry, also cultivate fields with the labour of agricultural neighbors and today live as minorities in agricultural villages (Beidelman, 1960; Rigby, 1985; Galaty, 1988). These peripheral pastoral groups are distinct from sedentary Maasai agro-pastoralists like the Arusha, Nkuruman, and Chamus, each of whom is closely linked in history both with the frontier Maa-speakers and with cultivating neighbours (Spear, in this volume). However, the development on the frontier of patterns of social dispersion and of complementary linkages with neighbouring non-Maasai may have led to their being perceived in similar terms by the incipient central Maasai sections, whose emergence and expansion would lead to significant conflict with their 'frontier' predecessors.

The Segmentation and Amalgamation of the Central Maasai

Today, the Maasai are divided into numerous autonomous political sections, which, in the past, formed larger sectional alliances, sometimes identified with their most prominent section. The four major alliances — the Kisongo, Loitai, Kaputiei and Purko 'clusters' — derived from periods of subdivision and expansion both within and outside the Maasai nuclear region.

The Kisongo were the first to emerge from the Maasai core. They moved to the area west of Mount Meru in northern Tanzania while the related Sikirari occupied the rich Sanya corridor between Mount Kilimanjaro and Mount Meru. Next to emerge were the Purko, associated with the Elementeita–Nakuru lake basin and the adjacent escarpments of the Rift Valley. Kisongo and Purko came to represent the southern and northern vanguards of the central Maasai, spearheading subsequent expansion and serving as the central nodes of later amalgamations.

By the middle of the eighteenth century, before the final period of expansion and intense internal conflict began, the political arrangement of the numerous Maa-speaking groups must have included the following: a nucleus of (core) groups in the central Rift Valley; an outer ring of groups less closely related to one another than each was to several core sections; two expanding vanguard groups projecting south and north in

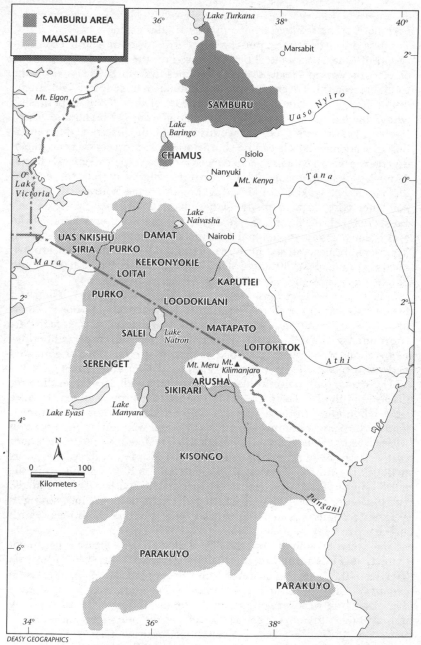

Map 3.1 Maasai Sections

an inner periphery and amalgamating other Maasai; and an outer periphery of the frontier groups previously discussed.

These distinctions presuppose a concentric (or even 'spiral') configuration of Maasai sections. They are based on the relationship between dialects in Vossen's lexicostatistical studies (Vossen, 1988) and on the spatial relations between sections in the nineteenth century. This model differs from the earlier ('diametric') model of the '*Iloikop* hypothesis', which divided Maa-speakers into two equal groups, Maasai and *Iloikop* (Galaty, 1977a). Within the concentric model, the historical differentiation of sectional dialects can be characterized in terms of their degree of divergence from a core in a set of concentric, geographical–lexical circles. A nucleus or inner core of dialects most highly correlated includes Damat, Keekonyokie, Loitai and Matapato in the central Rift Valley. An outer core, located on the adjacent plateaus, includes Kaputiei, Loodokilani, Dalalekutuk, Salei, Laitayiok, Serenget and Siria. Purko and Kisongo, the two vanguard groups of the inner periphery, spread over the northern and southern reaches of the Rift; and frontier groups, including Loogolala/Parakuyo, Uas Nkishu, Loosekelai, Laikipiak and Samburu, occupy the more distant peripheries (see fig.3.1).

It is impossible to reconstruct the processes of movement, fission and fusion that accompanied the creation of Maasai sections, but it would appear (by distribution of clans and sub-clans) that sections were in part constituted out of the residues of older groupings and dispersed peripheral sections which were absorbed as descent groups when fragmented and reassimilated (see Waller, 1979; and Sobania and Waller, n.d.).

There were four major fronts, each associated with a sectional alliance, involved in the Maasai expansion. The frontier groups appear to have been rebounding from the political and ecological limits of the rangelands at the same time that the nuclear Maasai were initiating their own wave of expansion. The ensuing conflict created the systematic chaos that we associate with this period of Maasai history. In the process, virtually all the frontier groups, with the exception of the Samburu in the north and the Parakuyo, who regrouped in the south, were eliminated and the loose, *ad hoc*, alliances which gathered around the four strongest Maasai sections created the social and political affinities which characterize Maasai society today.

The Loitai expanded from the Rift Valley up the western escarpment to the Loita Hills around 1800, expelling Loogolala and pushing the Siria back from the Loita Plains to the Mara River (Jacobs, 1972: 83). Loitai expansion into the Crater Highlands of Tanzania may have already stimulated the westward migration of small groups of Bantu-speaking hunters and cultivators, possibly as early as the mid-eighteenth century (Anacleti, 1977). In effect, it seems that south-western frontier Maa-speakers were realigned within a loose Loitai confederation, which included Siria, Laitayok, Salei and Serenget as well as Loitai, as the centre moved outward to absorb the periphery (Arhem, 1985).

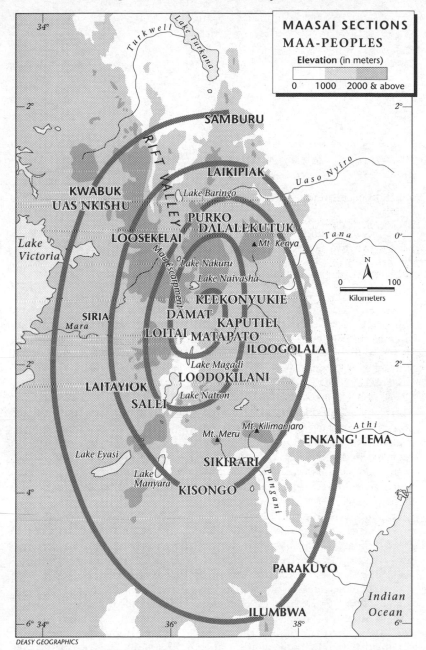

Fig. 3.1 Spiral Model of the Differentiation of the Maa-Speaking People

Tiyioki	c. 1791–1811
Merishari	c. 1806–1826
Kidotu	c. 1821–1841
Tuati I	c. 1836–1856
Nyangusi I	c. 1851–1871
Laimer	c. 1866–1886
Talala	1881–1905
Tuati II	1896–1917
Tareto	1911–1929
Terito	1926–1948
Nyangusi II	1942–1959
Iseuri	1955–1974
Kitoip	1967–
Kipali/Manjeshi	1983–/1990–

Fig. 3.2 Maasai Age-Sets
Note: Based on John L. Berntsen (1979a). Dates from 1881 are known; dates prior to that are calculated from average durations, as explained therein. While Berntsen employs a range of plus or minus 5 for such reconstructed dates, we indicate their tentative nature by 'c.' (eds).

Krapf (1854: 9) observed that 'the main strength of the Wakuafi is concentrated . . . in a country called Kaputie', where the Kaputiei alliance encountered the frontier Loogolala [*Kwavi*]. The alliance of the Kaputiei, Matapato and Loodokilani was forged during their south-eastern expansion. They (especially Kaputiei) assimilated many Loogolala and others fled southward to regroup with, or as, Parakuyo. While the Kaputiei seized control of the Athi River and plains, the Matapato and Loodokilani drove Loogolala out of areas south of the Kapiti Plains and the Loitokitok Maasai, a sub-section of Kisongo, replaced them in Amboseli (Western, 1983: 19). Krapf's informant reported that *Enkang Lema* (apparently a sub-section of, or group allied with, Loogolala) were 'nearly annihilated by the wild Masai' and had fled to Taveta and to the Pangani River to join the *Barrabuyu* [Parakuyo] (Krapf, 1854: 4–5).

In southern Maasailand, Loogolala and Parakuyo were systematically displaced by the Kisongo during the nineteenth century in a series of encounters recounted according to the chronology of Maasai age-sets (Waller, 1979). In the age of Il Merishari, early in the century, they took the Lake Manyara region from Tatog-speaking people, and in subsequent ages occupied Engaruka and the Ngorongoro Crater region. During the age of Il Kidotu, Maasai also seized the wells and swamps of Naberera and Losogonoi from the Parakuyo, with whom they had previously shared these critical resources. They then occupied the right bank of the Pangani River and Kibaya in the age of Il Twati and had taken over Talami and Kiteto in the far south by 1880 (Fosbrooke, 1948: 4–5; 1956: 193–195). The Parakuyo were either absorbed by the Kisongo or driven into districts adjacent to the Maasai plains. Here they have flourished in this century, some migrating during the last two decades to southern Tanzania and over the border into northern Zambia — now the southern frontier of Maa-speakers (Galaty, 1988).

In the north, there were 'three successive supremacies' in the nineteenth century: Uas Nkishu, Laikipiak and Purko (Weatherby, 1967: 133). Uas Nkishu dominated the region west of the Rift Valley before 1840, when they were attacked and defeated by the Laikipiak, perhaps as part of a wider conflict between Loosekelai, with whom they were aligned, and Laikipiak (Sobania, 1980: 82). Loosekelai were then defeated and dispersed by a Purko alliance (Jacobs, 1965: 68). Finally, just before 1870, the Purko, in alliance with the Laikipiak, invaded the Uasin Gishu plateau, leaving, in Thomson's words, 'not a man in the entire land' (Thomson, 1885: 243). Some Uas Nkishu refugees were absorbed by the Purko while others settled among the Nandi, the Chamus or the Luyia, whom they served as mercenaries. They were later moved to Eldama Ravine by the British colonial government and then to the Trans-Mara where they and their kinsmen, the Moitanik, now live in uneasy proximity to the Siria (Waller, 1984).

The Laikipiak, who had gained ascendancy over the entire Laikipia area, apparently 'withdrew' from the northern areas and moved southwards into the central Rift plains, coming into conflict with, and initially prevailing over, the Purko alliance (Sobania, 1980: 136, and in this volume). In the mid-1870s, however, the Laikipiak were utterly defeated and dispersed by the junior group (Left Hand) of the age-set Il Peles (or Laimer) in a diverse coalition of all four major Maasai alliances forged through the orders of the famous Maasai *loibon* Mbatiany (Jacobs, 1965: 74–75). The Purko were the chief beneficiaries of this victory. Subsequently, they absorbed numerous Laikipiak and assumed a hegemony over much of the Laikipiak plateau and the northern Rift Valley (Fosbrooke, 1956: 27; Sobania in this volume). The Purko became the dominant power in the north and centre during the age of Il Talala, and their power was only checked by the subsequent rinderpest and smallpox epidemics of the early 1890s and by the onset of colonial rule.

Processes of Expansion

From the historical and ethnographic record, Maasai expansion appears to be a matter of progressive social and linguistic differentiation, beginning with a mass of Sudanic peoples and ending with the emergence of individual Maasai sections. It is also clear that migration and social expansion are factors in the differentiation of particular linguistic and cultural forms which, in turn, take on distinctive identities. But, since more groups have withered or been assimilated than have proliferated and established separate identities, successful expansion seems the exception rather than the rule. Under what conditions, then, is this process stimulated or even accelerated?

Several explanations have been put forward to account for the motives and underlying causes of Maasai expansion, as well as for the process by which it occurred. Conflict and expansion themselves are manifestations of the evolution of economy and polity, not only within Maasailand itself but within a wider regional system of ethnic categories and subsistence forms. Maasai expansion was largely at the expense of other pastoralists, even other Maa-speaking groups, but specialized pastoralism, which was consolidated by the Maasai as a form of resource allocation and use, a system of labour allocation and production and a hierarchical pattern of social and economic value, evolved in reciprocal interaction not only with other types of animal production but also with the economic forms of non-pastoral neighbours. The evolution of pastoralism was thus only one part of a wider economic evolution, as the Rift Valley region experienced a 'refiguration' towards more specialized pursuits.

Two models have recently been put forward to describe the movements and interactions between East African communities. Turton identifies three types of movement: the breakaway from a parent group (Type A); the infiltration of one group by another across a stable ethnic boundary (Type B) and the gradual occupation of an area by an incoming group, resulting in a spatial shift in the ethnic boundary (Type C) (Turton, 1991). Waller distinguishes between 'attrition' and 'infiltration' (Waller, 1985a). The first, which resembles Turton's Type C (of which Type A is a specific case marked by rapid, distant movement), involves the securing of key resources so that victims must either withdraw or join the aggressors. The second, infiltration (Turton's Type B), implies the pervasive insertion of one group into the networks of another, so that the boundaries between the two gradually dissolve or shift. The two processes have quite different outcomes for the evolution of group identity. When attrition is involved, the integrity of each group is maintained; while, in the case of infiltration, the outcome may often be an altered identity for both, with a new synthetic structure and, perhaps, new symbols of identity emerging, or with a transformation in social content within the same form of identity.[11] While Maasai practised both attrition and infiltration, it is interesting to consider whether one or the other was more prominent at particular stages of expansion.

Two scenarios, of pastoral movement and age-set conflict, appear to recur, acted out separately or as successive stages in cycles of encounter and strife, encroachment and expansion. The first derives from the pursuit of specialized arid-land pastoralism. It might be called 'economic expansion', since it involves the appropriation of pastoral resources. The second, a related but conceptually distinct process, derives from participation in a highly elaborated system of age-organization. It is engendered by competition between rival age-sets and might be called 'political expansion'. While both of these institutionalized processes are widespread in pastoral Eastern Africa, their refinement has been particularly associated with the emergence and southward migration of the Maasai, and an examination of them is thus pertinent to an explanation of Maasai expansion.

Expanding Orbits of Pastoralism

The aim of pastoral mobility is to gain competitive access to scarce pasture and water resources, and pastoralism has been seen by some as an intrinsically expansionist mode of life (P. Anderson, 1974). In the short term, the nineteenth-century '*Iloikop* Wars' may have been precipitated by competition over the permanent water sources and more abundant pastures of the central Rift Valley and over the wells of the southern Maasai plains (Jacobs, 1968a; Waller, 1979), a point lent historical weight by the apparent coincidence of warfare with drought, epidemic and plague (Berntsen, 1977). Expansion, however, could be related equally well to the abundance of resources.[12] Abundance theories evoke expanding populations and the drive for new resources. In this sense, the central Rift Valley may represent a rich breeding ground for livestock which, figuratively, pushed the community out to new pastures.

General ecological explanations come into sharper focus when related to the actual judgements and predicaments of local actors (see Telelia and Spencer, in this volume). Movements of people and ripples of culture alike can be usefully situated in the context of the daily and seasonal movements of herds and households in cycles of nomadic and semi-nomadic herding. The most significant units of economic action for the Maasai (in ascending order of incorporation) are households, camps and neighbourhoods. The family is the stock-holding group, with responsibility for allocating herding labour and rights in the consumption of livestock products. Several families congregate to form a camp, within which coordinated herding, labour sharing and food redistribution occurs. The camps of a given neighbourhood, within which a political council may be formed, collaborate in allocating local resources, in providing for local defence, in scheduling access to watering points, and in organizing themselves for higher-order meetings, rituals, and combat. Households are linked through marriage and stock exchanges which cross neighbourhood and sometimes even section boundaries. This leads to the diversification of animal holdings, the consolidation of access to alternative areas of pasturage, and the establishment of networks of social relations marked by flows of people, animals and goods.

In addition to daily herding movements, households conventionally oscillate between wet and dry-season pasture areas. Given the occurrence of two wet and two dry seasons in the year in a bipolar rainfall system, this usually involves at least four moves per year. The main cattle herd, however, often splits off from the household to benefit from flushes of grass early in the rains or when showers break the monotony of the dry season, and then to move to distant and isolated highland pastures or to remote grazing in the height of the dry season when home pastures are exhausted.

Routine seasonal moves now usually occur within sections or localities, although the narrowing of herding range has been a fairly recent response to the demarcation of formal boundaries and the creation of administrative locations and sub-locations in the colonial period. Before 1905, when the region was vacated by Maasai in favour of British settlement, the Keekonyokie section occupied the Kinangop Plateau on the south-west slope of the Nyandarua Range during the dry season (January–March), moving down to the Naivasha plains with the wet season (April–June), where the waters of the lake were available, then using the Kinangop or the Ewuaso region during the cold, dry season (July–September), returning to the Rift Valley plains for the warmer wet season (November–December). In Keekonyokie now, many inhabitants of Kaputiei sub-location (not to be confused with the adjacent Kaputiei section) spend the wet season in the table-land pastures behind the Ngong Hills, and move cattle to the top of the escarpment in the height of the dry season; while inhabitants of Ewuaso location are concentrated near the Uaso Enkidongi river for the dry season, but move southward into the drier, lower plains of the Rift Valley with the wet season, or onto the sides of the rich but waterless Mount Suswa. Often, however, as the dry season advances and grass diminishes, herding orbits become distended and reach beyond the security of the section. In this way, members of different sections come into contact with one another, in interstitial zones between home pastures, in areas where particular water sources engender unseasonal growth of grass, in distant pastures after localized rains break the dry season or around long-established permanent water-points to which herds retreat with prolonged drought.

Numerous accounts of intersectional mingling emphasize the fact that herders from diverse sections often congregated without conflict. Sectional alliances allowed for shared access to pasture outside the 'home' section, such as the joint use of Lake Naivasha by Keekonyokie, Damat, and Dalalekutuk sections, which defined their collective identity as *Enaiposha* or *Il Kinopop*. In recent years, Kisongo have been granted use of a river in Kaputiei territory, thus signalling cooperation between two related alliances. Sections from alien alliances, and across the centre/periphery divide, however, were also known to mingle peacefully. The Kaputiei inhabited the Kapiti Plains together with Loogolala, and Kisongo jointly used the wells and pastures of the Maasai Steppe with Parakuyo. During certain periods, Samburu and Laikipiak lived closely together and the latter also shared the waters of the Rift Valley with the Purko. Today, the great Wambere and Usangu swamps in Tanzania are occupied by several pastoral groups, who converge on these final refuges at the height of the dry season (Galaty, 1988).

In historical perspective, however, we can see many of these periods of peaceful intermingling as precursors to conflict and preparatory to expansion. When conflict occurred, an informal segmentary logic shaped patterns of alliance. Those sections which lacked histories of ritual cooperation and reciprocity were invariably pitted against one another. Contemporary areas of tension are well-known and may have witnessed struggle in past epochs. The Uaso Nyiro plains between the Purko and Loodokilani and the Olkejuado River and swamps near the Mparasha Hills, between Matapato and Dalalekutuk, experience perennial competition today, and were loci of struggle between Maasai and Loogolala before (Galaty, 1980).

Pastoral resources are usually found within the section, or, rather, the territory has come to be defined over time in terms of the resources controlled by the section. Territories often overlapped, and the parcelling out of rights in water and pasture was in part reckoned according to structural relationships and in part according to power. Herd and household movements tend to occur within a framework of political relationships, manifested in action and discourse, by which shared exigencies are defined cooperatively, as when Loodokilani and Matapato exchange herders; competitively, as when Loodokilani and Purko clash; or in both ways successively, as was the case recently when Kisongo and Kaputiei, faced with drought and land-tenure conflicts, clashed over water sources (Galaty, 1982b).

Most instances just cited are cases of friction at the margin of herding orbits, where members of a more assertive section penetrate the peripheral pastures of another at the normal extreme of their march, then gain implicit rights in those pastures through continued, and often peaceful, use, and finally clash with, and, in some cases, muster sufficient force to expel, their hosts. Kisongo, for example, eventually infiltrated and pushed aside the Parakuyo on the Maasai Steppe. Similar processes occur at the margins of forests and cultivated land, where farmers are inhibited from extending the range of their grazing and tilling. A somewhat different process occurs when pressure leads young herders to move long distances to remote pastures where they often intermingle with other pastoral pioneers, exchanging security for space. Today the Usangu Plains, the southernmost reach of the semi-arid East African corridor, peopled by Parakuyo, Sukuma and Tatog pastoralists and agro-pastoralists, is such an area (Galaty, 1988). The central Rift Valley, between Lakes Baringo and Nakuru, and the southern Rift Valley, in the col between Mount Meru and the Mbulu Highlands, are locales of pastoral migration and mixing, where diversity was forged into the Maasai identity through the events previously described.

Deadly Jousts: Age-Set Combat and Expansion

Although some of the bitterest conflict occurred in the context of deprivation, 'need' as a motive rests on an edifice of pride, honour, jealousy and scorn engendered by the structure and ethos of age-sets. Constant reference has been made to Maasai aggressiveness and bellicosity.[13] Related characteristics of self-reliance and assertiveness have been attributed to herding experience, engrained in a 'pastoral personality' and codified in pastoral culture (P. Anderson, 1974; Edgerton, 1971). This psychological profile, although overdrawn, is surely not without some symbolic or behavioural basis, although when it is viewed in the context of age-based political socialization it is tempered by the obverse traits of congeniality and hospitality, respect and obedience which ideally obtain between age-mates or between *murran* and their sponsoring elders (Spencer, 1988). The 'pastoral profile' is, however, less an explanation for aggressive expansion than one part of the constellation of factors surrounding it. These values, inculcated through the age-organization and relevant to the exigencies of pastoral subsistence, represent internalized motives for action, which, under circumstances of age-related or resource-based conflict, are sufficient to stimulate intemperate bravery, ambition and self-sacrifice. What is required, then, is not affirmation or denial of Maasai 'bellicosity' but a way of setting their exercise of power in its regional context.

Maasai age-groups are constituted over time. A new age-division (*Olporror*) is opened every seven years, a successive pair of divisions forming an age-set (*Olaji*) on a fourteen year cycle. Alternative age-sets form 'streams' which link older and younger in relations of authority and political affinity (Galaty, 1985; Spencer, in this volume). In each section, the age-set which is assuming the leading political role as sponsors opens a new age-set for recruitment. However, the sponsors of the previous age-set which is just leaving *murran*hood continue to exercise influence in local meetings. Members of an age-set must respect their sponsors, but routinely experience tension and competition with adjacent age-sets, those immediately preceding and, in time, succeeding them.

Age-sets, based on time, cut across units of residential organization, from neighbourhoods to sections, which are based on space. Localized age-set units do, however, follow territorial divisions, beginning with local circumcision groups, neighbourhood cohorts (*Isirit*) with organized local *murran* camps (*Imanyat*), and culminating in sectional levels of overarching authority, manifested in the periodic creation of ritual villages. At the local level, informal leaders emerge, while formally designated spokesmen are chosen to represent larger divisions, one of whom serves as age-set leader for the entire section. Thus a structural hierarchy in the age system parallels and politically delineates the segments of a territorial section and provides the means for its integration.

Sectional politics involve two dimensions of age-group discussion and negotiation, between successive age-sets in the same locality and between divisions of the same age in different localities. Beyond ordering the process of advising and deciding in councils and conclaves, the culture of the age-set system provides a more pervasive structure for thought and action with regard to selfhood, ethics and morality, collectivity and individuality, and honour. Its social structure orients patterns of resource use and household movement, collective responses to aggression or mobilization for expansion. The Maasai age-set system underpins raiding and warfare, and, therefore, the process of expansion, through its provision of an ethos of assertiveness and a structure for organizing conflict (and its resolution) and for combining and orchestrating individual desires to attain honour and wealth.

During the period of *murran*hood which follows initiation, young men struggle and form alliances in classic in-group/out-group behaviour. Feelings of animosity and affectionate loyalty are instilled which are intense and lasting. Behaviour is narrowly channelled during this period and young men experience great freedom paradoxically combined with intense discipline. The *murran* values of bravery and 'respect' apply particularly to the behaviour of young initiated men, but the experience of *murran*hood casts a cloak of pervasive nostalgia over all subsequent experience, so that future action is also measured, if subliminally, against those great days of youthful vigour and self-esteem.

Despite, or perhaps because of, the emphasis placed on sharing and solidarity among peers, *murran* behaviour is also highly competitive. Groups and individuals vie with each other in displays of martial and sexual prowess to enhance their own reputations and that of their age. The structure of political affinities between competitors influences the nature and seriousness of conflict and serves to calibrate the scale of support marshalled by each side if matters escalate. Within the same neighbourhood, young men compete through wrestling and play, and when provoked fight without weapons. Between locations, members of different cohorts or *sirits* within the same section are expected to compete actively and, on occasion, to break out in serious fighting with non-mortal weapons. Conflict between members of allied sections should be avoided, or kept within these amicable limits, while conflict between non-allied sections of different confederations can quickly become quite serious, with mortal weapons used to deadly ends (Galaty, 1982b).

On many occasions, insult and encounter between individuals is defined as conflict between their respective age-groups, with escalation ensuing. Ceremonial age-set villages of different locations and sections were, and are, formed adjacent to one another, for joint celebrations or age rituals, and these also create an atmosphere of pageantry and challenge which was once associated with the joust in mediaeval Europe. Despite the efforts of responsible elders, such occasions often ended in organized clashes between age-groups, arrayed in long opposing lines with interlocked shields and sometimes with deadly weapons. Such occasions may have represented a sort of 'training with live ammunition'. They were often indistinguishable from 'live combat', or led to it.

Conflict between sections, which was earlier depicted as if political entities were actors, can be usefully described in terms of dynamic political relationships between individual *murran* and between age-based groups. All reports of the extended clash between Maasai and Laikipiak emphasize competition between their respective age-groups. Accounts of the defeat of Loogolala on Ol Doinyo Orok emphasize the bravery and ingenuity of Loogolala *murran* facing overwhelming odds. Again, the account of Kisongo expansion in Tanzania is a chronicle of the advances made by successive age-sets. In short, conflict and expansion represent not simply a struggle over resources but a political process with its own dynamic, in which competition between corporate age-groups involves questions of honour and reputation as well as booty.

While the ethos of *murran*hood provided some of the intrinsic motivation for conflict, age-organization also made it possible to mobilize age-set divisions at several different levels. The existence of a single system of age-sets common to all Maasai sections offered a social and conceptual framework for alliance and conflict. Divisions of a single age-set might amalgamate for ceremony or battle against other similar aggregations. Age-set ceremonies are still celebrated jointly by several sections, and we know from early colonial evidence that this practice was common within a sectional alliance and was an experience on which wider military collaboration might be based. Such a process of aggregation occurred routinely, as age-set ceremonies were celebrated at the level of locations, sections and clusters. For any given age-group, participation in section-wide ceremonies — *Eunoto*, for example — would occur every few years, cementing ties which would be reinforced during the interim, and, since age-sets constitute overlapping cycles, any given section experienced relatively frequent ritual aggregation. Most fronts of Maasai expansion seem to have involved links between sections within a single alliance, but tradition holds that for the Laikipiak war virtually all central Maasai sections — comprising the Purko, Kaputiei, Kisongo and Loitai clusters — banded together in self-defence. In times of conflict, the members of several successive age-sets could also mobilize jointly. The Maasai age system thus offered a framework for social and military aggregation, whereby significant 'massing', in Sahlins' (1961) phrase, could occur across age and territory, space and time, creating a potent force out of a widely dispersed population. Although the office of *loibon* played a consultative role in the process of ritual amalgamation and was evidently instrumental in mobilizing the coalition against Laikipiak, this factor of leadership probably depended on the structured linkages between age-sets across sectional boundaries (Berntsen, 1979b).

The ordering of the life-cycle by ritual and by collective, rather than simply individual, maturation (Spencer, in this volume) meant that many young men in effect became marriageable at the same time. For marriage, however, a young man should be economically secure in livestock and able soon to establish an independent pastoral household. Although the family herd is formally controlled by the father, the bulk is allocated among the sons of matricentric houses. While bridewealth involves a relatively small, ritually designated, number of livestock (4 to 6 animals), the marriageability of a young man depends in large part on the holdings of his family and the size of his own portion, a measure by which his reliability and future independence can be assessed. A direct connection between marriage, maturation and raiding has been drawn, since raiding allowed young men to accumulate enough animals for themselves to marry and thus to attain maturity (Tignor, 1972; Waller, 1976). Age-organization both defined the time and provided the means whereby the needs of young men could be met when, following *Eunoto*, marriage was ritually opened for the age-division. The mobilization of age units to carry out smaller raids and the consolidation of the entire age-group within the section — and in the past *several* sections — through the creation of ritual villages provided the mechanism for collective action. Through age-organization the structure of segmentary 'massing' was defined, while through ritual it was enacted. Periods of Maasai expansion are remembered through the age-sets which carried them out, as successive waves were set off by the ripple effect of a sequence of ceremonial age-set aggregations.

Maasai Expansion in Cultural Perspective

In the long run, Maasai expansion appears as an inexorable movement, a southward wave followed by outward ripples emanating from a central Rift Valley epicentre. Each front of expansion involved a historically specific set of encounters and each stage represented less a punctuated clash than a gradual process in which armed conflict was only one of many modes of interaction between Maa-speakers.

Maasai expansion was thus in large part incremental, with herd and household movements to marginal or interstitial areas in search of pasture and water bringing members of different groups and sections into contact. Often a period of peaceful mixing of herds and herders would precede a period of friction and armed clashes, concerning, for instance, the order in which herds used wells or the means by which dry-season pastures were made available. Serious conflict, however, generally arose through political differences centred on age-set competition, followed by the advance of one group and the retreat or assimilation of another. Expansion is associated less with the penetration of new territory in itself than with the seizure of livestock or critical water resources to the exclusion of losers. Thus the two economic and political moments of conflict and expansion, involving shifting pastoral orbits and age-set jousts, occurred simultaneously or in succession. Since they were inextricably interconnected, friction over resources leading to new economic gains was shaped both by larger political realities and by age-set conflict triggered by personal jealousies and resentments.

The expansion of the Maasai involved three major trends. The first was towards political differentiation and segmentation, as Maasai sections evolved within the Rift Valley nucleus and then moved out into an 'inner periphery' near the dominant frontier groups. The second was the consolidation of political alliances between sections which occurred during expansion onto the Rift Valley highlands, and which confirmed higher-order segmentary relations in some cases and redefined them in others. In this period, the Kaputiei, Loitai, Kisongo, and Purko 'clusters' emerged. The third trend was towards amalgamation. Most expanding Maasai sections assimilated individuals from groups being displaced, either peacefully or by wartime capture and adoption. After such wars, people followed the livestock into their new kraals and today many Maasai families can recall their origins in one of the groups dispersed in the nineteenth century (Waller, 1979). Kisongo and Purko, however, carried this out in a way, and on a scale, quite distinct from that practised by other sections, with important effects on both the size and the structure of both sections.

In a history of events, the 'frontier' groups were largely dispersed and annihilated as political entities, but, in a history of processes, most individuals from those groups survived through affiliation with other sections or groups, their identities evolving over time with their altered circumstances. Some sections were reconstituted in a different form — Loogolala becoming Kaputiei or Parakuyo — some, like Uas Nkishu, scattered only to re-form at a later date, and others were completely assimilated by the central Maasai, in particular by Kisongo and Purko (Sobania, in this volume). Had this amalgamation process not been curtailed by the devastations of the last two decades of the nineteenth century and the onset of colonial rule, large Maasai federations (or super-sections) of flexible pastoral units might have evolved, created through progressive assimilations and consolidated on the basis of sectional alliances, common identity and ideology, and a coordinated ritual process based on age-sets (Waller, 1979).[14]

Given that the process of expansion was both highly consistent and dependent on local conditions, to what extent is it possible to identify aspects of Maasai culture, economy or social organization which might have lent them a competitive edge over other Rift Valley societies? The Maasai have been distinguished in East Africa by their refinement of a specialized form of cattle pastoralism involving high levels of herd mobility, the potential for high rates of herd growth and an ethos of youthful aggression. Similarly, Maasai age-organization seems unique in having combined autonomous age-set villages, a ceremonial cycle involving age-set aggregation and massing, and constraints on marriage and livestock ownership which motivated young men to seek their fortunes through cattle raiding. Herd growth often led to a disequilibrium between livestock and pasture resources, a condition experienced in the form of seasonal scarcities and asymmetries of wealth between Maasai families, which in many cases stimulated pastoral drift and migration. High levels of pastoral productivity were also necessary to support the extensive system of age-set villages which provided Maasai with effective armed encampments of young men mobilized for defence and aggression. Many of these innovations were equally valued by other peoples in the region but none proved able to implement them to a comparable degree.

Although these economic, political and cultural factors were central to Maasai expansion, it is difficult to say whether they were causes or effects of this complex historical process. It seems clear, however, that expansion, even though tied to highly productive pastoralism, was not simply an outcome of local herd growth in an environment favourable for animal husbandry, or of periodic pasture insufficiency in a semi-arid zone. Such conditions were and are relatively common in pastoral areas. Rather, what seems distinctive and relevant in the Maasai context was social and political rather than ecological in nature, that is, their characteristic forms of organization and motivation. Territorial sections provided the collective framework for the appropriation and allocation of resources, the securing of regional systems of exchange, and the coordination of larger-scale action and expansion; while the age-set system offered a structure for sectional politics, a system of leadership and a cultural frame of reference. Age-grades and rituals demarcated and engendered motivations common to each stage in the life-cycle and, at the same time, provided the mechanism and opportunity for mobilizing warriors beyond the level of the locality.

Pastoral expansion is not inevitable, for the history of the East African plains is filled with traces of peoples who 'failed' and were eliminated through assimilation. This chapter has suggested that Maasai 'success' resulted not just from environmental pressures and opportunities, or from some peculiarly 'pastoral' character, but, rather, from a convergence of pastoral strategies and age-set organization, the critical factors in the development of the 'new pastoralism'. But we should be careful not to attribute a linear type of explanation to a long and complicated experience, which involved not only political expansion but also the emergence and refinement of the very factors of specialized pastoralism and age-set organization that may in retrospect seem critical to the expansion process itself. The 'Maasai Revolution' did not itself lead to expansion, but, rather, the characteristic innovations of a new pastoralism, the ideological, institutional and economic features of the Maasai identity, were created through it.

Notes

* This chapter represents the reworking of a chapter, entitled 'Pastoral Orbits and Deadly Jousts: Factors in the Maasai Expansion' in Bonte and Galaty (1991). I am indebted to other contributors to the present volume for comments and specifically to Richard Waller and John Sutton for illuminating pertinent areas of debate. Study among Maasai on which

this chapter draws was supported by the National Science Foundation (1974–75), the Social Sciences and Humanities Research Council of Canada (1983–90), the Quebec FCAR (1983–89), the International Development Research Centre (1984–87), and McGill University. I would like to acknowledge my research affiliation with the Bureau of Educational Research, now at Kenyatta University.

1. Early Pastoral Iron Age variants are associated with the (Elmenteitan) Southern Nilotes on the west side of the Rift Valley (1300–1100 BP), with Engaruka (in conjunction with specialized irrigation agriculture) and, most importantly, with the Sirikwa (beginning around 1200 BP) approximately where it is believed on linguistic grounds that Maa-speakers reached the central Rift (Ambrose, 1982: 129,135,143–144).
2. Lamprey and Waller (1990: 19), and Sobania and Waller (n.d.) provide an interesting comment on the implications of the lack of a more elaborate Maasai tradition of origin. It is not certain that *kerio* is to be taken literally as the Kerio Escarpment. The traditions merely stress a north-western origin — Berntsen, personal communication.
3. Lamphear's notion of the Sirikwa, drawn from the widespread oral tradition of an early pastoral people, should be distinguished from Sutton's use of the term to identify an archaeological complex by the presumptive community responsible for building it (see Sutton, in this volume).
4. For a discussion and refutation of the '*Iloikop* hypothesis', see Galaty (1977a, 1982a); Berntsen (1980) and Waller (1979, 1985b).
5. The great migrations of the Nguni and Oromo-speakers are other cases in point.
6. The history of Maasai migration and expansion is too long and complex to trace here in detail, but see Berntsen (1979a) and Waller (1979, 1985b), both of whose interpretations differ somewhat in detail from those presented here.
7. The Samburu emerged from three distinct groups: one from west of Lake Turkana (Labbeyok or Ngikuro), one from El Barta (Lorokishu) and one from Laikipia (Il Doigo). See Anderson (1981: 5) and Sobania (1980: 82).
8. Note that the early divergence of Uas Nkishu and Siria from the core cannot be derived from Vossen's data since both are linguistically close to other nuclear Maasai. It is based on oral tradition and inferences from the more recent history of the area. For a historical explanation of the linguistic convergence, see Waller (1984).
9. They may be the *Barabiu* noted north of Nyeri in Kikuyu tradition; see Waller (1979: 155) and Muriuki (1976: 65).
10. It might alternatively represent a memory of the earlier commonality of all 'new pastoral' Maa-speakers *vis-à-vis* 'old pastoral' *Lumbwa*.
11. For the Mursi, Turton has developed a link between long-term expansion and the emergence of group identity. In effect, the 'journey made them' (Turton, 1979).
12. Among the Nuer, as among the Maasai, cattle raiding is generally associated not with 'days of hunger' but with those of plenty (Evans-Pritchard, 1940). On the other hand, stock losses in the early 1890s also provoked widespread raiding (Waller, 1988).
13. *Iloikop* have been seen as particularly bellicose and Jacobs adopts a very Maasai point of view in contrasting them with the more pacific Maasai — a contrast which is not supported by the evidence (Jacobs, 1979). Historians have tended to stress peaceful interaction between Maasai and their neighbours and to note that warfare and raiding were never one-sided (Berntsen, 1979a; Waller, 1979). But this well-grounded argument may be taken too far when it is used to suggest that Maasai dominance in the pre-colonial period is a myth created by later distortions and that these 'peaceful pastoralists', in Jacobs' phrase, were merely one set of actors among many in the ethnic mosaic of the Rift Valley region.
14. In Waller's terms, the Maasai were not only 'assimilative' but also 'replicative', able to colonize through extension, and 'agglomerative', in the way that entire communities might be appended as clans to other Maasai sections (Waller, 1985b: 366).

Four

Four

Four

Aspects of
'Becoming Turkana'

Interactions & Assimilation
Between Maa- & Ateker-Speakers

JOHN LAMPHEAR

Although occasionally having to deviate from ideal social, cultural and economic practices, and even to abandon Maa speech, the Maasai peoples typically were the dominant party in interactions with their neighbours in the nineteenth century. Impressed by their 'cattle complex', military system, religious structures and a host of other cultural features, large numbers of outsiders were peacefully absorbed into Maasai society. In addition many other outsiders — occasionally entire communities of them — were swallowed up by Maasai advances as they came to control much of the central Rift Valley and the adjacent uplands.[1]

A survey of contacts between Maa-speakers and the Turkana and Karimojong communities of the Ateker branch of the Eastern Nilotes, however, presents a study in contrast. Far from being overrun and absorbed by Maa-speakers, it was Ateker[2] who predominated in these contacts, sometimes defeating Maa-speakers militarily and often absorbing them linguistically and politically. The means by which Ateker — especially the Turkana — were able to displace and/or assimilate their Maa-speaking neighbours throughout much of the nineteenth century emanated from a complex period of dynamic territorial expansion. Typical of such expansions elsewhere in Eastern Africa, that of the Turkana was intricate and multi-faceted, sometimes involving only a rather subtle territorial drift, but punctuated at frequent intervals by interactions, borrowings, adjustments, conflicts and assimilations. Again quite typical of similar expansions, the Turkana were to evolve an ever changing sense of selfhood and corporate identity from the experience. To paraphrase Turton's observation on the Mursi: the Turkana 'did not make a journey; a journey made them'.[3]

And yet, as will be shown in this chapter, two closely interrelated factors appear essentially to have underlaid this complex process. The first of these was favourable economic circumstances, entailing an early development of a 'new pastoralism', with wider patterns of trans-humance supported by efficient commercial networks, and later by the emergence of a more diversified pastoral economy. As we shall see, these circumstances gave Turkana a distinct advantage over their neighbours, especially in times of severe ecological stress and major epizootics. The second factor, the successful waging of inter-ethnic conflict, was derived largely from the evolution of a more efficient military organization. Ironically, this evolution stemmed in part from ideas and institutions initially borrowed from Maa-speakers, but then creatively adapted to meet the demands of a changing political and cultural environment.

This chapter, then, will attempt to provide a counter-case of an East African people *not* becoming Maasai and an analysis of how the Ateker were among the very few societies effectively to challenge the ascendancy of the 'Lords of East Africa'.[4]

The Ateker peoples are a branch of the same Eastern Nilotic language family to which the Maa-speakers belong. Historical and linguistic evidence suggests that Ateker were the last to leave a Nilotic cradle-land in the southern Sudan and join the migrational flow of other Eastern Nilotic communities down the Rift Valley. By the middle of the present millennium Ateker had pushed down into north-eastern Uganda and were experiencing close interactions with a variety of other peoples, including Southern Nilotic-, Luo- and Central Sudanic-speakers. The western, or Katapa ('Bread People'), branch of the Ateker, who had entered Uganda via the arable Acholi borderlands of western Karamoja, developed particularly close associations with their Luo neighbours. Heavy cultural borrowings flowed both ways and some of the Ateker became bilingual in their own and Luo dialects. At least one, the ancestral Langi, abandoned their original tongue altogether. Adopting agrarian techniques from their neighbours, these western Ateker groups developed economies largely focused on grain agriculture, augmented by hunting and gathering, and limited pastoralism.

In the meantime, the other Ateker sub-division, the eastern or 'Koten–Magos' group, also had pushed down into Uganda, following a more easterly route which brought them south via the drier country of eastern Karamoja into the rugged Koten–Magos hill country above the Turkana escarpment. In this more arid environment they developed a deep commitment to pastoralism, though their economy also rested on agricultural and hunting-gathering activities. While they did not experience quite such intense contacts with neighbouring peoples as had their Katapa cousins, they did form significant interactions with various agricultural, hunting and blacksmithing communities.

Until the eighteenth century, then, ethnic identities among the Ateker appear to have been rather fragile and transitory. Extensive, and essentially peaceful, intercourse between a wide variety of linguistic communities, practising wide range of economic activity, led to frequent bilingualism and multiculturalism, especially in the western parts of the

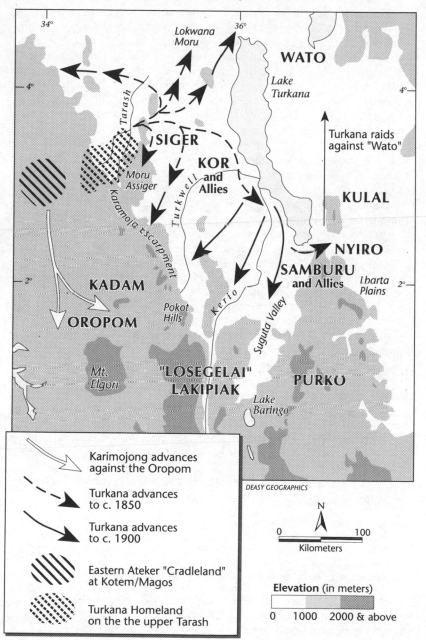

Map 4.1 Peoples of West Turkana

Ateker world. But then a dramatic change took place. Beset by mounting ecological problems, probably generated in part by the growing focus on cattle pastoralism, the eastern Ateker concentration at Koten–Magos began to fragment into individual groups, each with a mounting sense of unique identity. Ancestral elements of the Jie, Dodos, Toposa and Dongiro rapidly pushed out to the west and north, displacing and/or absorbing Luo, Katapa, Kuliak and other previous inhabitants, many of whom had been badly weakened by a terrible drought and famine remembered as the Laparanat. By the turn of the nineteenth century, other Ateker, who would provide important elements of Matheniko and Pian Karimojong, began moving southwards across the Apule River and into portions of southern Karamoja. The immigrants found the region in turmoil due to the effects of the Laparanat. Many groups of famine-stricken agriculturalists who had lived there in the past already were moving away, mainly to the west, in search of better conditions.[5]

Another community, the Oropom, far more pastoral in its economic outlook than the others, also had been weakened, but tried desperately to hold its grazing lands in the face of the Ateker advance. An aggregate of oral traditions (and some limited linguistic and archaeological evidence) depicts the Oropom as quite an exotic people. They are said to have built semi-subterranean structures, herded a distinctive type of black cattle with exceptionally long horns, and comprised families of skilled blacksmiths and potters. At least some spoke a Maa dialect (though other languages almost certainly were spoken too), and many traditions equate the entire community with 'Maasai'. There are indications of an especially close association with Uas Nkishu Maasai. Their cultural practices included cutting and stretching their ear-lobes, removing their lower incisors, daubing themselves with red ochre, using weapons of a 'Maasai' or 'Nandi' style and adhering to a hairstyle for men involving a long 'ponytail' and one for women featuring a cowrie shell dangling from a forelock. At least some elements practised circumcision.[6]

Despite determined resistance, Karimojong forays drove the Oropom back and by about 1825 they were in a crucial situation:

> The Karimojong kept beating the Oropom and drove them further and further south. Finally the Oropom became tired of running. They began killing their cattle to make leather ropes out of their skins. They tied themselves together with those ropes so that none could run away. They said, 'We are tired of running — it is better that we should all die here together.'[7]

Although this and other traditions emphasize the total 'destruction' of the Oropom, it is clear that they were not so much obliterated as absorbed into neighbouring communities. Considerable numbers of refugees fled in all directions: eastwards to find a haven on the Uas Nkishu plateau and with Pokot, southwards into the Toro–Nyanza area, westwards to join with Teso, and northwards where some were assimilated by Turkana and Tepes. A great many others were absorbed by Karimojong.[8]

As these developments transpired in southern Karamoja, other vigorous Ateker bands had been pushing eastwards down the escarpment from Karamoja into the upper Tarash River Valley. These Ateker, who would provide the ancestors of the embryonic Turkana, worked their way steadily down the Tarash until they found themselves nearing the threshold of an important ecological and ethnic frontier. At night flickering campfires on the surrounding hills revealed the presence of pre-existing communities of 'red people', who daubed their lighter-skinned bodies with ochre. Closest to the Tarash were the Siger (or Sigari) who inhabited the mountain which bore their name, *Moru Assiger*. Traditions portray them as a multicultural confederation whose various elements spoke Maa, Kalenjin and Cushitic dialects. As with the Oropom, the association with Maa-speakers is especially strong, and there are some indications of a close Oropom–Siger relationship. Certainly they shared cultural features, including the rearing of the distinctive black, long-horned cattle, and their women even had the same hairstyle with the dangling cowrie shell (*esigirait*, pl. *ngisigira*) from which the Siger are said to have derived their name.[9]

Coveting their rich highland pastures, the ancestral Turkana began to encroach on the Siger. Even as these confrontations were developing, however, the region was beset by a horrible drought, the *Aoyate*, 'the long dry time', and a resulting famine corresponding to the Laparanat of Karamoja. Siger herds were devastated and their community disintegrated. Many famine refugees who tried to push eastwards died of starvation near *Moru Eris*, but others found refuge with Dassanetch, Pokot, and Karimojong (where they formed important elements of the Matheniko section). Still others, impelled by Turkana pressures, raided down to the Uas Nkishu where they were known as *Kakesira*, and can be associated with the Losegelai (Siger = Sigerai = Losegelai) Maasai of that area. The remainder — quite a considerable number — became a new Turkana territorial section known as 'Siger', contributed other elements to the Bochoros section, and probably formed several new Turkana clans, including Siger, Swalika and Ngoleroto.[10]

Almost certainly these Oropom and Siger can be linked with the legendary 'Sirikwa' who feature in the traditional histories of many East African societies. In many important ways the Sirikwa are better regarded as a wide 'cultural phenomenon' than as any one distinct society. As such they usually represent 'old style' multicultural communities of pastoralists and semi-pastoralists who had inhabited many parts of Eastern Africa for centuries. The ubiquitous long-horned black cattle associated with the Oropom and Siger, quite apart from being an 'oral shorthand' to identify them as 'Sirikwa', in all probability refer to a specific type of cattle, cervico-thoracic humped sanga crossbreeds, apparently favoured by these 'old style' pastoralists. While somewhat hardier than various humpless breeds that had dominated East Africa in even earlier times, the sanga could not match the zebu, a later-arriving, short-horned breed, in its ability to survive in the adverse conditions of the drier grasslands. Indeed the zebu was to represent something of a 'bovine revolution' in East Africa, permitting the development of radically new patterns of transhumance and facilitating the emergence of 'new style' pastoralists better equipped to deal with even the harshest environments.[11]

Typical of these 'new style' pastoralists were the eastern Ateker, whose expansions out from Koten–Magos (entailing, as we have seen, their growing notions of unique corporate identity and the displacement/ absorption of aliens) apparently were fuelled by 'zebu cow power'. Facilitating the development of this 'new style' pastoralism was their easy access to vital ironware and grain supplies derived from their earlier interactions with western neighbours. The Ateker were not alone in the development of the 'new style' pastoralism, however. Maa-speaking peoples also had acquired the hardy zebu, and by at least the eighteenth century were pressing in on 'Sirikwa' communities as well, especially in the region of the Uas Nkishu plateau.

Acquiring a stronger sense of exclusive group identities similar to that of Ateker communities, rivalries also grew up among Maasai sections themselves, and it appears that some, impoverished by raids and displaced from their former territories, took refuge with Sirikwa groups, adding distinct Maasai characteristics to what were probably already culturally and linguistically diverse communities such as the Oropom and Siger, and so themselves became part of the 'phenomenon'.[12]

The notorious instability of pastoral communities, derived from the susceptibility of their herds to sudden and catastrophic decimation, is demonstrated by the rapid deterioration of the 'old style' Oropom and Siger in the early nineteenth century. Clearly their long-horned cattle were less able to withstand the worsening ecological conditions and died in far greater numbers than those of Ateker. Adding to their instability was the likelihood that both groups contained substantial numbers of recently impoverished and/or defeated peoples, and as such had weak political integrity. Certainly Siger traditions recall their expulsion from northern and eastern regions by Maa-speaking competitors and indicate that they had fallen back on the final refuge of the *Moru Assiger* highlands, apparently gathering in other refugees *en route*. The decimation of their herds, and, at least in the case of the Siger, the loss of their religious leadership (which will be discussed below), led to a rapid loss of cohesion and the eventual 'disappearance' of both communities. While Ateker raiding pressures may have brought things to a head, it is clear that environmental fluctuations and an outdated pastoral system underlay their demise.[13]

With the 'elimination' of the Oropom, Karimojong southern expansions came to a halt, and for the rest of the nineteenth century their main thrusts were against rival Ateker communities: Turkana to the east and Jie to the north. Although nearly absorbing the Jie at one point, conflicts with them and with the Turkana finally degenerated into a situation of 'reciprocal raiding' — a military balance in which unchecked escalations or permanent, deep encroachments were avoided. Most of the other Ateker communities found themselves in similar situations, and, as they encountered tougher resistance to continued expansion, made adjustments to their socio-political systems: Jie and Toposa, for example, developing the office of hereditary fire-maker as a source of new corporate solidarity, and Karimojong making some rather subtle changes to their age-class system. For their part, however, Turkana quickly embarked on a far more dramatic phase of expansion than any Ateker people had yet experienced. From their new footholds on *Moru Assiger*, the Turkana, now incorporating considerable numbers of Siger and Oropom, looked out to the north and east onto a region of desert-like conditions and searing heat. Except in a few favoured enclaves, grain cultivation was impossible.[14]

Inhabiting this hard country was another community of 'red' people, Maa-speaking *Kor*, the term which Turkana also use for the Samburu.[15] Traditions picture them as very numerous and living in pastoral association with *Rantalle* and *Poran*, the names used for the Cushitic-speaking Rendille and Boran. These powerful strangers were not 'old style' pastoralists clinging stubbornly to ancient ways, or dispirited remnants of military reversals, but a vibrant confederacy whose advances also had been fuelled in part by 'zebu cow power'. Adding valuable pastoral diversity were strange, long-necked creatures with humps on their back — the first camels the Turkana (at least those who had come down from Karamoja) had seen.

As the Turkana pushed further down the Tarash, driven apparently by ecological and demographic pressures, friction developed with the strangers and a need for additional manpower undoubtedly speeded up the absorption of the Siger, many of whom may have been at first regarded as allies or clients rather than as 'real Turkana'.[16] In addition to supplying manpower, however, the Siger apparently also were the source of some fundamental alterations to Turkana socio-political structures. The ancestral elements who had come down the escarpment from Karamoja brought with them a system typical of the other Ateker communities in which most religious, judicial and political power was wielded by congregations of senior elders whose pre-eminent status was derived from a generation-set system (*asapanu*). Clearly it was the elders who gave direction to the first expansions of Turkana raiding parties into parts of what was to become central *Eturkan* ('Turkanaland') and traditions recall them assembling as a single unified congregation through the early decades of the nineteenth century. By perhaps 1825, however, as Turkana advances pressed further afield it became impossible for the elders to gather collectively, and with the inauguration of a generation called Putiro some years later the whole generation-set system began taking on a new form. Instead of a system resting essentially on the distinction between alternating 'father–son' generations, a new one with a greater emphasis on biological age emerged. Now young men of the 'proper age' of initiation (about twenty) were inducted into age-sets regardless of generational status.[17]

Part of the effect for this dramatic alteration surely was to create a more efficient system of military mobilization. By now it is clear that the Turkana were experiencing much stiffer resistance from neighbouring peoples against whom their raids and territorial gains were being directed and the old generation-set apparatus was proving itself woefully inefficient in marshalling young fighting men. The lack of concurrence between biological and generational age meant that many young men had to postpone membership into corporate age-sets whose close-knit organization and *esprit de corps* underpinned military activity. Indeed, far from being a mechanism for military mobilization, the generation-set apparatus could better be regarded as a mechanism for *controlling* the aggressive tendencies of younger men whose excessive military activity could serve to undercut the authority and economic pre-eminence of the older men. As the elders began to lose something of their former central-izing authority, the alterations to the age-class system eliminated such inconsistencies, and far larger numbers of enthusiastic young fighting men now were mustered into corporate bodies.[18] Age-sets began to resemble military units to some extent and initiation itself became closely linked with raiding activity.

It has been suggested that these alterations may have been the result of spontaneous, even inevitable processes.[19] As I have argued else-where, however, the changes to the Turkana system surely developed far more from a process of conscious and creative adaptation to a range of new circumstances than from some 'automatic' process of atrophy or alteration.[20] The Turkana who drove out across the frontiers beyond the Tarash Valley were becoming very different from the Turkana who originally had arrived there from Karamoja. As they pushed further into the sprawling, intensely arid region west of Lake Turkana, they devel-oped a perception of themselves 'as expansion', and increasingly became freed of deep cosmological constraints that had bound other Ateker societies to graded, complementary gerontocracies in which generational dualism was strong.[21] The process was rapidly creating a new political identity, and in this transformed cultural environment the 'original' Turkana seem to have become susceptible to the influences of strangers who had been 'becoming Turkana' since the break-up of the Oropom and Siger.[22] In any event, Turkana oral traditions picture the Putiro generation, the first associated with the changes to the age system, as far more effective fighting men who rolled forward in an inexorable tide to crush the resistance of alien communities in several different parts of *Eturkan*.

Despite these traditions, however, the process of Turkana 'expansion' certainly involved large- and small-scale assimilations of rivals at least as much as actual armed invasion. In most fundamental aspects, the material culture, economic outlook, religious forms, social system (including the rejection of Maa-speakers' practice of circumcision), and — despite increasing bilingualism — the language of the evolving Turkana community continued to reflect earlier Ateker models. Even the important changes to the Turkana age-class system hardly represented any wholesale copying of the Maa-speakers' system. To the contrary, it was clearly a creative and selective adaptation born of new circumstances, and many of the strong generational aspects of the original Ateker system survived.[23]

In addition to providing a more efficient means of mobilizing manpower, the Turkana apparently understood that their new system could provide a mechanism to facilitate the absorption of strangers and consolidate relations with neighbouring communities. Once adopted it is very likely that the new organization rapidly helped to break down ethnic distinctions between 'old' and 'new' Turkana, and provided an internal integration similar to that derived by Nguni-speakers from their system of age-regiments.[24]

Some time before the mid-nineteenth century, Turkana, consistently well supplied with iron weapons and grain by their Jie allies and trading partners in Karamoja, had reached the western shores of the lake and occupied much of what was to constitute *Eturkan*. The main direction of most subsequent advances had then been down along the lake shores and into the southern plains areas, but they had finally stalled on the west bank of the Kerio River. It is not surprising that they should. The initial Turkana expansions had carried something of a momentum of their own, fuelled by impoverished individuals anxious to build up herds and by newly-initiated age-sets of the altered age-class system anxious to build reputations. The actual occupation of new territory had probably been a secondary, or even, as Galaty has suggested of such processes, an *unintended* consequence. Since the alterations to the age-class system, the power of the senior elders, already diluted by their inability to gather as a single congregation, was further eroded and it became difficult to achieve much coordinated direction over raiding forays. Indeed any strong sense of corporate Turkana selfhood probably was becoming more and more elusive. Increasingly most people were building a strong identification with local territorial sections, and substantial differences in dialect, dress and other cultural features became apparent. At least two groups of pre-existing strangers, the Kebootok cultivators and trappers of the Turkwel and the Bochoros farmers and fishermen of the lake shores, had been only imperfectly absorbed.[25]

Another powerful barrier to further Turkana expansion was presented by the emergence beyond the Kerio of the Maa-speaking Samburu community, who, as Sobania puts it, had been 'moulded by the pressure which emanated from the surrounding plateaux'. Much of that pressure had been imparted by the Turkana advances. Samburu traditions say that initial contact with them was made during the initiations of the Kipayang age-set (1823–1837) and they picture the invaders as a poor but belligerent people, anxious to capture livestock. Clearly many of the elements which would constitute the Samburu were the *Kor* and allied groups which Turkana traditions depict as retreating before the Putiro, but undoubtedly they also included Siger and other peoples, too.[26]

It was at this point that another fundamental alteration to the Turkana socio-political system, almost certainly inspired by Maa-speakers, manifested itself. Vivid Turkana traditions recall the existence of a powerful diviner (*emuron*, pl. *ngimurok*) named Lokerio under whose direction the Turkana gathered a fresh momentum and raided across the Kerio. Undaunted even by the vast expanse of water to the east, traditions picture him creating a dry path with his sacred stick through the lake in order to lead his armies across to capture vast herds of camels from peoples on the other side. While similar in some respects to religious leaders who dominated other East African societies including the Maasai and Nandi at this same time, Lokerio represents an institution foreign to all the other Ateker communities. His type of diviner, *ngimurok aakuj*, 'Diviners of God', was sharply different from the local healers and seers of the other Ateker, both in the universality of his authority, and in terms of the influence he exerted over the age-class apparatus and military affairs.[27]

It is most likely that Lokerio's family, the Meturona, were once part of the Siger confederacy, which apparently also was to contribute the *Kachepkai* diviners to the Pokot, the *Talai* diviners to the Uas Nkishu Maasai, the Nandi and the Kipsigis, and other families of diviners to the Sebei, Tepes and other people living in the vicinity of Mount Elgon. Despite tales extolling the great mystical powers of Apatepes, Lokerio's 'father' and the reputed founder of the Meturona line of diviners, however, it seems clear that no diviner before Lokerio wielded the same type of influence and control among the Turkana. Rather, Lokerio appears to have taken advantage of the 'power vacuum' resulting from the decline of the status of the senior elders gradually to gain control over important aspects of the new age-class system, and finally to supplant them as the director of military affairs. In his new role Lokerio did not have the same misgivings about the escalation of offensive operations that had constrained the strategic formulations of the elders in the old days. To the contrary, successful raids were of direct benefit to him socially, politically and even economically, as victorious raiding parties filled his kraals with the shares of captured livestock which were his fees for directing them. Adroitly manipulating the stiffening Samburu resistance to his advantage, Lokerio began to provide a strongly renewed sense of Turkana ethnicity, as is recalled by the powerful image of social transcendence inherent in the magical 'crossing of the waters' tradition.

Aspects of 'Becoming Turkana'

As with other East African pastoral communities, a period of escalating
conflict now provided a powerful stimulus to the process of Turkana
ethnogenesis. Under Lokerio's leadership of the Turkana, the Samburu
became 'something against which [the Turkana could] take shape' and
his office provided a mechanism by which the loose fabric of a widely-
dispersed Turkana community could be knitted together. Indeed, there
can be little question that in the second half of the nineteenth century it
was one's allegiance to the Meturona (and briefly the Katekok) diviners
which primarily defined one's status as a Turkana.[28]

It has been noted that, except under certain circumstances, age-sets,
in themselves, do not form a very effective basis for military organization.[29] Only as a society achieves a degree of political centralization, it
appears, do the age-sets begin to function as components ('regiments')
of a wider military structure. With the Nguni-speakers of southern
Africa, for example, a strongly monolithic hierarchical system took
shape as age-regiments mustered around powerful centralizing figures.
Apparently to an extent significantly greater than that of diviners in most
other East African societies, Lokerio now provided the burgeoning
Turkana community with a point of coalescence from which unprece-
dented military centralization could develop. Larger and better coordinated raiding parties struck at the Samburu and other enemies, and
Turkana settlements moved into the extreme northern and southern
limits of *Eturkan*. Once more, however, the process entailed assimilations
of aliens, not only of war captives and impoverished people, but surely
also those impressed by Lokerio's awesome mystical and political skills.
Somewhat ironically, although his office clearly was derived from Maasai
models, the Samburu, who now bore the brunt of his effective leadership
and military organization, lacked any comparably powerful diviner of
their own, and it can be surmised that many more or less voluntarily
'became Turkana' to enter into an association with this talented,
charismatic man.[30]

But, while derived initially from the institutions of Maa-speakers, the
Turkana did not, once again, simply copy their version of diviners.
Rather, they created a unique variation, distinguished by a greater
degree of centralizing authority expressed most dramatically in a
military context. It is feasible that this stronger notion of centralization may have developed from early Ateker exposures to the institution of Luo *rwodi* (s. *rwot*) priest-kings in Uganda. Certainly the
Turkana office of 'Diviner of God' was quickly usurped from Lokerio's
family by two others whose ancestry could be traced back to the old
Ateker concentration in Karamoja. Moreover, at least one of these
had had important ritual associations with Ateker hereditary fire-
makers whose own office clearly was influenced by the concept of
the *rwot*. Alternatively, it might have developed from — or at least
was strengthened by — Turkana territorial expansion itself, a process
typical of those in which Stanislav Andreski has discerned the

97

phenomenon of large-scale assimilations directly creating deeper senses of monocracy.[31]

But, even though Lokerio's dynamic leadership was of crucial importance in Turkana expansions into regions south of the lake, there were additional factors at work. Other Maa-speaking groups, including the Laikipiak and bands of Losegelai in the region north-west of Lake Baringo, also were pressing in on the Samburu at the same time. Sometime after mid-century the Turkana formed an alliance with the Pokot, and they too began making incursions against Samburu and against Maa-speaking Chamus in the Baringo area. Taking advantage of these turbulent conditions, Lokerio, exerting an even closer coordination of military affairs, further intensified his attacks, and soon Samburu were forced to withdraw to the north-east. Turkana raids also forced the Laikipiak to fall back from regions south-east of the lake before they themselves had to abandon some recently-gained regions upon the deterioration of their alliance with the Pokot.[32]

Then, by the 1870s, a series of events badly weakened the societies competing with the Turkana for access to these areas south of the lake. Both the Losegelai and the Laikipiak were dealt crushing defeats by the Purko during the intensifying Maasai 'Civil Wars'. Refugees from both peoples joined Turkana and one suspects that Laikipiak, who lost their family of diviners at this point, may have been especially impressed by Lokerio's burgeoning fame. Somewhat perplexing Samburu traditions, which portray continuing raids by both communities well after the Maasai, picture them as being 'totally annihilated' and 'ceasing to exist', may well refer to these refugee groups, who apparently formed an alliance with the Turkana for some time before being fully incorporated into their community. In any case, it must be emphasized that the dividing line between 'alliance' and 'assimilation' in such circumstances must always have been a very hazy one. While the Turkana only seem to link one of their clans, Komesoroko, with the Laikipiak, substantial numbers of refugees may actually have been absorbed, as is indicated by the (admittedly exaggerated) testimony of some of Hobley's informants, who declared that the Turkana community was nothing more than 'the survival of the Laikipikiah section of the Masai'. In the wake of the Laikipiak and Losegelai defeats, Turkana raids pushed against the Samburu and Rendille with a fresh vigour, carrying them even up the eastern shores of the lake.[33]

At the same time, the cattle of virtually all the inhabitants of the eastern Lake Turkana basin, with the notable exception of the Turkana, were beset by a serious bovine pleuro-pneumonia epizootic. About a decade later an even more catastrophic cattle disease, rinderpest, swept through the region. In some areas it was rapidly followed by a severe drought and then by a smallpox epidemic, constituting the 'Triple Disaster' which devastated many East African peoples. Again of all the pastoral societies of the area, the Turkana were virtually the only ones spared these ravages. Traditions claim this was because most of the Turkana cattle were isolated from the disease in central portions of *Eturkan* and in remote mountain pastures while it was mainly herds of goats and camels (which were not susceptible to the illnesses) that were being kept in areas adjacent to those affected by it. Those Turkana stockmen who did lose some cattle apparently fell back on their camels and small stock with relatively little disruption to their lives. It is clear, therefore, that the efficiency with which the Turkana had developed a diversified pastoral economy, similar to that of the Ariaal and Gurra, featuring cattle and camels alike, also helped them to avoid the crushing effects of the epizootics. Thus, as had been true in the initial phases of Turkana ascendancy, it was economic factors which again gave the Turkana an advantage over their neighbours in these later stages.[34]

In the wake of the devastation, many of the victims, in their determination to remain pastoralists or even in their grim struggle to survive, now 'became Turkana' in their turn. As terrible as these catastrophes were, however, they did not feature the 'obliteration' of entire communities as had happened with the Oropom and Siger. Most assimilations, therefore, were of smaller scale, consisting of impoverished individuals and small groups. In some instances Maa-speaking women were the ones absorbed into Turkana society as they married Turkana men so that their families could use the resulting bridewealth to begin restocking their herds.

Unlike most other options open to them — such as becoming hunters, fishermen or cultivators — the 'conversion' of Maa-speaking pastoralists to Ateker society did not entail, even temporarily, the painful necessity of undergoing an essential economic transformation or even of significantly altering a fundamental 'pastoral outlook'. Thus, if we accept Galaty's contention that: 'Maasai are pre-eminently pastoralists and all other values are thought to follow from that essential commitment, which occupies the conceptual and value centre of the notion of "Maasai"', we can readily discern a very powerful motive for so many Maa-speakers to 'become Turkana' at this point.[35]

By this same time the era of rapid Turkana expansion had begun to slow dramatically. In some places that expansion now took the form of a 'subtle demographic pressure', similar to the Mursi 'infiltration' of the country of the Bodi discussed by Turton. But, although still very fluid and ill-defined, many of the frontiers of *Eturkan* — especially those in the west and north marked by steep highlands and escarpments — had been showing a certain 'stabilization' for some time. In some places, close economic and social interactions resulted in very blurry ethnic identities. In many instances frequent intermarriage produced new conditions of reciprocity (even to the point where people from different communities settled together in common villages), similar to those Johnson has described as existing between the Nuer and Dinka. Additional 'semi-Turkana' groups reminiscent of the Bochoros and Kebootok, who long had functioned as 'half-way houses' in the assimilation of aliens, now came into existence along the frontiers with the Karimojong, Pokot and Dassanetch. Unlike earlier times, however, when these groups served mainly to incorporate strangers into the Turkana community, some now began to serve the opposite purpose of channelling 'peripheral' Turkana into the linguistic and cultural systems of their neighbours. As Lonsdale has noted of similar processes, 'who assimilated whom' in such circumstances is very much an open question. In other instances 'multicultural confederations', quite reminiscent of the Oropom, Siger or the western Ateker groups of Uganda, were created. Not infrequently the cooperating members of these new communities identified more closely with each other than they did with most other elements of the old societies. Everywhere, even along the still-contested south-eastern frontiers, Turkana military activity abated considerably. For a while the Maa-speakers of this region may have been too impoverished by the various epizootics to offer very tempting raiding targets, but even when hostilities did occur Turkana raiders frequently were contained by effective Samburu and Purko resistance and retaliation. A situation of 'reciprocal raiding' emerged in which a strong sense of tactical balance and limitation worked against strategic escalations.[36]

Although such limited military activity did continue in the south-east, important blurrings of ethnic identity also were taking place even here by the late nineteenth century. Somewhat ironically, the same Turkana sections which were most active in raids against the Maa-speakers and Rendille contained many recently assimilated people from those same societies, and bilingualism was very common. Early European visitors noted that many of the Turkana of this area were of 'the pure Samburu and Rendille type' and reported that intermarriage and other peaceful contacts were common. They also noted the 'great credit' enjoyed by Maa-speakers among the Turkana, and that the latter, while maintaining an essentially Ateker cultural identity, seemed particularly impressed by various aspects of the Maasai socio-political system.[37]

At least in part, the abating of the era of expansion and the 'stabilization' of frontiers can be attributed to a deterioration in the powers of the Turkana 'Diviners of God'. After the death of Lokerio in about 1880, a virulent rivalry grew up between his Meturona line and Lokorijam, a challenger from the Katekok clan, who eventually usurped the office by about 1895. The new line of diviners enjoyed only a short period of unrivalled ascendancy, however, before another bitter feud broke out between the Katekok and yet another contender, Loolel Kokoi of the Pucho clan, in the early years of the twentieth century. These rivalries substantially eroded the sense of Turkana corporate unity which had been bequeathed by Lokerio. In these circumstances, the same strong central coordination of military affairs became impossible to duplicate. This erosion of power quickly exposed the 'twisted and shallow' roots of Turkana ethnicity, and increasingly a stronger sense of identification with local communities — some of them newly formed from multi-cultural interaction along the borders — was reaffirmed. In such circumstances it was as likely that some Turkana might 'become Maasai' as vice versa.

Such mobility was not destined to survive into the colonial period, however, as Turkana experienced one additional powerful surge of 'nationalism' during their prolonged and determined resistance to imperial conquest, when the designation 'Turkana' increasingly implied opposition to the British and their 'pacified' African allies, many of them Maa-speakers. Then, following the final crushing of Turkana resistance, the creation of administrative boundaries based on inflexible notions of ethnic identity produced an even more monolithic 'tribe', thus excluding, for whatever reason, outsiders from 'becoming Turkana', as so many had done in the past.[38]

Notes

1. See, among others, John L. Berntsen 'The Maasai and their Neighbours: Variables of Interaction', *African Economic History*, (1976: 5–7); John G. Galaty, 'Form and Interaction in East African Strategies of Dominance and Aggression' in D. McGuiness (ed.), *Dominance, Aggression and War* (New York, 1987: 240–241). Richard D. Waller, 'Interaction and Identity on the Periphery: The Trans-Mara Maasai', *IJAHS*, 17, 2 (1984: 250, 281); William L. Lawren, 'Maasai and Kikuyu: An Historical Analysis of Culture Transmission', *JAH*, 9, 4 (1968: 571–583).
2. The term 'Ateker' replaces 'Central Paranilotes' used in some of my earlier writings. The group includes the Turkana, Jie, Karimojong, Dodos, Nyangatom, Toposa, Jiye and Teso (both of Uganda and of Kenya). Sommer and Vossen (this volume) refer to the group as 'Teso–Turkana'.
3. David Turton, 'War, Peace and Mursi Identity', in Katsuyoshi Fukui and David Turton (eds), *Warfare Among East African Herders* (Osaka, 1979: 204).
4. Acknowledgements to Richard Waller.
5. For a fuller account see John Lamphear, 'The Persistence of Hunting and Gathering in a "Pastoral" World', *SUGIA*, 7, 2 (1986: 235ff); idem, *The Traditional History of the Jie of Uganda* (Oxford, 1976: 61ff).
6. Oral interviews, termed 'Historical Texts', conducted in Uganda and Kenya in 1969–71 and 1976, are abbreviated as follows: 'J' for Jie, 'BK' for Bokora Karimojong, 'MTK' for Matheniko Karimojong, and 'T' for Turkana, followed by the chronological number of the interview. Thus 'T-56' refers to Turkana Historical Text number 56. The interviews from which the foregoing information was derived include: BK-2, BK-6, BK-7, BK-9, and J-2. Also J.G. Wilson, 'Preliminary Observations on the Oropom People of Karamoja', unpublished typescript, Moroto (c. 1969); John Weatherby and Ralph Herring, a personal letter to Bertin Webster concerning the Oropom, 19 June 1973, and cf. C.A. Turpin, 'The Occupation of the Turkwel River Area by the Karamojong Tribe', *U.J.*, 12, 2 (1948).
7. John Loyep and Esero Lobanyang, BK-2.
8. Turpin, 'Occupation' 162; John Weatherby, 'Ethnological Aspects of the Tepes', unpublished typescript, Moroto (n.d), p. 3; Wilson, 'Preliminary Observations'; Pamela and P.H. Gulliver, *The Central Nilo-Hamites* (London, 1953: 72); J.B. Webster et al., *The Iteso During the Asonya* (Nairobi, 1973: 28ff), and cf. John Mack, 'Material Culture and Ethnic Identity in the Southeastern Sudan', in J. Mack and P. Robertshaw (eds), *Culture History in the Southern Sudan* (Nairobi, 1982: 121); also Galaty, 'Form and Interaction': 240.

9. Interviews including BK-7, MTK-1, MTK-2, MTK-3, T-4, T-14, T-18, T-19, T-54; J.R. Nimmo, 'Handing Over Notes, Lokitaung', Kenya National Archives (*KNA*)-*HOR/886* (1948: 2); Weatherby's and Herring's letter; Wilson, 'Preliminary Observations'; Lamphear, 'Hunting and Gathering', 244–246; also see Neal Sobania, 'The Historical Tradition of the Peoples of the Eastern Lake Turkana Basin, c. 1840–1925, unpublished Ph.D. thesis, University of London, 1980: 67–68.
10. Interviews including T-5, T-6, T-8, T-15, T-18, T-19, T-56, BK-7, MTK-3; John Lamphear, 'The People of the Grey Bull: The Origin and Expansion of the Turkana', *JAH*, 29 (1988: 32–33); Alan H. Jacobs, 'The Traditional Political Organization of the Pastoral Masai', unpublished D. Phil. thesis, Oxford, 1965: 67–70; Waller, 'Interaction and Identity', 250.
11. Lamphear, 'Hunting and Gathering': 248–253; *idem*, 'Grey Bull', 31–33; H. Epstein, *The Origin of the Domestic Animals of Africa*, 1 (New York, 1971: 372–377, 409, 541–543); Nicholas David, 'Prehistory and Historical Linguistics in Central Africa', in Christopher Ehret and Merrick Posnansky (eds), *The Archaeological and Linguistic Reconstruction of African History* (Berkeley, 1982); *idem*, 'The BIEA Southern Sudan Expedition of 1979', in Mack and Robertshaw, *Culture History*, 55.
    For another view on the development of 'new style' pastoralism, see Galaty, this volume. Likewise, a different interpretation of the Sirikwa and the role of zebu cattle in the 'pastoral revolution' is contained in Sutton's chapter, this volume.
12. Lamphear, 'Hunting and Gathering', 251–253; *idem*, 'Grey Bull': 36–37; Jacobs, 'Pastoral Masai': 54–59; and *cf*. Waller, 'Interaction and Identity': 251, 279; *idem*, 'Ecology, Migration and Expansion in East Africa', *African Affairs*, 84 (1985: 350, 358); and Charles H. Ambler, *Kenyan Communities in the Age of Imperialism* (New Haven and London, 1988: 32).
13. Interviews including T-10 and T-11; David, 'Prehistory'; Sobania, 'Historical Tradition', 69, Waller, 'Ecology': 350, 359, 364; and *cf*. P. Bonte, 'Cattle for God: An Attempt at a Marxist Analysis of the Religion of East African Herdsmen', *Social Compass*, 22, 3–4 (1975: 388) for the argument that a pastoral society that loses its herds loses its very social definition. See also John L. Berntsen, 'Maasai Age-Sets and Prophetic Leadership, 1850–1912', *Africa*, 49, 2 (1979: 135).
14. John Lamphear, *The Scattering Time: Turkana Responses to the Imposition of Colonial Rule* (Oxford, 1991), ch. 2; *idem, Jie of Uganda*, ch. 7; *idem*, 'Historical Dimensions of Dual Organization: The Generation-Class System of the Jie and the Turkana', in David Maybury-Lewis and Uri Almagor (eds), *The Attraction of Opposites: Thought and Society in the Dualistic Mode* (Ann Arbor, 1989: 252–53).
15. I much prefer the spelling 'Sampur' for this group, and have used it in most of my recent writings. In order to conform to the spelling used by other contributors to this present volume, however, I am using the form 'Samburu' in this chapter.
16. Lamphear, 'Grey Bull', 30–33; and *cf*. Waller, 'Ecology', 365; A. Gold, 'The Nandi in Transition: Background to the Nandi Resistance to the British, 1895–1906', *Kenya Historical Review*, 8 (1981: 93–95); Douglas H. Johnson, 'Tribal Boundaries and Border Wars: Nuer–Dinka Relation in the Sobat and Zaraf Valleys, c. 1860–1976', *JAH*, 23 (1982: 187).
17. John Lamphear, 'The Rise and Fall of the Turkana *Ngimurok*', a paper presented at the Seers, Prophets and Diviners Conference, London, December, 1989: 6–7.
18. Lamphear, *Scattering Time*, ch. 1; see also, among others, several contributions to Fukui and Turton, *Warfare among East African Herders*, especially Uri Almagor, 'Raiders and Elders: A Confrontation of Generations Among the Dassanetch'; and P.T.W. Baxter, 'Boran Age-Sets and Warfare', 92.
    As late as the 1970s under conditions similar to those described here, the Nyangatom people began to fear their community was 'finished', and considered 'becoming Turkana' *en masse*. See Serge Tornay, 'Generational Age-Systems and Chronology', a paper presented at the Archaeology and Ethnohistory of the Southern Sudan and Adjacent Areas Seminar, SOAS, London (1980).

19. See Paul Spencer, 'The Jie Generation Paradox', in P.T.W. Baxter and U. Almagor (eds), *Age, Generation and Time* (London, 1978); Harold K. Muller, *Changing Generations: Dynamics of Generation and Age-Sets in Southeastern Sudan (Toposa) and Northwestern Kenya (Turkana)* (Saarbrucken and Fort Lauderdale, 1989: 35–36, 137–139).
20. Lamphear, 'Dual Organization', *passim,*
21. Lamphear, 'Dual Organization'; and *cf.* Katsuyoshi Fukui and David Turton, 'Introduction', in Fukui and Turton, *Warfare*, 11–12, for their argument against the 'soldier ant' theory of migration; also Turton, 'Mursi Identity', 197.
22. *Cf.*, among others, Berntsen, 'Maasai and Neighbours': 8; Lawren, 'Maasai and Kikuyu', 579, 583; Robert A. Levine and Walter H. Sangree, 'The Diffusion of Age-Group Organization in East Africa', *Africa*, 32, 2 (1962: 98).
23. See Philip H. Gulliver, 'Turkana Age Organization', *American Anthropologist*, 60 (1958).
24. Interviews including T–3, T–5, T–13, T–15, T–19, T–53 and T–54; Lamphear, *Scattering Time*, ch. 1; A.K. Rennie, 'Ideology and State Formation: Political and Commercial Ideologies among the South-Eastern Shona', in Ahmed Idha Salim (ed.), *State Formation in Eastern Africa* (Nairobi, 1984: 185); also see Morimichi Tomikawa, 'The Migrations and Inter-Tribal Relations of the Pastoral Datoga', in Fukui and Turton, *Warfare*, 15ff and 30.
25. Galaty, 'Form and Interaction': 249, fn. 8; Lamphear, 'Grey Bull': 36–37. Although they do not exactly correspond to any of the three types of 'expansionist' societies described by Waller ('Ecology', 366), the Turkana most resemble his 'assimilative' type.
26. Sobania, 'Historical Tradition', 782; Paul Spencer, *Nomads in Alliance* (London, 1973: 148–155); Lamphear, *Scattering Time*, ch. 2.
27. Lamphear, 'Turkana *Ngimurok*', 1–2, 10.
28. Waller, 'Interaction and Identity', 249; Lamphear, 'Turkana *Ngimurok*': 8–10; *idem*, 'Grey Bull', 37–38, and *cf.* Robert Harms, 'Oral Tradition and Ethnicity', *Journal of Interdisciplinary History*, 12 (1979: 78); Katsuyoshi Fukui, personal communication, 1990; Elliot Fratkin, 'A Comparison of the Role of Prophets in Samburu and Maasai Warfare', in Fukui and Turton, *Warfare*, 61
29. See, for example, Baxter, 'Boran Age-Sets', 93.
30. See John L. Berntsen, 'The Enemy is Us: Eponymy in the Historiography of the Maasai', *History in Africa*, 7 (1980: 5, 13); Fratkin, 'Role of Prophets': 53; Lamphear, 'Grey Bull', 38; Muller, *Changing Generations*, 36.
31. Stanislav Andreski, *Military Organization and Society* (Berkeley and London, 1954: 13–14); Lamphear, *Scattering Time*, especially ch. 2 and Conclusion; *idem*, 'Turkana *Ngimurok*; *idem*, *History of the Jie*, especially chapter 6.
32. Sobania, 'Historical Traditions', 81–83, 97–101; Lamphear, *Scattering Time*, ch. 2; K.R. Dundas, 'Notes on the Tribes Inhabiting the Baringo District', *JRAI*, 40 (1910: 51–52, 56, 69); Mervyn Beech, *The Suk* (Oxford, 1911: 4–5); G.H. Chaundry, 'A Short Account of the West Suk Tribe', *KNA–HOR/886* (1931: 2).
33. Lamphear, *Scattering Time*, ch. 2; interviews including T–12; Sobania, 'Historical Traditions', 136–137, 141; also see Sobania's chapter, this volume; C.W. Hobley, *Eastern Uganda* (London, 1902: 480).
34. Lamphear, *Scattering Time*, ch. 2; *cf.* Waller, 'Ecology': 359.
35. John G. Galaty, 'Being "Maasai"; Being "People of Cattle": Ethnic Shifters in East Africa', *American Ethnologist*, 9, 1 (1982: 4, 7); also Berntsen, 'Enemy is Us' 13; David, 'Southern Sudan Expedition', Sobania, 'Historical Tradition', 187; Dundas, 'Baringo District': 66; John Lonsdale, 'When Did the Gusii (or any other group) Become a "Tribe"?', *KHR*, 5 (1977: 127).
36. Turton, 'Mursi Identity': 196; Lamphear, *Scattering Time*, ch. 2; Sobania, 'Historical Traditions': 147; Spencer, *Nomads*, 152; Galaty, 'Form and Intention': 238–239; Johnson, 'Tribal Boundaries', 183, 186, 190; Lonsdale, 'Gusii', 12; also see Peter Robertshaw and David Collett, 'A New Framework for the Study of Early Pastoral Communities in East Africa', *JAH*, 24 (1983: 293).

37. Interviews including T-8, T-12, T-14, and T-19; H.B. Kittermaster, 'History of the Turkana', *KNA-PRB/211* (Jan. 1911: 50); E.D. Emley, 'The Turkana of Kolosia District', *JRAI*, 57 (1927: 190); Dundas, 'Baringo District', 66, 69; L. von Höhnel, *Discovery of Lakes Rudolf and Stefanie*, 1 (London, 1894: 230).
38. Lamphear, 'Rise and Fall', 10–16; Ambler, *Kenyan Communities*, 157; Mack, 'Material Culture', 121; Margaret Hay, 'Local Trade and Ethnicity in Western Kenya', *African Economic History Review*, 2, 1 (1975: 11).

Five

Defeat
& Dispersal

The Laikipiak & their Neighbours
at the End of the Nineteenth Century

NEAL SOBANIA

Among the Maasai the military defeat of the Laikipiak by a Purko–Kisongo alliance is legendary. According to Maasai tradition the curses and prophecies of their *loibon*, Mbatiany, so weakened the Laikipiak that, when the warriors of the alliance attacked the Laikipiak warrior village of Il Kileti, they were able to gather unseen during the middle of the night in the centre of the village. The warhorn blew, the Laikipiak stumbled sleepily from their houses, and were summarily destroyed or 'finished'. The crucial fighting of this period, which tradition represents in this single devastating defeat, probably occurred between 1874 and 1876.[1] And it is said that after this the Laikipiak disappeared as a social-political unit.

Indeed, from the view-point of the Purko–Kisongo and the other Maasai, all of whom lived to the south and west of this fighting, the Laikipiak did cease to exist. And from this perspective, heretofore the only one recorded, it was not inconsistent to conclude that the few Laikipiak encountered after the mid-1870s were merely 'remnants' of this former enemy. For the Maasai such 'remnant' populations were not new. The traditions of pastoral peoples often recall individuals and families 'being lost', i.e. lacking a viable herd both to sustain themselves physically and to maintain the relationships necessary to exist socially. For the Maasai, evidence that the Laikipiak were 'lost' was clear. They had been militarily defeated and their prophet, Koikoti ole Tunai, had fled to the Trans-Mara region of western Maasailand. Their grazing lands, which stretched from at least Naivasha to the Leroghi Plateau, had been abandoned, and across the region large numbers of defeated Laikipiak were assimilated by the Purko, Kisongo and others whose lands were contiguous to those of these once powerful neighbours.

To the north, however, among the peoples of the eastern Lake Turkana basin, this conceptualization of a defeated people was vastly at odds with the Laikipiak population with whom they had to reckon.

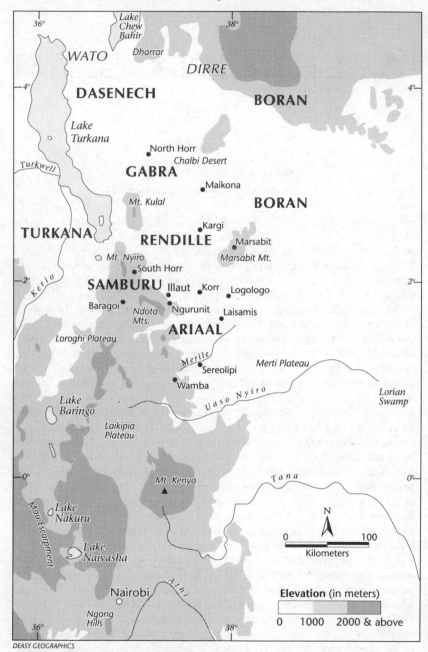

Map 5.1 Peoples of East Turkana

Instead, in this more northern region, wherein are found all the principal places with which the Samburu, Rendille and Boran traditionally associate the Laikipiak, a significant Laikipiak element continued to raid and plunder.[2]

These two distinct sets of tradition, which at first appear to be at odds with each other, are in fact most helpful in exploring Laikipiak identity. Since no Laikipiak socio-political unit exists today, and since individuals or particular families identified as having once been Laikipiak are few and scattered across Kenya and Tanzania, any reconstruction must of necessity rely on the traditions of others about the Laikipiak. What the southern set of Maasai traditions record is a period that extends to the mid-1870s, a time in which, from a Maasai perspective, the Laikipiak disappeared. What the northern traditions document, however, is a second period of Laikipiak history. This period lasts into the early years of the twentieth century when the Laikipiak really do cease to exist as an identifiable community. But, until that time, the Laikipiak were very much an extant population and, for the neighbouring communities of Samburu, Rendille and Boran herders, had anything but disappeared.

Each set of traditions presents the 'reality' from the particular vantage point or perspective of those communities who had to contend with the Laikipiak, and in the context of those encounters. From the perspective of the southern traditions Laikipiak identity is seen in the context of territory: the ouster of a formidable neighbour from an area from which they could have expanded southwards, deeper into the heartland of the Central Rift. The perspective provided by the northern traditions is one of Laikipiak identity in the context of survival and assimilation: recovering first from their defeat at the hands of the Purko–Kisongo alliance, and later in the 1880s and 1890s from the epizootics that destroyed their remaining herds.

The two perspectives provided by these distinct vantage points and contexts highlight the serious problem encountered in using traditions that describe a community as 'being' Laikipiak, and which describe a people or enemy as being 'finished', with the implication of a total defeat or of stock loss disastrous to the point of annihilation and obliteration. But are a people in fact 'finished' when they lose their territory? Or is a community 'finished' only when it loses its ethnic or cultural identity?

In this chapter it is argued that the traditions about the Laikipiak as a defeated and dispersed people, an identity in the context of territory, obscure not only their continued existence, but the process by which pastoralists, be they groups or individuals, in fact survive such setbacks. Thus, the shift of the Laikipiak to the north and the traditions of their raiding the Samburu, Rendille and Boran can be seen as an initial attempt to recoup the losses they had so recently suffered at the hands of the Purko–Kisongo. Later, especially in the 1880s and 1890s, their resort to raiding is part of long-established pastoralist strategy for surviving the catastrophic natural disasters that periodically devastated the herding communities of East Africa. An examination of the northern traditions not only clearly documents the continued existence of the Laikipiak well beyond their defeat at Naivasha in the 1870s, but allows their loss of cultural identity, which in fact occurred only some thirty years later, to be more fully understood.

Defining Laikipiak Identity

The Laikipiak presence to the north of the Central Rift, their identification with the Leroghi/Laikipia Plateau and their confrontations with the Purko–Kisongo alliance lead to a number of possible explanations as to who the Laikipiak were. From a Maasai perspective, where the importance of prophetic leadership by a *loibon* was well established, the Laikipiak may well have been seen as the followers of the prophet Koikoti. But such a definition seems unnecessarily narrow and tied too closely to the traditions of the Purko–Kisongo victory and Koikoti's departure from the region.[3] Such a link to prophetic leadership would, moreover, require that one argue for there being no Laikipiak prior to the emergence of the *loibonok*, which not only is unnecessarily didactic, but moves backward into the categorical distinctions of a Central Maasai nation and *Iloikop* or *Kwavi* groups (see Galaty, this volume). And, while the exact units of the Laikipiak are not known in detail, sectional identities could and did stand on their own without Koikoti just as Samburu unity existed and continues to exist without the blessings of a strong class of *loibon*.

A broader definition might focus on language, specifically Maa-speakers of the area. Here, dialect differences can be useful for determining linguistic relationships between, for example, the language of the Laikipiak as distinct from that of the Samburu and other Maasai (see Sommer and Vossen, this volume).[4] But, for reconstructing more recent history from oral texts, definitions of identity that focus on language use are made problematic by the bilingualism and multiculturalism of the region (see both Fratkin, and Klumpp and Kratz, this volume). Extensive networks of exchange and reciprocity linked neighbouring communities in an interdependent regional economy (pastoralists to pastoralists, pastoralists to agriculturalists, and hunter-gatherers to both) that not only underpinned a society's adaptation to the environmental, social and political conditions of a given area, but fostered the bilingualism and multiculturalism known to have existed.[5] Given the independent adaptation of cultural forms, the mere use of language can not define identity.

Yet another way to define the Laikipiak is to identify them, as the Maasai often do, as those cattle-herders who had a particular attachment to the Laikipia/Leroghi plateau region.[6] But the evidence suggests that such a territorial definition is too contrived since the Laikipiak were clearly more broadly dispersed — across a region that ran from Naivasha in the west along the Uaso Nyiro River to the Lorian Swamp in the east, and at least as far north as the Laisamis area, but probably to beyond Marsabit Mountain.[7] Adding to the problem, however, is that the relationship of the various groups across this region is unclear. Establishing the range of Laikipiak occupation does not clarify the relationship of the communities identified as Laikipiak that lived within it. And the lists of Laikipiak subgroup names compiled in the first decade of this century by Hollis, Hobley and Dundas only add to the confusion.[8]

Waller suggests that these lists include references to sections, clans and geographic areas, but that there are correlations with Maasai tradition.[9] He concludes that while these names may represent 'a number of independent sections, loosely organized in a federation under the name Laikipiak', they may also suggest a closer relationship.[10] Arguing for the latter, that the Laikipiak were much more than an autonomous territorial section (*iloshon*), and of the order of a sectional alliance of the greater Maasai nation (a constellation of sections such as were the Uas Nkishu and the Iloogolala), is the considerable alliance that was required to repel them from their southern reaches. This interpretation is even more persuasive when one takes into account the considerable success enjoyed by the Laikipiak against the Samburu and others to the north following that ouster. The northern traditions that depict the Laikipiak as a people distinct from both the Samburu and others called more generally the Maasai give further credence to this reconstruction of Laikipiak identity. To examine these traditions, however, requires a shift in focus to the more northern reaches of Laikipiak territory and a brief survey of the lands on which these pastoralists herded their stock.

An Ecological and Strategic Overview

Ecologically the rangelands upon which East African pastoralists herd their stock are quite different. The extensive plains of the Central Rift Valley with the permanent lakes of Naivasha and Nakuru offered significantly better pasture lands than did the more arid north. The scrub bush of the plains that surround Lake Turkana is broken by low lava plateaux that hide isolated springs, but even here there is a difference, for the lands east of the lake are better watered than the lowlands to the west from which people have historically tried to break out (see Lámphear, this volume), and where the Turkana have of necessity had to herd both cattle and camels to survive.

East of the lake the plains are broken by isolated mountains with hidden valleys of perennial grass and permanent water; it is this area that was home to the cattle-keeping Samburu and camel-herding Rendille. Still further north and east are the escarpments from which the Oromo-speaking communities of Gabbra camel-herders and Borana cattle-herders were pushing south. Thus, both east and west of Lake Turkana, the land occupied related very directly to the pastoral adaptation followed and the type of stock herded.

Between the Central Rift and the more northern plains lay the higher elevations of the Leroghi/Laikipia plateau whose perennial grasslands and montane forest were the domain of the Laikipiak. From this upland area the Laikipiak held a strategically powerful position. Here they were a barrier to Turkana expansion from west of the lake — an ongoing, dynamic process of territorial extension addressed in detail by Lamphear in Chapter Four of this volume. At the same time their strength curtailed any attempts by the Samburu or Rendille to expand southwards. From the mountain outcrops that extended from north-east of Lake Turkana to Mounts Kulal and Nyiro in the south, and south-eastwards to the northern banks of the Uaso Nyiro, and in the valleys interspersed between them, the Samburu tended their cattle. The Rendille with their herds of camels moved between the shores of the lake and the springs at the margins of the Chalbi desert, the region's central, and most arid, core. And in the eastern part of this region they ranged from Marsabit Mountain to south and east of the Merille River, sometimes pushing eastwards to the Merti Plateau and the western margins of the Lorian Swamp.[11] Yet in this era the Samburu and Rendille record their finest grazing lands as being in the extreme north at a place called 'Wato', inland from the Dasenech-occupied north-eastern shore of Lake Turkana.[12] In all of these areas the traditions of the Samburu, Rendille and Boran-speaking communities aver that the Laikipiak were unwelcome competitors.

The Northern Traditions of Continued Laikipiak Strength

Just as on the central plains of the Rift Valley, the last decades of the nineteenth century were a time of significant change in northern Kenya. Raids in this region by the Laikipiak occurred at least as early as the middle of the nineteenth century, although rarely are these recalled as specific incidents. Among the Samburu these are associated with Mounts Nyiro and Kulal. In c. 1879–1880, however, perhaps remembered because of the extreme northern location, as well as having been the year the Rendille age-set of Dibgudo married, a confrontation of some magnitude occurred east of Marsabit at Kurikude-Intargeta (Lorrok-Lontargeta to the Samburu). Here the Rendille record their having killed and chased away Laikipiak intruders.[13] Similarly, the Samburu record a victory over the Laikipiak in the same area and recognize two other nearby locations, Susukh and Longosori, as places where they fought the Laikipiak at this time. The number of these hostile encounters suggests that they were less skirmishes with parties of raiders and more in the nature of deliberate campaigns. This is further supported by the fact that many Samburu had recently shifted from Wato to the Marsabit area and that the Rendille shifted westwards following these events because they feared further attacks.[14] In this same period the Laikipiak also carried out raids against Rendille herdsmen who had pushed too far south into grazing between Laisamis and Serolipi.[15]

For the Samburu and Rendille, the defeat of the Laikipiak by the Maasai had consequences which went far beyond the mere increase in northerly incursions by Laikipiak warriors. On one hand the Laikipiak withdrawal and subsequent dislocation partially released the Samburu in the Nyiro-Kulal area from the yoke under which they laboured. At the same time the Maasai defeat of the Laikipiak unleashed the Turkana in a movement that has not abated to this day. Allowed to push eastwards in the absence of Laikipiak resistence, the Turkana conducted forays along the entire eastern shoreline of Lake Turkana in the last two decades of the nineteenth century.[16] In reality the threat posed by the Turkana presented no significant change in the situation previously endured under the Laikipiak. In these southern reaches, just as before, the Samburu (and Rendille) were limited to the upland areas in the mountains and, because the numbers this terrain could support were limited, they were not in a position to mount much opposition to the more numerous Turkana on the plains below.

Like the Samburu, the Rendille were also forced to abandon the shores of Lake Turkana in the face of increased Turkana raiding in the region.[17] Apparently over-extended in an arc-like occupation around the interior desert region, the single clan-based settlements of the Rendille were not always able to mount a strong enough response to the raids directed against them. In the late 1880s the raids with which the Laikipiak harassed those Rendille (and Samburu) who kept their herds and flocks in the south became more resolute, and once again the intruders succeeded in penetrating the Marsabit area. This time these Laikipiak incursions came when the Rendille were already facing Somali, and sometimes Kamba, raids from the east and suffering under severe drought conditions.[18] Despite frequent Rendille and Samburu claims of victory against these Laikipiak raiders, the most frequently recited account of their greatest success suggests otherwise. In a series of confrontations in 1889, the Rendille record having to battle their way back into the Marsabit area from Derati well to the north-west before finally being able to push them out of the region altogether.[19] To these Laikipiak the Rendille attribute the motivation of wanting 'to capture the land'.[20]

In the same year it is recalled quite specifically that the Laikipiak attacked a Rendille settlement of the Sale clan. (The particular events of this are described at some length not only to illustrate the detail recalled in tradition and ascribed to the time, but to allow a picture of Laikipiak strength to emerge.) Upon discovering that the settlement contained only women, old men, girls and uncircumcised boys, the Laikipiak are said to have claimed it as their own. 'Each [Laikipiak] warrior said, "This will be mine" choosing his goats from the Rendille herds; some chose their own camels. Others said, "These goats are mine". Some even chose Rendille wives.'[21]

The traditions ascribe the absence of Rendille warriors to their having gone to the Koroli area to hunt and eat meat; but the Laikipiak are said to have been told that the settlement had no warriors. The conditions of extreme drought which coincided with these Laikipiak incursions would have entailed the warriors being absent for extended periods of time, travelling great distances with the *fora* (mobile stock camp) camel herds in order to find adequate grazing and water.

After this Rendille settlement had been forced to shift locations a number of times, the early months of 1890 found it located on the north bank of the Merille River.[22] From a nearby encampment the Laikipiak warriors continued to dominate the Rendille:

> 'This herd is mine', they'd say. 'These camels are mine.' 'This herd of small stock is mine.' Every one of them had his own herd in the [Rendille] settlement . . . The Rendille then said, 'Now these people are finishing us and all our animals. Let us begin to fight them. If they defeat us, they take the animals. If we defeat them, we take the animals.'[23]

Once again the Laikipiak ordered the settlement to shift southwards, but this time the move would have taken the Rendille into what was Laikipiak country. '. . . if they moved then the Laikipiak would be the only men in the world and if they [the Rendille] didn't fight, they would be like women.' The Rendille refused to move.[24]

At the same time the Rendille warriors are said to have returned to the area, and in the nearby bush they roasted meat in preparation for the war that was certain to follow. Tradition records that one of these warriors went to the Laikipiak and 'with his spear stabbed up all the meat on their fire for himself. The Laikipiak asked among themselves, "Is this foolish or is it greedy?" '[25] Another Rendille, a warrior of Sale, rode his horse around the Laikipiak camp taunting them: 'You women; the Rendille are waiting for you. Come and fight!'[26]

Prepared to fight, the Laikipiak approached the Rendille settlement and were met by the Rendille warriors in what one informant referred to as an 'arranged' battle. The tradition's emphasis on both groups of warriors eating roasted meat in preparation for this confrontation reinforce the notion of a pre-arranged engagement. And the portrayal of the Rendille settlement on one bank of the Merille River and the Laikipiak in a nearby encampment, perhaps a warriors' *manyatta*, conveys an image of a developing battle not unlike that at the encampments of Laikipiak and Purko Maasai depicted in 1883 by Thomson's informants in the region north of Lake Naivasha.[27]

Further, the portrayal of the Laikipiak attacking the Rendille warriors who stood outside, in front of their settlement, is consistent with the latter's defensive posture in such confrontations. Traditionally the Rendille positioned themselves in three concentric circles around their settlements. With an ox or bull camel tied to the gate the warriors are said to have stood at the entrance facing the enemy, having vowed never to turn their backs unless they fell in battle. Only if this outer fence of the settlement was breached would the women and children flee to the bush for refuge. Although in their fighting the Laikipiak, Rendille and Samburu followed a code that did not condone the killing of women, children and old men, they were not above kidnapping young girls and boys.[28]

When the confusion of battle at the Merille River cleared and the warriors disengaged, the Rendille are said to have emerged victorious. They record that they lost five men and that eighty Laikipiak were killed and others were captured. For the Rendille, this event marks the time when the Laikipiak were 'finished'. Chased to the south, it was the last time the Laikipiak are recorded as having brazened their way into the land of the Rendille.[29] Other evidence, however, suggests that the forays mounted by the Laikipiak were not brought to so sudden a halt, again raising the issue of what is meant when traditions describe an enemy as being 'finished'. But, before moving on to the pastoralist assumptions implicit in such remarks, the Boran accounts of this time are noteworthy.

For the Borana and Gabbra this same period marked a time when they were shifting south off the escarpments that today serve to demarcate the frontier between Ethiopia and Kenya. Boran tradition records that their confrontations with the Laikipiak had been on-going since at least the 1880s and at times were of the order of an invasion. The magnitude of these incursions forced the Borana deep into the Dirre and Megado regions of the escarpment area.[30] Again, as with the Rendille and Samburu, the Boran-speakers are quite specific that their confrontations were with the Laikipiak (*Kibiyi*) as distinct from the Maasai (*Maasai*) or the Samburu (*Korre*). And, equally, these traditions recall the Laikipiak as intent on taking over Gabbra and Borana land.[31] Only with the added support of mounted reinforcements from Liban in the Boran heartland was a Borana–Gabbra alliance able to dislodge the Laikipiak and force them back south. Like the Rendille triumph over the Laikipiak in 1890, the Borana and Gabbra mark this period as the point in time after which they no longer regarded them as a major threat, but it was still not by any means the end of the Laikipiak. At the south-east end of Lake Turkana the Samburu again found themselves having to repulse Laikipiak raiding parties.

Samburu traditions about this period continue to record Laikipiak raiding parties and especially attacks in the Ndoto Mountains, and the penetration of the [South] Horr Valley. In c. 1892–1893 a party of Laikipiak, under the 'leadership' (*oloingoni* or war leader) of an individual named Loldapash, struck at Mount Nyiro while a second group advanced on Mount Kulal. 'Merikon were warriors then; Terito were boys, not yet circumcised. And our fathers [Merikon] had married but we were not born. Some were with one child and some were with two.'[32] At the same time, these traditions are quite explicit about there being the added complication of rinderpest, a point returned to below, and of both the Samburu and Laikipiak being victims of the destruction wreaked by epizootic on the cattle herds of the region. 'They are the ones that came at the time of rinderpest [*lodwa*]; at the time of rinderpest the Laikipiak raided when they [the Samburu] were slaughtering those dying animals. They took what they took, and left what they left.'[33]

In the 1890s the valleys and forest retreats on Nyiro, Kulal, Oldonyo Mara and other mountains in the Ndoto chain teemed with impoverished Samburu who had retreated from the destruction caused by the spread of rinderpest. In particular, it is said, these were the Samburu who had come from the Wato region in the north. Besides providing food in the forms of roots, berries and wild game, the mountains were a more easily defensible sanctuary in which to nurture their depleted stock back to viable herd size: 'They [the Samburu] preferred it because the paths are small and good to kill enemies.'[34] The forays led by Loldapash are especially remembered by the Samburu as being unequalled because they breached the mountain fastness of Nyiro and Kulal. At Kulal the confrontation was marked by the capture of a man called Lesanchu, while at Nyiro the hostilities are recalled as having been broken off when Loldapash was killed by Lentumunai, a warrior of the Merikon age-set.[35] For the Samburu the defeat of the Laikipiak under Loldapash and the capture of Lesanchu represent the end of the protracted confrontations in which these two societies engaged across the southern reaches of Samburu country during the last half of the nineteenth century.

Short and Long-Term Strategies of Survival

The array of traditions that recall the Laikipiak to the north of the country with which they are traditionally associated, like those that record the Purko–Kisongo defeat of the Laikipiak, focus on the most dramatic of their encounters. Couched in terms of confrontations over cattle, they represent underlying tensions over access to and control of grazing. Yet these major clashes were both preceded and followed by more numerous raids and skirmishes. Because their traditions are associated with warrior age-sets, the way in which the Maasai order events over time, it is only the more dramatic of these encounters that are remembered; they are the ones that highlight and support the ideals of *murran*hood. And, while the outcomes are likewise notable for documenting the territorial claims of individual sections, they represent much longer-term processes. Further, the recording of these combative relationships masks the existence of cooperative networks between herders. The evidence for these is less obvious but no less convincing, and taken together there emerges a more dynamic interpretation of Laikipiak dissolution.

As already noted, the defeat of the Laikipiak in the 1870s led many individuals and groups to seek refuge among the Maasai victors. But even in this traditional evidence of success there are indicators that the Maasai victory was not total. For example, Maasai attribute the routing of the Laikipiak to the Il Aimer age-set (c. 1866–1886) and yet recount that these same Laikipiak were only assimilated during the following warrior age-set of Talala (c. 1881–1895).[36] Equally telling, the principal grazing of the Purko and Kisongo remained much as it had been prior to the major confrontations with the Laikipiak, centred south of Naivasha and extending well into what is today northern Tanzania.[37]

Other Laikipiak took refuge among neighbouring agricultural communities, including Meru and Kikuyu (see Waller, 1985b). And still others joined existing bands or formed their own communities of hunting and gathering *iltorrobo*. At one level the traditions of *iltorrobo* groups in this region have also been used to support the view of Laikipiak annihilation. However, when such groups are placed in the overall context of the dynamic social and economic regional systems that structured the pre-colonial period, these same traditions are equally consistent with a continued Laikipiak presence. For example, among these *iltorrobo* are a number of communities whose identity includes either origins in or significant linkages to the Laikipiak.[38] Following Blackburn's contention that bee-keeping is a possible key to differentiating which hunter-gatherers are 'defeated' pastoralists and which have a longer-standing existence as 'true' *iltorrobo*, at least half the thirteen groups who claim ties with the Laikipiak may indeed have once been pastoralists.[39] This notion of a significant element of one-time pastoralists drifting off to various hunter-gatherer groups, as well as to neighbouring herding and agricultural communities, is consistent with the adaptations that pastoralists have always made to recurrent crises. The existence of 'Laikipiak' *iltorrobo*, who would have been actively seeking to return to the cattle-keeping economy rather than tacitly submitting to what was for them a demeaning hunter-gatherer existence, is thus merely part of the transformation, realignment and remodelling of communities that has always been an active feature of East African history.[40]

Whether the Laikipiak who continued as an identifiable community in the northern reaches of their original territory were firmly situated in a pastoralist subsistence mode or merely on the fringes can only be surmised. The scattered locations of these encounters — Nyiro-Kulal and Laisamis to Marsabit and Dirre — suggest a picture of a disparate and dispersed population. Their raiding across this region of the Samburu, Rendille, Borana and Gabbra can be seen in a number of ways, but the eventual loss of cultural identity as an independent community with pockets of Laikipiak households in the process of being absorbed and assimilated at the end of the nineteenth and into the early twentieth century suggests the following scenario.

In the immediate aftermath of defeat by the Purko–Kisongo in the 1870s it can be argued that Laikipiak raiding was an attempt to recoup recent losses. As easily made is the case that these skirmishes and battles were the means by which the Laikipiak established a defensible frontier zone with their competing pastoralist neighbours. In all probability elements of both were at work in this period. Later confrontations, however, in the wake of the bovine pleuro-pneumonia and rinderpest epizootics of the late 1880s and early 1890s, were more clearly an adaptive response to this despoiling of their herds. The failure of the Laikipiak to emerge from these crises suggests not only the severity of the defeats suffered at the hands of the Purko–Kisongo in the Central Rift, but the inability of the Laikipiak to manipulate successfully (or in some cases possibly the failure even to have established) networks of exchange and obligation in the more northern reaches of their lands.

The vagaries of the environment in which East African pastoralists existed necessitated adaptations that allowed for responses to the ever present dangers of drought, disease and stock-raids. Not infrequently these triggered shifts in location or the migration and absorption by neighbouring communities of both households and larger groups. The loss of pastoral viability for households of various economic potential was a reality with which herders had to contend. Recourse to the complementary modes of subsistence in neighbouring ecological zones through individually established networks of exchange, contact and obligation with agnates, affines and bond partners/stock partners provided the potential sources of assistance and the avenues of access that all herders required to survive as pastoralists. As part of an accumulation strategy an extensive range of such contacts provided opportunities for the loan and transfer of stock, labour and needed trade goods. As part of a survival strategy they included points of social contact purposefully developed within and across societal boundaries that provided a defence against times of severe adversity. And when coupled with claims of kinship and descent, a metaphor that supported links between even mutually hostile or geographically distant societies, a system of overlapping social environments existed into which people could shift both temporarily and permanently to survive.[41]

These strategies, which had proved so useful in the past, might also have served to prevent their ultimate demise this time were it not for the complication of the Samburu and Rendille shifting south to consolidate in this same period their own hold on the region. As such it was mutually beneficial for the latter to absorb those Laikipiak who were no longer able to survive as independent herders. For the Laikipiak, acceptance of client status to these neighbours allowed them to remain within the pastoral economy, avoid the stigma attached to hunting and gathering, and retain hope of one day re-establishing their existence as independent pastoralists. For the Samburu and Rendille the addition of Laikipiak households and their *murran* added strength and momentum as they confronted Turkana encroachment to the west and Boran advances in the north. In a process of penetration and consolidation the Samburu and Rendille absorbed people and captured stock that enabled them to occupy and hold the vacant and abandoned land once identified as that of the Laikipiak. In the same way the Turkana and Borana absorbed people and took stock to consolidate their positions.

Given the ever present reality of extreme conditions and the possible demise of one's herds, the keeping of stock was never a guarantee of a secure existence. As a result, ethnic mobility has always been a characteristic of East Africa. The response of the Laikipiak to their defeat by the Maasai and then by their northern neighbours in combination with the devastation of the epizootics striking down their herds was not an innovation, but rather the tried and tested action of generations of herders before them. In the end it was a process from which the Laikipiak never re-emerged, and in the light of which it is possible to understand more clearly what a people being 'finished' really means.

Notes

1. J. Berntsen, 'Pastoralism, Raiding and Prophets: Maasailand in the Nineteenth Century', unpublished Ph.D. dissertation, University of Wisconsin, 1979: 243, 252-254; R. Waller, 'The Lords of East Africa: The Maasai in the mid-Nineteenth Century c. 1840-1885', unpublished Ph.D. thesis, Cambridge University, 1979: 388-389; J. Thomson, *Through Masailand* (London, 1885; repr. 1968: 240-243). Cf. S.S. Sankan, *The Maasai* (Nairobi, 1971: 5-6).
2. See, for example, Samburu Historical Text (hereafter SHT) 50,53,64,66,83. Oral interviews, denoted as 'Historical Texts', were conducted in Kenya in 1975-77 and 1978-79, and are numbered sequentially in the order in which they occurred. Interviews with Rendille and Boran informants are similarly identified, but with 'RHT' to indicate Rendille Historical Text, and 'BHT' for Boran Historical Text.
3. Cf. John L. Berntsen, 'The Enemy is Us: Eponymy in the Historiography of the Maasai', *History in Africa*, 7 (1980).
4. Also see SHT 29, an interview with a woman called Neng-guya, who said she was born Laikipiak. This claim was supported by her responses to a linguistic research word-list in which she consistently gave Maasai words for those items which have unique Samburu words. These include the words for blood, day, egg, hippo, nine, seven, thirty and war. I am grateful to Rainer Vossen for his assistance at the time of this interview.
5. For more on interdependent regional economies and networks of exchange and reciprocity see N. Sobania, 'The Historical Traditions of the Peoples of the Eastern Lake Turkana Basin, c. 1840-1925', unpublished Ph.D. thesis, University of London, 1980; 'Fishermen Herders: Subsistence, Survival and Cultural Change in Northern Kenya', *Journal of African History*, 29 (1988: 41-56); and 'Feasts, Famines and Friends: Nineteenth-Century Exchange and Ethnicity in the Eastern Lake Turkana Regional System', in P. Bonte and J. Galaty (eds) *Herders, Warriors and Traders: the Culture and Political Economy of African Pastoralism* (Boulder, 1991).
6. Cf. C.H. Stigand, *The Land of Zinj* (London, 1913: 206-207); Berntsen, 'Pastoralism, Raiding and Prophets', 243.
7. See, for example, Kenya Land Commission, *Evidence and Memoranda*, 2 (London, 1934: 1604). The name Laisamis is said to be derived from the Samburu word *inkimsamis* (bad smell), which is said to have resulted from the stench of corpses following a battle on that site between the Samburu and Laikipiak. The well and an *mbao* game board fashioned in rock at Laisamis are also attributed to the Laikipiak.
8. Charles W. Hobley, *Ethnology of the A-Kamba and Other East African Tribes* (London, 1910; repr. 1971: 160); A.C. Hollis, *The Masai: Their Language and Folklore* (London,

Becoming Maasai

1905, repr. 1970: 26); K.R. Dundas, 'Notes on the Tribes Inhabiting the Baringo District, East African Protectorate', *Journal of the Royal Anthropological Institute*, 40 (1910: 55).
9. Waller, 'Lords of East Africa', 146–151.
10. Waller, 'Lords of East Africa': 144–148.
11. Cf. W.A. Chanler, *Through Jungle and Desert* (London, 1896: 73, 121). Cf. Kenya Land Commission, *Evidence and Memoranda*, vol. 2, 1604.
12. See Sobania, 'Historical Traditions': 97–102.
13. Interviews including RHT 8,12; SHT 73.
14. See, for example, RHT 8,12; SHT 44,46,54,68,70,73.
15. SHT 27,48,50; RHT 8.
16. Cf. L. von Höhnel, *Discovery of Lakes Rudolf and Stefanie*, vol. 2 (London, 1894: 73–74,112).
17. RHT 22; also 6,21; A. Donaldson Smith, *Through Unknown African Countries* (London, 1897: 351); Chanler, *Jungle and Desert*, 314,321; H.S.H. Cavendish, 'Through Somaliland and Around the South of Lake Rudolf', *The Geographical Journal* 11 (1898: 383).
18. See for example, RHT 6,8,12,26; cf. Smith, *African Countries*, 351.
19. RHT 6,10. The Rendille make use of a very accurate calendric system in which they identify each year. From this it is possible to establish in the Gregorian calendar the Rendille year referred to in tradition. Details of this system can be found in A. Grum, 'The Rendille Calendar,' unpublished manuscript, n.d.; P. Spencer, *Nomads in Alliance* (London, 1973: 65–71); Sobania, 'Historical Tradition', 16–17).
20. Cf. Kenya Land Commission, op. cit.
21. Interviews including RHT 1,19,21,30; SHT 47,51,62,71,78.
22. RHT 6,10. This date is calculated from the Rendille calendar system as this was 'the dry season of *Ahad* waiting for the rains'.
23. RHT 21.
24. RHT 10; also 6.
25. RHT 30.
26. RHT 23; also RHT 1. As late as the 1950s the Rendille could still be found in possession of horses, albeit few. These were either acquired through trade or in battle from the Borana, and are said to have never been bred by the Rendille. See, for example, RHT 1,4,5,30 and the copy of a colour slide in the possession of the author which clearly shows Rendille warriors and their ponies (original slide taken in 1956 by the late Colonel R. Mayer of Voi, Kenya, while District Commissioner in the area).
27. RHT 10; Thomson, *Through Masailand*, 347–348. Another tradition, which records an early conflict between the Rendille and Turkana, also suggests this type of set-piece battle, see RHT 7.
28. See Sobania, 'Historical Traditions' for further examples and details about their assimilation into other households.
29. RHT 1,6,8,10; SHT 43,62,71.
30. See especially BHT 2,7,8,11,13; C.H. Stigand, *To Abyssinia Through an Unknown Land* (London, 1910: 127); L. Aylmer, 'The Country Between the Juba River and Lake Rudolf', *The Geographical Journal*, 38 (1911: 296). Also Chanler, *Jungle and Desert*, 298.
31. P.W. Robinson, 'Gabbra Nomadic Pastoralism in Nineteenth and Twentieth-Century Northern Kenya: Strategies for Survival in a Marginal Environment', unpublished Ph.D. dissertation, Northwestern University, 1985, 1: 292–293; 2: 622–628.
32. SHT 76. The Merikon began to marry in c. 1891–1892, and in theory remained warriors until the circumcision of Terito in c. 1893. Cf. Chanler, *Jungle and Desert*, 298.
33. SHT 37; also 52,66,73.
34. SHT 36; also 37; Lt. A.W.S. Lytton, 'Northern Frontier District Handing Over Report' (1924), KNA/DC/NFD/1/9/1.
35. Interviews including SHT 52,58,64,73,76. For texts which attribute Loldapash and Lesanchu to earlier age-sets see SHT 59,60,61.
36. Berntsen, 'Pastoralism, Raiding and Prophets': 255; A.H. Jacobs, 'The Traditional

Political Organization of the Pastoral Masai', unpublished D.Phil. thesis, Oxford University, 1965: 75; and J.M Weatherby, 'Nineteenth-Century Wars in Western Kenya', *Azania*, 2 (1967: 141).

37. Thomson, *Through Masailand*, 200, 240–243; also G.A. Fischer, 'Bericht über die im Auftrage der Geographischen Gesellschaft in Hamburg unternommene Reise in das Masai-Land', *Mitteilungen der Geographischer Gesellschaft in Hamburg* (1882–83: 79).

38. For a detailed analysis of these *iltorrobo*-Laikipiak ties see Waller, 'Lords of East Africa', 147–151. Publication of Urs J. Herren's recent, extensive research in the Mukogodo area will also shed new light on this discussion.

39. From this perspective the Lemarmar, Dondoli, Lesupukia, Lngwesi, Ndigiri, Lanat and Momonyot, none of whom keep bees, might all have been part of a greater Laikipiak nation. R.H. Blackburn, 'The Okiek and their History', *Azania*, 9 (1974: 139–157); *idem*, 'Okiek History', in B.A. Ogot (ed.), *Kenya Before 1900* (Nairobi, 1976: 53–83). Also, Spencer, *Nomads in Alliance,* 201–203; Berntsen, 'Pastoralism, Raiding and Prophets', 243, D.M. Rosen, 'Preliminary Report of Research among the Mukogodo, Laikipiak District', mimeo, Institute of Development Studies (University of Nairobi, 1968).

40. See Sobania, 'Historical Traditions', and 'Fishermen Herders'; Waller, 'Lords of East Africa'; N. Sobania and R. Waller, 'Oral History and the End of Time' (unpublished paper).

41. Sobania, 'Historical Traditions', and 'Fishermen Herders', and R. Waller, 'Ecology, Migration and Expansion in East Africa', *African Affairs*, 84 (1985: 356–359).

Six

Being 'Maasai', but not 'People of Cattle'

Arusha Agricultural Maasai in the Nineteenth Century

THOMAS SPEAR

If Maasai commonly saw themselves and were seen by others as 'People of Cattle', then the designation 'Agricultural Maasai' would seem to be a contradiction in terms.[1] Given the degree to which Maasai social relations and cultural values were a function of pastoral economy, Maasai social institutions should have been dysfunctional to an agricultural economy whose needs for organizing resources, production, and labour were significantly different. Given also the cultural arrogance expressed by pastoral Maasai towards others, it would seem equally remarkable that non-pastoralists would have embraced such values as their own.

We have already seen, however, that Maasai embraced a number of such perplexing paradoxes (see Spear, 'Introduction', this volume). Peoples of the Rift were highly specialized economically, and yet such specialization necessitated widespread economic interdependence if each people was to live successfully in its own ecological niche. Hunter-gatherers, farmers, and especially pastoralists each relied on others for many of their basic necessities. High degrees of ethnic differentiation generated by economic specialization were thus balanced by inclusive cultural categories that facilitated social and economic interaction among different groups. Thus Kisongo pastoralists, Okiek hunter-gatherers, and Arusha farmers all participated to some degree in Maasai social institutions together. Expressions of cultural superiority and exclusivity by some were countered by shared values and institutions that encouraged the inclusion of others.

These inherent paradoxes of being Maasai have usually been viewed from the perspective of pastoralists and have given preference to the pastoral way of life. It was the pastoral economy which needed access to others; social exclusivity and inclusion operated on terms favourable to and dictated by pastoralists; and hegemonic Maasai culture was pastoral culture. Given military dominance of the plains by pastoralists in the nineteenth century, such a perspective makes some sense, but it does not help us to understand what being Maasai meant to those who were not pastoralists. How and why did they seek to maintain their identity as Maasai?

The Historical Roots of Maasai Agriculture

This is a naive question in many ways, because the roots of Maasai agriculture are older than Maasai themselves, going back more than two millennia to their Eastern Nilotic forebearers in the Sudan. All Maasai speak Maa, an Eastern Nilotic language derived historically from Ongamo–Maa, Lotuko–Maa, Teso–Lotuko–Maa, and Eastern Nilotic successively (see Sommer and Vossen, this volume). Ancestral Eastern Nilotic-speakers probably practiced a mixed agro-pastoral economy, raising dry land cereals, for their vocabulary included terms for 'millet', 'eleusine', 'sesame/seeds', 'dig', 'reap', 'field/garden', 'axe', 'to grind', 'flour', 'porridge', 'millet beer', 'charcoal', 'fire', and 'hearth'.[2] This lexis is consistent with archaeological evidence for mixed agro-pastoralism over much of the past two millennia in the southern Sudan and central Kenyan Rift.[3] Thus, even through pastoral Maasai subsequently abandoned agriculture during the 'pastoral revolution' of the eighteenth and nineteenth centuries, as indicated by the fact that Maa today retains little inherited Eastern Nilotic vocabulary concerning cultivation, farming has long been practiced by their ancestors on the plains and continued to be pursued by their closest relatives, the Ongamo.

The agro-pastoral tradition also accords with the accounts of nineteenth-century travellers who reported that agricultural Arusha Maasai raised maize, millet, sorghum, cassava, beans, sweet potatoes, yams, sugar cane, bananas, and tobacco in irrigated fields at Arusha Chini in the Pangani River valley and at Arusha Juu on the sides of Mount Meru in Tanzania.[4] While the non-grain items mentioned — beans, bananas, sweet potatoes, yams, cassava, sugar cane, and tobacco — were new crops, borrowed from their central Kenyan and north-eastern Tanzanian highland neighbours, the others were historically plains crops raised by Eastern Nilotic-speakers. Thus the roots of grain production lay deep in Eastern Nilotic history, while those Maasai who became farmers also adopted new crops and techniques specific to the highlands environment from their more established Bantu-speaking neighbours.[5]

By the time the first Europeans entered East Africa and romanticised the nobility of pastoral Maasai culture, the only Maa-speakers who practised agriculture had been driven to the fringes of the plains by the dominant pastoralists during the wars of the nineteenth century. These became known generically as *Loikop*, a doubtful ethnonym but convenient shorthand for those Maasai on the periphery of the Purko–Kisongo confederacy of pastoral Maasai who dominated the central Rift.[6] *Loikop* included such groups as the Loogolala of south-eastern Kenya and Parakuyo of southern Maasailand and the Pangani Valley who were driven out of the pastoral economy or dispersed by Kisongo during the wars of the early nineteenth century, many of whom retreated into mixed agricultural communities, such as Taveta or Arusha, or re-formed further south to find refuge in and amongst Bantu-speaking farmers.

Agricultural Maasai: The Arusha

Arusha was one of the small agricultural communities composed wholly or partly of Maasai refugees from the Maasai wars in the Pangani Valley. Taveta, Kahe, Kimengalia, and many of the trading settlements on the caravan routes were others. In these other communities Maasai joined pre-existing Bantu societies, but, while they exerted some influence on the cultures, never came to dominate them. Arusha, however, was a Maasai society. Arusha spoke a dialect of Maa closely related to that of the Kisongo of the plains. They belonged to common Maasai clans shared with Kisongo and other southern Maasai. They participated in Kisongo age-set rituals, belonged to the same series of named age-sets, and followed the Enkidongi ritual leader (*loibon*) at Monduli. In spite of the large numbers of Meru and Chaga whom they assimilated subsequently, they continued to define themselves as Maasai and to follow Maasai customs.

Arusha trace their origins from Arusha Chini (Lower Arusha), a fertile oasis south of Moshi where the rivers flowing down Kilimanjaro join those from Mount Meru to form the Pangani. The inhabitants of Arusha Chini probably derived from Parakuyo defeated by Kisongo advancing into southern Maasailand early in the nineteenth (see Galaty, 'Maasai Expansion', this volume). While many joined the Kisongo, fled south, or took refuge in the hills with Shambaa, Chaga or Pare farmers, Arusha settled at Arusha Chini, where they established irrigated farms in the midst of the semi-arid plains. By the end of the nineteenth century, Arusha Chini was well-known as a valuable source of food for pastoral Maasai and passing caravans.[7]

Sometime after the conquest of south-eastern Maasailand by Kisongo during the Kidotu age-set (c. 1821–1841), however, some Arusha left Arusha Chini and followed the Pangani and its tributaries west to settle at Arusha Juu (Upper Arusha) on the south-western slopes of Mount Meru. Settling adjacent to Meru who had colonized the south-eastern slopes more than a century before, Arusha soon became known for their fertile irrigated farms and for the market they established at Sanguwezi to trade with pastoral Maasai and long-distance caravans. Clearing the virgin forest, Arusha planted bananas, maize, millet, sorghum, cassava, beans, sweet potatoes, yams, sugar cane, and tobacco in the rich volcanic soil watered by dependable semi-annual rains and irrigation drawn from the innumerable rivers flowing down the mountain year-round.[8] They also raised cattle, sheep, and goats on small mountain pastures that were rotated with annual crops to maintain the fertility of the soil. The basic productive unit was a man, his wives, and their children, with each wife allocated land to cultivate for and with her children. As sons grew up, the older ones tended to leave the family homestead to pioneer farms of their own higher up the mountain, while a man's youngest son usually inherited his land. Over time, then, small groups of descendants of a founder tended to develop around ancestral land holdings, but such lineages remained shallow because of the constant movement of older sons to pioneer land elsewhere.

Arusha colonization of Mount Meru was closely associated with pastoral Kisongo Maasai, who inhabited the adjacent plains, and with the Enkidongi lineage of Maasai ritual leaders (*loibons*) settled at Ngosua near Monduli. One set of traditions claims that they were settled at Arusha Juu by *loibon* Supeet to provide grain, tobacco, honey, and labour to pastoral Maasai, but relations between the two were reciprocal.[9] Arusha shared the same clans with Kisongo. They fell within the Kisongo definition of *iloikop* (compensation-paying groups), consulted the Kisongo *loibon*, and participated fully in Kisongo age-set ceremonies as members of the same named age-sets. Kisongo and Arusha dialects of Maa are more closely related to one another than either is to any other Maa dialect; intermarriage between Arusha and Kisongo was frequent; and Arusha placed their herds with Kisongo stock partners on the plains. Kisongo, on the other hand, obtained food, honey, tobacco, and herdsboys from Arusha, and, during the disastrous series of droughts and diseases that ravaged pastoral societies in the 1880s and 1890s, many Kisongo took refuge with Arusha age-mates, agnates, and affines.

Arusha–Kisongo relations varied according to circumstances and the needs of each, as shown by shifting patterns of intermarriage between the two. One pattern predominated during times of relative prosperity among pastoral Maasai, when they had a surplus of cattle relative to available labour. Under these conditions, pastoral Maasai married Arusha women in exchange for cattle, thus gaining women and children as labour, while at the same time ridding themselves of excess cattle from their herds. In the process, they also gained Arusha affines who could provide herdsboys, access to agricultural products, or potential refuge in times of need. Conversely, Arusha were almost always short of cattle required for marriage or of sufficient pastures on which to graze the stock they did have. In obtaining cattle from pastoral Maasai, they also gained affines with whom they could place cattle surplus to the restricted pastures on the mountain as well as social resources to move into pastoral society should they wish to do so. Since all Arusha and Kisongo *murran* participated in the same age-set rituals and often shared in the same *murran* feasts, such marriage alliances were easily arranged among age-mates in the two societies.

A second marriage pattern obtained during periods of drought and cattle diseases on the plains. Such disasters rarely struck the mountain with the same degree of severity as they struck the plains. The mountain received much higher and more reliable amounts of annual rainfall, and the streams flowing down it provided water year-round for irrigation, assuring Arusha of adequate produce in good years as well as in most bad ones. Arusha cattle were kept in small groups on isolated mountain pastures, thus insulating them from the epidemic cattle diseases which spread rapidly among the large Kisongo herds on the plains, especially during drought conditions when herds were concentrated on restricted dry-season pastures and around the few available waterholes. Arusha thus usually had adequate supplies of food and cattle which they could exchange for women and children with Kisongo at times when destitute Kisongo suffered from a shortage of cattle and a surplus of people. Kisongo women and children frequently sought food and refuge among Arusha affines and age-mates during famines, while Kisongo men remained on the plains to try to preserve whatever cattle remained and to rebuild their herds with stocks from Arusha and elsewhere afterwards. Kisongo were thus able simultaneously to obtain food, to reduce their surplus population, and to acquire a nucleus of cattle or small stock to rebuild their herds, while Arusha obtained women, wives, and agricultural labour to increase their own production precisely at those times when there was increased demand from their pastoral kin. Given the different ecologies and economies, the demands for cattle, food, women, and labour in the two societies were thus complementary and synchronized with each other over time.

Arusha assimilated large numbers of pastoral Maasai during the 1880s and 1890s, when a series of droughts, famines, diseases, and civil wars on the plains drove many Kisongo, Sikirari, Matapato, Loitai, and other pastoral Maasai to seek food and refuge with their Arusha neighbours, relatives, and age-mates.[10] The complementarity of farming and pastoral economies was thus reinforced by stress and led over time to the development of wide-ranging interdependent socio-economic networks — for which common age-sets and intermarriage served as the basic common denominators — which ensured that mountain-dwelling, agricultural Arusha, whose daily needs and lives differed so dramatically from those of their pastoral cousins, would continue to see themselves and be seen by other Maasai as integral components in the wider construction of Maasai identity, even as the terms of their association varied over time.[11] Arusha thus came to serve as a vital and sustaining link between the plains and the highlands. By remaining within the pastoral cultural nexus while pursuing an uplands agricultural economy, they were able to help ensure the long-term survival of pastoralists on the plains while strengthening their own position on the mountain *vis-à-vis* their Meru neighbours.

Arusha relations with their Chaga-speaking highland neighbours were less intense than those with Kisongo and were frequently marked by conflict. Arusha at Arusha Chini had traded salt for iron hoes with Chaga on Kilimanjaro, but there is little evidence of more enduring relations. With the move to Mount Meru, however, Arusha came into potentially close contact with Chaga-speaking Meru long established on adjacent slopes of the mountain. Since both peoples shared the same ecology, raised the same crops, and had the same needs for land and labour, however, they tended to compete with one another for access to resources rather than to complement one another. Much of Arusha success in colonizing the mountain was based on the ability of their *murran* to obtain cattle, women, and even access to land in raids on Meru and Chaga. Arusha raided Meru with increasing success from the time of Nyangusi (c. 1851–1871), acquiring large numbers of Meru women, men, and cattle in the process. The women were circumcised, married, and incorporated into Arusha social and economic life as wives and mothers, while Meru men joined the appropriate age-set as fellow *murran*, acquired cattle themselves in raids on other Meru, married locally, and settled in Arusha with their age-mates. Arusha society, like that of other Maasai, was remarkably open in assimilating immigrants, and Arusha hegemony ensured that others would seek to join it. Ethnic background and descent counted for little among Arusha Maasai; if one was properly circumcised and a member of a Maasai age-set, one was Maasai, even if one did not speak Maa or own any cattle.[12]

By the time Talala started initiation c. 1881, Arusha had assimilated considerable numbers of Meru and had succeeded in pushing back the border between them from the Temi to the Songota River, thus creating a buffer zone between the two that was predominantly Meru in background, but which was bilingual and participated in Arusha social institutions in practice. Other Meru began to enlist in Maasai age-sets in self-defence, joining with Arusha and Kisongo to initiate Talala (c. 1881–1905), Tuati (c. 1896–1917), and Tareto (c. 1911–1929). Meru warriors copied their Arusha age-mates' weapons, dress, hair-styles, and military tactics, and joined with them on raids against Chaga and pastoral Maasai, returning to Mount Meru with cattle and women as spoils of their own.[13] When the first two missionaries visited Mount Meru in 1896, Arusha and Meru warriors conspired together to kill them, and they joined in opposing succeeding German military expeditions until they were finally conquered in 1900.[14] With the establishment of colonial rule and the end of raiding, however, Arusha dominance began to decline; Meru slowly ceased joining Maasai age-sets; and Arusha assimilation of others slowed considerably.

By the 1870s, Arusha and their Meru allies were also raiding as far afield as Kilimanjaro, usually in alliance with one Chaga chief against another in the endemic wars for political control that marked Chaga politics at the time. Arusha mercenaries were prominent among the ranks of Chief Mandara's warriors in Moshi throughout the 1870s and 1880s, but they were also found among those of his enemy, Sina of Kibosho.[15] Many of the raids were on eastern Chaga (Rombo and Usseri) and enabled Arusha to return home rich in cattle, together with more women and children to be incorporated within Arusha society.[16] By 1900, then, Arusha had established an important role for themselves around Mount Meru. Dominant on the mountain and adjacent plains, their population had grown rapidly from the assimilation of large numbers of Meru, Chaga, and pastoral Maasai as wives and mothers, rapidly overtaking the Meru who had preceded them on the mountain by more than a century.[17] Within seventy years, they had transformed themselves from a small community of immigrant plains herders and farmers to well-established mountain farmers by capitalizing on their Maasai identity and cultural heritage.

Being Maasai Farmers

While the benefits of pastoral cultural hegemony combined with symbiotic economic relations with farmers and hunters are readily apparent for pastoralists, for farmers to embrace a pastoral culture would seem dysfunctional and counterproductive.[18] Land, unlike cattle, was a fixed resource and demanded steady labour inputs to be productive. Thus most farming societies were organized on descent principles, with control of the land vested in the descendants of those who first brought the land into production and labour provided by small continuing lineages under the overall direction of the eldest males. As family groups grew too large for the available land, lineages segmented and brothers sought land elsewhere. Farmers thus possessed a profoundly localized vision, bounded by fields and family. Social organization based on descent reinforced that vision, consolidating the control of local groups over land and the labour needed to work it. Pastoralists' vision, on the other hand, swept across the plains to the hills and peoples beyond, and was reinforced by wide-ranging associations of age-mates and clansmen. Descent groups thus limited access to wider contacts, while age-sets enhanced it.

Farmers had little need for such broad access, however; their labour and reproductive needs could be satisfied by intermarriage with neighbouring descent groups and by the affinal networks that resulted. It thus does not seem likely that the combination of an attenuated pastoral Maasai descent system and wide-ranging age-organization would have served Arusha farmers' needs well. Furthermore, intensive irrigation farmers like Arusha would hardly desire to limit labour by allowing able-bodied young men to retire to *murran* villages for extended periods of ritual seclusion during their teens and early twenties while restricting marriage and wives to men in their late twenties or thirties. The very culture of the *murran*, who gorged on meat and disdained to eat agricultural products while developing the martial arts and solidarity with their age-mates, seems antithetical to agricultural economic and social values.

Arusha were, however, able to adapt pastoral social relations and cultural norms to their own needs in the process of settling Mount Meru. The first Arusha settled on the lower reaches of the mountain around modern Arusha town and, as families matured, older sons pioneered land further up the slopes, while the youngest sons inherited their fathers' homesteads, following Maasai inheritance patterns. Unlike Meru, where brothers expanded up the mountain together creating vertical slices of land controlled by a single localized descent group, Arusha age-mates tended to pioneer new land together when they retired from being junior *murran*, married, and settled to farm. Thus localized sections of age-sets, rather than descent groups, became a prominent form of local social organization, and age-set spokesmen (*laigwenak*), rather than lineage or clan elders, became important local leaders.[19] Descent did come to play a limited role in Arusha society, however, as shallow, local lineages developed over time among those who remained near their ancestral family homestead, and lineage elders assumed responsibility for adjudicating claims relating to land and for honouring ancestral spirits. But lineages tended to become dispersed so widely that they were not an effective means of wider social organization.[20] Arusha thus modified Maasai age-organization to serve many of the same functions as descent in Meru.

Arusha household economy was organized in much the same way as that of pastoral Maasai, where a man allocated cattle to each wife and wives were organized into alternate sections within the household. The basic unit of production in Arusha was a man, his wives, and their children. Wives were settled on alternate sides of the gate entering a homestead and allocated fields for their individual use where they raised food for their children. Those on each side of the gate formed a division (*olwashe*) within the household, and the wives and children of the right or of the left often cooperated with one another and were considered to be more closely related to one another than to those of the other side.[21]

Arusha were also able to adjust *murran* seclusion and late marriage to suit their labour needs, on the one hand, as well as to adapt their labour needs to the practices of the *murran*, on the other. Arusha *murran* did not withdraw to their own *manyata* like their pastoral brethren, and so their periods of seclusion were much shorter, confined to the immediate periods when ritual events took place and often timed to accord with the agricultural calendar.[22] The rest of the time they were available for work when needed. Arusha *murran* also tended to marry and advance to elder status earlier. With their successful acquisition of cattle and women in raids on Meru and Chaga, *murran* were able to marry and settle prior to their formal promotion without gaining the approval of their seniors, thus forcing the elders to recognize reality and allow them to be promoted earlier than the elders might have wished.

Arusha labour needs were also highly adaptable. Unlike shifting agriculture where peak labour demands during the rains mandated intensive use of all available labour for the duration of the planting season, labour demands of irrigated mountain agriculture were spread more evenly throughout the year as perennial crops of bananas, supplemented by a succession of seasonal crops, replaced episodic annual crops. During the nineteenth century, Arusha farming was combined with cattle-keeping on small mountain pastures that were rotated periodically with annual crops to maintain the fertility of rich volcanic soils in permanently farmed fields.[23] And irrigation channels were simple and easily maintained by local groups of users. Labour needs were thus spread fairly evenly through the year and closely matched the consumption needs of the family. All grown members of the family worked, men tending the bananas and women the cattle and annual crops of grains and beans; land was plentiful; and people were able to produce what they needed. The main variation in labour demand was related to the developmental cycle of the family. Young families with only parental labour and young dependants had to work harder than mature families with plenty of labour and few non-working dependants. By the time Arusha boys became *murran*, family needs for their labour were thus not as great, and they could contribute to ongoing labour demands as needed in between times of ritual seclusion.

If Arusha were able successfully to adjust pastoral Maasai culture to the needs of agriculture, then, there must have been some rewards for the effort. It would, after all, have been all too easy for the small number of Arusha settlers to have assimilated to the numerically predominant Meru already successfully settled on the mountain, as Maasai who settled in Taveta and elsewhere did. Retention of Maasai ethnicity, social relations, and cultural values conveyed a number of advantages for Arusha. It enabled them to continue to play the economic role which they had played at Arusha Chini. Meru did not participate in the regional economy of the plains. Travellers along the caravan route noted their distant presence in the hills, but visitors actually stopped and traded with Arusha at Sanguwezi at the foot of the mountain. Participation in the regional economy allowed Arusha to continue to maintain a strong presence in the cattle economy. Sanguwezi was best known as a cattle market where Arusha and pastoral Maasai exchanged cattle, small stock, and foodstuffs. Pastoralists also frequently visited Arusha neighbours, age-mates, and affines to exchange cattle, arrange marriages, recruit herdsboys, and establish stock-partnerships. Arusha elders, in turn, were able to maintain the diversity of their own economy by building up stock capital on the plains which could be used either to maintain a more varied diet than Meru or to facilitate marriage and the growth of large family groups to clear and colonize the virgin slopes of the mountain.

Arusha benefited regardless of the terms of trade in the pastoral economy. During times when cattle were plentiful and relatively inexpensive, they built up social capital, while, during the periodic disasters that afflicted pastoralists, they absorbed women and children to expand the agricultural economy. Arusha have continued to shift investments between cattle and agriculture since. During the early 1940s, for example, when wheat prices increased, some Arusha sold cattle and bought land, tractors, and combine harvesters to raise wheat on the plains, but, when prices declined after the war, they sold the land and equipment and reinvested in cattle.[24] And today land-short Arusha mobilize relations with pastoral Maasai to obtain land on the plains (see Galaty, 'Inclusion', this volume).

While complementarity among different social and economic groups was the rule on the plains, competition and conflict between similar groups seeking access to the same resources was the rule on both Mount Meru and Kilimanjaro. Here Arusha were able to turn their maintenance of Maasai age-sets to dramatic advantage in their successful raids against Meru and Chaga. The rapid growth of Arusha population during the late nineteenth century was one of the most important factors enabling Arusha to dominate the mountain and adjacent plains so quickly. Not only do Arusha greatly outnumber Meru today, but they are also the largest single Maasai section and comprise some one-third of all Maa-speakers. While other enclaves of Maasai farmers at Nkuruman and Chamus remained very small, numbering today in the 100s or 1,000s, Arusha became a large and substantial society of 156,000. No factor contributed to population growth more than the capture and assimilation of large numbers of Meru and Chaga women by Arusha *murran*. Arusha raids on Meru air during the 1850s to 1870s were so successful that Meru joined Arusha age-sets in self-defence. The focus of the newly united *murran* then shifted to Kilimanjaro, where political conflicts among competing chiefs had reached new heights during the 1880s and 1890s. Arusha and Meru warriors were in great demand as mercenaries, and large numbers of women and cattle were obtained as spoils.

Murran success in obtaining cattle and women dramatically improved their status within Arusha society by allowing them to marry, settle, and advance to elder status earlier than they might have been able to do otherwise. Marriage and social advancement in Maasai societies were traditionally controlled by the elders. As the patriarchs of their families, elders controlled the family herds used for bridewealth, while, as members of the senior age-sets, they also determined when *murran* could advance to junior elders and marry. In both cases, elders often sought to restrict marriage and promotion of their juniors in order to be able to continue to monopolize cattle, women, and power for themselves. With their successful raids of Meru and Chaga, however, Arusha *murran* became increasingly able to acquire cattle and women for marriage without recourse to their elders. Newly married, they were then able to obtain land by clearing virgin forests further up the mountain with the assistance of their age-mates, thus further freeing them by effectively establishing their own age-set as a separate unit of local social and political organization. As *murran* married and settled on their own prior to their formal advancement to elderhood, they effectively forced the elders to acknowledge their status and promote them, thus confirming their own achievements and further accelerating the expansion of Arusha settlement and agriculture in the process.

Arusha success in raiding their neighbours thus had a number of effects on Arusha society. It enabled them rapidly to expand their agricultural economy at the expense of Meru by providing resources of land and labour in abundance. Arusha population grew apace, so that by the end of the century they had cleared and settled virtually all of the south-western quadrant of the mountain, pushing Meru to the east in the process. Within Arusha society, it had the effect of shifting power to younger men, facilitating their social advancement, and, by shortening the period of *murran*hood, shifting more men into farming and family-hood at an earlier age, thus further increasing the labour resources available for farming.

Capture of large numbers of people is one thing; however, assimilating them peacefully into a cohesive social fabric is quite another. Here Arusha could rely on the cultural traditions of Maasai hegemony and homogeneity; their military success and projection of cultural superiority attracted others to them, while the open nature of their social institutions made it easy for others to join. Meru who joined Talala with Arusha and Kisongo Maasai did so in spite of the fact that they neither spoke Maa nor had cattle to give to the *loibon* for their initiation. A gift of carved stools was their cattle and, once circumcised and initiated into a Maasai set, they were considered to be Maasai. Such assimilation was likely to be uneven, however. It was most effective in the core Arusha areas during the height of their power in the later nineteenth century, but it was less effective in the marginal borderlands between Arusha and Meru, especially after the Germans put an end to raiding in the early twentieth century. Nevertheless, foreigners still figure prominently in Arusha genealogies today, a fact Arusha are not loath to admit.[25]

Arusha were thus successful in both the complementary environment of the plains and the competitive one in the highlands. Since they were not competing for access to plains resources with pastoralists, they rarely came into potentially disastrous conflict with them until the civil wars fought over succession of the *loibon* and the endemic droughts and epidemics of the 1890s so weakened the pastoralists that Arusha were able to extend their domination to the plains adjacent to the mountain as well. Being Maasai thus served Arusha well in the particular circumstances facing them during the tumultuous years of the nineteenth century.

Being Maasai

Thus not only have people who considered themselves and were considered by others to be Maasai farmed throughout Maasai history, but they have occupied a critical place in wider Maasai society and culture. Prior to the 'pastoral revolution' of the eighteenth and nineteenth centuries, many Maasai practised a mixed agro-pastoral economy in order to supplement pastoral products with those of farming and hunting. Following the economic specialization and ethnic differentiation that took place during the pastoral revolution, a multitude of economically specialized Maasai groups, not just pastoral, developed to ensure that a mixed economy still existed on a wider level.

The development of complementary groups of pastoralists and irrigation farmers is a case in point. While normally thought of as representing radically divergent levels of development, pastoralism and irrigation agriculture are, in fact, two sides of the same ecological coin. Semi-arid conditions may favour pastoralism, but pastoralists also require access to water for their herds and to agricultural foodstuffs for themselves in order to survive. Given that rainfall is rarely adequate for rain-fed farming and standing water is usually limited, highly concentrated forms of agriculture must be developed in the few well-watered areas that exist within the pastoral economy. It is thus not surprising that a number of farming communities developed in the midst of pastoral areas, and that such communities practised highly intensive irrigation agriculture.

Arusha was not the only Maasai agricultural community in the nineteenth century. Others existed at Nkuruman at the foot of the escarpment south-west of Lake Magadi, Chamus (or Njemps) south of Lake Baringo, Taveta east of Mount Kilimanjaro, and, later, Ngong on the edge of Kikuyu. All were oasis communities, occupying small irrigated niches in or on the fringes of the otherwise semi-arid plains. While pastoral Maasai also had relations with Bantu-speaking agricultural peoples surrounding the plains, the oasis communities were a unique source of agricultural products in their midst, and were themselves either Maasai or heavily influenced by Maasai.

These 'Arcadian' oases in the midst of the arid plains also became frequent rest and provisioning stops for long-distance trading caravans in the nineteenth century. The best known was Taveta, the first major stop inland on the trade-route from Mombasa. A heavily fortified riverine community located in a forest at the foot of Mount Kilimanjaro, Taveta was a diverse community of Pare, Shambaa, Chaga, and Maasai who maintained a highly diversified economy. Taveta raised bananas, yams, and some maize in forest clearings; trapped animals and gathered honey in the forest; and kept some stock. The Taveta community was already well-established before the wars of the early nineteenth century forced many Maasai to take refuge there. Maasai cultural influence was thus moderated by earlier influences in this multicultural community where many became bilingual in Pare and Maa and followed Maasai age-sets and customs, but Pare language and culture ultimately predominated.[26] A similar community developed later at Ngong, where Maasai who had lost their cattle on the plains settled on the edge of the highlands. While initially Maasai, Ngong later became a mixed community, similar to Taveta, as Kikuyu came to predominate numerically over time (see Waller, 'Acceptees and Aliens', this volume).[27]

By contrast, Nkuruman and Chamus were, like Arusha, Maasai societies.[28] The inhabitants of both areas spoke Maa and were closely affiliated with adjacent pastoral Maasai. Both farmed on the semi-arid plains, employing irrigation drawn from the rivers flowing down the escarpment or out of Lake Baringo, and both moved back and forth between agriculture, pastoralism, and fishing as conditions permitted. Neither, however, developed into as large or stable an agricultural community as Arusha. Both occupied small, remote, highly restricted environments incapable of expansion, thus making them more dependent on the changing fortunes of pastoralism and the caravan trade. Chamus, for example, expanded considerably from the 1840s to 1870s with the influx of many Samburu and Laikipiak refugees from the pastoral wars and the expansion of the caravan trade, but subsequently went into decline with a downturn in trade and loss of population, until floods destroyed the irrigation system in 1917 and people took advantage of the colonial pax to resume herding on the plains.[29]

While most oasis communities were thus limited by their situation to small, remote areas, Arusha were able to expand the limits greatly by moving from Arusha Chini on the plains to Mount Meru, where the mountain provided abundant resources of land, water, and people. In settling on the mountain, they potentially joined a world of Bantu-speaking mountain farmers who normally maintained their distance from the plains, but, by settling on the margins of the plains and continuing to interact intensively with pastoral societies, Arusha were able to exploit the mountain on its own terms at the same time as participating actively in the economic and cultural world of the plains to establish a strong stable agricultural society.

Their success was at least partially attributable to the flexibility inherent in Maasai culture. The projection of pastoral Maasai cultural hegemony is often taken as evidence of the arrogant exclusivity of Maasai culture, but we have seen that it also represents the flip side of social openness and inclusivity. Maasai identity rested more on control of resources and on social practice than it did on background, allowing the free movement of individuals through various Maasai societies and others beyond what was necessary for survival in the unpredictable world of cattle. While a highly specialized pastoral economy was a complete economy some of the time, it could not survive in isolation over the long run. Pastoralists had to retain social access to resources outside the pastoral economy if they were to survive the vagaries of climate and cattle. Thus cultural hegemony had to be balanced by homogeneity, ethnic exclusion by inclusion, socially restrictive practices and conflict directed towards others by easy assimilation, and economic specialization by economic interdependence. Arusha capitalized on these cultural values, and their attendant social institutions to adapt to the new environment of Mount Meru and to assimilate the large numbers of people needed to exploit its resources.

At the same time, they were able to maintain a strong Maasai cultural base and identity within broader Maasai society. Starting during the tumultuous years of the wars of the nineteenth century, they were able to go from defeat to establishing a secure position with other Maasai. Their peaceful relations with other Maasai were characteristic neither of the pastoral world of the plains nor of the agricultural world of the mountains at the time, as endemic conflicts in both areas over access to resources continued throughout the century. Arusha were not in competition with other Maasai for resources, however; on the contrary, their needs and those of pastoral Maasai were complementary, ensuring largely harmonious relations between them. Arusha only became involved in intra-Maasai conflicts during the late 1880s and early 1890s when different sections, the Kisongo and Loitai, were competing for dominance over the adjacent plains during the difficult 'Time of Troubles'. Coinciding with the death of the *loibon* Mbatiany and the struggle between his sons, Senteu and Lenana, to succeed him, Arusha were forced to take sides, allying first with Senteu and the Loitai and subsequently with Lenana and the victorious Kisongo. In the process, however, Arusha began to assert their own claims to cattle, grazing lands, and farm land on the plains, bringing them into potential long-term conflict with pastoral Maasai. That threat was partially averted, however, when the Germans defeated the pastoralists and confirmed Arusha claims, but renewed Arusha expansion onto the plains since the 1940s has brought on new competition between the two.

If relations with pastoral Maasai were largely complementary, those with their agricultural neighbours in the highlands were highly competitive as both sought to control access to the same resources of land and labour. It was there that Arusha were able to mobilize Maasai social institutions and cultural values to assert a dominant role through raiding and assimilation of others. Being 'Maasai' was thus an integral component in their success, not as 'People of Cattle', but as 'People of the Soil'.[30]

Notes

1. The terminology is adapted from John Galaty, 'Being "Maasai": Being "People of Cattle"; Ethnic Shifters in East Africa', *American Ethnologist*, 9/1(1982: 1–20).
   The following paper is based on research conducted in Tanzania during 1988 under the auspices of UTAFITI and the Department of History of the University of Dar es Salaam and was supported by grants from the National Endowment for the Humanities and Williams College. I am grateful to them and to the many individuals who facilitated my research, including Dr N.N. Luanda, Mr Wolfgang Alpelt, Mr Chikote, Mr J. David Simonson, Revd Mesiaki Kilevo, Revd Erasto Ngira, and the Arusha and Meru elders who kindly agreed to be interviewed. I am also grateful to Richard Waller, Elliot Fratkin, John Galaty, and David Anderson for their helpful comments.
2. Rainer Vossen, *Towards a Comparative Study of the Maa Dialects of Kenya and Tanzania* (Hamburg, 1988); *idem, The Eastern Nilotes* (Berlin, 1982).
3. While there is no direct archaeological evidence of agriculture (e.g. seeds) among Southern Cushitic or succeeding Eastern Nilotic cultural traditions, the presence of grinding stones and pestles provides indirect evidence for grain farming.
4. J. Rebmann, 'Narrative of a Journey to Madjame in Jagga', *Church Missionary Intelligencer*, 1 (1849–50: 309); T. Wakefield, 'Routes of Native Caravans from the Coast to the Interior of Eastern Africa . . .', *Journal of the Royal Geographic Society,* 40 (1870: 304–305); J.P. Farler, 'Native Routes in East Africa from Pangani to the Masai Country and Victoria Nyanza', *Proceedings of the Royal Geographical Society*, 4 (1882: 733–734); H.H. Johnston, *The Kilima-Njaro Expedition* (London, 1886: 312); J.C. Willoughby, *East Africa and its Big Game* (London, 1889: 179); A. LeRoy, *Au Kilima Ndjaro* (Paris, 1893); L. von Höhnel, *Discovery of Lakes Rudolf and Stefanie* (London, 1894: 65–67, 165).
5. For a more extensive linguistic analysis of the origins of Arusha farming, see Thomas Spear and Derek Nurse, 'Maasai Farmers: The Evolution of Arusha Agriculture', *International Journal of African Historical Studies*, in press.
6. John Berntsen, 'The Enemy is Us: Eponymy in the Historiography of the Maasai', *History in Africa*, 7 (1980: 1–21); Richard Waller, 'The Lords of East Africa: The Maasai in the mid-Nineteenth Century (c. 1840–1885)', Ph.D. thesis. Cambridge, 1979: 268–284. Galaty ('Maasai Expansion', this volume) suggests that *Loikop* may have been 'old-style' pastoralists in contrast to 'new-style' Purko–Kisongo who came to dominate the plains in the eighteenth to nineteenth centuries.
7. *Arusha Historical Traditions (AHT); Arusha District Book*; Hans Cory, 'Tribal Structure of the Arusha Tribe of Tanganyika' (Hans Cory Papers, University of Dar es Salaam, 1948); P.H. Gulliver, *Social Control in an African Society* (London, 1963: 10–12). See also Waller, 'Lords', 137–156, 305–317, 378–381; John Berntsen, 'Pastoralism, Raiding, and Prophets: Maasailand in the Nineteenth Century', Ph.D thesis, Wisconsin, 1979: 128–143.
8. See Note 4, above.
9. *Arusha District Book*; Cory, 'Tribal Structure'; P.H. Gulliver, 'A History of Relations between the Arusha and Maasai', *Conference Papers of the EAISR* (Kampala, 1957: 1–2). See also Berntsen, 'Pastoralism', 129–144; Waller, 'Lords', 147–156, 284–288, 373–381.
10. For details of 'The Troubles', see Richard Waller, '*Emutai*: Crisis and Response in Maasailand, 1883–1902' in D. Johnson and D.M. Anderson (eds), *Ecology of Survival* (Boulder, 1988: 73–113); Berntsen, 'Pastoralism', 276–297.
11. Thus the waning degree of Maasai identity among Arusha identified by Philip Gulliver 'The Conservative Commitment in Northern Tanzania: The Arusha and Masai' in Gulliver, P.H. (ed.), *Tradition and Transition in East Africa* (London, 1969: 223–242) in the 1950s may have resulted from the contrast between 'progressive' ideologies then

current in Arusha and more conservative ones among Kisongo; while increased Maasai identity among Arusha today may be a function of enhanced Maasai political influence in the Tanzanian government and Arusha mobilization of pastoral relations to obtain land on the plains (see Galaty, 'Inclusion', this volume).

12. Ngole ole Njololoi (*AHT* 4); Longoruaki Meshili (*AHT* 6); Eliyahu Lujas Meiliari (*AHT* 8).
13. *Meru and Arusha Historical Traditions.*
14. Höhnel, *Discovery*, 135-151; J. Thomson, *Through Masailand* (London, 1885; repr. 1968: 81-84).
15. C. New, *Life, Wanderings and Labours in Eastern Africa* (London 1873: 413); Thomson, *Through Masailand*, 81-84; Willoughby, *East Africa*, 112; Höhnel, *Discovery*: 198; LeRoy, *Au Kilima Ndjaro*: 290-292.
16. Ngoilenya Wuapi (*AHT* 5); Longoruaki Meshili (*AHT* 6); Jonathan Kidale (*AHT* 7).
17. The estimated population of Arusha in 1921 was 22,000; that of Meru 12,000; *Arusha District Book*. Gulliver calculated that 44 per cent of Arusha lineages came from Meru, 22 per cent from Chaga, and 3 per cent from pastoral Maasai; Gulliver, *Social Control*, 12. Meru, Chaga, and pastoral Maasai women still figure prominently in Arusha genealogies today; *Arusha Historical Traditions.*
18. As indeed it appeared to P.H. Gulliver, 'The Arusha: Economic and Social Change' in P. Bohannan and G. Dalton (eds), *Markets in Africa* (New York, 1965: 250-284).
19. Gulliver, *Social Control*, 71-75.
20. With increasing land shortage and the tendency of older sons to remain at home to divide their patrimony today, localized descent structures have become much more important in preserving claims to land, thus perhaps explaining the prominence Paul Spencer attributes to them in his reanalysis of Gulliver's data: 'Opposing Streams and the Gerontocratic Ladder: Two Modes of Age Organization in East Africa,' *Man*, 11 (1976: 153-175). My hypothesis is that descent played a lesser role in the nineteenth century, when land was still freely available and lineages quickly became dispersed, as confirmed by Gulliver, *Social Control*, 75-100. Another indication of the absence of a strongly developed descent ideology was the limited practice of ancestor veneration, witchcraft, or sorcery in all but the heavily Meru districts of eastern Arusha. Donald Flatt, *Man and Deity in an African Society* (Dubuque, Iowa, 1980).
21. P.H. Gulliver, 'Structural Dichotomy and Jural Processes among the Arusha of Northern Tanganyika,' *Africa*, 31 (1961: 19-35).
22. Spencer, 'Opposing Streams', 154-160.
23. This also contrasts with the current situation. With increasing land shortage and resultant agricultural intensification from the early twentieth century, labour demands have increased considerably: cattle have been stalled, mountain pastures planted, fodder has to be laboriously carried up from the plains, and manure must be carried out onto the fields. Some of these increased demands have been offset by the use of oxen for ploughing and other labour-saving technology, and men now undertake a greater amount of agricultural labour than previously.
24. N.N. Luanda, 'European Commercial Farming and its Impact on the Meru and Arusha Peoples of Tanzania, 1920-1955', Ph.D thesis, Cambridge, 1986: 165-173.
25. Ngole ole Njololoi (*AHT* 4); Longoruaki Meshili (*AHT* 6); Eliyahu Lujas Meiliari (*AHT* 8).
26. Ann Frontera, *Persistence and Change* (Waltham, 1978).
27. John Galaty, 'Maasai Pastoral Ideology and Change' in P.C. Salzman (ed.), *Contemporary Nomadic and Pastoral Peoples* (Studies in Third World Societies, No. 17, Williamsburg, Va., 1982: 11-16).
28. See, e.g., Thomson, *Through Masailand*, 263.
29. David Anderson, 'Cultivating Pastoralists: Ecology and Economy among the Il Chamus of Baringo, 1840-1980' in D. Johnson and D.M. Anderson (eds), *Ecology of Survival* (1988: 241-260); Alan Jacobs, 'The Irrigation Agricultural Maasai of Pagasi: A Case Study of Maasai-Sonjo Acculturation,' *MISR Social Science Research Conference Papers, C: Sociology* (1968).

30. In a study of cultural boundaries between contemporary Chamus Maasai and their neighbours, Hodder concludes similarly that cultural distinctions between adjacent peoples are made most strongly where there is the greatest competition for basic resources while they are most blurred in complementary situations. I. Hodder, 'The Maintenance of Group Identities in the Baringo District, W. Kenya' in D. Green *et al.* (eds), *Social Organization and Settlement* (BAR International Series, No. 47, 1978: 47–58).

PART THREE

Being Maasai

Introduction

We shift focus now from 'becoming' to 'being', from the broad outlines of Maasai history to some of the detailed processes through which Maasai and others have affirmed and negotiated their identities. Our focus continues to be on instrumentality — how and why ethnic ideology is evoked, especially in situations regarding others; for ethnicity, by its very nature, presupposes an other in defining not only who one *is*, but also who one *is not*. That said, however, it is precisely the apparent 'primordiality' and 'naturalness' of ethnicity that provides its evocative power, establishing apparent fixed ground rules and also the limits of the moral community. But norms are rarely unambiguous or non-contentious. Once established, they provide a new language of struggle as people seek to articulate, uphold, and dispute moral values. Ambiguity, in turn, leads to negotiation as people seek to establish exclusive moral boundaries (i.e. ethnicities) which then become the subject of further disputation by parties contending over their definition. 'Becoming', it seems, never ends, for, just as people seem to come to be, struggle commences anew to determine and control their new bases of social reality.

Spencer's and Telelia's chapters put forth normative views as seen by Maasai, even as they acknowledge that individual everyday reality could, in fact, be very different. The anomalous presence of married *murran* and their wives in the *manyata* is a dramatic case in point. Spencer focuses on one such normative value, time, to show how Maasai socially construct themselves in the highly elaborated structures and attendant values of their age-sets. Formally progressing through life corporately with one's peers in an age-set, Maasai men move both chronologically and morally from self-abnegating warriorhood to serious, self-interested patriarchy, internalizing the values of Maasai society in the process. His analysis reveals the degree to which Maasai self-identity is embedded in their most fundamental values, and demonstrates why one of the most open and frequent means of non-Maasai to enter Maasai society is through participation in the age-set process by which even Maasai themselves must become Maasai.

Telelia's account affirms the moral authority of elder males established by the age-sets even as she conveys the divergent perspective of a Maasai woman. While explicitly affirming male authority, she equally stresses the degree to which men are dependent on women, and therefore the real power which women have in the society. Sons depend on their mothers to be initiated into Maasaihood and to receive their first cows, while husbands' stomachs are like children, requiring constant nurturing. Yet there is ambiguity in this account. While strongly articulating Maasai norms and values, Telelia nevertheless conveys a strong sense of women's powerlessness in face of the abuse of male authority.

Galaty's and Klumpp and Kratz's chapters, by contrast, focus directly on ambiguity and negotiation, as different parties argue over, dispute, and mock established values in attempts to redefine them to accord with their own purposes. Galaty focuses on the ways in which ethnic boundaries shift as individuals cross, expand, and relabel them and demonstrates how ethnicity provides a structured means of discourse. Here, establishing ethnic claims is a game with set rules, understood and accepted by all, that plays on difference as a means of managing relationships, persuasive in their apparent stability, continuity, and inevitability. Thus, although ethnicity is indeed socially and culturally constructed, it is nonetheless real and compelling in providing institutional structures and sets of values by which individuals and peoples navigate their lives.

Klumpp and Kratz deal with a situation in which the rules set by one group are not necessarily accepted by another. Their meticulous analysis of Maasai and Okiek aesthetics provides a detailed study of how beadwork provides a grammar of social communication by which women, literally, 'wear' their ethnicity in ways that are easily 'read' and interpreted by all. But a grammar that is universally understood can also be transformed, accented, reinterpreted, or disputed to provide highly distinctive messages that may range from acceptance to commentary to satire. Interaction and assimilation thus provide opportunities for people not simply to change their identities, but to comment on them, play with them, and transform them. Ethnicity becomes not simply something to negotiate, but the means by which people do so. Ethnicity provides structures of thought as well as of social action. It is as good to think as to be.

We thus move in these chapters from the normative view of the centre conveyed by Spencer and Telelia and that of the periphery given by Galaty to the anarchy depicted by Klumpp and Kratz that reigns beyond the fringes. For Spencer and Telelia, the boundaries of Maasai identity are firmly fixed by values established through the age-sets and enshrined in patriarchy, whereas for Galaty the boundaries of Maasai identity themselves contribute to forming and maintaining that identity. And, while the boundaries themselves are not negotiable, they do provide a framework for negotiating with others over them. From the perspective of pastoral Maasai, for example, agricultural Arusha Maasai may well be seen to share the values and operate within the terms of the pastoral moral universe, but, from the Arusha perspective, those values may, in fact, be reformulated radically. Arusha may even hold alternative ones, as shown earlier by Spear. Finally, for Klumpp and Kratz the world beyond the boundaries is viewed by Maasai as uncivilized chaos, in which people who do not know any better consistently 'get things wrong', but, when viewed from the Okiek perspective, 'getting it wrong' may be a deliberate act of moral inversion and self-assertion that makes a mockery out of what they see as Maasai priggery in much the same way that Maasai *murran* themselves taunt elders and flout their authority through privately encoded songs. In sum, then, no single set of norms or analytical perspectives can account for the variety of ways that ethnicity is employed and deployed. Rather it is in the manifold ambiguities between and within them that history is made.

Seven

Becoming Maasai,
Being in Time[1]

PAUL SPENCER

This chapter examines the process of becoming 'Maasai' for those that are born as Maasai within the Maasai area. They have to learn to identify themselves as such, giving a sense of purpose and meaning to their existence: an orientation that is bound up with an awareness of the continuity of their society. To become a Maasai is to develop a world-view with the concept of 'Maasai' at its centre. The notion that as members of a territorial section (such as Keekonyokie, Kisongo, Matapato, etc.) they belong to a Maasai federation of sections is of course an important feature of this world-view. However, this is part of a broader cosmology extending beyond territory and the erratic course of the seasons to a sense of being and becoming in time. This is especially true of their age system which structures their existence. With their age system intact, the Maasai have a culturally defined sense of time encompassing the life course of men, pervading aspects of womanhood, and linking directly with their oral traditions of earlier times. It is useful at this point to outline this system using a series of models that apply to different aspects of the process of ageing in Maasai.

Models of the Maasai Age System

In describing any system of age-organization, it is necessary to distinguish between age grades and age-sets. *Age grades* are the successive statuses to which individuals are ascribed in the course of their lives. An *age-set* comprises all those within a broad range of ages who are formed into a group of peers with their own separate identity. Maasai women do not belong to age-sets, but at marriage they are in effect promoted to a higher age grade. All Maasai men belong to an age-set following their initiation, and with their peers they pass as a body from one age grade to the next. If one imagines a queue climbing up a ladder, then this replicates the age system, with each successive climber representing an age-set and each rung an age grade (Spencer, 1976: 153–154). Among the Maasai, climbing onto the bottom rung of the ladder represents initiation for individual youths as they become members of their age-set, and thereafter they climb together as an age-set. Towards the top of the ladder, the leading climber represents the oldest surviving age-set.

A simple model of the Maasai age system relates the major groupings by sex and age grade. This model draws attention to the power that is retained by the elders by delaying the marriages of younger men — the *murran* or 'warriors' — creating a surplus of marriageable girls as brides for the elders themselves, enhancing their chances of polygyny. From this point of view, the survival of the *murran* system throughout the present century when peace has prevailed may be seen as less to do with a reserve force of warriors and more to do with gerontocratic power. This may be described as a gerontocratic model as shown in Figure 7.1, and it could be elaborated by propping the age ladder against the left-hand side of the diagram to emphasize the process of ageing. Ostensibly, it is a system that demands a high degree of respect for older men, but this conceals a concern for retaining the underlying privileges associated with their status. Relaxing restrictions on *murran* would lead to earlier marriages and clearly indicates the elders' concern for retaining the monopoly over women against younger men. Women are regarded as dependants throughout their lives, but seniority of status among women, also associated with age, is rigidly acknowledged within the domestic domain and again demands respect. The gerontocratic model may be described as the dominant premise of Maasai society, providing a framework within which their age system operates. It is so fundamental to their lifestyle and manner of thought that among Maasai it does not require explanation.

This model points to the anomalous position of one of the most characteristic features of Maasai society: the *murran*. The *murran* are suspended somewhere between boyhood and full adulthood and are placed in limbo for an extended period of adolescence that stretches well into their twenties. They are trapped in a regime imposed by the elders and yet at the same time are a law to themselves, a society within a society. The gerontocratic rule of the elders and the control they claim over the disposal of women is tempered by the extent to which they have only partial control over young men (Spencer, 1965: Chapter 5; 1988: Chapters 7 and 8).

An alternative model focuses especially on the *murran* in terms of the cycle of ceremonies associated with each successive age-set during the most flamboyant period of youth. This ritual cycle extends over about fifteen years and varies between tribal sections, but typically entails two half-cycles forming successive 'sides' of the age-set. Each side performs the same series of ceremonies during their *murran*hood. In these two half-cycles, it is the first, the 'right-hand' side, that is

Being Maasai

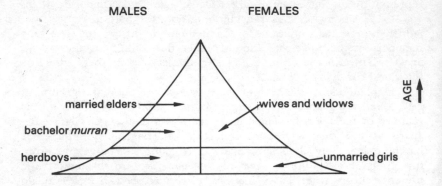

Fig. 7.1 *The Gerontocratic Model: Distribution of Status by Age and Sex*

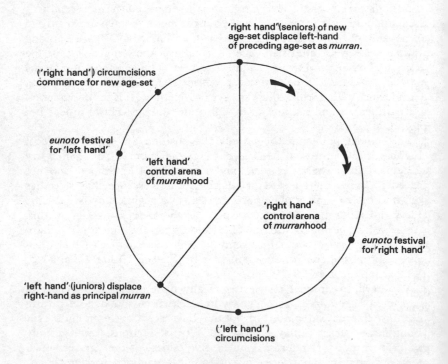

Fig. 7.2 *The Fifteen-Year Cycle of Murranhood, Typical of the Kenya Maasai*

more prominent, with larger numbers of *murran* and persisting for a longer period than the second, the 'left-hand' side. But each half contains its own period of initiation, building up its numbers, and then later a peak of fulfilment as *murran* at its *eunoto* ceremony, when the *murran* are granted a certain seniority with increased privileges and status. When the left-hand side takes over the arena of *murran*hood, those of the right-hand side remain as *murran*, but assume a more dignified and less flamboyant lifestyle as a first step towards elderhood. The cycle of *murran*hood is shown in Figure 7.2, which replicates the Maasai view when they suggest that their age system goes 'round and round', with special reference to the ceremonial cycle of *murran*hood. It is a cycle that marks out the passage of time for Maasai. Following this cycle, and after a further lapse of years, the two sides are united into a single age-set at their 'unifying' ceremony, *olngesher*, to become elders.

The cyclical model emphasizes the presence of a standing force of *murran* in their physical prime, ostensibly for defensive purposes, but conspicuous in their attire, their *murran*ish ways, and the ritual constraints that keep them apart from the rest of their society. This contrasts with the gerontocratic model, which drew attention to the extent to which political power is ultimately in the hands of the elders, beyond their physical prime and more inconspicuous, but overshadowing the *murran* in wielding these ritual constraints and ultimately legitimizing the superficial glamour of *murran*hood. The age ladder could be superimposed on the left-hand side of the gerontocratic model to draw attention to the continuous process of ageing, promoting individuals to higher statuses as they in effect climb up the page. The process of ageing is also implicit in the cyclical model, but only so far as it concerns the *murran* in their prime, displaying themselves at the centre of their arena. The model cuts off at the point at which they are displaced from this arena by a new age-set of younger men.

A more comprehensive and elaborate model seeks to extend the cyclical model to the male life course as a whole, placing it within the gerontocratic framework of the first model. The fifteen-year cycle of age-set time coupled with the movement up the age ladder may be portrayed as a spiral, extending beyond the period of *murran*hood, combining the fifteen-year cycle with the linear process of ageing. To envisage this, imagine a revolving barber's pole, held vertically and with a coloured line wound round it in an upward spiral, representing the ageing of males. If we view this pole in our mind's eye from above, then we have a replication of Figure 7.2, revolving once every fifteen years and referring specifically to the newest age-set during the peak years of their *murran*hood. If we view the revolving pole sideways, then it replicates the upward movement on the gerontocratic ladder of Figure 7.1. The coloured line appears to move upwards because our eye remains still while the pole revolves; and this replicates the process of ageing as perceived by the observer, with new age-sets and indeed

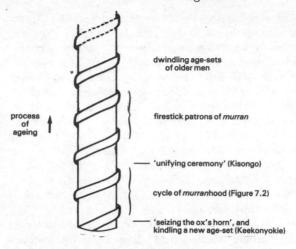

Fig. 7.3 *The Upward Spiral of Ageing*

new generations replacing their precedessors as they pass from bottom to top (Figure 7.3).

This spiral model can be further elaborated, adding more nuances of the Maasai age system, but these lie beyond the scope of the present chapter (Spencer, 1989: 300). There is, however, one feature that is especially relevant to this model. Elders acquire an enhanced political and moral seniority when the age-set that replaced them as *murran* is in turn replaced by a new age-set fifteen years or so later. It is the responsibility of these elders to kindle a fire that ritually brings to life the new age-set of *murran*, two age-sets below their own. These elders are the 'firestick patrons' of these *murran (ilpiron)*, with a potent power to bless or to curse the *murran*. Thus, as the *murran* of an age-set mature and retire into elderhood, passing through their physical prime, so their firestick patrons, who are broadly thirty years older, pass through their political prime, eventually retiring into old age. During this period of about fifteen years, there is a notional 'firestick' alliance between these two age-sets in opposition to the intervening age-set, who are eclipsed during this period but will emerge as firestick patrons in their own right to a new age-set of novice *murran* in due course. When this occurs, they come out of eclipse, and power in the arena of Maasai affairs switches to this age-set and the novice *murran* as the alternative firestick alliance for about fifteen years. It is this structure of alternating alliances that seems to account for the fifteen-year cycle of the age system: over a period of forty-five years, from the age of about twenty until perhaps sixty-five, adult males pass through their physical and then their political prime. Before this period they are mere boys and afterwards they are a dwindling array of ageing men.

If men aged more slowly, then the periodic cycle of age-sets would extend beyond fifteen years.

These models draw out different aspects of the Maasai age system. They also have a bearing on the variations in age-organization between different Maa-speaking peoples. An earlier study of the Samburu, the most northern of these peoples, focused on the gerontocratic model with particular reference to the delinquent tendencies of the *murran*, reacting against their vacuous position (Spencer, 1965, 1973). In contrast to this, a study of the Arusha Maasai, neighbours of the Kisongo in the south, focused on the spiral model and the dynamics of competition between the firestick alliances (Gulliver, 1963; Spencer, 1976: 157-168). More recent fieldwork among the Maasai proper has suggested that these models represent the extremes of a north–south continuum (Spencer, n.d.). In other words, both models are relevant to all Maasai, bringing out different aspects of their age system with a shift in emphasis from north to south. Among the more northern Maasai, it is the division between *murran* and elders — between age grades rather than age-sets as such — that is emphasized. Further south, it is the competition between adjacent age-sets rather than age grades that is more pronounced. The firestick relationship is essentially concerned with the authority of older men over dangerously independent *murran* in the north, and with the union of alternate age-sets in the south. Within the age cycle also, there is a certain process of transformation when first one model and then the other is more appropriate (Spencer, 1989: 315-316).

Finally and relating in a different way to this north–south continuum, a fourth model has a bearing on the Maasai perception of their territory as a federation of largely autonomous tribal sections. While they differ between sections in the exact timing and details of the cycle of age ceremonies and in the division into right-hand and left-hand sides, the notion that they are all Maasai relates to sharing a single age system in its more fundamental aspects, and the age-sets themselves are synchronized throughout the area. This synchronization is achieved through the performance of two ceremonies, one of which anticipates the cycle shown in Figure 7.2, whereas the other follows it after a lapse of several years. At the inauguration of each new age-set, before any circumcisions into it can be performed, the Keekonyokie Maasai, in the north, act as hosts in mounting a competition between boys from northern sections to seize an ox's horn. It is at this point that the firestick patrons kindle their fire, bringing the new age-set to life. Versions of this ceremony are performed among tribal sections to the south, but none of these can be mounted until the Keekonyokie have done so. In this way, it is the Keekonyokie who inaugurate each new age-set, extending to all Maasai. The other ceremony synchronizing the age system is performed among the Kisongo Maasai in the deep south and at the other end of *murran*hood. This is the 'unifying ceremony', *olngesher*, marking the final and complete transition into elderhood, and again no other

Maasai tribal section can perform this ceremony or its equivalent until the Kisongo have done so. Thus the importance of *olngesher* in Kisongo is not only the celebration it marks for them, but also its significance in making possible the promotion of *all* Maasai of this age-set finally to elderhood.

Thus at different points of the fifteen-year age cycle, but on the spiral and lying beyond the slice that constitutes Figure 7.2, before it and after it, there are two major ceremonies, one in the extreme north and the other in the deep south. At one point, the Maasai in all sections look towards the north for one cue, and at another point they look towards the south for the other cue. It is these two ceremonies, linking their local variations in the age system to a synchronized Maasai whole, which gives them a sense of belonging together in space also. The federation which persists in time also exists over a continuous space stretching from north to south.

Summarizing these models, the Maasai age system is organized in a recurring cycle of about fifteen years with attention focused on the most recent age-set of *murran* and leading on to an upward spiral into elderhood as they gather seniority. It marks the passage of time. Figuratively speaking, with each ceremonial stage, time is ticking away, marking the discontinuous process of their ageing very publicly. The Maasai are a very age-conscious people. Despite their reputation for being egalitarian, the premise of equality only operates within the age-set. Beyond this, there is a premise of inequality based on age differences and built into their concept of ageing and of time itself. To become a Maasai among the Maasai, that is to acquire a sense of being a Maasai, is to enter into this premise of age inequality from the bottom rung and ultimately to have a role in perpetuating it as one climbs upward.

The Sense of Time and the Upward Spiral

The age system extends beyond territorial sections to encompass all Maasai and is a topic of constant gossip and appraisal. Its public nature is marked by the fixed sequence of ceremonies associated with promotions of the age-set, each with implications for preceding and succeeding age-sets and responding to the demographic profile of ageing. Ceremonies and demographic pressures are complementary aspects of the age system. The ceremonial gatherings are the nodes, the events that mark the points of transition, while it is the process of physical ageing that provides the main-spring, propelling boys into *murran*hood, easing older *murran* into elderhood, and robbing older age-sets of the will to hold on to their power as they are nudged into retirement. Those in a position of prominence, whether as *murran* in their physical prime or elders in their political prime, might wish to stop the clock, but time is on the side of those waiting to step into their shoes. Each transition is inevitable, and very broadly it can be expected to occur when the time is ripe, as measured by a combination of demographic and political factors. It is not so much the ceremonies themselves as the way in which they are mounted that indicates the changes that are taking place. In other words, the age system has a fixed sequence of events, but it is the interpretation of each event and the spirit and panache of the occasion that lie at the heart of 'being Maasai'. The reputation of those responsible for mounting the ceremony, elders and *murran*, hinges on their performance.

This is an aspect of the Maasai age system that Philip Gulliver (1963) noted in relation to the Arusha, although he discounted the importance of the *murran* and of ceremony itself, highlighting instead the jostling element of performance among elders in the ambiguous context of their social ageing. Here, in order to make my point, I wish to downgrade ceremony in a different way. This is not to relegate it purely to the realms of celebration, as Gulliver did, but to note the extent to which there is a damp squib element whereby the performance is not always quite as successful as is often suggested by Maasai: Murphy's Law takes its toll. Typically, plans to hold a ceremony are deferred; then after a halting start there is repeated confusion on matters of procedure with heated arguments among elders and accusations of disrespect directed towards younger men; concern over extraneous issues detracts from the main thrust of the ceremony; many who are expected to attend stay away, and then there may be an unexpected surge of interest with too many to feed at once, undermining expectations, and leading to complaints of hunger and meanness; precautions are taken against sorcery, but rumours can build up unexpectedly of hidden malcontents spoiling the occasion and anxiety spreads, even leading on rare occasions to panic (Spencer, 1988: 222–223).

Seen in retrospect, it is as though there has been a long slow, repeatedly delayed build-up and then a general sigh of relief when it is all over, but not always a particularly significant event in between. Many do not attend these ceremonies anyway; and, even for those who do, it is mostly only for the brief climax and when so much is happening that they cannot possibly experience more than a portion of the whole. This is, I hasten to add, a one-sided view that glosses over the more impressive aspects of a ceremony during the brief period of its climax, and over the political dimension when the confusion is itself an aspect of rivalry between age-sets and between elders competing for influence. However, this slant does serve to emphasize an aspect of ceremony that goes beyond the event itself: a build-up and then a climb-down. In describing their age system, Maasai tend to dwell on the minutiae and glitter of their ceremonial performances as a display that encapsulates the essence of 'Maasai'. Becoming a Maasai for a child is to enter into this world — one day. But the glitter of these descriptions is part of the build-up of 'Maasai' for Maasai. Conversely, the discrepancies between different descriptions are an aspect of the confusion at the event itself; and subsequent gossip relating to these confusions and their political implications of disrespect among *murran* and incompetence among older men are part of the climb-down, looking at the process of ageing from a greater distance. At the risk of overemphasizing the damp squib element, I am trying to establish that the throb of community existence does not depend on attending lavish displays, or even on the displays being particularly lavish — but on a sense of orientation in time, an awareness of the pulse, of events that take their place in due course, and of the course itself. This course is entwined with the life courses of individuals. For those directly involved, it *is* their life course. For others — men or women — it marks the changing configuration of their network of relations and of the ebb and flow of power with age. The significance for them is that the ceremony *has* taken place. At a distance, gossip leading up to the event switches in the aftermath from anticipation to reminiscence, and from reminiscence to the faint anticipation of the next event in an unending series. Viewed from a greater distance still, anticipation and reminiscence are aspects of the event itself, not as a unique occurrence, but as a node in the throb of Maasai time and in the perception of ageing: everyone's ageing.

On the more positive side, there is a very strong sense of occasion when large numbers gather together for a ceremonial purpose, and this too should not be underestimated, again in relation to Maasai time. To argue that Maasai identity is closely involved with this orientation in time has an intriguing parallel with Durkheim's analysis of what he regarded as the most elementary forms of religion (1912). Durkheim noted that, among remoter peoples who are normally scattered, there is the sense of a divine presence when they congregate in ceremony, of some omnipresent force that rises above the mortal destiny of individuals. This awareness of the sacred, he suggested, is an expression of their reverence for the sheer scale of their collective presence: the perception of God or of clan deities or ancestors in such instances is their perception of the omnipresent moral force of society at large.

Turning to the ceremonial context of Maasai beliefs, their God is felt to be close and yet quite unknowable. In as much as God has human attributes, they are not of sex or size or shape as of extreme old age. Respect for the knowledge of the oldest living men and their ritual power to bless and to curse is magnified in the profound respect for the all-powerful and all-knowing God. Highly respected elders with their blessings and ritual understanding are invariably a central feature of any Maasai ceremony; and each ritual transition is a step towards old age and metaphorically a step towards God. The critical event of all the major ceremonies is a sacrifice, which, in sharing the meat, brings all participants closer to God. It is at this point especially that stringent precautions are taken against the possibility of sorcery. Rather like the devil in Christian belief, the shadowy figure of some sorcerer is felt to be lurking somewhere out there, in the bush, poised to spoil the occasion and bring chaos in its wake. At this point of transition, the age-set is at the same time both close to God and yet vulnerable to some anti-God, threatening its very survival and the structured process of their age system at large. In their age-set ceremonies, there is a sense of confronting Providence, or at least of taking one more significant and providential step in a never-ending process. Providence ultimately is an aspect of God, with the elders acting as intermediaries. The damp squib element apart, the success of each ceremony is to emerge one step further along the providential if not altogether predestined path of the age-set and of the succession of age-sets. In becoming older as they see it, the celebrants become 'greater', closer to God, and Maasai in a fuller sense. Such ceremonies are seen as the essence of Maasai (*vide* the glittering accounts) and of an unquestionable moral order. Thus while Durkheim surmised that the sense of the sacred was a sense of society itself, the Maasai are almost explicit on this point. It is a very Maasai sacredness and focuses on people becoming *murran*, becoming elders, becoming 'greater', keeping at bay the forces of chaos. Through their age system, it is the process of being and becoming Maasai.

Thus, having argued that the wider process through time is more important than the ceremonies themselves, using the damp squib argument to emphasize the point, this is not to discount the relevance of an argument that draws attention to a Durkheimian firework display. The climax of the ceremony *does* matter, but so does its wider context that links ceremonies into a sequence, and the sequence into a more inclusive concept of successive age-sets that are assumed to continue for ever. The concept of the self among Maasai relates to a consciousness of being Maasai and of being caught up in the structured sequence of Maasai time, structuring the life course within an endless stream of ageing age-sets. It is to be a part of the Maasai cosmos.

The Shifting Horizons of Becoming a Maasai

For a Maasai male, there are two quite distinct strands in the life course. The first is as a pastoralist with a very direct involvement in the chequered process of building up a herd, surviving periods of drought, and establishing a family, with striking differences of achievement and wealth. The second strand is a developing involvement with his age-set. The confidence that Maasai display in their culture and their sense of identity as a distinct people is bound up with the second strand which emphasizes the equality of peers and the irrelevance of family and differences in wealth. Primary socialization is learning to accommodate the first strand; becoming a Maasai is adapting to the second. Family and herd provide an economic base upon which the ideology of Maasaihood is constructed.

For boys, the distinction between these two strands is essentially between work and play. From the earliest age, they are primed to become herdboys and learn about stock as a prerequisite to becoming adults. That their herding experience primes them to become Maasai *murran* is a side issue of the daily routine; and, when fathers and older brothers foster this aspiration, an element of play intrudes into a strictly economic role, rather as herdboys may play at being warriors among themselves but face the full consequences if they neglect their herds in doing so. The point I wish to elaborate is that the age system provides the stage on which the Maasai play up to an image they have of themselves. Increasingly, so far as herding duties permit, the ideal of *murran*hood is held out to the boys as one they must be prepared to fight for to be worthy of the image. Again, as with ceremony, the ideal exceeds performance. *Murran* have not been warriors in any meaningful sense for two generations or more. Many *murran* do not live in warrior villages (*manyat*, s. *manyata*), which in any case no longer provide a permanent or universal protection for the herds and frequently have a somewhat deserted appearance. A significant minority of young men do not even become *murran*. Nevertheless, the thrust of a new age-set focuses on those who do become *murran* and on their acquiring the 'privileges of *murran*hood'. These are the rights they flaunt to behave in certain ways and to wear certain adornments that older men have discarded and younger men are denied. Ultimately, the privileges centre on their right to establish their *manyat* as defenders of Maasai herds. It is as much the display of the privileges as the *manyat* that is popularly upheld as the ideal of *murran*hood. Boys covet this ideal and see it as being at the heart of Maasai identity. Once an age-set of youths have been initiated and have acquired these privileges, typically around the age of twenty, they have without any doubt become Maasai in a very full sense. As *murran*, they develop loyalty, discipline and higher qualities. 'Play' merges into a cultural ideal that becomes larger than life. It is being together as a group, sharing in everything — company, food, and even the girls who become their lovers. Being Maasai among *murran* is being accountable almost obsessively to one another, and especially to their *manyata*, even for those who do not live there. In so far as they have an identity, it is identifying themselves with the *manyata* and beyond this with their age-set at large. They parade their unity and strenuously deny any individual existence apart from the group. Detracting from this, the *murran* are regularly accused of disrespect for the elders and are suspected of adultery with their wives and theft of their small stock, but they would not be suspected of disloyalty to one another. Their unity is inviolate.

There continues to be a strong element of play in the mixture of group-indulgence and adolescent exuberance. In popular travelogues and similar media, it is the playboy image of the *murran* that is highlighted. In official circles, this view has been generally shared, implying that the Maasai are out of touch with the wider realities of the twentieth century. Among the Maasai elders, the dancing, panache and bravado of the *murran* are treated as young people's play, and the arena of *murran*hood as a sideshow. An aspect of their ambivalent relationship is that the elders simultaneously deplore the impulsive whims of the *murran* and yet hold up the ideal of *murran*hood with fond memories of the *murran*ish lapses of their own pasts. *Murran*hood has a fascination for all sectors of Maasai society.

It is in the elders' interests that the *murran* — as bachelors in a highly polygynous society — should manage their own affairs. And, if this leads to a certain overstepping of their privileges, then these delinquencies may be seen as the price that the elders have to pay for their own indulgence in denying the *murran* the means to settle down sooner in marriage. However, in leaving the *murran* to their own devices, the elders lose control over them, and this poses a threat to the wider Maasai society. The elders have to be prepared to act as a concerted force at any time to demonstrate their superior power. They have to contain the *murran* with the ultimate threat of their curse. Through the ceremonies promoting the *murran* in particular, the elders establish a more serious and profound dimension to being Maasai. *Murran*hood, seen by boys as an immediate ambition, is treated by the elders as merely a step towards a further goal. There is a further horizon and becoming a Maasai ultimately entails discarding the privileges of *murran*hood and becoming an elder. Thus being a Maasai in terms of knowing and understanding and controlling Maasai is the province of elderhood. The elders have moved through *murran*hood to become the guardians of Maasai culture.

Among elders the element of collective 'play' never quite disappears. When conditions permit, they enjoy a more ludic, extraverted and gregarious form of existence, but it is contained within a wider collective commitment that is neither trivial nor irrelevant. The wider understanding and control of the older men is the aspect of elderhood that they hold up when they congregate together, and especially at times of ceremony. Their mediating role closer to God adds a further dimension to Maasai existence.

There is, however, another aspect of elderhood that involves a radical shift of orientation from peer-group to self-interest and a return to a concern for herd and family as they marry and settle down. When their resources are at first limited and especially in times of drought, elders fall back as individuals to the care and survival of the family and herd. To this extent elderhood represents a shift away from a purely Maasai ideal towards a pragmatic concern for their pastoralism: from group-indulgence to self-indulgence. Devotion to building up the household is a general expectation at this stage, and in this respect is an aspect of Maasai elderhood shared with boys. However, the opportunities for growth — of the herd on the one hand and through polygyny on the other — are so unfettered that there is a competitive edge to their ambitions, emphasizing the element of self-interest. When elders migrate to smaller villages in remoter areas and pursue their own interests, they isolate themselves from community affairs. To the extent that they are less available as age-mates or kinsmen, they betray a selfish streak that is anathema to any Maasai ideal. Given the widespread concern for sorcery, the popular image of the sorcerer may be regarded as a grotesque caricature of the isolated elder: an envious malcontent pursuing his own malicious ends. It is a concern with the unwholesome aspect of elderhood. The sorcerer is in effect an image of what Maasai should not be: he is the Godless inversion of the Maasai ideal, a nefarious being somewhere out there in the bush while others congregate. in ceremony. In public, elders strain to portray themselves as utterly generous and worthy. But this is a conscious effort to distance themselves from an aspect of elderhood that is more concerned with personal gain. Elders recognize this aspect as a liability that does not infect *murran*hood. For the *murran*, the image of elderhood is of patriarchal power and concerted selfishness; and their own ideals of sharing are explicitly pitted against what are seen as the selfish indulgences of married elderhood, maintaining their own distance and their ideals.

Paradoxically, the horizon of becoming Maasai in the sense of becoming an elder is the antithesis of *murran*hood. The elders are not just more than *murran* but are also less than *murran* in their private lives, and, in this respect at least, they are less than Maasai. As Maasai, the ideal of *murran*hood leads on to the ideal of elderhood, and just as the ideal of *murran*hood is tainted by a rougher side that betrays their immaturity, so the ideal of elderhood is at best only one side of elders' lifestyle. It is an ideal that is achieved to a considerable extent by many elders and these have the respect of their fellows. However, it is characteristic of elderhood that many others, including some of the richest men, are thought to fall short of this ideal, gaining wealth at others' expense. The *murran* are seen as tainted by their youthfulness, but they are innocent of hypocrisy. This is the disability of elderhood where the unified integrity of the age-set is broken. Being a Maasai among elders, notably at their ceremonies and meat feasts, is to reinvoke briefly the ideals of fellowship in *murran*hood at a higher level and to disavow the selfishness of their lifestyle more generally. At the same time, their concern for some sorcerer who may be lurking in the bush beyond the circle of the feasting may be viewed as a nightmarish spectre of their other selves: an awareness of a more solitary side to their existence that has lost the gregarious innocence of youth and in its selfishness is cut off from Maasai ideals. Becoming a Maasai elder has its unbecoming aspect.

Women and the Maasai Ideal

Among the Maasai, only men belong to age-sets and control of the age system is firmly in their hands. This raises the question: how far are women incorporated into an ideal of Maasaihood that parallels and perhaps even complements that of men? A point to stress is that gender relations play a central role in the age system. The transition from boyhood to *murran*hood to elderhood entails a changing configuration of men's relations with women, and with one another through women (Spencer, 1988: Chapter 10). At each stage, there is a modification in their relationship with mothers, sisters, lovers, and ultimately their own wives and, indeed, other men's wives, culminating in the supreme avoidance of 'daughters'. It follows that for women, the process of maturation entails a series of transformations of *their* relations with men and with each other through men. It also follows that their avoidance of all 'fathers' is supreme. By extending this avoidance to all members of the father's age-set, this slots a girl into the age system: she may have brothers in several age-sets, and similarly, in due course, sons and even successive husbands, but there is only *one* father's age-set and this identifies her from a very early age as Maasai. The avoidance of the father's age-set is regarded as fundamental to Maasai morality — and pride. Because they are married while still very young, and often betrothed years earlier, daughters are brought up almost from infancy to behave in a way that makes them highly eligible as wives. They are primed as a future gift from father to husband; this is also treated as an arrangement between their families but especially between their age-sets. With regard to each age-set shunning all thought of marriage with their 'daughters', one may refer to a form of 'age-set exogamy'. The uniqueness of the avoidance of 'daughters' is the uniqueness of the marriage bonds that cut across age-set rivalries; and brides are the prized chattels that seal this bond. Thus, while women are regarded by elders as peripheral to Maasai affairs, and in a subordinate role with no control over their individual destinies, they are at the heart of the Maasai age system, and to this extent they are unquestionably Maasai.

The less passive aspect of women's role in the age system is as critical onlookers. The expectations and disappointments in the ceremonial cycle of *murran*hood that give a sense of Maasai time are as much an experience of women as of men. Women are the principal spectators of the arena of *murran*hood. As girls and lovers, they respond to the *murran* in their dances and in private. Later as proud mothers of *murran*, their huts become a venue for *murran*, even to the extent of being led away from their husbands' villages to live for a period in the *manyata*. Even the elders' young wives, who should avoid *murran*, add to the glamorous and rakish reputation of the arena of *murran*hood as prime suspects of adultery with the *murran*. Women in all categories dote on *murran*hood.

Towards older men, women are altogether more ambivalent. When the *murran* eventually pass through the final ceremonial stages to elderhood, the humiliation of those that have fallen short of certain expectations is more complete because it is highlighted in the presence of their mocking wives. As they mature, women have it within their grasp to humiliate any man who has infringed on their domain. At a time of their choosing, they may mount a collective raid against the homestead of any elder who has violated certain sexual avoidances (bearing on the avoidance of daughters) or even against one who is merely suspected. In this sense, paradoxically, it is women who are the bastions of a morality that underpins the age system, which in turn is largely responsible for the subservience of women (Spencer, 1988: Chapter 11). The elders' view of their wives is not just as placid dependants who breed and nourish their children, but also in general as the source of disorder in their adulteries and their perverse wilfulness at all times. The response of the women among themselves is to belittle the elders, pointing up their weaknesses in precisely those areas where they fall short of the Maasai ideal. In various ways, and especially in relation to elders' sexuality, it is the women who uphold the ideal. While they submit ultimately to the power of the elders within the family and in the community, it is the women who make very public the selfishness and duplicity of the elders in the loud gossip of their songs and dances, when they create a central arena of their own.

Underlying women's protests are serious anxieties concerning their fertility. In establishing their own arena in their dances, women explicitly assert themselves as the counterparts of *murran*. Rather as *murran* face the hazards of the bush and are regarded as the prime defenders of cattle, so women face the hazards of childbirth and must defend their procreative powers, their unborn children, and future generations of Maasai. It is in fulfilling this aspiration to have children that women come closest to being Maasai. They are 'in time' in the sense of bearing future generations; whereas elders who give their private interests priority and take sexual liberties are felt to threaten this vital process. In this way the Maasai ideal assigns women a special role. The most protected part of their society — women and children as dependants — is the part that is crucial for the future of Maasai. There is a general belief that, at times of childbirth, life is especially precious and God is especially close. Only women can attend the occasion. A new life holds a new aspiration for the family and for the Maasai more generally. The fact that women's dances focus attention on their fertility betrays their anxieties, but it also proclaims an inviolable domain that is close to God and barred to men.

Conclusion: Unbecoming Maasai

A striking feature of contemporary Maasai society is the tenacity of the ideal of being Maasai which owes much to the positiveness of their view of the life course and the negativeness of any obvious alternatives for those that remain in the area. It is this Maasai construction of time, spiralling upwards with age, that seems to underlie their general lack of interest in the monetary economy where time is appropriated in a different way. The Maasai certainly have a comparable capitalist ethic in relation to their cattle, but find the opportunities of translating these into cash a poor investment in an alien economy where the rules seem invariably geared towards profits elsewhere (Spencer, 1984). Within the traditional pastoral framework, young men acquire a foothold in Maasai society during the prolonged transition from boyhood to elderhood and have little incentive to take risks with their slender capital as non-pastoral entrepreneurs. Those who regard themselves as Maasai-and have cattle are slotted into a time dimension that is the antithesis of short-term strategies for uncertain gain. Within their pastoralism, they sense that they have a secure economic base on which the ideology of being Maasai rests.

Quite common among Maasai are an odd category who never quite manage to aspire to pastoralist ideals. They are interesting by way of a conclusion because they are a negative instance to this chapter — men who never fully 'become' Maasai. Some boys never quite settle down to herding, and respond to the exhortations and beatings of their fathers and older brothers by withdrawing further. Maasai suggest that even some of the best families may have a wastrel son and there is nothing that can be done. 'Wastrels are like the wind of God', they say: quite unpredictable. Some improve as they grow older. All of them are expected to become *murran* in a very full sense and may return from the *manyata* with a new interest in herding, cured of their wastrel tendencies. Others do not. Yet others, after a normal boyhood and *murran*hood, lapse to become wastrels in later life. Those who fail to make the transition from *murran*hood to elderhood at the appropriate time or who later turn to drinking and fritter away their opportunities are despised and are seen as not worthy of Maasai. It is the wastrels of Maasai society who are thought to be most likely to be tempted to take short-cuts through sorcery. Serious accusations of sorcery are rare, but the incidence of dropping out as a wastrel is relatively widespread and a matter of general concern throughout Maasai.

This opens up intriguing questions concerning the process of 'becoming a wastrel'. I have only fragmentary data on this, but it seems to reflect the highly competitive nature of Maasai pastoralism. The fact that wastrels may become successful *murran*, generous and gregarious, fulfilling all the expectations of their peers, suggests that the 'play' element of being Maasai poses no problem. But the differences in wealth between the successful and the unsuccessful and the emphasis on achievement within the stock economy appears to be too intense for those who lack an unflinching commitment. Even rather small boys may be identified as wastrels when their fathers perhaps expect too much of them. Others who become wastrels as adults may be responding to severe loss, as when an elder I knew mourned the death of his favourite wife. The Maasai have no folk theory of late development, or of mid-career crises. Thus rather as the image of the sorcerer is in effect the inverse of an ideal Maasai, so the wastrel has a similar image, not necessarily unintelligent or ungregarious or ungenerous, but still disoriented and unnatural. It is the wastrel who lacks the will to persist, and in later life, if he also lacks social graces, becomes isolated.

While the wastrel is one who in effect drops out of being Maasai and is disowned, a stranger who becomes assimilated into Maasai society is the opposite. There would normally be some unusual circumstance that has led to his immigration; typically he would come as a stockless herdsman and work for a rich Maasai. For such a man there can never be more than partial assimilation, even though he will be identified up to a point with a particular age-set. However, if he establishes himself, building up a herd of his own, marrying and living in harmony with his Maasai neighbours, then it becomes possible for his children to be fully assimilated if they have grown up among Maasai. His daughters would be married to Maasai and his sons would become *murran*. For the sons, making friends among their peers as herdboys lays a useful foundation for the life-long bonds that are consolidated during *murran*hood. As young elders, they might have some difficulty in acquiring wives because of their father's limited network, but, if they live up fully to the expectations of their age-mates, then they could build up a wide network of friendship, making them indistinguishable from their Maasai peers. It would be the son of an immigrant who fails to adapt to these Maasai ideals, even after *murran*hood, whose assimilation would be less than complete and whose non-Maasai ancestry would be seen as a contributing factor. A stranger who has certain attributes of a wastrel is prime suspect for sorcery and liable at some stage to be expelled from the society of Maasai.

Becoming Maasai is a very stereotyped affair. To become a Maasai is to fit into a mould and to pass from one mould to another as the age-set spirals up to elderhood; and this extends to all facets of Maasai existence. To fail to fit into this mould, like a woman who fails to become a mother, is to be outside the image of what is fitting for a Maasai. The richness of their society is that they will contemplate no other.

Notes

1. Fieldwork on which this chapter is based was undertaken among the Maasai in 1976–77 with a grant from the Social Science Research Council and leave of absence from the School of Oriental and African Studies. A fuller account of the present argument has been published in Spencer, 1988. What I wrote there concerning the Matapato is generally true for all Maasai so far as the present argument is concerned.

Eight

The World of Telelia

Reflections of a Maasai Woman in Matapato

TELELIA CHIENI & PAUL SPENCER

Introduction (by Paul Spencer)

Telelia expressed her world-view on which the present chapter is based towards the end of 1976, It was the most critical period of a severe drought made worse by the spread of East Coast Fever along their herds which killed off most of the calves. I had begun my fieldwork among the Matapato Maasai at the village where Telelia's husband, Masiani Ole Chieni, had three wives. She was the fourth and most senior wife, who was living at the time at a warrior village (*manyata*. pl. *manyat*) four miles away. This was one of three self-governing *manyat* set up in Matapato, ostensibly to defend the herds in the area, but serving also to separate young men, *murran*, temporarily from their fathers. Several years earlier, Telelia had been taken away by the *murran* of the *manyata* to accompany her youngest son and a foster nephew along with other selected mothers of *murran*. No-one could visit the *manyata* without first obtaining permission from the *murran* there. Telelia's oldest son Kinai ('Nasira's father') negotiated this permission for me and it was with him that I first met Telelia inside her hut at the *manyata*. She was slightly built, although with a resilient vigour in her conversation and movements that gave few concessions to ageing or to hunger caused by the drought. On her shaved head there was just a hint of grey stubble, and her face showed strong, lined features with an extraverted expression. She seemed to merge easily into the company of the other women there, all displaying a string of beads from one ear that identified them as *manyata* mothers. Telelia was probably the oldest among them. From comments in her narrative, she would have been about 63 years old.[1]

I next met her back at her husband's village as the drought became steadily worse and food became scarcer. Masiani himself had just moved away with one of his wives and the bulk of his herd in the hope of finding better conditions for the cattle elsewhere. Because of the worsening situation and the compelling excuse of the difficult pregnancy of her daughter-in-law ('Nasira's mother'), Telelia was one of several *manyata* mothers that had been given permission by the *murran* to return temporarily to their husbands' homes for respite. At Masiani's village, in exchange for money to buy the food they needed so desperately, other members of the family had agreed to record conversations with me (Spencer, 1988: 288–289), and it was in this context that Telelia too told me her own narrative in her own way.[2] This chapter is a Maasai woman's view of her world during a period of hardship that was so familiar to Maasai. In the story, drought and hardship always seem to be just round the corner, but never despair. It is the zest and uncomplicated certainly of being a Maasai wife in Matapato that prevails. The names I have given the characters here are fictitious, but the narrative is as close to the original as translation coupled with intelligibility permits. In other words, I have tried to give our series of disconnected conversations a certain continuity, cutting down the repetitions and inserting words and phrases where these seem implicit in her presentation and necessary for the flow of the narrative. My aim has been to edit the text as she or any other Maasai might conceivably have edited it for a non-Maasai audience.[3]

The family background of this narrative is important and this is summarized in the diagram below. Telelia was the senior of Masiani's seven wives of whom only four now remained. As the son of a widow, Masiani had been allowed to marry her when he was young by Maasai standards, and Telelia kept reminding me that they were of a similar age and had been together since childhood. It is this repeated emphasis and not just her seniority that places her above the other wives in the narrative. One of these ('Karaini's mother') was Masiani's current favourite. Another ('Simpiri's mother') was the companion who had moved away with him in search of grazing. At the time of our conversations together, Telelia had returned from the *manyata* but was still separated from her husband. Masiani himself seemed wholly unsentimental, yet in his own narrative, when he mentioned that his second wife had been his lover as a *murran* and had died young — perhaps forty years earlier — there were tears in his eyes: *she* had been his real favourite. Telelia gives the impression of being Masiani's only wife while she was young, but it is clear that she had rivals for his attentions early in her marriage as well as more recently. The significance she attaches to the middle years when they built up and lost a large herd and then migrated to the hot lowlands of Loodokilani is that she was his only wife during the whole of this gruelling period, emphasizing again their closeness before he acquired three more wives. There is a rhetorical licence in her claim to have built up a herd of over three thousand cattle. Matters of numerical as well as of ceremonial accuracy are not strong features of this narrative. 'Three thousand' should be read as 'an inconceivably large number' and again intended to emphasize.

The World of Telelia

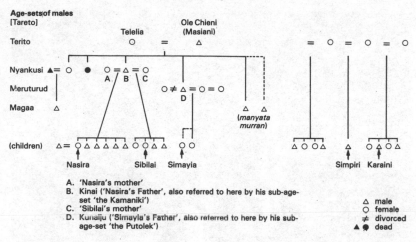

A. 'Nasira's mother'
B. Kinai ('Nasira's Father', also referred to here by his sub-age-set 'the Kamaniki')
C. 'Sibilai's mother'
D. Kunaiju ('Simayia's Father', also referred to here by his sub-age-set 'the Putolek')

△ male
○ female
≠ divorced
▲ ● dead

Fig. 8.1 Telelia's Family

the success of their joint enterprise after Masiani had lost his earlier wives and before he replenished his homestead. Masiani's youth at marriage is confirmed by the fact that his first son — the third of Telelia's children — belonged to the next age-set after Masiani; and Telelia's seniority was evident from the fact that her grandchildren in Masiani's village alone outnumbered the children of his other three wives.

The importance of ties between mother and child pervades the narrative, endowing the mother with a special importance. One of Telelia's earliest memories is of a *murran* invoking his mother in his dying gasp. In the most dramatic episode experienced by the family, she becomes a central character held captive in a *manyata* determined to recruit her reluctant son Kunaiju ('Simayia's father'). As long as the *manyata murran* hold her hostage as Kunaiju's mother, he is obliged to follow her there. At the *eunoto* ceremony when the *murran* take a significant step towards elderhood and become 'great', the principal act of the *manyata* mothers is to shave off the braided hair of their *murran* sons, and this creates a striking shift in the appearance of the *murran* towards elderhood. The *eunoto* shaving is depicted in the accompanying photograph (on p. 160; see also front cover colour photograph), where Telelia and her *murran* son are watched by two other characters who feature in his narrative: her oldest child who is by now herself a *manyata* mother, and also Sibilai, Telelia's grand-daughter who has been helping her at the *manyata* as part of the girl's upbringing to instil a respect for Maasai values. As a mother and grandmother, Telelia sees herself as always available to help her children and their families. In her repeated references to childbirth, she casts herself in the role of mother or mother-in-law in control of the young and inexperienced bearer of the new child.

159

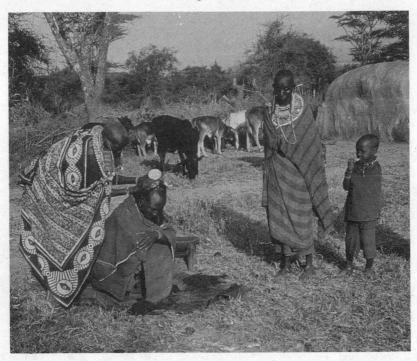

Photo 8.1 Telelia Shaves Off the Murran Hair of her Youngest Son at Eunoto (Oldoinyo Orok, June 1977)

The image Telelia projects in this narrative is that of a very experienced granny, a ubiquitous factotum for the whole family. She lives in a society where men are in charge — her father when she was a child, her husband when she married, and her sons when she accompanies them to the *manyata*, and again her sons at some future point if her husband dies first. She does not pretend to understand the world of men, but she asserts the importance of the world she shares with other women. For Telelia it was not a matter of defending the equality of women in Maasai but of affirming their vital role in domestic affairs and in legitimizing the various roles adopted by men: a son only has a right to cattle allocated to his mother; a *murran* can only belong to the *manyata* where his mother is installed and she plays an essential part in his *murran*hood; the status of an elder ultimately hinges on the fertility of his wives which is central to the domain of women. It is not just women whose position is defined in relation to men, but also the reverse. The whole transition for a male from boyhood to elderhood hinges on the transformation of relations through women (q.v. Spencer, 'Becoming Maasai', this volume).

There is in this narrative an uncertain boundary between actual historical events on the one hand and Telelia's presentation of herself on the other. There are various ways in which she seems to elaborate her past to project her closeness to Masiani. Her ordering of events surrounding her initiation, for instance, seems improbable. Was she really given away as an unshaved initiate to be looked after in the impoverished home of the spirited young Masiani? Or was she embroidering the sequence in her attempt to project an image of closeness to her husband and of the confidence that her father had in them both? As a husband, Masiani is made to seem positively reasonable in the extent to which he restrained himself in beating his wives, although his junior wives gave quite the opposite impression in separate discussions. Generally, Telelia seemed to be siding with the elders. She evaded my attempts to draw her into discussion on movements among Maasai women asserting their temporary independence (q.v. Spencer, 1988: Chapter 11). Instead, her narrative gives a benign account of the women's fertility dance which endows the elders with an honoured place: the money extorted from their dancing is used to brew beer for the elders and she emphasizes the harmony of the whole episode.

In siding with her husband and with the elders at large, Telelia appears to conspire with them in maintaining a regime that subjects younger women in a way that she herself has had to endure (q.v. Foner, 1984: 78–91). In the Maasai instance, this extends to female circumcision, an arranged marriage, wife-beating, and subservience to men at all normal times (their dances are not 'normal'). In the Maasai idiom, all women — even resilient widows — are 'children' (*in-kera*), and need to be under the protection of some man. Even the rights Telelia claims in her allocated herd or in her own hut are arbitrated by men. Women have the right to appeal above the heads of their husbands or sons, but only to other men. Those who react to this regime are the ones who run away — to some other man. However, Telelia proudly asserts that, since her early marriage, she has never run away. Her younger co-wives have run away, two of them for good, but she has stood beside her husband. She has emerged from all this on the side of the elders, and as such expects to be honoured with gifts as a dependable wife and mother.

In all this a deep loyalty is evident, and also a dignity in the way in which she presents her family as individuals. Formal terms are used, appropriate when talking to an outsider: 'Ole Chieni', the family name, for her husband, Masiani; 'Nasira's father' and 'Simayia's father' for her two married sons. She makes no mention or criticism of the fact that her husband in moving impulsively to another area has just made a monumental miscalculation which is costing them their herd. From a Western standpoint, the types of situation she describes are full of ambivalence. However, the presentation, strung together by Maasai clichés, is of an unambiguous state of grace, a faith in the integrity of her family and of the Maasai culture which they represent. Disregarding the uncertainties of her time and the ravages of drought, see how she radiates effortlessly the certainty of being Maasai.

The Narrative (by Telelia Chieni)

When I was a child, I had an older brother who was a *murran* of Tareto age-set, but I was too young to join him at their *manyata*. However, my mother did take me to see their *eunoto* festival, when the *murran* become great. I don't really remember much for I was only as big as Sibilai [*i.e. five or six years old*]. I remember one scene, though. Matapato *murran* shared the same festival with the Kaputiei Maasai at that time. I was with a group of children just outside the village where we had found some berries and were sharing them together. While the *murran* were dancing, a fight broke out between them. A Matapato *murran* threw a stone and hit a Kaputiei on his head. We saw his as he staggered crying: 'ooOWooo . . . ! My mother!' He ran right towards us and then fell to the ground, struck to death. He was as close to us as that tree. We stayed there, quite quiet. How could we know he had been killed? We were only small children.

Another child at that time was Ole Chieni [Masiani], whom I later married. He and I were about the same age. We had been children together when our lower teeth were taken out. We had grown up together. And then we were together when his ear-lobes were pierced so that he could be circumcised and become a *murran*. That is an old story. He was a poor boy with no father, and had to live with an uncle, a brother of his father, until he was old enough to be circumcised. Meanwhile, he could not stop his uncle taking away his cattle all the time.

One day, Ole Chieni had had enough and said to his uncle: 'Papa, I want to be circumcised.' The uncle replied: 'Did you say "circumcised"? The son of a widow! No! No! No!'

So Ole Chieni decided to get his ears pierced somewhere else as a first step towards circumcision. We were out herding the calves and we pierced his lobes with thorns and put twigs in the holes so that they would not close up. When he returned to the village, his uncle exclaimed: 'What have you done to your ears!'

Ole Chieni replied: 'I had them pierced because I want to be circumcised. I hate being nobody. How can I stay like this?'

The uncle then beat up the boy, hitting him, tearing out the twigs, and breaking his arm. It was two months before it healed.

One day after this, we were out herding and one of Ole Chieni's cows bore a calf in the bush. He carried his calf back to the village to his mother's hut. His uncle came and took it away to his own hut. Ole Chieni was furious. He took hold of a spear and threw it at the old man. It went through his blanket, through his shoulder-cloth and stuck right in the ground. This time it was Ole Chieni who had 'beaten' his uncle. My father belonged to the same age-set as Ole Chieni's dead father, and he joined the other elders when they were considering what to do after this incident. He knew how the boy had been treated and could understand why he had thrown the spear at his uncle. He therefore went along to the meeting and said to the uncle: 'Leave it at that and stop fighting. Circumcise the lad and I will give him my daughter to marry.' That was how my marriage came to be arranged. I was promised to Ole Chieni.

So, when the Terito age-set was formed, Ole Chieni was among the first to be initiated into it. Then he moved to the Maparasha area, while we were living with my father near Oldoinyo Orok (the Dark Mountain). I was still a small girl but I was growing up. It was the *murran* of this area who led me to their meat feasts in the forest. At first, I was uncertain about following them in case my father did not want me to go. Even today, a Maasai girl has enormous respect for her father. Everyone else respects him, and she should not be separated from anything he wants her to do, for he would hate it. This respect that the girls have for their father really is great. But, until I was actually initiated and married, I also belonged to the *murran* in this area and could not refuse them. They insisted that they had come to lead me away, so I felt I had to go. We once stayed in the forest long enough to slaughter seven oxen before coming home. Another time, we stayed to slaughter two. Every girl had to have a lover who also protected her from other *murran*, and one of the *murran* who slaughtered oxen for us to eat was my lover.

Then, five months after Ole Chieni, I was initiated to be married. I stayed in my father's home for four days and, on the fifth, I was led away before dawn to Ole Chieni's village while I was still only an initiate. My father said to me: 'Here you are, my child, I have looked for a husband for you and this is the man I give you to.' And to Ole Chieni: 'Take her away to your village. Go and give her fat. Give her food so that she does not run away to some other man.'

So Ole Chieni came, long ago, to lead me to my new home when I was still only an initiate. We stayed there for a long time, and he slaughtered cattle to feed me and help me grow. His mother was also there, for my own mother was still at my old home with a son of her own to look after. I stayed there for two years, and then, in the third, I returned to my father's village to have my hair shaved and end my period as an initiate. I was shaved in the evening, then we got up early to go back to our own village — the village of Ole Chieni. And there I remained, now as his wife.

[It was at this time that the Terito age-set formed their *manyata* (c. 1928).[4] Ole Chieni's was at Olkitatin (Maparasha), while Telelia's former lover was at the *manyata* near her father's home at Oldoinyo Orok. Beside their mothers, a number of unmarried sisters of the *murran* would stay at the *manyata* where they had *murran* lovers. The image of *murran*hood was of bachelorhood with no domestic ties, and those that had married for personal reasons were expected to leave their wives behind at their father's village. Because several married *murran* like Ole Chieni had no father, they were allowed to bring their wives to the *manyata* on sufferance. There, these wives were in an anomalous position with no role. They were avoided by their own husbands and despised by the other *murran*, and also by the unmarried girls who identified closely with the *murran*. This anomaly was only brought to an end when the *murran* went to celebrate their *eunoto*. At this point, these wives were obliged to return to their parental homes while the *murran* took a major step towards elderhood and anticipated marriage on a larger scale.]

Now the Maparasha *manyata* at Olkitatin was huge with several hundred *murran* and just seven of us young wives. We were not allowed to go with the *murran* when they took the uninitiated girls into the bush to slaughter cattle. At their feasts, they would save some meat and take these to their mothers to give us to eat on our own. The *murran* did not want their wives at the *manyata* and we were frightened of the *murran*, for the Terito age-set were vicious. They did not even want to see any of their wives passing by them inside the village; if a *murran* saw one, he would throw a club at her. We were not allowed to go into the communal area of the village at any time. We dared not even go round the outside of the *manyata* to visit other huts, for the *murran* would beat us, they were that bad. Then in the evening when we just had to go out to milk our cattle and put the calves back in their pens, the *murran* would stay right away over there so that no married *murran* would accidentally stumble across his own wife in the twilight. They avoided us and hated to see a young wife in the village. You would go to the hut of your mother-in-law to sleep. When it got light, there was just the gap between the hut and the outside fence where you could go. Once the cattle had gone out grazing, your mother-in-law would lead you outside to rest right over there in the shade of a tree beside the other young wives of *murran* and cover you with a cloth.

I hated it at the *manyata* and came to loathe my husband. So I ran away to my lover near the mountain at Oldoinyo Orok. Then after a time I returned again to my father's home for I did not dare go back to Ole Chieni and the *manyata*. My father made me promise not to run away again and I tried to forget my lover, for I never wanted to be separated from my father's wishes again.

It was after this, while I was still staying at my parents' home, that my *murran* lover came to me at night. There were five *murran*. Four stayed outside the village while my lover crept through the gateway to the hut where I was sleeping near a small vent in the wall.

He came and poked me through the vent with a stick and whispered: 'Come. Let me lead you away, back to the mountain.'

This time, I refused to go with him, for I did not want him any more.

I told him that I only wanted to obey my father, and he had given me to Ole Chieni.

Altogether he came four times that night, poking me and calling me, calling me again and again to follow them to the mountain. And I refused each time. In the morning, I told my mother, and she told my father. When he heard, he came to me and said: 'Leave that man alone, my child. I have told you I don't want it, for you have your husband. If he comes for you again and you follow him, I will have you tied up and beaten by your brothers.'

I did not want to leave Ole Chieni again for I respected my father as a daughter. I had great respect for him. My father also called my lover and told him to leave me alone. That's how it happened. After this, my lover never came again for we had all rejected him. I never ran away again to the mountain, and I have never run away from my husband since that time.

When Ole Chieni heard of all this, he was furious. He did not want any other man to have me and certainly not one from another *manyata*. In those days when he was a *murran*, he really was strong and would fight and beat any other *murran*. He always has been strong, like a bull. He is weaker now that he has become old and no longer has the strength and he does not beat women or children. But even now he will still stand up to any man who has offended him, even an age-mate who was at his *manyata*, and he will hit him straight away.

Ole Chieni came to fight that man who had poked me in the night with a stick. They fought, and how many times do you think Ole Chieni clubbed the head of that lover of mine, my protector? Three! But Ole Chieni had no right to do this while I was still with my father, and this was no way to settle the issue. So my father called him. 'What's all this?' he demanded. 'You hit that man and now you want to take back my daughter?'

Ole Chieni replied: 'Papa. Take this heifer. Take this beer. Take this blanket. Forgive me. Take them, and let me have my wife and I will look after her.'

So he led me back to the *manyata*. I was his first wife and we were there for three years before I became pregnant. This was the time when the Terito age-set were going to their *eunoto* festival and the young wives had to return to their own parents' home. Ole Chieni's mother went with the *murran* to the *eunoto*. So, when I became pregnant, my own mother came to take me home to look after me during the birth, while Ole Chieni's mother stayed over there at the festival. Another elder of our family led along an old woman who knew how to deliver a child. I gave birth to my daughter Sinyet later on the same day as the sacrifice which made her father's age-set great. Her 'fathers' of Terito age-set were at the *eunoto*, and I was at the home of my own father. We stayed for some time so that the baby could grow strong. When it was time to move, my mother moved with us to Ole Chieni's village which was now at Nkiito. There Ole Chieni brought some fat for the children and drove along some milk cows. Once the child had grown — it was as big as this and could play — Ole Chieni killed a sheep for my mother and she returned to her own home.

Then we too moved to the village where Ole Chieni had first led me. We stayed there for a long time. I had another child, the only one who has died, and then Nasira's father, the Kamaniki. Now we had our own home right out in the bush. I had three growing children and Ole Chieni's mother was with us all the time. I no longer yearned for my lover. I only wanted mv own home and to be with Ole Chieni. Then I became well established. If Ole Chieni and I did not always speak with one mind, it was just the tongue that was different, for these were always trifling matters. We had grown up together — since we were as big as Benet — and we have always been together. We stayed to look after our cattle. My father approved, and so did I for his sake, and so did my husband. And my lover went completely out of my life and never came back.

I only once nearly ran away. I had forgotten that a calf was outside the village when I was penning the others before the cattle came home. Then I noticed and asked the children: 'Where is the calf?'

'It's in the hut,' they replied.

When we were milking the cattle, I heard the calf crying out in the bush, 'aaAAa'. 'aaAAa . . .' I cried. 'A hyena has eaten it,' and I started to run away.

Then I thought: 'Ai. There are my children at home. I won't leave them, even if Ole Chieni beats me. Let him beat me. I won't leave my children.' So I came back and went to the far end of my alcove in the hut and remained quiet. Then Ole Chieni came home.

'Children!' he said, 'Where's your mother?'

'We don't know. She's gone,' they replied.

'Where?'

'We don't know. She said she was going to run away, for you would beat her.'

'She's gone? Oi. We're done for. Who will give my children food now?'

I coughed quietly and said: 'I haven't gone.'

'You haven't gone you good-for-nothing [*anaka ipusu*]? I'll beat you now,' he exclaimed. 'Come on out, for I will not argue with you inside the hut.' So I came out, wearing my cloth over my arm like this so that I could ward off his blows. Then I went over to continue milking the cattle, and still he didn't beat me — then or later.

He did beat me at other times though, when I did wrong. He would run up to me and lash out with his stick and I might want to run away, but it was always over with just one blow. I would plead with him: 'enough . . . enough . . . enough . . .' Or I would run to my hut and stay there, and he would leave it at that. I never actually ran away on any of these occasions. Never. Never. Never. I don't know about running away.

The World of Telelia

At first we only had three heifers. We looked after them, and herded them. And out of this herd poured three thousand, one hundred cattle. The children grew and we had all those cattle. Then, when I had my fourth child, an epidemic killed off all our cattle except eleven, and we had to sell the hides to buy enough to eat.

Then another terrible thing happened. Ole Chieni's mother went to sell some hides and to fetch water at the same time. While she was lifting water from the deep well at Partimero, she slipped, fell in and was drowned, weighed down by all her clothes and ornaments. Now things really did become hard for us, for we had all those children to look after.

[At this point in the narrative (c. 1946), Ole Chieni migrated with his family to live among the Loodokilani Maasai. The Loodokilani were neighbours and long-standing allies of the Matapato who lived in the hot low country of the Rift Valley. This provided ideal conditions to rear sheep and goats, a demanding but quick way of recovering his lost stock to feed his family.]

So we went down to the low country at Loodokilani. There I had another girl. We all of us helped to build up our flock of sheep and goats. We brought up our young sons and as they grew they could be left to herd by themselves. One boy might drive the flock to that distant hill over there, and then back home by himself. It was me and Ole Chieni and our young sons who made these herds what they are.

It is the men, of course, who control things, but the wives do not mind, for they do not want to interfere in matters that belong to the men. I can only tell you my story. It is the same as Ole Chieni's, for we are the same age. The other things he has to tell you that are none of my business — news about men fighting — I really don't know anything about that. However, I do know the woman's business about looking after her family and I know how to bear children. I can do all the women's work. All the Maasai have their work to do. This includes the wives and the children they bear and the celebrations after children are born.

Sometimes a woman has a miscarriage. Then the other wives will come and beat this woman who has killed her child, and they will cut some flesh from her brow. Have you seen . . . . . 's mother's brow? Ha. Ha. They slaughter cattle and the elders eat one side of the animal and the wives eat the other side.

At other times, the Maasai women have their fertility dance [oloiroshi], they all process singing from village to village. At each village, they greet the other wives and go into their huts for some food and are given whatever they ask for: a sheep, money. Animals are killed for them and their clothes are smeared with fat. When it is morning, they sing in the corral and sprinkle grass round about. Then they bless

167

the home and process to another village where they are given whatever they want. There is respect in the country at such a time. The elders show respect for the women and the women show respect for the men. There is nothing bad or spiteful. The women use the monev to buy sugar to brew beer. Among the gifts is a goat which is given to the elder who acts as host in the final part of the ceremony. At his village, he slaughters a pregnant cow and the wives have chalk smeared on their foreheads and backs and the animal's foetal fluid is smeared on their stomachs. After eating the meat, they dance around in a large circle, while the elders drink the beer. The wives then dance and sing until the sun sinks low and the celebration finishes on that day.

Young men also have their dances. When each of the boys had grown, he would join other boys in their initiation dance [*inkipaata*]. Then after being circumcised, they would make bows and arrows to shoot birds for their feathered head-dresses. After this, they were shaved and became *murran* — and hooligans [*imalimali*] for they were Maasai. They fought everywhere, but they got over it. They even fought other *murran* inside the villages, but they got over that as well. When your son is a *murran* and wants to go somewhere, he simply leaves and you do not know where he has gone. Then later he may come back to see you some other month.

[Telelia's oldest son, Kinai, had an uneventful *murran*hood, became an elder, and Ole Chieni arranged his marriage. However, when her next son, Kunaiju 'the Putolek', was initiated into Meruturud age-set the family faced trouble (c. 1966). Kunaiju had spent most of his childhood in Loodokilani and regarded it as his true home. In order to join his Loodokilani friends as *murran* at their *manyata*, he had to accompany Telelia and some cattle: by custom a *murran* cannot be separated from his mother and her 'herd', if she is at a *manyata*. However, the family still had strong roots in Matapato and, while in Loodokilani, Ole Chieni and his son Kinai had only obtained wives from Matapato. This confirmed the general expectation that the family would return to Matapato sooner or later.]

It was when the Meruturud age-set became *murran* and we were still in Loodokilani that we had a hard time. A party of young *murran* from Matapato came down to force us to return there so that the Putolek [Kunaiju] and I could go to their *manyata* and not the one in Loodokilani.

The Putolek was elsewhere at the time with other Loodokilani *murran*. There were just me and Ole Chieni and Nasira's father [Kinai]. I had recently come out of hospital and was still quite ill. The Matapato *murran* told us that they wanted to take the Putolek back with them but asked me if I was well enough to go as well. For, if they took me and some cattle, then the Putolek had to follow.

'Can you move?' they asked.

'Yes,' I replied. 'Here, take this hide. Make me a new pair of sandals and then let's go back to our country before it gets too light.'

So Nasira's father rounded up the donkeys for the *murran* and said: 'These are ours. Take hold of these.' He and his father, Ole Chieni, also selected some cattle and said to them: 'Take these as well.' I then slipped away with the *murran* to Matapato, here, without the Putolek, for he was still with his friends in Loodokilani, while here I was among the Matapato *murran* without my son.

When we had arrived inside Matapato, we stayed ten days at the *manyata* at Intumuleni without the Putolek. When the Loodokilani *murran* found out, they took up arms to fight, for they wanted to snatch me and the cattle back. The Matapato *murran* knew this would happen and discussed what to do next. They left the *manyata* singing, and returned driving all their cattle into the central corral at midday, so that they could defend their herds when the Loodokilani *murran* arrived to fight them. Then, with their cattle penned up and safe, they slaughtered four oxen to eat while they were waiting for the Loodokilani *murran*. They said to me: 'We will not let you go. Only the Intumuleni *manyata* will have you.'

Meanwhile in Loodokilani, the *murran* there were preparing to come and snatch us back. However, it did not come to that. There was no fighting because the Loodokilani elders intercepted the Loodokilani *murran* and detained them. The Putolek, my son, wanted to remain there with his friends, but it was the elders who persuaded him to change his mind. Elders are fine for they do not allow their children to fight. If the elders had not intervened, then the Loodokilani and Matapato *murran* would have fought over us. So the Putolek realized that he would have to leave his Loodokilani friends and come to Matapato. A messenger was sent from Loodokilani to tell the Matapato *murran* that I should be allowed to go to an elders' village, for the Putolek did not want either me or the cattle in the *manyata* while he was not there. He would slaughter some cattle to feast the Loodokilani *murran* and get their blessing. Then he would come to Matapato to follow his mother and cattle.

So the Loodokilani *murran* came together to bless the Putolek, and then led him to a place near the boundary with Matapato. There, some Matapato *murran* were waiting for him, and they led him to the *manyata* here at Intumuleni. That was how we came back to our own country where we are now.

Now Ole Chieni had to face the Loodokilani elders. They told him: 'You were responsible for all this, encouraging those *murran* to take back your wife. Now, you must leave us. Go back to your own country.'

Ole Chieni replied defiantly: 'Yes. I let them go. For, when I came to Loodokilani, we were all poor and my sons came barefooted. All the time I have been here, I have been generous with you and have given you one of my daughters, and you never gave a single child to help me:

no girls to marry and no boys to help me herd. When I return to Matapato, I will remain there.' Then Ole Chieni and Nasira's father returned here as well.

It's fine when the *murran* lead you to the *manyata* as one of their mothers for there you are a very senior woman among your children. The *manyata* was a village of *murran*, and it was they who were in charge of it, but not when they came to rest inside my hut, for that belonged to me. While I was a mother there, the Meruturud stayed as *murran* — as *murran*. They would go off to the forest to eat cattle — as *murran*. Then they went to their *eunoto* festival and became great. There was this huge and wonderful ceremony, and again they danced their *enkipaata*, just like the boys. When it was all over they retired to become elders, I returned to Ole Chieni's village, for no decent woman throws away her husband's home. It is fine there also. The *manyata* or your husband's village, it is fine to be at either. Your children are there and there is nothing you can dislike, for they are all yours. So the Meruturud age-set in their turn rested and they were 'given milk' to drink and they became elders and married wives. The Putolek has had three wives altogether; although one of these ran away and he now has only two left.

Altogether, Ole Chieni has had seven wives. One died, two ran away. Now we have grown to be four households, but I was first, and I am the senior one of them all. I have had three daughters [and a fourth was adopted]. One of these is now at Oldoinyo Orok, another remained in Loodokilani, another is near here, and the oldest [see photo] is now a *manyata* mother at the Maparasha *manyata* right over there.

When a woman has a child, she has other wives to help her look after the baby. When your daughter becomes pregnant, your son-in-law visits your husband and asks his permission to have your help. He then leads you back to his village. While you are there, you must prevent your daughter eating too much. She cannot eat meat or milk from a diseased animal like other Maasai. She should remain hungry, and simply eat a little plain porridge [*kurma*] so that she will be strong and have a fine child. There you stay until she has had her child and for two months more. Then, on the third, you return home for the baby will have grown and you will have taught her how to hold her child. While you are there your son-in-law will buy you cloths to wear and give you money. He will slaughter an ox for you as his mother-in-law and give you some fat. Then returning to your own home, you carry this fat on your back, for your work there is over. That's how the Maasai do it.

Each wife is given cattle to look after, and I really would hate it if Ole Chieni took away one of my cows to give to another wife. If I had a son and this other wife had a son, then they would quarrel and fight over that cow of mine when they grew up. So the Maasai don't let elders take away cattle from their wives like that. If my husband did so, then I would wait until my boy, the Kamaniki [Kinai], could get it back for me, for I am his mother. When your son grows — as high as this — you give him a cow. The Kamaniki now has some of my cattle. I was his mother and gave them to him and to my other sons. It is the youngest — the *murran* — who is expected to look after me when I grow old and he will inherit all the cattle I have left; while Nasira's father [Kinai] as our most senior son will look after Ole Chieni in the same way, and it is he who will inherit Ole Chieni's things. Simayia's father [Kunaiju] is the middle son and he is not expected to look after either Ole Chieni or me. However, any of these children of ours will feed us and none of them would refuse us a cow. This has always been the way of the Maasai from the time they first emerged.

I do things for Nasira's father and for Simayia's father, and they buy me a cloth and say: 'Here, take this from me, mother.' Or tobacco: 'Here, take this from me, mother.' Or tea: 'Here, take this from me, mother.' There's no-one who will not give me something. 'Here, take this from me, mother.' When Simayia's father's wives become pregnant, I'll come along and help get them ready so that they can have their children and become strong. And then I will return to where Ole Chieni is. I belong to all the family homes and, whenever they are in need, I will be there to help them, so that they can pull through without selling off their cattle. I am the mother of them all.

A woman knows how to look after the home, taking care of this child or that cow. You feed your husband and get to know his stomach. His stomach is like a child. You give him food at all times, and there's no time when he has to go hungry between meals. Just now the cattle are finished by this drought and the hunger that this brings is bad for an old man. However, Ole Chieni has never had this while he has been with me.

We stayed looking after our stock for years and years. We stayed together as a family and never divided the cattle between wives into separate herds. Then with the next circumcisions, it was the turn of the Magaa age-set who are still *murran*. When they too came to lead me away to their *manyata*, this time with my youngest son, that was fine. Ole Chieni did not mind, for we were in our own country again. He slaughtered cattle and goats for the *murran* to eat when they came to lead me away, for they had come to their father's home.

So my hut is at the *manyata* of the *murran* again. There, it is the young *murran* who dance in the centre of village and bring meat to us mothers and tell us what to do. Ole Chieni is not there, for the *manyata* is a place for young people, and I am no longer young. My head has now grown white, my back aches, and it is a long way to fetch water. My grand-daughter Sibilai·[see photo] is here and she helps me. But she is only a small child. How much can she carry?

And now our cattle are finished once again, so here. I am, back at Ole Chieni's village, where Nasira's father is the senior elder as

Ole Chieni has moved elsewhere [about a week earlier]. While I have been living over there at the *manyata*, he has been living with his younger wives. I have noticed that he has become very thin recently, as if he is going to die. When we are together, I give him plenty of food and his body stays fat. Now his younger wives that are looking after him are just children and he has become thin. Milk from their cow gets drunk first by others. Their porridge gets eaten, and they don't even know how to prepare it. They spoil it and then he does not want it, for he's an elder. However, I am the same age as him and I know how to do everything properly.

I should be at the *manyata* of the *murran*, of course, but there is no food there any more. I have come to his village to help Nasira's mother have her baby, for just now she is very weak. I will stay here for two or three months and then, when she becomes strong again and can look after her own baby, I will return to the *manyata*, for the *murran* want to go to their *eunoto* when it rains. They need to go very badly — have you heard? Do come and see how fine it is and see how everything I say is true. You did say you would come.

Just now, however, I am frightened. For it is not Ole Chieni or Nasira's father who is in charge of me, but the *manyata murran*. They may come at any time to lead me back, and say: 'Come on! let's go.' What can I say? For I have deserted them. I'll say: 'Alright, alright, alright. I'll come, but just let me stay a little while so that Nasira's mother can have her baby and get well. When it rains, then I'll come back to your *manyata* and we can all set off for the *eunoto*.' However, the *murran* may come and say: 'The *manyata* is moving *now*; and we are setting off for the *eunoto* site over there.' If they say that, then I will have to go.

They are not moving yet, they will decide very soon now. They will come dressed for battle as warrior posses [*impikasin*]. They will spread out to round up their mothers, driving them from villages in the low country, from here, and from Nkiito, taking all their mothers again to the *manyata*. They have begun rounding up the mothers who have left the *manyata* during this drought so that they can be ready to set off. When they have all the other mothers, then they will come here and say: 'Now *you too*. Come along you. Let's go, for the *manyata* is about to set off for *eunoto*.' Then I will have to leave Nasira's mother and Nasira's father and go back to the *murran* village. Then we can all move to the *eunoto* and see the *murran* have their celebration and become great.

When this is all finished, the *manyata* will have to disband and I will go back to Ole Chieni's village, wherever he is. I'll stay together with Ole Chieni, not with Nasira's father or with Simayia's father, the Putolek, for it is Ole Chieni who is the father of these young men. By then I will be very senior and the younger women can fetch the water and my back will get better. I don't want to go to another *manyata.* Why should I? Where are my children? I have no more sons to become *murran*.

Tailpiece

The drought broke with torrential rains shortly after my conversations with Telelia. One month later, Nasira's mother died in childbirth where she had been attended by her own mother and her mother-in-law, Telelia. She had found successive pregnancies debilitating, and the Maasai practice of underfeeding pregnant mothers to ease the birth may have contributed to her weakness on the present occasion. The child, her sixth son, was weak and survived for twelve days. Telelia's *murran* son was then detailed by the other *murran* to escort her back to the *manyata.* A few weeks later they followed the other Matapato *manyat* to join together at their *eunoto* festival (again q v photo). Ole Chieni joined her there during the ceremonial climax. Then the *manyata* dispersed and Ole Chieni and his four wives came together at another village to rebuild their herds.

Notes

1. Telelia indicates that she was five or six years old when the *eunoto* festival of the Tareto age-set was held in 1918–19. This would have placed her birth around 1913 and she would have been 63 years old by 1976.
2. For a fuller reconstruction of the fortunes and misfortunes of the Chieni family derived largely from this series of interviews, see Spencer (1988: 288–289), indexed under 'Masiani'. An introduction to Masiani's own narrative as a self-portrait is also being published in Spencer (1992).
3. The original texts for all these interviews are available as 'Chieni Texts'. In successive topics of the present chapter, the following grouping of paragraphs has been made from Section B of the texts: Tareto *eunoto* (231–233); Ole Chieni's childhood (114, 162–163); meat feasts with *murran* (166, 222, 228); initiation and marriage 112, 166–167, 225); Terito *manyata* (234–237); affair with her lover (119–121, 214–225); birth of first child (113, 155, 167–169); subsequent early marriage (116–117, 121, 171, 223); wife-beating (174, 211–213, 215); growth and loss of herd (116–117; 171–172); period in Loodokilani (114–116, 125, 127, 153, 158–159, 281–291); critical episode of return to Matapato (251–264); back in Matapato (118, 123–126, 128, 136, 142–5, 154, 156–159, 271–272, 292–295, v. 30f); the Magaa *manyata* (116, 122–123, 138–139, 161, 241, 265, 311, v. 31b); concern over daughter-in-law (138–141, 242–245).
4. In a previous account of this marriage (Spencer, 1988: 173), I assumed that Masiani married Telelia after he had gone to the *manyata.* In Telelia's narrative the marriage appears to have preceded the *manyata* by several years. Her version would have made this marriage unusually early, even for a *murran*.

Nine

'The Eye that Wants a Person, Where Can It Not See?'

Inclusion, Exclusion & Boundary Shifters in Maasai Identity*

JOHN G. GALATY

Ethnicity & Identity in Context

The term 'Maasai' is currently used to mark two different cultural realities, the first being the gamut of Maa-speaking people and groups in East Africa, the second the set of central and primarily pastoral Rift Valley Maa-speaking sections for which the term marks their distinctiveness. The first represents an 'objective' notion of ethnicity (that is, the subjectivity of external observation), used to describe the extension of a language and cultural community, such as 'The Russians', 'The Serbo-Croatians', 'The Rendille', or in this case the community which emerged out of the complex process of the Maa expansion. The second, which involves the complex and 'subjective' world of 'ethnic' politics presented from a particular point of view, is ambiguous, contextually variable and often contested; this is the ethnic usage of 'White Russians', Serbs versus Croats, 'pure laine' French Canadians, 'White Rendille', and Maasai 'proper'. Barth's (1969: 13) suggestion that ethnicity involves how a group defines its 'most general identity' appropriately focuses less on the history of linguistic and cultural diffusion and more on an anthropology of signs, used to constitute and delimit boundaries of affinity. What is, of course, culturally problematic and politically at stake is just where the line of 'most general identity' should be drawn, and how its content defined. The inclusion and exclusion of individuals and groups tends to be historically contingent, dependent on the context, circumstances, motives and aims of interaction, so ethnicity — as well as other orders of identity — tends, in Cohen's words, to be 'situational' (1978: 388).

In the long run, whether a group tends to be 'inclusive' or 'exclusive' in its subjective interactions will likely influence the growth and spread of a cultural or linguistic community. In East Africa, the Rendille say they 'sort people out' and, since 'they discriminate, segregate and differentiate', they have ended up a small community (Schlee, 1989: 49). In contrast, the Maasai, and other groups such as the Somali, have tended to be 'assimilative' (Waller, 1985a: 367), as the title of the chapter implies, and this may be one aspect of their historical expansion and growth. At the same time, however, they have tended to hone a sharply defined notion of 'Maasai' as 'people-of-cattle', which has been used — socially and rhetorically — to 'cut away' or distance those who deviate from a pastoral ideal; yet, when circumstances have demanded it, Maasai have embraced whatever subsistence strategies were necessary (Waller, 1985b). It is this dialectical pattern of inclusiveness and exclusiveness, and of discrimination and opportunistic openness, that lends Maasai identity its complexity and makes it desirable that we call upon notions of context and the indexing functions of 'shifters'[1] in describing their use of what are apparently 'ethnic' terms and notions.

Today, the concept of 'ethnicity' has come into its own, in part to fill the gap left by the demise of the notion of 'tribe', which implied a type of self-sufficiency and autonomy that has proven not only inadequate as an account of current affairs but also unconvincing as a model for the past (Cohen, 1978; Comaroff, 1987). The ethnic concept usefully implies a multiplicity of general identities within a complex cultural field of the past as well as the present; as Cohen (1978: 389) comments, 'ethnicity has no existence apart from interethnic relations'. But, apart from what Barth observed to be its generality and its implicit emphasis on a group's origins or background, 'ethnicity' has no necessary content. In an earlier comment on the subject, I suggested that, the 'the concept dissolves into a plethora of features such as "shared blood", "one origin", "common history", and "similar kind"', all deep-seated symbols of the 'natural' in human groups (Galaty, 1982a: 2). Thus, 'ethnicity' may be usefully seen in Lévi-Strauss' terms as 'totemic', representing

> . . . a correspondence between the cultural level of human classes and the natural level of substantial-historical features, wherein each level provides the operative principle that constitutes the other (*ibid.*).

Further, within a Maasai ethnosociology, there is an identity established between what people are (their 'nature') and what they do (their 'culture'), more specifically between their substantive identities and their place within an occupational system (*ibid.*:5). In a very similar way, Comaroff (1987: 304) has identified two properties of ethnicity:

> . . . the subjective classification, by members of a society, of the world into social entities according to cultural differences . . . [and] the stereotypic assignment of these groupings — often hierarchically — to niches within the social division of labor.

The first principle underlies totemism, the second principle class, while the two principles together underlie ethnicity (*ibid.*: 304). Further, he suggests that totemism tends to establish symmetrical relations between similar groups, while ethnicity originates in the 'asymmetric incorporation of structurally dissimilar groupings in a single political economy' (*ibid*.: 307). However, it may be worth considering whether the tendency to 'naturalize' or 'substantialize' a society's division of productive labour may not be socially pervasive. If so, a fundamentally 'totemic' form of classification may be intrinsic to the cultural ordering of all three forms of what Comaroff has identified as totemic, ethnic and class consciousness.[2] For our purposes here, the question we should ask is whether and how hierarchy based on economic differences — and in the end a system of regional stratification — tends to apply to forms of Maasai social classification.

As suggested at the outset of this paper, one notion of ethnicity is that it is an objective attributional *state* possessed by a community, a commonality of language, kinship or cultural practice, while the second notion is that it is an attributional *process*, in which a certain overarching identity is assigned to individuals or groups by virtue of properties perceived, qualities defined or features selected. From the latter perspective, ethnicity may guide behaviour or its interpretation, but is not part of the order of social groups but rather of discourse about it. Ethnic status is never acquired simply by doing something, unless that behaviour becomes an element, chosen out of available cultural fragments, in an identity constructed by and for a person or a group. Ethnicity involves less identifying an attribute than attributing an identity — often through naming or labelling — of someone, by someone, often in the context of someone else, to paraphrase Peirce's famous definition of a sign (Peirce, 1931–1958). Implied is that ethnicity is not a state of affairs or a quality of persons; rather, it is a process in which identities are fashioned through the creative use of signs to constitute notions and intuitions of selves and others. To understand Maasai ethnicity, then, we should ask when, how, and by whom the label 'Maasai', in contrast to and among other markers, is attributed to someone, and in what context and with what import.

Ethnicity often appears to the reflective observer — both foreign and culturally engaged observers (the latter being, after all, the source of most schematic accounts of ethnic attributes presented as 'anthropological') — as an objective quality of groups, expressed in the properties of shared systems of language, culture, kinship or economic life. Unlike the micro-level of individual, family or community identity, which is always situated in particular contexts, the macro-level of ethnicity appears bounded and fixed in nature, despite its evolution over time. But over time there is no necessary concurrence between the spread of a language and culture, the recognition of a single origin, the practice of a common form of economic life and the defining of a shared identity, as seen from within. Boundaries can be collapsed as well as constructed, can experience decay or be maintained. This dynamic aspect of identity, witnessed by residential shifts across boundaries and longer-term shifts of boundaries and marked by multilingualism and code shifting, has led some scholars to suggest that ethnicity in pastoral East Africa, in this case the Maasai, tends to be 'fluid' or 'mutable' (Waller, 1985b; Sobania, 1991).

What are the implications of intermarriage, bilingualism, residential mobility and economic variation, now part of the Maasai ethnographic record, for the identity of a people that has defined itself in terms of a language, a culture, and an intensive and specialized form of pastoral practice? To interpret such phenomena, the concept of ethnic 'shifters' may prove useful, by illuminating the diverse cultural projects people pursue across ethnic lines; cultural realities which appear 'fluid', 'blurred' or 'mutable' may in fact lie within the well-understood repertoire of a community, their domains of competence being made subject to play, parody or pretence (cf. Klumpp and Kratz, this volume). Their projects surely include straddling a boundary, striving for assimilation, claiming another community's benefits, establishing a friendship, or simply trying to 'pass'. 'Shifting', while perhaps not rule-bound, may represent innovations coherent only in light of a community's shared competence regarding the conceptual objects of play. Hodder (1982: 18), reflecting on shifts in ethnic presentation within the regional culture of ethnic groups in Baringo, noted that

> . . . there is usually very little ambiguity or blurring about the tribal group to which a person belongs . . . The people themselves know very clearly whether at any one moment they are identifying with the Pokot, Njemps or Tugen.

Changes in residence, especially by women, often lead to adaptations in dress and adornment to conform with one's hosts:

> . . . whatever a woman may feel she really is, she can outwardly express different identities, and there is rarely any ambiguity about which identity she is overtly expressing at any one time (*ibid.*: 21).

We can apply a concept of 'shifting' to at least three distinct processes concerned with identity, ethnicity and spatial or social movement:

(1) the contextualized 'shifting' in the sense or reference attributed rhetorically to ethnic labels (an individual is deemed a Maasai in one context, not in another; 'Maasai' connotes pastoralist in one context, a Maa-speaker in another);
(2) the 'shifting' of individual, family or community identities by, as it were, 'crossing' — literally or metaphorically — a recognized ethnic boundary (as when Maasai 'became' Torrobo, a Kikuyu herdsboy 'becomes' Maasai); and
(3) the 'shifting' of the geographical or social boundaries (linguistic

or otherwise) of groups or communities (as when the Torrobo of a region 'become' Maasai, or Uasin Gishu are assimilated to the 'Maasai' idiom).[3]

To explore the implications of movement and interaction for identity, a number of cases and several bodies of discourse will be presented, bearing on questions of inclusion in and exclusion from Maasai identity, and the ongoing cultural debate and contestation regarding the 'Maasai' attribution. There is reason to believe that the name 'Maasai' may be relatively recent, since it nowhere appears as a name traditionally attributed to Maasai or Maa-speakers by their neighbours. It may well have historically emerged during the Maa expansion to define the loose unity forged by the pastoral sections of the central Rift Valley.

The Maa expansion involved the spread and efflorescence of a language, the differentiation and subsequent refiguring and realignment of territorial sections, the spread and refinement of a specialized form of cattle pastoralism, and the creation and diffusion of cultural and institutional forms, including social organization based on age-sets. As developed in the chapter by Klumpp and Kratz, Maasai identity was marked by signs of ethnic display and commitment: a distinctive apparel of flowing red robes or sheets and beaded jewellery, age-, sex- and status-coded hair style and armaments, and a strongly internalized system of personal mores and interpersonal ethics which, in Maasai eyes, set them apart from morally lesser people. Yet these same markers have served to publicly validate the incorporation and assimilation, often through marriage or adoption, of countless individuals, families and community fragments swept into the Maasai vortex.

But these qualities and attributes, although representing a striking movement of cultural boundaries through time and space, did not necessarily signify an encompassing identity as seen from within. Indeed, in one way or another the notion of 'Maasai' arose in contra-distinction not only to non-pastoralists, the cultivators and hunters with whom pastoralists formed a regional 'triangle of economic types' (Galaty, 1982a: 6), or as the *Ilomet* class of ordinary herders to the internal classes of blacksmiths and diviners in a pastoral division of labour (*ibid.*: 11), but also to other Maa-speaking pastoral groups, whose divergence in fundamental identity from Maasai was only represented by superficial differences of language, culture, economy and organization. The signification of 'Maasai' at this level can only be understood in terms of pure attributions of identity. The final stage in ethnic evolution is still underway, with the increasing use of the 'Maasai' nominal currency by all Maa-speakers to identify themselves within the complex national settings of multi-ethnic politics in Kenya and Tanzania, a conceptual hegemony within the Maasai region comparable to the political hegemony established by central Maasai in the nineteenth century. The Maasai name is now attributed to the assimilated Uasin Gishu and Siria sections and is often used to identify themselves by Parakuyo,

Arusha and Chamus (but not to my knowledge by the Samburu). To speak Maa is increasingly equated with being Maasai, pastoral or not.

The first set of cases presented concerns interaction between central Maasai and other Maa-speaking communities, two pastoral (the Siria and Parakuyo) and one agricultural or agro-pastoral (the Arusha). The second set concerns interaction between Maasai and groups of non-pastoralists rooted in their own languages and cultures (though often bilingual in Maa), one of which pursues cultivation (the Kikuyu), the other hunting-gathering (the Torrobo). Two key issues regarding processes of and plays on identity will concern us: first, in what way are shifters involved in inclusion or exclusion across lines or boundaries of social identity; second, in what way can notions of symmetry or hierarchy be used to characterize Maasai/Other relations, in order to shed light on the ethnic aspect of regional systems?

'Only We Can Tell the Difference': Shifters & Internal Boundaries

Early missionary observers reported that 'Masai' were distinguished from the 'Wakwavi' or 'Wakuafi', 'the brothers of the Masai'; Krapf stated that 'the two kindred tribes, the Wakuafi and Masai, hate each other mortally' (Krapf, 1860: 360–361). Krapf described as 'Wakuafi' the inhabitants of Kaputie, specifically the 'Engang-lima', and the 'Barrabuyu' on the Pangani (Krapf, 1854: 4–5), groups the Maasai probably called by the name 'Loogolala'. However, the term 'Wakwavi' was later used by Wakefield (1870) to identify other Maa-speaking groups, including the Laikipiak, the Uasin Gishu and the Siria, as well as 'poor Wakwavi' of Nkuruman and Baringo forced to cultivate after losing their cattle to Maasai, and the Arusha as 'descendants of the Wakwavi' (Wakefield, 1870: 304–306). Krapf had earlier noted that both 'the Wakuafi and Masai . . . call themselves "Orloikob", or "Loikob"', both being pastoral (Krapf, 1860: 358; des Avanchers, 1859). The first categorical reference to agricultural Maasai was by Farler, who tentatively observed that 'The Wakuafi . . . seem to be an agricultural branch of the Masai people' (1882: 731). By the onset of colonial rule, after decades in which Maasai had militarily defeated and dispersed the Uasin Gishu, Laikipiak and Loogolala–Parakuyo, a distinction was made between the settled agricultural Loikop (or Kwavi) and the pastoral and nomadic Maasai (Eliot, 1905). Thus, regardless of their respective subsistence pursuits, through most of the nineteenth century a symbolic distinction was consistently made between 'Maasai' and other communities speaking the same language, although it is doubtful that any greater cultural commonality or political unity obtained between non-Maasai Maa groups than between them and the Maasai; Bernsten observed that ' . . . there is little evidence to indicate any kind of lasting unity between the various Maa-speaking people called Kwavi' (1977).

Being Maasai

Although both Hollis (1905, repr. 1970: iii) and Krapf (1860: 358) speculated that Loikop signified 'the possessors-of-the-land', after the root for 'land' (*En-kop*), the term has a quite specific sense, to designate the crime of murder and the pollution or guilt associated with a murderer who has not yet paid blood-wealth compensation to the family of the victim or performed rituals of cleansing (Galaty, 1977a: 39–40; Bernsten, 1980: 12).[4] While the term applies most specifically to individuals, a group which traditionally does not receive 'blood-wealth' (*Enkurou*) payments from another group may call them *Iloikop*, while warriors or groups may call themselves *Iloikop*, with connotations of fierceness, 'yielding no quarter'. Previously commenting on the question, I suggested that:

> The term *Iloikop* is thus potentially pejorative as well as laudatory, and thus clearly applicable to one's own group as well as other 'foreign' groups. It clearly must be seen as an attributional label, but used in certain contexts to predictably refer to certain groups, thus assuming certain 'naming' functions (Galaty, 1977a: 40).

The term 'Wakwavi' may have been derived from the term *In-kuaapi*, a plural form of *En-kop*, which signifies 'other lands' or 'foreign areas' (*ibid.*: 41), making it a Maasai-centric label for non-central Maa. However, it is also possible that the terms 'Kwavi' or 'Kapi' represent a series of Bantu corruptions of '*Iloikop*', the outsiders' version, if you will. Similarly, terms such as 'Humba' are clearly variants of the Maa term Lumbwa, which referred to the earliest Maa inhabitants of southern Maasailand but was later attributed to the Parakuyo.

General terms of identity such as 'Maasai' or 'Kwavi' are not of the same order as names of groups, such as Kisongo, Keekonyokie, Siria, Arusha or Parakuyo, which take as their referents particular communities with local organization. The question here is how attribution of the term 'Maasai' has been used to define boundaries internal to the Maa-speakers, or at a certain point in time or under certain circumstances to transgress or even to eliminate the boundary. The two key symbols associated with the Maasai idea were the practice of pastoralism and competence in the Maa language, as well as community solidarity, marked by reciprocal recognition of blood-wealth. The following Maa-speaking groups were not, in the nineteenth century, part of the Maasai system of political solidarity, but two were pastoral practitioners (Siria and Parakuyo) while a third (Arusha) was closely tied to the neighbouring Kisongo.

Siria and Parakuyo: The Pastoral 'Other'

Two groups of Maa-speaking pastoralists illustrate the processes by which some came to be deemed 'Maasai' while others did not. The Siria of the trans-Mara region were among those earlier deemed 'Wakwavi', but today they are considered wholly 'Maasai'. An account of their origins is instructive with regards to shifts in Maasai identity:

All these people now known as Siria came from different corners. I do not
know how they reached here. Let me consider the sections in our area. I belong
to the Kaputie in this area. These Kaputie are the same as those found in
Kaputie (Kajiado), but they just ran away and came here. So after the wars,
all those sections were here with their clans . . .

There were people living here previously. Torrobo were here from before,
living in the bush . . . They never had any ceremonies and didn't want any
cattle. They just wanted meat. Other small groups joined them until they
were many.

The Loitai later fought the Siria. You know that their *loibonok* are strong,
. . . and the Siria were chased [to Luoland] by them . . . The Kaputie were
also attacked since they possessed cattle and had warriors.[5]

Kaputie immigrants thus joined with earlier inhabitants (see Wakefield,
1870: 308) and others to form the Siria of today.

Loitai Maasai were alternately antagonists and allies of the Siria.
For years the Siria attended Loitai ceremonies in a subordinate position,
taking home the charms which allowed them to celebrate their own
local rituals. Now they have begun celebrating their own age-set rituals
in consultation with the Loitai *loibon* and have even begun to speculate
on how they might free themselves of that subordinate tie by establishing
their own independent *loibon*, a descendant of the Loitai *loibon* Senteu.
Siria are thus now considered to be Maasai, based on their participation
in pastoralism and age-set ceremonies. But these attributes have only
been claimed relatively recently as Siria altered their economic practice
to signify a Maasai-like commitment to pastoralism and as they acquired
direct social and ritual links to the Loitai section. Maasai social and
conceptual boundaries have thus expanded to include the Siria, just
as they have for their Uasin Gishu neighbours.

Parakuyo, on the other hand, have apparently never been viewed
as 'Maasai' from the central Maasai point of view, but in a Tanzanian
setting where they have been unacceptably labelled 'Kwavi', they continue to assert that, in addition to being Parakuyo, they are, indeed,
Maasai (Beidelman, 1960; Rigby, 1985). While greeting an external
aid mission visiting Morogoro District in 1985, a spokesman presented
himself and his village as 'Maasai' and was visibly embarrassed when
asked whether he was not, in fact, Parakuyo. With the claim to Maasai
identity dropped, the spokesman discussed relations and cultural differences between Parakuyo and Maasai.[6] Johnston (1886: 407) recounted:

> If you ask the 'Wakwavi' [Parakuyo] of Mazindi what they are, they will
> reply at once, 'Masai'. And if you ask a nomad Masai . . . what he calls
> his congeners of Mazindi — who perhaps a generation ago were fighting in
> the same clan — he will answer contemptuously 'Embarawuio' . . .

Noting 'competing claims to the same identity', Waller (1985b: 116)
cites an anecdote with a similar theme. Ironically, the term ol-Parakuoni
signifies an individual rich in cattle (Mol, 1978: 136), and is used by
Maasai themselves as an age-set name.

The boundary between Maasai and Parakuyo has been maintained despite the fact they they often shared the same pastures in Naberera and Kiteto, used the same wells, and often occupied the same village. A Maasai elder from Monduli Juu, referring to Parakuyo, recently stated:

> If you meet warriors from Lumbwa [Parakuyo], they are no different from ours. And women and men are the same. Everything is the same and it is only we who can tell the difference.

In a similar fashion, Kaputie earlier lived side by side with Loogolala until the two clashed and the Loogolala were annihilated and dispersed, only to regroup as Parakuyo in the south.

There may not be a satisfying explanation, apart from a history of linguistic and cultural differentiation, of why Kisongo and Parakuyo, sharing residences and resources, perpetuated a profound gulf between them until, with the southward dispersion of Parakuyo, the question of shared identity became mute. But there seems to be a growing awareness by Parakuyo today that the pastoral ideal they pursue is best symbolized by effecting an identity as Maasai, probably due to the eclipse of the pastoral federation in which they formerly participated. In contrast, the Siria, long a significant force in their region, seem to have embraced the larger Maasai identity both as an act of fealty to the Loitai *loibon* and as a means of signifying their pastoral values within a system of ethnic meanings refashioned by the devastation and assimilation by Maasai of most other Maa-speakers.

Kisongo and Arusha: Shifting Boundaries; Shifting Dominance

The Arusha of Mount Meru in northern Tanzania are also Maa-speakers, but differ from Parakuyo in their pursuit of cultivation and complementary patterns of exchange with pastoral Sikirari and Kisongo Maasai. What is remarkable, however, is how the forms of ritual and cultural domination exerted by Kisongo over Arusha in the nineteenth century have been effectively reversed as the Arusha population and economy have grown in the twentieth. Gulliver (1969) notes, for example, that Arusha developed a myth in the 1950s relating how pastoral Maasai came originally from Arusha in a transparent attempt to make the past accord with the economic realities of the present. Despite Gulliver's predictions that continued acceptance of Maasai ritual dominance by Arusha would prove untenable, however, Arusha have continued to participate in Kisongo ritual ceremonies directed by the Kisongo *loibon* as recently as December 1988.[7]

Arusha have expanded dramatically from the crowded slopes of Mount Meru onto the Kisongo plains south and west of Arusha town over the past twenty years. Today they completely dominate the town of Monduli (Monduli Chini) and live intermingled with Kisongo on the grassy plateau of Monduli Juu (Jacobs, 1978). While both appear equally Maasai from the outside, there is a firm awareness within the community of who is Kisongo and who is Arusha. Both sides concur in perpetuating the distinction, but many Arusha also stress their identity as Maasai, particularly when seeking access to land in traditionally pastoral areas. Fellow Maa-speakers, living side-by-side, thus continue to maintain a firm boundary between themselves, despite engaging in many forms of social discourse and interaction with one another.

The Monduli plateau lies at the margins between highland forest and a sharp descent into the Rift Valley. The village of Emairete adjoins an area of seepage lower on the plateau, while the village of Enguiki is higher, with gardens marking the line of forest. A survey of 20 households in Emairete and 15 in Enguiki revealed that equivalent numbers of Kisongo and Arusha are intermixed, with a total of 16 Kisongo and 19 Arusha-headed households across both villages.[8] Although Kisongo and Arusha often inhabit the same residential area, they unambiguously reported the ethnic affiliation of the household and all its children as that of the male head. We can thus examine the effects of mixed residence on factors pertinent to identity, namely, marriage patterns and economic pursuits.

The 16 Kisongo men are married to a total of 43 wives, of whom 31 are Kisongo and 12 are Arusha. The 18 Arusha men are married to 36 wives, of whom 5 are Kisongo and 31 are Arusha. The degree of in-marriage is more striking if the two villages are compared. Of 61 married women in Emairete, there are only 8 who are married across the two groups (4 Kisongo women to Arusha men and 4 Arusha women to Kisongo men). This 'cross-over' rate of 13 per cent contrasts strikingly with that of 50 per cent in Enguiki, largely accounted for by marriages between Kisongo men and Arusha women in a village with few Kisongo women. In fact, the cross-over rate of Kisongo men and Arusha women (28 per cent of their marriages) is twice that of Kisongo women and Arusha men (14 per cent). Kisongo men have a somewhat higher polygyny rate than Arusha (2.69 wives per man vs 2.0), but the differences between the two villages is even greater, with a rate of 3.1 in Emairete and only 1.33 in Enguiki. Family sizes also differ in similar directions, greater for Kisongo than Arusha (11.8 vs 9.6 members) and for Emairete than Enguiki (12.0 vs 8.7).

Clearly, there is a strong maintenance of ethnic marriage boundaries in Monduli, with appreciably greater permeability for Arusha than Kisongo women. Other differences in family structure may originate in cultural and economic differences, since wealth in animals and land is crucial to marriage and building a large family. While it is Arusha who have carved large farms out of pastureland and forest for the cultivation of maize, beans, wheat, and barley, virtually all Kisongo households on Monduli also practise agriculture, though usually on a smaller scale than Arusha. Conversely, Arusha also practise animal husbandry, though to a lesser extent than Kisongo. Kisongo have larger family herds than Arusha in both villages (74 head per family for Kisongo vs 44.5 for Arusha), but, since Kisongo have somewhat larger families, differences in per capita holdings are somewhat less (6.3 cattle per person for Kisongo vs 4.6 for Arusha). Differences between the two villages exceed those between the two communities, however, with inhabitants of the lower village, Emairete, having an average of 4.2 cattle per person while those of Enguiki have 7.8. Small stock holdings are spread throughout Monduli, but they tend to represent a smaller proportion of total livestock holdings for Kisongo than for Arusha and for Enguiki than for Emairete.

There thus appear to be consistent social and economic differences between Kisongo and Arusha, but in most cases these are exceeded by differences between the two villages. What is to be concluded, then, concerning the maintenance of ethnic boundaries between the two Maa-speaking communities? Monduli Juu lies at the geographic boundaries both of agricultural Arusha centred on nearby Mount Meru and of pastoral Kisongo inhabiting the surrounding plains. Suitable for farming and herding, it evidences a mix of both and a merging of subsistence strategies. The region is also mixed culturally. All houses are built in the Arusha style, and both peoples continue to participate in Maasai age-sets and rituals. Kisongo practice has thus moved towards Arusha and vice versa. Kisongo and Arusha also appear to accommodate each other when living together, and each appears to resemble their co-residents in each of the two villages more closely than either resembles their ethnic counterparts in the other village.

Despite shifts in economic practice, however, a clear ethnic line is maintained between the two communities. This is seen in the relatively low rates of intermarriage, in the categorical recognition of patrilateral ethnic filiation, and in the insistent reproduction and regeneration of various social markers between the two groups, including distinct age-set cohorts, dances and songs, forms of dress and hair styles, and ways of speaking. Such differences are sustained by negative stereotypes each have of the other, such as the common Kisongo complaint regarding Arusha women who marry Kisongo men, invite all their brothers to cultivate near them, and then evict the Kisongo husbands when their herds disturb the crops. Conversely, each also embraces a distinctive ethnic ideology that affirms its own distinctiveness: We Arusha, though like the Maasai, are industrious, aggressive, and shrewd, and dominate the Maasai in the modern world. We Maasai, though tolerating and benefiting from our neighbours the Arusha, are richer in wives and in animals, have a sense of timing and grace, possess a great land, and dominate those who labour. Though 'flowing' together, Arusha and Kisongo Maasai conceptually meet with sharp and well-honed edges.

Hierarchy & Difference on the Non-Pastoral Margin

The assertion of 'pastoral honour' is virtually a trope of Maasai identity. Non-pastoralists are not only assessed as neighbours, but defined according to a set of stereotypic notions — such as *ilmeek* cultivators and Torrobo hunters — drawn from Maasai ethnosociology (Galaty, 1982a). The relative merits of various forms of labour, kinds of food and types of social organization have served to order hierarchically the conceptual Rift Valley world according to a pastoral logic. This ideology has served as a symbolic backdrop for the much more complex interactions between pastoralists and non-pastoralists, justifying the set of ethno-economic boundaries which are in reality traversed by individuals and families linked within a regional system of interethnic trade, exchange, and discourse. The key relations maintained by pastoral Maasai of the central Rift Valley have been with Okiek, known by Maasai as 'Torrobo', and Kikuyu.

'Now We Are Maasai': Assimilation and Hierarchy at the Torrobo Border
Scholars have long debated whether the differences between Torrobo[9] and Maasai are ones of ethnicity, of caste, or of class; that is, whether Torrobo have a distinct origin from Maasai, whether they are separated from Maasai by intra-societal restrictions on marriage and conviviality, or whether they are identified primarily by their pursuit of hunting in a regional ethnic mode of production (Spear, 'Introduction', this volume; van Zwanenberg, 1976; Kratz, 1980).

Maasai views are also ambiguous. A Maasai informant condescendingly listed three differences between Torrobo and Maasai: Torrobo smell like faeces and urine; they were brought up without cattle and eat wild animals; and they speak Maa imperfectly. More generously, an Enkidong informant from Loitai (whose first wife was said to be Torrobo) stated:

> Torrobo are just like Maasai, except they hunt; and nowadays they have cattle and they have houses. They can be married and it is not 'bitter' . . . Originally they had their own *iloshon* [sections], . . . but then they came here . . . [where] they have no Torrobo *olosho*, but are just Maasai.

Torrobo themselves vary as well. A Torrobo woman, whose father was an Nguesi who lived with Purko on Laikipiak and was later adopted by a Purko family near Naivasha, noted that, although her mother was a Purko Maasai, they did not consider themselves Maasai until her father was subsequently adopted by Purko. Now they are Maasai. A Torrobo circumciser among the Narok Purko stated Torrobo were:

> . . . always together with the Maasai. When we came to this land we were one, but we were poor . . . We got the name [Torrobo] because we were poor. We had no cattle and it was said we were Torrobo because we ate

wild animals of the bush . . . We are now Maasai, however, because we have left the bush behind and we now have cattle.[10]

Are Torrobo Maasai, then? Well, yes and no. Van Zwanenberg (1976) asserts that, when Torrobo accumulate livestock or are adopted into Maasai families, they stop being Torrobo. But Kratz (n.d.:3) comments that most of those who still identify themselves as Okiek in Narok District now keep domestic herds, cultivate shambas, and tend increasingly to accumulate rather than slaughter the livestock they acquire.

> Acquisition of livestock is not simply a matter of economic diversification for Okiek, but is also a factor in changing attitudes in ethnic relations with their neighbours . . . The fact that Okiek now have domestic animals does not instantly eliminate Maasai condescension or the arrogant and domineering way they sometimes talk about or to Okiek, but it is an important part of the rhetoric of ethnic equality . . .

And would Maasai be called Torrobo if they began to eat wild game? Hobley (1902) observed that there were many poor Maasai who had lost their cattle in the disasters of the 1890s living among Okiek (see also Waller, 1985b:128; Berntsen, 1976). But the Torrobo circumciser said no; Maasai have eaten wild animals before and they were not called Torrobo.

There seems little doubt that Maasai and many Torrobo communities have exchanged populations in the long run, and that the distinction between them is essentially an economic one, reinforced by other social boundaries. In the past, relatively specialized hunting and bee-keeping may have evolved out of communities of pastoro-foragers as the rangeland niche became increasingly monopolized by more specialized pastoralists (Ambrose, 1984). But it seems doubtful that Maasai were simply 'assimilated' by Okiek communities or local Torrobo 'absorbed' into Maasai ones (Blackburn, 1974; Kratz, 1980). Ethnic assimilation and absorption are complex processes which occur over generations, not within the few years of a drought or similar crisis.

It is also important to distinguish between short-term, contingent practices, which are easily explained, such as eating wild game or even donkeys or skins during a famine, and characteristic practices by which people choose to define themselves. 'Adoption' may seem an unambiguous shift across a clearly recognized line if it 'takes', which it often does not as assimilees return to their homes when a crisis is over or opportunity beckons, but Maasai memories are long and one's origins may not be ignored. More often the conceptual line shifts, as Torrobo are 'in' or 'out', depending on circumstances and motive, what is meant, and what is at stake. In the mid-1970s when land was being adjudicated in Nairragie Enkare, Torrobo communities suddenly reasserted distinct separate identities many of them had long sought to discard in order to validate their claims to land, while Maasai suddenly insisted that Torrobo were and always had been fully Maasai and so should join together with them to form ranches and farms. As the line shifts, the *notion* underlying identity may shift as well: language now outweighing practice, affinity transcending culture, or kinship outweighing shared residence. Though complex, this cultural 'game' has both explicit and tacit rules and assumptions. People are rarely confused; while the rules themselves may change, it is likely that this will be understood as well.

If eating game allows some to call certain Maasai 'Torrobo', or owning cattle some Torrobo to call themselves (or be called) 'Maasai', the characteristic practices associated with their personal heritages provides equal justification for either to assert continuity in their identities. Waller (1985b: 129-130) notes:

> At times, the dividing line between herders and hunters may become very thin and is easily crossed. This issue is complicated by the ambiguity of Maasai attitudes towards the 'Dorobo' and by the fact that perceptions are affected by the context in which they are expressed. At different times, both 'Dorobo' and Maasai have chosen to emphasize either assimilation or separation and have presented their interpretation of the relationship accordingly.

Ethnicity does not, then, entail being situated on one side or another of a boundary, or of simply 'crossing over', changing identity as one changes one's residence, one's occupation, or one's speech. As Kratz (1980: 366-367) points out, Okiek are not 'really' Maasai (or Kipsigis or Kikuyu), but 'everyone, including the Okiek, wants to keep the question open and the lines between them slightly obfuscated'. In the case at hand, we see 'ethnic shifting', the strategic drawing on codes of competence, practice, and affinity to claim, or to be proffered, a particular identity qualified by context and motive. Herding and hunting practices are easily interchanged when warranted, and aspects of assimilation or separation can be highlighted as the contexts of unity or difference demand. The negotiation of such conceptual boundaries, while involving subtle gradations of attribution, are not 'fluid', but rather are complex in very specific ways. Ethnic shifting is only effective if the signs used to evoke particular forms of identity are in fact understood and tacitly accepted. Complex and open for 'play', full of diverse forms of meaning, yes; but, if ethnic signs were fluid or obscure, they would not work (cf. Klumpp and Kratz, this volume).

'We Were Not Kikuyu; We Were Maasai': Fluidity and Exchange on the Kikuyu Border

The question of identity gains a sharp edge when it concerns relations and shifts between language communities with divergent practices and values, such as between Kikuyu farmers and Maasai herders along the eastern edge of the Rift Valley where open pastoral grassland shaded gradually into highland farms. For Maasai, Kikuyu in the highlands were a secure source of agricultural foodstuffs and refuge, while, for

Kikuyu, Maasai provided a constant supply of cattle required for food, bridewealth, and other social exchanges. While such complementary relations might have sharpened ethnic, linguistic, and cultural distinctions, however, social boundaries shifted and became blurred over time so that, by the end of the nineteenth century, as Waller (1985b: 124) notes:

> . . . ethnic identities and modes of subsistence imperceptibly merged as one ecological zone shaded into another, from forested ridge to open grassland, 'Kikuyu' to 'Maasai'.

Colonial conquest and the enforced movement of Maasai south into the Maasai reserve distanced Maasai from Kikuyu along all but the southern frontier between Kiambu and Ngong with Kaputei and Keekonyokie Maasai. With increasing shortage of land in the highlands, however, Kikuyu sought to mobilize their prior relations with Maasai to obtain cultivable land in Maasailand, leading colonial officials to complain constantly of Kikuyu 'penetration' of the legally 'closed' Maasai districts. Maasai responses to Kikuyu immigrants were mixed, as Waller details extensively in his essay later in this volume. Maasai fears of losing control over their land frequently led them publicly to cooperate with colonial authorities in sharpening ethnic boundaries and expelling Kikuyu, while, at the same time, concerns for their own Kiyuku clients and relatives led them privately to try to circumvent such regulations.

A vivid personal account of boundary 'crossing' is provided by a Kikuyu woman married early in the century to a Maasai elder.[11] As a girl, many Maasai settled in her village to escape the ravages of drought and to cultivate while waiting for their fortunes to improve on the plains. She began to learn Maa from their children, and soon was able to serve as a translator between the two communities. She also frequently took foodstuffs to her brother and other Kikuyu employed as herders by the Veterinary Office at Embakasi, where she liked to flirt with the Maasai *murran*. A Maasai elder, Ole Karriaki, observed her there, however, and offered her father so many cattle 'he swept away his whole herd': 'The eye that wants a person, where can it not see?' Maasai and Kikuyu elders were friendly and, like many Kiyuku, her father coveted the cattle gained from marrying one of his daughters to a Maasai. He thus ordered her to forget the *murran* and marry Ole Karriaki.

Once in Maasai she learned to intersperse cultivation with the annual movements of cattle in order to be able to continue to farm. She also continued to learn to speak Maa and raised her own children in that language, noting:

> Their fathers did not allow us to speak to them in Kikuyu. But I could not dislike Kikuyu. How can I dislike the language I was born into? I was born into it. But when a Kikuyu woman gets married, she is not allowed

to speak to her children in her language. However, I still dream in Kikuyu and think in it, even as I sit here now.

She also often dreamed of visiting her own people, which she did infrequently, but noted that none of her relatives had come to live with her in Maasai, explaining that they did not need to bring their cattle there and were, in any case, prohibited from doing so by colonial restrictions. When asked if she had had any trouble living as a Kikuyu in Maasai, she replied: 'Which Kikuyu? We were not Kikuyu. We were Maasai.'

Kikuyu wives were not common in Keekonyokie, however; she could only name seven others, all married early in the century. Family surveys carried out on the residents of two recent Keekonyokie ceremonial villages illustrate the rarity of marriage to non-Maasai or even non-Keekonyokie women within this group today. In one survey of 45 male-headed households only fourteen non-Keekonyokie wives were recorded (four Purko, two Loodokilani, and eight other Maasai) while in the other, only one half-Kikuyu, one Samburu, and two Purko wives were noted.[12]

Thus, while Maasai frequently sought refuge with Kikuyu during famines in the past, settling among families with whom they had ties, they tended to return to their home country and to pastoralism as soon as conditions permitted, a trend noted elsewhere among Samburu and Dassanetch (Sobania, 1991). Temporary co-residence in Kikuyu did not usually imply any long-term shifts in subsistence practice, language, or culture. Some form of bilingualism usually developed, but the tendency was for others to learn Maa, and there was a strong tendency for Maasai to insist that their children be raised in their own language, even at Ngong where the Kiyuku presence was so pervasive.[13]

Maasai with Kikuyu relatives need to be distinguished from the relatively well-defined group of Narok Nusui, who represent not simply the children of Maasai and Kikuyu but bilingual bicultural families and individuals, now distanced from the pastoral economy, who participate in education, farming, trade, and land acquisition much more frequently than pastoral Maasai. While cultivation is practised elsewhere throughout Narok District, it is often done by non-Maasai, on their own, as wives, or as employees of Maasai. Those Maasai who cultivate tend to do so only sporadically. Oloomocheene built a water tank and created a small irrigated shamba on his ranch at Oloishoibor as part of his family's self-conscious strategy to modernize themselves in accord with their Christian beliefs, but, when the crops did not do well and the water tank sprang a leak, they ceased cultivating.

The recent movement of Kikuyu into Keekonyokie is only the latest stage in the historical expansion of Kikuyu southward from Kiambu. Whereas Kikuyu initially sought trading partners and the use of cultivable land, they now seek to purchase land under individual title, often for speculation or collateral for loans. Little of this land has been occupied or cultivated, and Maasai continue to use it for pastoralism. Indeed, there is a tendency for Maasai to move back into regions of the Rift Valley lost to white settlement long ago and subsequently occupied by Kikuyu, since these regions have proven relatively unproductive for agriculture. Many of these changes have increased the residential proximity of Maasai and Kikuyu, especially in Nairragie Enkare, but have not in general altered the ethnic boundary, marked by language and subsistence orientation, between them.[14]

In short, the ethnic boundary between the Maasai and Kikuyu is not 'fluid' and permeable, but is 'negotiable', as the two communities are selectively linked with one another during a period of regional change.

Conclusion: Shifting Boundaries, Boundary Shifters

This essay has presented case material that illustrates the complex social relations between, and nominal identities of, diverse communities in Maasailand. Given the social and economic variation of the history and the contemporary situation of Maa-speakers in Kenya and Tanzania, we have seen how attributions of identity have served as strategies of exclusion and inclusion in particular contexts. These 'variations on a Maasai pastoral theme' considered the status of Maa-speaking pastoralists (Siria and Parakuyo) and cultivators (Arusha) as well as that of communities who do not speak Maa as their first language, the non-pastoral cultivators (Kikuyu) and often bilingual Okiek hunters (Torrobo). The material reviewed here has considered the process by which members of these groups have negotiated their identities with members of various Maasai pastoral communities, Siria with Loitai, Torrobo with Purko and Loitai, Kikuyu with Keekonyokie, Arusha with Kisongo.

While not untouched by the spread of mercantile relations during the pre-colonial period, or with the inexorable commercialization of the regional economy in this century, the ethnic and cultural configuration of the Rift Valley region is clearly the outcome of a local dialectic, of economic specializations strengthened through reciprocal trade and social exchange. From one point of view, pastoral value and Maasai regional political dominance provided an encompassing framework of hierarchy within which other groups were ideologically arrayed and socially and economically interrelated. But if hierarchy characterizes the linkages within a regional subsistence triangle (Galaty 1982a; Waller 1985b), between Maasai pastoralists, Bantu and Arusha cultivators, and Torrobo hunter-gatherers, how can we characterize the ties of Maasai and other Maa-speaking pastoralists?

For an earlier epoch, it is quite likely that Maasai perceived such groups as Loogolala, Parakuyo, Uasin Gishu, and Laikipiak, as honourable pastoral 'others', comparable to but even closer than their *Ilmang'ati* 'enemies', the Tatog. Prior to the nineteenth century, each

Maa-speaking group very likely exercised comparable influence over their respective corners of the Rift Valley. What is intriguing is the tendency of Maasai in the nineteenth century, in the wake of conflict and strife, increasingly to define their enemies in pejorative terms, as their own regional dominance grew. The symmetry of Maasai and 'Kwavi', expressed in mid-century by Krapf, had become a definite asymmetry of victors and vanquished by the 1880s, Kwavi assuming a new connotation of 'farmer', given that many pastoralists took up cultivation — often temporarily — in the wake of defeat. In the twentieth century, the only nominal marker of pastoral status remaining was that of Maasai identity, thus accounting for the spread of that usage up to the present day.

It is clear that 'ethnicity', if we can apply the term to these diverse dimensions of identity, is not static, either in its form or content, but undergoes historical change and demonstrates variation between contexts. The powerful engine of Maasai assimilation lies in a process of attribution, which is simply the most visible and convincing aspect of shifting identity, summing up diverse changes in residence, labour, language competence, ritual participation, marriage and affinity, and social affiliation. At the same time, however, the compelling nature of 'ethnic' identity stems in large part from the stability, continuity and even inevitability its ideology conveys.

This account has reviewed at least three senses of ethnic 'shifting', each of which involves both change and persistence in the content of Maasai identity. The first type of 'shifting' is between different uses of ethnic labels, to convey different senses in different contexts ('I am Kikuyu; we are Maasai').

The second is the shift of people across recognized ethnic boundaries, often through marriage (like the Kikuyu and Arusha women). In the first generation, however, such shifts are often seen as short-term straddling. W.H. Auden recently commented:

> Though I've lived more than half my life in the States, am an American citizen . . . I cannot, of course, call myself an American. I do, however, think of myself as a New Yorker.[15]

One could paraphrase the life story of the Kikuyu woman in very similar terms: 'Though I've lived most of my life in Keekonyokie, am accepted by and have given birth to Maasai, and am a citizen of Maasailand, I cannot, of course, call myself a Maasai. I do, however, think of my rightful home as Ewuaso Enkidong.' Only in the second generation, after having been born and raised in a given place, will people claim unqualified identity, although they may still retain alternate claims ('We still have land among the Meru', or 'my father still has cattle among the Purko') and may still be subject to contextualized and pejorative exclusion ('After all, he is just a Kikuyu anyway').

The third is the long-term 'shift' of Maasai boundaries and pastoralism through expansion, of a people, a language, or a practice.

Intensive intermarriage or co-residence may, in fact, produce a new interstitial and often bilingual and bicultural ethnic category with stability over several generations: the Gira between the Turkana and Samburu, the Nusui of Narok, or the Ariaal, who inhabit the cultural, geographical and economic space between Rendille and Samburu (Spencer, 1973; Fratkin, 1987a and this volume).

Ethnic shifting is unsettling, for external observers and cultural participants alike, because it appears to contradict our often unspoken assumptions regarding ethnic continuity. But the material presented here clearly demonstrates that the articulation of ethnic groups does not necessarily entail ethnic fusion (or confusion). Ethnic shifting may, in fact, represent a coherent cultural process of managing long-term intergroup relationships and the negotiation of ethnic boundaries is a way of defending and reproducing, not obscuring or erasing, lines of demarcation between communities. The way Maasai identity is defined and transformed is not unique, although it appears startlingly complex given the naive simplicity of folklore concerning their pastoral identity. The interplay of linguistic, cultural and economic symbolism; the existence of boundaries marking distinctions of honour, status and class; and the negotiation of identity between distinct groups joined through affinity and co-residence may be quite general phenomena in the construction of identities and the creation of communities. Where Maasai experience may be noteworthy is in the emergence of a strongly pronounced sense of personhood and group character which has been historically strengthened rather than weakened as the group has served as an ethnic vortex, providing itself with recourse in times of stress by pulling neighbouring people into an orbit and, selectively, defining them as 'Maasai'.

Notes

* This essay benefited from research carried out in 1974–75 with the support of the National Science Foundation and in 1983–90 with the support of the Social Science and Humanities Research Council of Canada, the FCAR of Quebec and the International Development Research Centre. For assistance in carrying out the research, I am indebted to the late Mosinko Ole Tumanka, Jeremiah Ole Tumanka, and Rueben Ole Kuney, and for research affiliation to the Bureau of Educational Research in Kenya and the Rural Development Training Centre in Monduli, Tanzania.

1. For more elaboration of how the linguistic notion of a 'shifter' can be applied to the problem of ethnicity, see Galaty (1982a). The concept of a 'shifter' will be somewhat widened in this paper to include the social outcomes of the cultural process of 'indexing' relations, that is, 'shifting' of individuals or groups over a boundary, and the shifting of a boundary.

2. One merit of Comaroff's account is that it overcomes the classical debate over whether class or ethnicity is more fundamental, yet avoids the pat solutions that ethnic consciousness is either reactionary, or simply an expression of class differences. My point is that the use of economic signifiers to define and 'naturalize' social differences may be even more widespread than we have realized, appearing in such diverse forms as the beliefs that small-scale 'totemic' groups are internally related to subsistence

pursuits, and that people 'belong' in the classes in which they find themselves in complex societies.

3. The latter two forms of shifting resemble the two basic types of population movement described by Turton (1991: 161), involving gradual infiltration of a population across a stable boundary, or the concerted occupation of a region by a group, resulting in the boundary shift. The chapter on the 'Maasai Expansion' in this volume discusses these types of movement at greater length.

4. *Iloikop* (*Oloikopani*, sing.) further signifies the 'murderers' and the murdered ones. It remains unclear whether the term derives from the *En-kop* stem or to the term *Il-oik*, signifying not only 'bones' but the guilt and taboo incurred when one breaks another's bones, for which compensation also must be paid (Galaty, 1977a: 40).

5. Interview with Ole Madala, Ole Kanoi, and Ole Tumanka at Olmotonyi, January 1988. In his detailed account of the trans-Mara Maasai, Waller (1984: 247) notes that the 'Kaputie' who were integrated into the Siria were 'almost certainly Iloogolala, Maa-speaking refugees from the wars of the 1840s and 1850s' and their *loibon* Koikoti ole Tunai. See also Berntsen, 1979a.

6. Interview with P. Moreto, Kambala, Moroguro, August 1985 during FAO Livestock Project Development Mission to Tanzania.

7. Note, however, the different interpretation of Kisongo–Arusha relations from an Arusha perspective, stressing complementarity rather than dominance, in Spear, 'Being Maasai', this volume (eds).

8. The survey of Emairete was carried out by Athumani Ally, that of Enguiki by George Lowassa, both in November 1989.

9. I purposely use the somewhat pejorative Maasai term *Il-torrobo*, a term for 'poor people' elevated to a class label, rather than the term Okiek, which highland hunting people who speak an Eastern Kalenjin dialect apply to themselves. The Maasai term applies not only to those people who are either monolingual or bilingual Maa-speakers and live close to Maasai, but also to the larger group of Kalenjin-speaking Okiek. My aim here is to give an account of social and conceptual boundaries of identity essentially from a Maasai point of view. For the Okiek perspective, see Kratz, 1987, 1990; and Klumpp and Kratz, this volume.

10. Interviews in Kisokon (Loitai) and Leshuta (Purko), Narok District, 1975. For an elaboration of Maasai ideology regarding Torrobo, see Galaty, 1986.

11. Interview with the wife of Ole Karriaki and M. Ole Tumanka, Ewuaso Enkidong', Keekonyokie, September 1988.

12. The *enkipaata* survey was carried out in February 1990 by J. Ole Tumanka; the *olngesher* survey in June 1989 by M. Ole Tumanka. Two possible factors which may have biased the surveys should be noted: (a) The possible tendency of men not to report non-Maasai wives, but, since the clan and sub-clan of each wife's father was given, hiding a wife's origin would have required more subterfuge than simply omitting to mention the fact. (b) The possible tendency of men married to non-Maasai wives to be overlooked or even excluded from participation in the two ceremonies, thus making such a survey unrepresentative of the section as a whole.

I believe this might have occurred, as many men married outside Keekonyokie had already distanced themselves from intense involvement in the local age-sets. Thus the survey can not be used as evidence that intermarriage is limited throughout Keekonyokie society (a conclusion that could only be made on the basis of a random sample), but only that those men at the centre of ceremonial life tend strongly to seek mates first from their home area, secondly from their section, and finally from other sections, especially Purko, with whom Keekonyokie have been traditionally allied.

13. Justin Lemenye (1955–56: 53) reported in his autobiography that a 'Kwavi' who had settled in Taveta after being defeated by Kisongo told him: 'We were not prevented from following our own customs . . . Our warriors danced their own dances and the Taveta came and joined in . . . The Taveta requested that their children should join in our circumcision ceremonies.' He also noted that the Chaga chief, Mandara, knew the Maa language (*ibid.*: 44).

14. My interpretation here, stressing the apparently fluid ways people live and meld together while maintaining a sense of identity and continuing subtly to demarcate ethnic boundaries, contrasts with those of Waller and Campbell (this volume), who see a general hardening of ethnic boundaries as a result of increased Kikuyu immigration over the course of this century, especially since the 1960s.
15. *New Yorker*, September 10, 1990: 104.

Ten

Aesthetics, Expertise, & Ethnicity

Okiek & Maasai
Perspectives on Personal Ornament[1]

DONNA KLUMPP & CORINNE KRATZ

'If Kopot Edina gets dressed up with beads, you'd think she was Maasai.'
'Who [in the picture] is Kopot Edina?'
'This one.'
'You can't see clearly that this is Kopot Edina.'
'You'd think it's a young Maasai woman.'

This snatch of conversation comes from commentary made by Kaplelach and Kipchornwonek Okiek as they looked at pictures of themselves.[2] Had a Maasai woman been present to view the pictures, her remarks might have been quite different. Instead, she might have picked out what she would regard as glaring errors and inconsistencies in the way the lovely young Okiot woman was dressed as she came out of seclusion after initiation.

The central purpose of this paper is to consider processes through which ethnic identity is claimed, advertised, and negotiated by looking closely at a key visual index of ethnicity in eastern Africa, beaded personal ornament. Personal ornament provides a prominent example of the way people can constitute a common ground of understanding and identity through a set of signs with general similarities of both form and function, and yet simultaneously differentiate among those who use the common signs. The distinctions they emphasize can be formal, functional, and/or evaluative.

The young Okiot woman in the picture, for instance, wears a necklace that a Maasai woman would see as incongruous because *her* understanding is that it is worn only on or after a woman's wedding day. Okiek wear the same ornament, but have a broader definition of when it is appropriate. Details of the young woman's ornaments show similar disjunctions between Okiek and Maasai understandings of acceptable aesthetic form, but only Maasai condemn them because the differences offend only their sensibilities. Maasai-like ornaments are recontextualized and redefined in Okiek practice, incorporated into Okiek understandings and evaluations. Yet they are similar enough to those of Maasai that they can also be perceived and evaluated through Maasai understandings. In that case, differences Okiek introduce are often regarded as flaws.

Okiek hunters and honey-gatherers and Maasai pastoralists have lived in adjacent areas in Kenya for at least several centuries. Throughout that time, they have been interacting with each other in various ways, and with varying degrees of intensity at different times of the year, and under different historical and personal circumstances. The highland forests of the Mau Escarpment are the heartland of Kalenjin-speaking Okiek, while Maasai stay mainly on the more open, bordering savannah. Their seasonal movements and patterns of land use in the past over-lapped chiefly in the forest fringes, where Maasai grazed herds in the dry season and Okiek hunted large animals and collected honey from the flowerings of lower-altitude trees. Of course, visits and other meetings could and do take place at any time of year.

The complementarity of Okiek and Maasai productive activities, as practised in distinctive, adjacent ecological zones, figures prominently both in their own views of their interrelations and in scholarly discussions of Okiek and Maasai identities, placing them within a larger, regional perspective in both cases. Agreement on basic economic and ecological particulars of the situation, however, does not constitute consensus on how those distinctions are understood, valued, and experienced or on how such values are embodied, created, represented, and transformed in daily life.

For instance, Okiek and pastoral Maasai create and wear beaded ornaments which are in many ways very similar; other agro-pastoral Maasai and people of other ethnic groups also make and wear ornaments of related style and design. From the pastoral Maasai perspective, however, other groups modify the forms and uses of ornament in ways that show their inferiority just as much as their deviance in practice from the pastoral ideal. Indeed, to Maasai the two are interlinked. Aesthetics and expertise in beadwork, pastoral production, and ethnicity are all bound together in the Maasai self-image of domineeringly ideal perfection. However, Okiek understandings and evaluations of design and aesthetics in beaded ornament and their own ways of using ornaments present an alternative reinterpretation which deflates and counters Maasai cultural hegemony.

Maasai innovations in beadwork are creative variations within their aesthetic bounds, while Okiek also introduce variations which question those very boundaries, broadening strictly defined Maasai patterns of colour, design, composition, and use. They simultaneously follow the rules in general and break them in detail. These playful-seeming twists demonstrate the arbitrariness of aesthetic boundaries and thereby question the superiority presumably correlated with them as well. Okiek consider their ornaments beautiful, but Maasai find some of them unacceptable, ugly, or peculiar, though very close to their own. Is it surprising that they deny the beauty of variations that simultaneously undermine the supremacy they assert?

There are several important reasons for considering questions of ethnicity through Maasai and Okiek beadwork.[3] First, there is a widely recognized shift in the nature and significance of ethnic boundaries in East Africa beginning around the late nineteenth century. Ethnic boundaries began to harden, become more exclusive, and be politicized in a different way, with different implications (Lamphear, Waller, this volume). The introduction of great quantities of coloured trade goods, especially cloth and glass beads, coincided with this shift. Beads, cloth and cheap aniline dyes brought about a revolution in East African art which developed in conjunction with the new politics of ethnicity. Colour preferences and designs became highly visible resources for advertising hardening ethnic distinctions within a broadly shared cultural understanding of the body (i.e. appropriately clothed and decorated). They became a critical visual idiom for claims about and shifts in ethnic identity.

Second, those who were making those colourful claims and engineering those visual shifts were the beadworkers: women. The inclusion of Maasai and Okiek women in particular as creative actors in the calculus of ethnicity is long overdue. Previous studies of Maasai ethnicity concentrate on domains of male activity and interests, conveying the implicit impression that women are subsumed as well, with their conceptions of identity shaped only by the same interests and interactions. Women's influences and perspectives on ethnicity have yet to be factored in. We elaborate on this matter below.

Third, the inescapable fact of individual design and creation of ornaments brings the personal side of ethnicity to mind as well as the role of individuals as agents in the negotiations and interactions through which ethnicity is constituted. 'As implemented by the historic subject, the conventional value of the sign acquires an intentional value, and the conceptual sense an actionable reference' (Sahlins, 1981: 69). The negotiated aspect of ethnicity is a major focus of other papers in this volume, but the ways in which ethnicity is also always a personal reinterpretation sometimes slips from view.

Finally, questions of ethnicity and identity are refocused in certain ways as a result of combining this female- and agency-oriented perspective with the study of ethnic identity through visual, material media, a combination which is unavoidable in focusing on Maasai and Okiek personal ornament. A number of assumptions which underlie standard discussions of ethnicity thus emerge as not only questionable, but perhaps objectionable.

Being Maasai

Understanding Identity: Perspective, Personal Experience, and Effect

Scholarly discussions of ethnicity in areas where Maasai live and interact with others have followed pastoral Maasai interpretations in the main, whether they look at relations with Okiek or those with other Maasai groups who combine agricultural and pastoral pursuits (cf. Spear, this volume). They thus emphasize the superiority Maasai attribute to the ideal of a purely pastoral way of life, and the pollution, inferiority, and moral deficiency associated with non-pastoral Maasai and non-Maasai, including those Maasai categorize as *il Torrobo*, such as Okiek (Galaty, 1977a, 1982; Jacobs, 1965; Klumpp, 1987). These attitudes also informed early ethnographic and historical reports on the Okiek (usually under the name Dorobo) in which they were characterized as Maasai 'serfs', or as degenerate Maasai who had lost their cattle and gone to the bush. This answer to the question of Okiek origins thus dismissed their viability as an ethnic group with an identity and history different from that of Maasai, following Maasai categories which construct an *il Torrobo* 'Other' (cf. Kenny, 1981).

The few scholars who have studied Okiek culture over the years insist that, contrary to Maasai assertions, Okiek are *not* Maasai and do not see themselves as such (Huntingford, 1929, 1931; Blackburn, 1974, 1982; Kratz, 1980, 1986, 1988b). Alternative answers to the question of Okiek 'origins' suppose them to be either autochthonous residents of the region who later adopted Kalenjin speech or else a very early group of Southern Nilotic-speaking immigrants. The question may never be resolved, but both of these answers recognize cultural and historical differences between Maasai and Okiek as well as certain cultural and linguistic affinities among the diverse Okiek groups. Approaches which emphasize different perspectives — Maasai or Okiek — may also reflect a collapsing of historical and geographic variation in relations between pastoralists and hunters (not all Okiek) (Waller, 1985b: 128–133). Okiek themselves discuss their long history of Maasai interaction with ambivalence, sometimes stressing the length of individual friendships, and sometimes the antagonism with their 'enemies' (*puunik*), the Ikwopik,[4] as Okiek call Maasai (cf. Galaty, 1977b).

However, recent scholars of Maasai and Okiek ethnicity all stress the intrinsic negotiability and permeability of ethnic categories, a critically important insight which developed out of earlier work on cultural identity (e.g. Leach, 1954; Barth, 1969).[5] Some Okiek certainly have 'become Maasai', e.g. Okiek women who were given to Maasai in marriage and stayed there, along with their offspring and some male relatives with cattle who went to reside with Maasai affines. Similarly, some Okiek groups who now live in the midst of Maasai, such as Omotik, may have become culturally closer to Maasai at this point in time than to their Okiek kin on the Mau. Most Okiek live among other Okiek, interacting with Maasai only on occasions that bring them together with their neighbours. Nonetheless, some of them find it easier in certain circumstances to temporarily 'pass as Maasai' (or as Kipsigis), e.g. in towns where they can 'blend in' with the more numerous Maasai crowd, and where Maa is a lingua franca.

While the majority of Okiek[6] share some outward signs of Maasai identity with their pastoral neighbours and participate in common social organizations with them in certain ways, those signs and social memberships are simply part of a wider set of cultural options, with a significance quite different from that understood by Maasai. Whatever the outward sign — be it language, costume, social membership, song, beadwork, or whatever — it is recontextualized as it becomes part of Okiek practice. This means it is open to reinterpretation as it becomes part of another people's history and modes of expression, understood within the values and interests that inform their lives rather than Maasai ones.

For instance, most Kaplelach and most older Kipchornwonek are multilingual, with some ability in Maa in addition to Okiek, their own home language. Yet Okiek uses of Maa are not limited to encounters with Maasai neighbours, or to situations which call for Maa as a lingua franca in the area (cf. Fratkin, this volume). The language also becomes part of the linguistic and cultural repertoire through which Okiek create and express aspects of personal and cultural identity among themselves through code-switching, lexical borrowing, and alternations (Kratz, 1986). Distinctions of linguistic repertoire within the Okiek population are part of these indexical processes as much as they are a product of varying Okiek histories of Maasai interaction.

The same Okiek can also name their clan affiliation, in many cases a clan found among Maasai. But, among Okiek themslves, clanship is a virtually irrelevant social category. It is evoked chiefly when seeking a relationship with someone (usually not an Okiot) who cannot be related in another, closer and more fundamental way. For Kaplelach and Kipchornwonek Okiek, then, clan membership is a contextually useful (at least potentially) but minimally applicable affiliation. These patterns of linguistic and social extension were common long before Okiek began to farm and acquire livestock. Participating in certain ways in social institutions which are critical to Maasai pastoral production does not mean joining the cattle-centred mode of production.

For their part, Maasai have virtually no reason to 'pass' as Okiek or Torrobo, but they have sometimes relied on Okiek communities in times of hunger. Maasai who 'become Torrobo' in this way, however, most often do so on as temporary a basis as possible. Moreover, while they may 'become Torrobo' (i.e. poor Maasai without livestock, relying on non-pastoral foods), they do not 'become Okiek', learning neither to speak Okiek, nor to make beehives, climb trees etc.[7] This uneven directionality is duplicated in Okiek–Maasai intermarriage. Maasai take

Okiek women, but they give their women to Okiek only in exceedingly rare circumstances.

This directional imbalance has been coupled with the persuasively insistent Maasai assurance of their intrinsic superiority to produce the curious assumption which seems to lie behind some discussions of ethnic identity: that Okiek (or others) would really like to be Maasai. 'Impressed by' aspects of Maasai life, they somehow decide their own life and traditions are as worthless as Maasai believe and switch over to the better brand of culture. No one would like to recognize themselves in this caricatured overstatement of peculiarly motivated change of ethnic affiliation, but in more subtle ways the attitude informs the language and rhetoric of many analyses.

The objections to it are two-fold. First and most obviously, it endorses and authorizes one perspective over others within a multi-ethnic setting. Maasai might indeed enjoy overt social and cultural dominance in a region, but their interpretation of the situation is not necessarily shared by others, even if they participate in and perpetuate the dominance in various ways. Furthermore, the other, ignored interpretations may counter and contradict the supposed superiority of the chosen perspective. As Said comments on Orientalist attitudes: 'imaginative geography of the "our land–barbarian land" variety does not require that the barbarians acknowledge the distinction' (1979: 54).

Second and more insidiously, the assumption often appears in tandem with a notion of cultural identity that remains essentialist in its dynamics despite avowed appreciation of the negotiability of ethnic categories. Thus, movement between ethnic groups may be recognized and stressed, yet ethnic affiliations and shifts are often attributed with the help of a list of cultural features — such as language, clan, age-set membership, and costume — which are themselves treated as givens, in essentialist terms. The overall picture of negotiated shift is treated as smaller shifts between essential elements which are identifiable, unshaded, undifferentiated, and in some sense unchanging.

In terms of costume, for instance, the many peoples who have adopted general Maa beadwork styles would be treated as having a Maasai costume feature as part of their identity and affiliation. Negotiations, shifts, and restatements within the media of costume are invisible under this treatment. Also hidden are processes through which people negotiate distance and closeness to their neighbours without making relatively clearcut ethnic switches. We have already pointed out parallel difficulties that arise when similar assumptions about language ability vs language use or about clan membership are made.

From the way ethnic identity is often discussed, people would seem to change identities like chameleons or lizards shedding old skins. An important question, rarely asked, instantly qualifies this outlook: what remains if someone changes ethnic affiliation? The fluidity and interpenetration of both ethnic categories and characteristics return clearly to view. Changes of ethnicity appear less as total transformations than as new orientations, redefinitions of social networks, and shifts in the relevance and priorities of issues and values.

No matter what the reason for a change of ethnic identity, the result is an expansion of cultural and social resources to be minimized, maximized, indexed, or downplayed according to circumstances. Former networks, relations, orientations, and values remain both as mobilizable potential and as personal history and identity (cf. Waller, this volume). The more personal sense of lived ethnicity that emerges from this perspective emphasizes the interplay between 'cultural features' as resources which mark identity in a gross sense and the ways they affect and are affected by individuals and their choices, actions, and decisions.[8]

This more elusive realm of shifting social networks and shades of emphasis can be posed in terms of ornament as well. Does an Okiot woman marrying into a Maasai family immediately abandon her Okiek ornaments and adopt unaccented Maasai ones? Such stylistic processes have yet to be documented, but it is likely that her beadworking style changes over time as she is incorporated into the community and experiences a corresponding fashion reorientation. The complexity of aesthetic rules in Maasai beadwork composition, outlined in the next section, is enough to suggest that instantaneous reorientation is unlikely.

Interethnic marriage is an example that also raises other important questions, directing our discussion of perspective, personal experience, and individual effect in ethnic identity to gender. Did the Okiot woman go to her Maasai husband gladly or forcibly, with the blessing of her whole family, or with dissension in the ranks? How do these different scenarios shape interethnic affinal relations and ethnic identity over time? Most previous discussions of Maasai interethnic shifts, mixtures, and exchanges concentrate on male-dominated economic and political pursuits such as cattle- and camel-keeping, integration and fragmentation due to military encounters, or reorganization and adoption of social groups of male membership, such as age-sets.[9] Women's places in these accounts have largely reproduced one kind of Maasai representation of women — as a human equivalent of cattle and another important sign of men's wealth and status (e.g. Spencer, 1988). Llewelyn-Davis (1981) shows that there are other viewpoints, such as female manager of a household of children competing with others, respected mother-in-law, or female 'owner of the village', rich in progeny, but these viewpoints are not taken up.

Thus, women and their children are captured in war, or they serve as hooks into other communities through marriage out (cf. stock partnerships) or as magnets to bring others in, also through marriage. The experiences of those women and their other effects receive no further comment. Yet the role of women as crucial cultural transmitters, conservators, and creators is well documented in matters of language, oral tradition, and stylistic form and design of material culture — all important resources in defining cultural identity (Herbich, 1987, 1989; Klumpp, 1981; Labov, 1973; Roe, 1980; Sakata, 1987; Sherzer and Sherzer, 1976).

Created entirely by women and worn mostly by women, personal ornament makes one final and public statement of ethnicity in areas of Maasai influence, regardless of what kind of animals a man keeps, who his wife is, or who won the last battle. Beadwork is a Maasai woman's personal wealth, comparable in many ways to a man's cattle (Klumpp, 1987: 107–113).[10] Like cattle, beaded ornaments also become pawns in sociopolitical relations (often domestic politics, and by implication affinal politics).[11] They are material signs of personal involvement and relations, of ceremonial occasion, and above all of personal and social identity of various kinds. For instance, women's stylistic innovations in beadwork are distinctive markers of successive male age-sets; wearing the appropriate ornaments is one way to claim and demonstrate age-set membership for men and elective affinity for women.[12]

But we are not using ornaments here as a way to concentrate exclusively on female domains of exchange, value, and wealth or on how they are involved in the representations and negotiations of Maasai and Okiek gender relations, as the ever-growing literature on 'women's things' pioneered by Weiner (1976) commonly does. Rather, we are looking at the important roles and effects of women on the signs and collective understandings of ethnic identity in many different domains of Maasai and Okiek life, for men and women alike (cf. Strathern, 1981). Our focus on beadwork helps emphasize these roles and effects because of the visibility of ornaments as material objects and because of their personal nature as individual body ornament.

Whether Maasai ethnicity is seen as a question of identity, of politics, of aesthetics, or of survival, beadwork is part of the process. Ethnic groups on the social periphery of pastoral Maasai all seem heavily influenced by the visual persuasiveness of Maasai colour and ornamental codes.[13] Yet their 'naive' adoption of these codes, as well as their integration of their own codes with Maasai ones, serves to advertise and reinforce ethnic distinction through nuances of personal appearance.

What does this mean in concrete and specific terms? When Maasai Nairurari sits with her tin of multicoloured beads on the savannah to make an ornament for her son, Lerionka, how does she decide what to make, how to start, which colour of bead is followed with which? How do Nairurari's choices and artful products differ from those of Niniye, her Okiot counterpart in the forest? How does each create the signs of her ethnicity (and those of the men whose ornaments she makes) from the range of materials and techniques at her disposal? And how does each view her own results and those of the other in the larger cultural dialogue?

Manifesting Identity: Common Yet Distinctive Codes of Costume

Certain common parameters constitute a broadly shared code of costume and personal decoration within Eastern Africa, where the human body is the primary medium of concrete aesthetic expression. Within a basic shared body profile and set of material resources, however, differences of technique, composition, colour preference and combination, motif, and ornament type and elaboration can simultaneously mark distinctions of ethnic group, sex, age grade, age-set, region, ceremonial status, aesthetic canon, and personal preference.

There is a general Kenyan costume 'type', what the fashion industry would call 'the East African silhouette'. A composition of costume and ornaments of generally similar shape, with ornamental foci and emphases in the same areas of the body, the silhouette is a basic visual and structural ideal shared across ethnic groups (see Figure 10.1). Starting from the top down, the East African silhouette consists of a short projection centred at the top of the head, earrings in the upper and extended lower ears, and a concentration of ornaments at the neck. For men, neck ornaments tend to be relatively small and reserved. For women they are more voluminous, either flat or dishlike, radiating out toward the shoulders or ballooning between ears and shoulders. Upper and lower arms, waist, calves, and ankles are other points of ornament, in some cases as accents and in others as focal points.

The uniquely Maa silhouette is an elaboration of the basic East African silhouette. They follow the same basic arrangement, but Maasai wear more, bigger, brighter, and freer ornaments. Okiek contiguous to Maasai conform to the Maa silhouette. In addition to creating for themselves a profile indistinguishable from that of Maasai, Okiek design and construct their ornaments like Maasai ones, resulting in an ornament assemblage that seems identical to outside observers.

Okiek and Maasai use many of the same materials as other ethnic groups: glass beads imported from Czechoslovakia, chains, wire, leather, rubber, plastic sheet, a variety of metal dangles and recycled pins, zippers and buttons, and thread of sinew, sisal, plastic or nylon. Different ethnic groups are distinguished, however, by techniques they favour as well as by their choices among available materials.

For instance, Bantu-speakers to the east of Maasailand (Kamba, Taita, Taveta) and ethnic groups living on the coast use conus shell discs, foreign to Maasai-style beadwork. That distinctive material is only one characteristic that sets their beadwork apart, along with technique, colour choices and combinations, motif and composition. Instead of constructing their ornaments with wirework, they use satin stitch to embroider large areas of skin or cloth solidly with beads or make tight networks or twined gridwork on a loose hanging warp. They sometimes

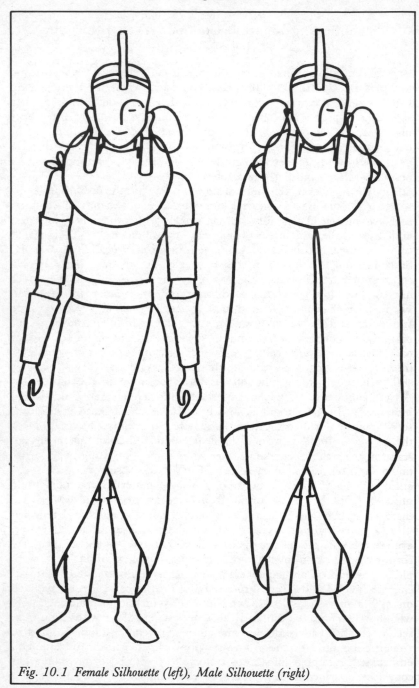

Fig. 10.1 *Female Silhouette (left), Male Silhouette (right)*

make patterns with no 'cuts', essential dividers in Maasai pattern. Geometric figures floating on white grounds or covering large areas in repetition are also non-Maasai features in the beadwork patterns of these groups.

In comparison with such numerous discontinuities of technology, material, form, pattern, and colour, beadworking differences among various Maasai groups and between Okiek and Maasai are relatively minor. Maasai and Okiek both construct beaded ornaments using stringing, sewing, wrapping, and wirework techniques.[14] The differences lie chiefly in their use of colour, in the composition of individual ornaments, and in the composition and balance of ornament combinations on the body. These are also important areas of difference in the beadwork of other peoples who have come under Maasai stylistic influence.

As Kenyan ethnic groups elaborated and developed their nineteenth-century colour codes from a common tricolour foundation of red, white, and black to the more diverse twentieth-century systems with brightly coloured glass beads, certain colours and colour combinations became diagnostic indices within the ethnic groups who share beadworking techniques with Maasai. Pink, for example, is characteristic of Kikuyu ornaments, while turquoise beads are a good sign that a Kipsigis or Nandi woman made a particular necklace or beaded leather skirt. Individual colours become diagnostic when used chiefly by a single ethnic group. But in each case the colour is part of a general colour code and aesthetic which delimits the full palette normally used (including colours used by many other ethnic groups) and how they should be combined and composed in ornaments.

Colour is a crucial factor in defining Maasai ornaments, though no individual colour instantly indicates Maasai-ness. Well-defined colour sets and rules of colour order and balance, however, are cultural means through which a woman demonstrates understanding (or misunderstanding or disregard) of Maasai aesthetics. By implication, she simultaneously demonstrates her understanding of Maasai culture and her ethnicity through her use of colour in beadwork. Maasai share certain motifs and patterns structured by colours with other ethnic groups, but they are 'spoken' by Maasai and by Okiek alike with a Maa 'accent'.[15]

The basic precept of Maasai colour organization is 'to catch the eye', i.e. to maximize visual impact by juxtaposing colours of maximum contrast and complement. Black/white is the most contrasting and complementary of colour pairs. The original red–white–black colour set, called *narok* (black) and still one basis of ornament design, capitalizes on this. *Narok* stands for *Enkai Narok*, the black aspect of God. As a whole, the colour set counts as the black member of a pair of colour sets that replicates the black/white contrast.

The most important and strongest contemporary Maasai colour set embellishes the red–white–black triad by dividing the end colours into complementary pairs: red–green–white–orange–blue.[16] This quintet is one of two colour sets called 'beautiful colours' (*muain sidain*). The other set of 'beautiful colours' is a compositional counterpoint to the first, restating it with yellow for green and black for blue: yellow–red–white–black–orange. Each is considered equivalent to white when taken as a whole in the composition of ornaments and ensembles on the body, appearing in opposition and complement to the *narok* colour set. However, the two sets of 'beautiful colours' are used very differently. The final contemporary Maasai colour set, red–yellow–black, is based on blanket patterns and the colours of the national flag. It was developed relatively recently, and at least in part in response to a shortage of white seed beads in the early 1980s.

Taken together, the four colour sets delimit both the range and orderings of colours which are aesthetically acceptable. Women incorporate these ordered colour sets into the design of individual ornaments in many ways, according to other structural and aesthetic conventions. The precept 'to catch the eye', however, carries beyond individual ornaments to define criteria of acceptable and pleasing combinations in the way ornaments are worn. At this level of ensemble composition, definitions of entire colour sets as 'black' or 'white' are most relevant.

Thus, ornaments made with the first set, considered 'black' (*narok*), can stand alone in an ornament but must be balanced on the body with ornaments of the first 'white' set of 'beautiful colours'. Ornaments made with the first set of 'beautiful colours' must include that full set in order and be accented and balanced with ornaments made with the 'black' set. This creates an overall black/white combination. These 'beautiful colours' cannot stand alone in an ornament either, but must be completed with at least a small component of the *narok* set. Ornaments with the other set of 'beautiful colours' must be accompanied by one or both of the first two. The last set can stand alone in one ornament, but must be balanced on the body by another ornament of either the first or second set.

The composition of ornaments and their placement on the body is based on the symmetrical alternation of 'black' and 'white'. If a woman wears a red–white–black bangle on one wrist, for instance, she must wear a green–red–white–blue–orange bangle on the other. Upper and lower arm alternate with each other and with the opposite arm. Ankles alternate with each other and also with the wrists. Ears alternate with each other and can also alternate with arms and legs. All of this means that even if a non-Maasai woman successfully reproduces Maasai colour combinations and patterns in her ornaments, the way she chooses to wear them can still manifest a non-Maasai aesthetic.

These same rules of combination concerning colour sets apply to the composition of individual ornaments. There they are commonly realized with the most important and ubiquitous of motifs in Maasai art, the cut.[17] Visually a cut is an interruption, termination, or enclosure of a field of contrasting colour. Maasai cuts are always constructed of colours that are complementary or contrasting to the colours being separated or framed. For example, Purko women use red–white–black cuts to divide and border an ornament with fields of colour drawn from a set of 'beautiful colours', thus also incorporating the necessary combination of colour sets.

The cut is universal in the ornament of Bantu- and Nilotic-speaking peoples of Kenya, although some ethnic groups also use ornaments without cuts (e.g. Kamba). Like colour sets, the cut is a diagnostic feature of Maa or non-Maa beadwork, and the pattern of cuts also marks internal differentiation among Maasai groups. Internally, different cuts are signs of section, region, or historical period. For instance, contemporary Purko Maasai use only the red–white–black sequence to cut, either in equal one-bead widths or with the white alone two beads wide. Keekonyokie Maasai make wider equal cuts of two beads each with the same colour sequence; the structure of the cut is the differentiating factor.[18] Externally, variation in cuts is more marked; different peoples construct cuts in different ways and with different colours. The standard sequence of a Kipsigis cut, for instance, is turquoise–dark blue–yellow–red–white.

Maasai associate cuts in an ornament with natural and cultural phenomena like slashes in a piece of roasting meat, breaks in a line of cattle or people, or the short interruption when a Maasai woman fills a cup by pouring a bit of milk, stopping, and then pouring again to fill it up. They have a general cultural attitude toward these different 'cuts': nothing should be continuous and unbroken. Maasai purposely 'cut' patterns in beadwork and activities such as pouring because to create pure fields of colour or a continuous flow of milk would seem to claim the purity and power attributed only to God. Moreover, the initial cut in any Maasai beadwork is a black line, associated with God.

Since nothing should be continuous and unbroken, mixture is a fact of life. But mixtures must be appropriately balanced. Just as the basis of colour organization is high contrast and complement, the bases of Maasai pattern structure are the size, distribution, and relationships of patches, fields, blocks, or stripes of contrasting or complementary colour. Though colour combinations may be eye-catching, they will not work well unless their patterns establish balanced mixtures of light and dark. The proportions of light and dark which are aesthetically acceptable closely parallel certain patternings within the range of cattle coats and of the natural environment. Patterns which Maasai distinguish by name are often recognized in several of these domains.[19]

Up to this point, we have chiefly been describing materials, techniques, and aesthetic principles of design which figure in the creation of Maasai beadwork and its identification as Maasai. We also hinted at interrelations between Maasai understandings of beadwork design and cultural attitudes towards and idioms for other spheres of Maasai life. The repertoire of ornament types (including who wears which ones and when) adds a final wrinkle to the complexities of creating, wearing, and interpreting personal ornament as an index of ethnic identity.

Gender, age-set, social status, progress through the life cycle, and ceremonial involvement are all marked and displayed with personal ornament. There are important differences, for instance, in the ornaments worn by a young Maasai girl before initiation and after, when she has become a young married woman.[20] After that, some changes in a woman's ornaments are tied to changes in the status of her husband or sons. Other shifts reflect the gradual, ceremonially unmarked progress of a woman's career of childbearing and motherhood. Some types of ornament, such as the wrapped wrist bangle (*enkirina oonkaina* (Maa); *enkirini* (Okiek)), are worn by both men and women; their exchange between and among men and women figures in the development and public acknowledgement of friendships.

These distinctions are as blatant and obvious to Maasai as the difference in someone's ears before and after their lower lobes have been pierced and stretched (and, incidentally, made available for further ornamentation). Anyone who is not fully conversant with the significant details of personal ornament, however, does not know how to 'read' an ensemble. Those people can interpret neither its full range of sociological clues nor the signs of its aesthetic and cultural accord with Maasai canons. Without appreciation of the diverse and complicated principles governing Maasai beadwork down to the smallest detail, those significant and telling signs are easily overlooked. They can thus perceive an entire ensemble as an overall sign of Maasai ethnicity or influence, even if the individual ornaments are not appropriately designed, properly composed as an ensemble, or worn as they should be.

With so many ways to go wrong in 'imitating' or 'adopting' Maasai style in personal ornament, it is actually quite remarkable that Okiek get so much *right*. In fact, some beadwork made by Kaplelach and Kipchornwonek Okiek is more like Purko Maasai beadwork than that made by either Arusha or Loitai Maasai. But does either verb — 'imitating' or 'adopting' — really capture what Okiek and others are doing in the process of their long intercultural interactions? Perhaps 'affecting', 'appropriating', 'modulating', or 'interpreting' would be more apt. The change of verb would dictate a parallel change of perspective and attitude: if they are not trying to 'imitate' Maasai, then perhaps the differences in their beadwork are not 'wrong' or 'ugly', except to Maasai eyes and according to Maasai rules and judgements.

For the moment, we bracket this question to discuss Okiek beadwork. Moreover, as we describe examples of Okiek work in the next section, we adopt a Maasai viewpoint. The strict Maasai canons of colour combination, design, composition, balance, and appropriate use provide a useful measure through which to compare and relate Maasai and Okiek ornament. In adopting the viewpoint of Maasai aesthetic judgements in the next section, we will talk of what Maasai would call Okiek 'errors'. We temporarily bracket the related questions of perspective and evaluation only while we show how Okiek personal ornament is exceptionally close to, yet critically different from, that of Maasai.

What's Wrong with This Picture?

This discussion is based on three sets of objects: (1) a group of bracelets made by a single Okiot woman (Kratz's co-wife,[21] considered a knowledgeable beadworker by Okiek); (2) beaded Okiek ornaments which are part of the Blackburn collection made in the late 1960s (available to us in Kenya through Klumpp's photographs of the objects); and (3) photographs of Okiek that Kratz took in the course of her research. The textual basis includes many conversations during which Maasai discussed their own ornaments, explicitly articulating and pointing out examples of their rules of colour, balance, and composition. Okiek commentaries cover their own ornaments as well as some diagrams and pictures of Maasai ones.

We do not have extensive Maasai comments focused specifically on Okiek ornament, though we recorded their reactions to some particular examples. However, we can talk about other Okiek examples because one of us has been trained to look at ornaments with a 'Maasai eye'. On the basis of aesthetic rules articulated in her discussions with Maasai, Klumpp can pick out 'flaws' and variations in beadwork as a Maasai woman would.[22] In adopting the Maasai perspective to describe Okiek ornaments here, we also use their value-laden language and judgements. The Okiek viewpoint will return again in the final section. We first summarize the kinds of distinctions, many of them matters of detail, that give Okiek beadwork away as non-Maasai, and then provide a few specific examples.

In general, Okiek ornaments use the elements of Maasai style in ways closely parallel to Maasai. The colour sets are there, cut in appropriate places, and the repertoires of ornament types overlap considerably. These alone can account for the overall impression of overwhelming similarity. But a closer look shows that, in many Okiek pieces, details at virtually all levels of composition are off from a Maasai perspective. At the level of finest detail, there are colour indiscretions, with colours out of sequence or unseemly colour juxtapositions (e.g. green–orange, or green–blue). Cuts are missing here and there (e.g. the initial black cut for God is often absent), done in the wrong colours, or made too thin.[23]

In total ornament composition, alternations between sections of an ornament or between two parts of a pair of ornaments are absent or oddly constructed. At times it seems as if the Okiot beadworker begins correctly, but without a sense of the way her beginning will develop, or without an overall plan. As she continues, compositional 'problems' develop that she can't work out or doesn't recognize. This results in peculiar sections in the ornament, and sometimes in the kind of colour indiscretions noted. According to Maasai principles, most Okiek ornaments lack the balance, proportions, and alternations that make their own ornaments beautiful and exemplify Maasai aesthetics.

Being Maasai

Three examples will illustrate these kinds of aesthetic 'flaws', the first a young man's beaded sword belt (*enkeene pus* (Maa); *aanweet ap rootweet* (Okiek)) (Figure 10.2), the second an adult woman's earring flaps (*inkonito onkiyiaa* (Maa); *muuenik ap iitiik* (Okiek)) (Figure 10.3), and the third a pair of beaded flywhisk handles, one Okiek and the other Purko Maasai (Figure 10.4). The key explains how different colours are represented in the diagrams.[24]

The sword belt includes all the necessary 'beautiful colours', but uses them in the wrong order. It has the right colour contrasts, but arranges them in the wrong way. For instance, in the lower left section where the belt is patterned with vertical bands of colour and narrow one-bead cuts, the artist has placed blue and green fields next to each other with a red cut; blue and green fields are also juxtaposed in the centre of the section. The first green field is followed by a white cut and an orange field. The cuts are perfectly acceptable, but a Maasai woman would bring together neither blue and green fields nor green and orange ones. On the right triangular tab at the top of the belt, an orange cut is the outer edge of a blue field. This is an indiscretion Maasai would diplomatically describe as 'her taste', in other words not so wrong as to be revolting but demonstrating lack of understanding of what is acceptable.

The leather earrings are also missing cuts, for instance between the blue/black sections and the white and red wedges on the lower half of the left earring. A glaring colour indiscretion in the top half of the left earring places a green border next to an orange field. Another type of compositional flaw can be seen at the base of the earrings, where the required colour alternation is constructed with two different patterns instead of the same pattern as Maasai would do it. One earring has divided wedges of red and white at the base, while the other uses a full semicircle of red, placing the alternating green in a border around its base. Maasai would find the other alternations between the two earrings of such poor quality that they would question whether the two flaps are even part of the same pair.

The Okiek flywhisk handle illustrates problems of colour order and juxtaposition in both its cuts and its wide bands of colour, problems which are ultimately difficulties of composition. A Maasai woman can plot the entire colour scheme of a belt or another piece done on leather with couching stitch by first placing the cuts. Purko always follow the same cut sequence: red–white–blue–red–white–blue. With this sequence of cuts in place, the 'beautiful colours' fall into place almost automatically, with appropriate cuts in appropriate places. However, this way of working is impossible in beadwork which is strung, wrapped, or wired.

The Purko woman nonetheless followed the rule for cut sequences on her beaded handle, a rule already familiar to her from her earlier (and easier) exercises in belt-making as a young girl (*entito*). The Okiek handle, however, does not follow the proper Purko cut sequence of red–white–blue, and also includes cuts of green (about a third of the way down from the whisk) and orange (at the base). About two-thirds down from the whisk end, the Okiot woman has also put a blue cut next to a green section (not enough contrast for Maasai), and has also juxtaposed wide sections of green and orange, 'leaving out' a wide white section between them and putting in just a narrow white cut.

Okiek beadwork also shows aesthetic influences from other neighbours. Most jarringly notable from the Maasai perspective are Okiek pieces that include colours, cuts, and motifs found in Kipsigis personal ornament. Yet other Okiek ornaments seem to have a Uas Nkishu flavour, or to retain patterns from previous ages now out of fashion to contemporary Maasai.[25] While most beadwork by Kaplelach and Kipchornwonek Okiek approximates the canon of their Purko neighbours, the eclectic inclusion of these other accents and mixtures is distasteful and unbecoming to the strong Maasai sense of aesthetic perfection.

What Maasai would regard as mistakes in Okiek usage of personal ornament can be illustrated with our final example, the photograph Okiek were discussing in our opening epigraph (see p. 214 and back cover colour photograph). The young woman they were talking about, Lakwani (Kopot Edina), is on the far right, shown the day she and her pictured co-initiates completed initiation.[26] Leaving aside here questions of colour and composition, she still presents Maasai with a confusingly mixed image because of the variety of ornaments she wears. The long wire *imunai* earrings in her upper ears are typically worn by Maasai girls and women, but she also has leather earring flaps in her lower ears. To Maasai, these are a sign that a woman is already married. Furthermore, she wears the flat brass coils (*isirutia*; *taaook* (Okiek)) that Maasai women don only after they have sons who are warriors. The initiate in the middle of the picture wears a wedding necklace (*enkarewa*), though it is not her wedding day and she is still single.

Lakwani appears to be an odd social conglomerate to Maasai, a young single woman simultaneously and inappropriately wearing the ornaments of a girl, a married woman, and an older woman with adult sons. She presents no such confusion to Okiek, who simply and immediately recognize her as a young woman recently out of seclusion and/or recently married. The occasion of the photograph has no exact Maasai parallel, as Maasai girls are not secluded during initiation. Okiek have defined the costume appropriate for their ceremony using the full array of Maasai-like ornaments. The young woman's progress through the Okiek ceremonial sequence is clear to them, signalled in part by changes in her headdress (Kratz, 1988a). Maasai share neither the headdress nor the specifics of the ceremonial process. This now brings us back to the question temporarily bracketed, that of perspective, attitude, and evaluation.

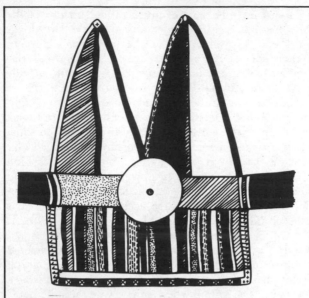

Fig. 10.2 *Young Man's Beaded Sword Belt*

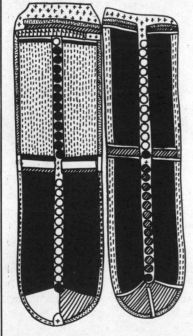

KEY

 BLUE/BLACK

 WHITE

 DARK RED

 ORANGE

 GREEN

 YELLOW

 NO BEADS

ZIPPER

Fig. 10.3 *Adult Woman's Earring Flaps*

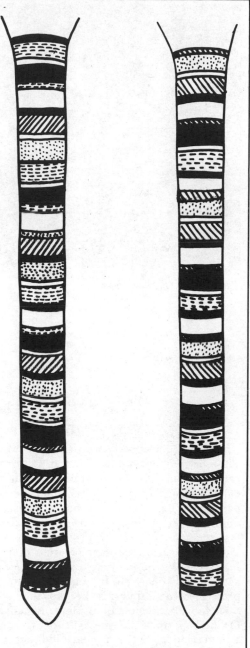

Fig. 10.4 Beaded Flywhisk Handle: Okiek (left), Purko (right)

213

Photo 10.1 Okiek Initiates

Who Says Something's Wrong?

Maasai interpret all these differences in Okiek beadwork as mistakes —
wrong, ugly, inexpertly constructed, and, in their most dismissively
summary judgement, non-Maasai. However, the last example of appropriate costume for *Okiek* ceremonies which violates *Maasai* definitions
of appropriate usage suggests that Maasai, Okiek, and others whose
personal ornament approximates Maasai ideals may have somewhat
different perceptions of perfection, aesthetics, appropriateness, and
fashion.

How do Okiek see their creation of beaded ornaments that super-
ficially seem to appropriate and reproduce Maasai styles? Maybe Okiek
are mocking Maasai by making their ornaments just slightly off
prescribed Maasai norms. Perhaps they are deliberately demonstrating
their non-Maasainess by using ornaments in ways Maasai would not.
Or perhaps they are simply copying something they think is pretty
and making it prettier. Never mind that the new initiate wears earrings
that Maasai reserve for married women; she looks good and that is
the important thing.

Is there, then, something decidedly Okiek about *their* personal ornament? There obviously are Okiek costume conventions that differ from Maasai ones, such as what young women wear when completing initiation.[27] And what of Okiek colour schemes? A Maasai man was present one day when Kratz was in her principal research area, showing people photographs of Okiek from there. He pointed out many minute features in one picture of a young Okiok woman, including details in the placement of colours and an extra line of beads on her headband, that made it clear to him that she was not Maasai, or at least not Purko. However, he could not pick out anything that identified her positively as an Okiot. Later, several groups of Okiek looking at the same picture all agreed that there was no difference between her beadwork and that of Maasai. They, too, said there was no way to tell she was an Okiot simply by looking at her.

From these and other discussions with Okiek, it seems colour is not their focus for ethnic self-differentiation in personal ornament. It is difficult to describe characteristics of Okiek ornament in positive terms with respect to colour and composition; differences are most readily defined negatively, in contrast to strict Maasai rules. Okiek talk about the same colour sets, sequences, and combinations as Maasai, but they are not as elaborately specific about alternations and balance. Nor are they as derisively uncompromising about following what they articulate as the main aesthetic rules of composition. To them, it's alright to use other combinations from time to time if they look nice. Maasai rules of aesthetics do not allow that anything else could look nice. If other patterns appeal to other people, it is simply another sign of their inferiority and lack of judgement.

Okiek uses of personal ornament may be more amenable to description in terms of contextually and socially specific definitions, combinations that make sense to them but are sometimes unacceptable to Maasai. Yet the way those definitions overlap, intermix with, and contradict comparable Maasai rules of wear are still an important aspect of them to be reckoned with. Similarities of costume, of ceremonial marking of the life cycle, or of social organization can help make interethnic relations and intercultural communication possible, though in each case the details and how they fit together may be quite different. At the same time that broad similarities can facilitate such interrelations, however, points of detail can simultaneously be understood as insurmountable differences and evaluated quite differently. The bases for justifying cultural hegemony to one group may be regarded as inconspicuous and irrelevant variation by another.

Maasai beadwork is the basis of a visual lingua franca that now joins different Maasai sections with Okiek and with a number of other peoples who neighbour Maasai. Like coastal speakers of Kiswahili, Maasai regard it as bastardization when others 'simplify' their visual language or 'speak' it with an 'accent'. Nonetheless, those 'speakers' communicate effectively, even if they do not recognize all the subtleties to which Maasai themselves pay attention.

If there *must* be something, *some* particular object to be held up as 'Truly and Uniquely Okiek' (which we would suspect to be an academic insistence, not a Maasai or Okiek one), then perhaps it would be a few particular ornaments which Maasai do not use, like the transitional strand of beads worn as initiates leave seclusion. More notable, perhaps, are certain other material objects associated with Okiek forest life, such as honey baskets and elephant spears. But why should there be some material embodiment of ethnicity to hold up? Why should ethnicity be concentrated and contained in a single object or set of objects, other than for the convenience of scholars or collectors who need to label and/or sell them? The 'Okiek' strand of beads is made according to the colour sets shared with Maasai, even if they do not have that form and occasion in common. That strand, too, is part of the regional system of aesthetics, history, and their circumstances. It is liable to change shape, colour, definition, or use, just as Maasai colour sets and styles have gone through various developments that can be traced to late in the last century but which surely extend further into the past.

Okiek are participating in an aesthetic system of personal ornament with what Maasai would regard as imperfect knowledge of it. It seems they make 'mistakes' without realizing (or caring) that their slight variations in colour and pattern identify them as non-Maasai 'imitators' of the Maasai standard. Yet their greater tolerance of such variations, their broader interpretation of what is acceptable, may be one tellingly different ethnic marker. Attempts to specify it in terms of rules are frustrated by the elusive negativity that results from that tolerance; it is more a difference of attitude and elaboration than a difference of rules.

The cultural attitudes that Maasai and Okiek bring to personal ornament seem to exemplify Sieber's contrast between an explicit, articulated aesthetic and an unvoiced aesthetic which is understood more implicitly, with little elaborate verbal formulation (1973). Both aesthetic systems readily accommodate changes of style, pattern, and material over time, though, judging from this example, the latter might accommodate wider ranges of variation. Verbal elaboration and formal elaboration coincide in Maasai beadwork, providing a Maasai vocabulary of cultural as well as aesthetic judgement.

One familiar lesson here is that ethnicity can not be objectified and enshrined, frozen, or isolated from historical circumstances. Ethnic identity has to do with cultural attitudes, understandings, and values towards various modes of social and economic organization in particular circumstances. We can only try to understand ethnicity by studying the processes by which these are interlinked through the experience of individuals, processes through which those attitudes, values, modes of organization, and circumstances are both reproduced and transformed.

When Lerionka wears the beadwork style of his age-set, it is a step towards identifying with others in social groupings of various kinds, groups which operate at a number of levels of inclusion. One facet of the way he understands and defines himself with respect to others, it also testifies to the kinds of networks and resources on which he can rely (including women with appropriate aesthetic knowledge and skill to make him ornaments) and to the kinds of values and priorities most relevant to him. It further lays an implicit basis for future claims to resources and networks of other kinds.

A means of publicly identifying with particular others, his personal ornament simultaneously includes criteria for exclusion and discrimination. Okiek and Maasai share a great deal of cultural knowledge about how to construct beaded ornaments and about the chronology and development of beadwork styles through successive age-sets. But, in the colours and patterns of their beadwork, Maasai also encode more complex aesthetic requirements, related to their most important cultural values. They are tuned in to those subtleties in ways Okiek are not. Okiek do not proceed from the same philosophical bases and do not use the same aesthetic code to distinguish fine points of their social and spatial organization in the same way.

Differences of aesthetic specificity further complicate the politics of ethnic identity when Okiek deny the differences between their ornaments and ensembles. Their denials might be affrontery to Maasai, but are more likely to be taken condescendingly as further evidence of their ignorance. For Okiek and other non-Maasai, their less-nuanced understanding means their public persona always includes an identity qualifier, always maximizes their options for Maasai affiliation or 'passing' if it makes convenient sense.

The different attitudes Maasai and Okiek bring to the aesthetics of beadwork and the politics of ethnic identity resonate with descriptions of other spheres of Maasai life. Spear's discussion of Maasai exclusivity and inclusivity is relevant here (Introduction, this volume). He talks about the seeming paradox created when 'the projection of Maasai cultural hegemony' with its exclusive and arrogantly superior stance is confronted with the flexibility inherent in the openness and inclusivity of Maasai social organization. Maasai might sneer at the work on an Okiot's sword belt, but they don't exclude him if they are planning a joint cattle raid as age-mates. Okiek, it seems, extend a comparable sense of inclusivity to some of their neighbours' cultural practices as well as their social groups, incorporating and reinterpreting them as their own in the process.

The nuances of personal ornament have provided one focused example of this in this chapter. Maasai and Okiek women put similar resources to different but related uses, within understandings analogous though distinct. Okiek and Maasai beadwork differ sometimes in form, sometimes in function, and most always in the evaluation and attitude which

Maasai and Okiek bring to it. While they may understand the type of claims suggested to Maasai by wearing a style of beadwork, Okiek may or may not participate in the same social groups and may or may not feel that their own attire makes similar claims to networks and resources. This introduces both ambiguity and irony into Okiek assertions of identity. Both are useful defences in circumstances in which Maasai assertions of cultural hegemony are often accompanied by a regional sociopolitical dominance. Ambiguity in such matters can also assist people who *do* begin to reorient their activities, networks of interaction, and goals in a more Maasai-like direction.

We looked closely at one way through which Okiek and Maasai women actively mediate ethnic identity in daily life, even in situations less dramatic and clear than people changing ethnic allegiance. They advertise their own identity through the beaded ornaments they create and wear. Even when they are absent, they also help state and negotiate that of their husbands, sons, brothers, and friends who wear their creations. Finally, they help create one of the principal marketed versions of Maasai-ness with the beaded ornaments sold to tourists and others, and with the displays of beadwork in popular images of Maasai.

Notes

1. Thanks to Ivan Karp, Fiona Marshall, Tom Pilgram, and Tom Spear for comments that helped us revise an earlier draft of this chapter.
2. The photographs were part of a recent exhibition at the National Museum, Nairobi, called Okiek Portraits, Photography by Corinne Kratz. It was shown there in 1989 and is currently travelling in the United States. A copy of the photographs has been donated to the National Museums of Kenya for research and documentary purposes.
3. Our joint reflections on Maasai and Okiek identity and personal ornament began in 1982, when we were engaged in research within thirty miles of each other. Klumpp was working with Purko Maasai in Lemek, looking at Maasai art in the form of ornamental beadwork. At the same time, Kratz was with Kaplelach and Kipchornwonek Okiek on the Mau Escarpment. These are Okiek that Maasai call Ilpalagilak Torrobo, in contrast with Lomoot (Omotik) who now live on the savannah near Maasai, some within Klumpp's research area. Kratz was concentrating on processes through which Okiek construct gender and identity through language and ceremony.

   We already knew from our previous work and from the Blackburn collection at the American Museum of Natural History that Okiek living near Maasai make and wear ornaments almost exactly like Maasai. Those close to Kipsigis make similar ornaments, but with clear Kipsigis influence on colour use and motifs. This was the start of an ongoing dialogue whenever we met in Narok or Nairobi and became a wider exchange as we extended those conversations into our research areas. This chapter reports some of our conclusions after talking with Maasai and Okiek as we all tried to clarify issues involved in our different perspectives on beadwork.

   Klumpp's research was supported by the Wenner Gren Foundation, Fulbright-Hayes Program, the Richard Lounsbery Fund, and the Explorers Club. Support for Kratz's work came from National Science Foundation, the Joint Committee on Africa of the Social Science Research Council and the American Council of Learned Societies, Wenner Gren Foundation, Institute for Intercultural Studies,

Fulbright-Hayes, and the University of Texas at Austin. We appreciate their assistance as well as that of the Institute of African Studies and the Sociology Department, University of Nairobi for academic affiliation and the Office of the President, Government of Kenya for permission to conduct our studies.

4. Cf. *kwapi/kwavi*.

5. Bentley (1987) sketches this development, two major schools of thought concerning ethnicity, and some of the difficulties with the division they create.

6. To be more specific, this is true of the majority of Okiek on the southern and eastern parts of the western Mau Escarpment, where interaction with Maasai has been an important part of their history. Okiek on the western side of the escarpment are oriented, rather, towards Kipsigis and participate in shared modes of social organization with them, such as their age-sets and clans.

7. We do not want to rehash here the arguments against those who assume Okiek are Maasai who have lost their cattle, overgeneralizing the circumstances of some people Maasai categorize as Torrobo (e.g. van Zwanenberg, 1976; Chang, 1982).

8. Waller (1988) shows how this sense of personal choice and variability emerges historically.

9. Most of the papers in this collection show these very concentrations.

10. There are two critical and confining differences, however, which are related and are defined and produced through Maasai gender relations. First, 'until tourism and urbanization became important economic factors in Maasailand, the accumulation of ornaments was an economic dead end. There was no additional gain or return that increased the owner's wealth . . . [Second,] ultimately, women's art is based on men's surplus wealth and is used to support, reinforce, advertise and entertain men' (*ibid.*).

11. Talking about how women handle unhappy marriages, an Okiot woman related her own early marriage history of frequent flight to her natal family. She noted that the only thing she carried with her when she ran away was her handbag with her beads and the ornaments she was currently working on. Bianco (n.d.) is an interesting discussion of the social and political dimensions and uses of Pokot women's belts.

12. Styles and patterns in personal ornament thus constitute a historical sequence that parallels age-sets, and at times influences the names given to ages (e.g. *il Kishili* (*il Gecherei*) 'the ones you can't take your eyes off') (cf. Winter, 1977).

13. Reciprocal aesthetic influences exist, but are harder to identify once they have become incorporated into the Maasai fashion canon. Tracing such influences is part of our ongoing research.

14. Okiek and Maasai use a common vocabulary for beadworking techniques, though in translation as calques (e.g. both talk of 'cutting' patterns and colours, *a-dung'* (Maa) *-til* (Okiek)). Many Okiek names for beads are also the same as Maasai terms. Techniques are discussed in detail in Klumpp (1987: 72–78).

15. Within the basic Maasai rules of colour use, some variations, preferences, and combinations also indicate the Maasai group to which a woman belongs. For instance, Chamus and Arusha follow the basic Maasai colour scheme of green–red–white–orange–blue. Unlike pastoral Maasai groups, however, they sometimes place orange next to red, or yellow next to blue. Sectional preferences in colour emphases are also related to the major ecological and ceremonial division of Maasai into the cool, wet highlands (Enaiposha) and of the hotter, drier, lowlands (Olkaputiei). Sections of the Enaiposha coalition of western Maasailand prefer darker shades of red and blue, cold colours to the Maasai, and they use less white than those of Olkaputiei in eastern and southern Maasailand. The latter like lighter, warmer shades of red and blue, more white and almost no black. These colour preferences are also related to general preferences in cattle colours: red for Purko, black/blue for Loitai, yellow for Keekonyokie.

16. Because each of these four colours is darker than white, they can be considered black if placed next to white. Blue and black are equivalent in design and both called *narok* (Maa) or *tikiik* (Okiek). They are distinguished, when necessary, as 'black' and

219

'very black'. Further discussion of relations between paired colours as strong/weak, of changes in colour interpretation based on juxtaposition, of the further elaboration of subdivisions of this quintet and other colour sets, and of ways the development of contemporary colour sets relates to the history of available beads can be found in Klumpp (1987: 82–85).

17. Other Maasai motifs are either geometric abstracts with no particular symbolic meaning or abstracts which resemble and are therefore named for parts of a cow, the human body, natural or household objects. They include patterns such as the eye, the buttocks, the window, the stool, the stem of a plant called *sinoni*. The use and/or rendering of these and other motifs in beadwork can also indicate cultural and aesthetic knowledge and ethnic affiliation, but in the present summary treatment we only consider the cut.

18. Kaputiei and Loitokitok Maasai sometimes use yellow or green with red in cuts. This sometimes makes their beadwork unrecognizable as Maasai to Purko, whose lands are not contiguous with either group.

19. For example, there are names for very large patches of colour, alternating bands, zebra stripes, vertical striations, and dots of various sizes. To give one example, *uas* or *euas* refers (1) to cattle with widely spaced, large dark spots of regular size on a light ground, (2) to rolling grasslands dotted with small clusters of bushes and trees as in the trans-Mara area, and (3) to a pattern of arranging green–red–white–black–orange beads such that white predominates with narrow blocks of the other colours (Klumpp, 1989). Uas Nkishu is the name of a Maasai section which once had many *uas* cattle and still prefers mottled *uas* ornaments. As of the late 1980s, however, *uas* ornaments were in usage only by the Loitokitok and Kisonko Maasai in far eastern Maasailand. Other Maasai recognized the possibility of *uas* patterning, but considered it too . white for their liking. Cf. Lienhardt's (1961) discussion of colours and patterns that cross domains of experience to unite such things as a cow, a bird, a mood, and an event.

20. There is more detail on ornament distinctions of gender, age, and life cycle in Klumpp (1987: 134–170) for Maasai; Kratz (1988a) discusses changes in Okiek ornaments during initiation.

21. Her fictive kin relations are based on a position as 'second wife' in the Kaplelach home where she stays.

22. This is comparable to the process through which art historians learn to work on the products and aesthetics of another period. Using aesthetic rules and judgements available in historical sources and discussions of particular works written during that period, they can develop a 'period eye' so that they can extend the same aesthetic principles to other paintings that are not explicitly discussed in similar sources (Baxandall, 1972). Baxandall (1985) also discusses these issues in Chapter Four.

23. The thin cuts in some Okiek pieces gives them an archaic look to Maasai eyes because older Maasai pieces used thinner cuts. The historical development of cut construction (width and colour) can be traced like that of contemporary colour sets.

24. For a number of Each African peoples, red, orange, and even yellow are relative colours, conceived less as absolutes and more on a sliding scale that depends on context and juxtaposition. A light shade of red, for instance, may be defined as orange next to a darker shade of red, though the same colour would be considered red next to a more yellow or less saturated red mixture. When beads of various colours are unobtainable, even orange can be red, while yellow becomes its orange.

The Okiek examples are part of the Blackburn collection at the American Museum of Natural History in New York: sword belt 90.2/7560, ear flaps 90.2/7528a/b, flywhisk 90.2/7534. Thanks to Enid Shildkraut and for providing colour slides of the objects.

25. For example, work with narrow cuts or narrow colour alternations. Some of the pieces we are talking about were collected by Blackburn in 1969, but Klumpp also saw Omotik Okiek beadwork with very narrow colour bands in the early 1980s and some of Kratz's bracelet collection also has narrow bands.

26. In the epigraph, people referred to her by her current teknonymous name, Edina's mother. At the time of the picture, she was not yet married or a mother.

27. It is worth noting that Okiek and Kipsigis headdresses also differ during this ceremonial progression, a set of occasions which they share. These distinctions are a good example of how similar contrasts can be differently marked, and of how the same ornaments can be used in slightly different but related ways. After initiation, young Maasai women wear a blue beaded headband with cowries and chains all around. They do not wear a wedding necklace until the day of their marriage. Okiek girls in seclusion wear a headband somewhat similar to the Maasai one (or to the Maasai one pictured in Adamson, 1967). As they go through their final initiation ceremonies, however, that is replaced first with a single strand of blue beads with a centred red grouping (worn before their heads are shaved), and then with the *enkishilit* shown in Photo 10.1 after their heads are shaved. They wear the same ornaments the day they leave seclusion and at marriage. The difference of occasion is shown by grass put on their forehead in a marriage blessing and by the things the bride carries on her back. Kipsigis girls wear very different head coverings in seclusion, and their headdress when finishing initiation is a cap of cowries with a flat beaded circle at the top.

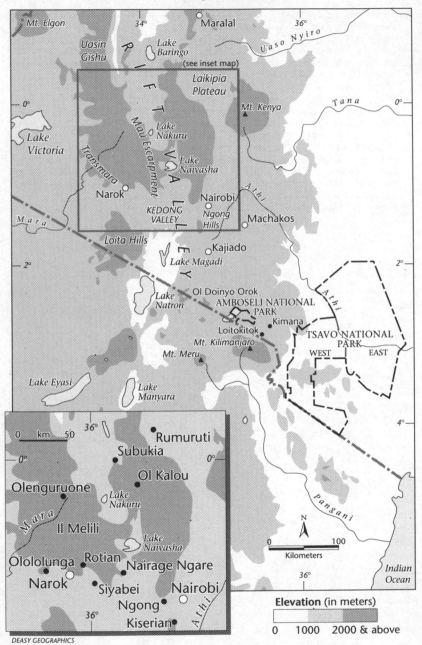

Southern Maasailand

DEASY GEOGRAPHICS

Elevation (in meters)

0   1000   2000 & above

PART FOUR

Contestations
&
Redefinitions
Introduction

While cattle occupied a central position in the pastoral economy and, therefore, in struggles over definitions of 'being Maasai' in the nineteenth century, land and markets have increasingly became the central resources and arenas in the twentieth. The establishment of African reserves, in both the highlands and the plains, sharply restricted Maasai access to pastoral resources and put them increasingly in competition with highlanders seeking fertile agricultural land on the plains. As available land became increasingly limited, it came to be seen more as a *resource* which could be appropriated by individuals rather than as a communal *territory* containing resources for all (see Campbell, Chapter Twelve). Increasing penetration of the market has also provided Maasai with an outlet, albeit an uncertain one, as they now sell both cattle and labour for cash. The implications of their integration into a wider economy for what it means to be Maasai are enormous, as we are only beginning to understand. For, if cattle have been critical in defining Maasai views of themselves and have been the main means of mediating relations between themselves and others, what does a future bode in which land and market relations — privately conducted — replace cattle — held in communal trust and widely shared — as the primary economic resources?

Waller examines the early stages of this process under colonialism, as control over land became in itself as significant for Maasai survival as access to cattle had been hitherto. As scarcity of land in the highlands pushed increasing numbers of Kikuyu farmers to settle in Maasailand, Maasai fears over losing land encouraged them to cooperate with colonial authorities to restrict the immigration of outsiders. At the same time, however, the increasing difficulty of maintaining their pastoral economy encouraged Maasai to accept individual Kikuyu as client cultivators and even to adopt farming themselves. Maasai responses to outsiders were thus conflicting. On the one hand, they seemed to acknowledge

223

colonial ideas regarding their ethnic exclusivity while, on the other, they continued to interact with Kikuyu and protected individual Kikuyu clients from removal by the colonial authorities. This resulted in continual negotiation over stereotypes. To a degree, the idea of the Dorobo 'other' was supplanted by that of a Kikuyu 'other' in the minds of both Maasai and colonial administrators. But the increasing number of Maasai cultivators within their own society raised the awkward question of whether there was not, in fact, a Maasai 'other' as well. To cope with this, and to find a place for themselves which would enable them to straddle ethnic and economic boundaries, those Maasai who had for various reasons espoused the idea of colonial modernization now attempted to forge a new Maasai identity which included 'modern' farming and education as well as 'traditional' values.

Campbell's and Fratkin's studies of the increasing importance of the market, land, jobs, and education in Maasai political economy extend Waller's analysis of earlier history and point us to the future. Campbell finds that, as land has been alienated to white and African farmers, game parks, and individual Maasai ranchers over the course of the century, the Maasai community as a whole has increasingly come to lose access to sufficient pastures and water to maintain a viable pastoral economy. Wealthy Maasai who once invested their cattle in wives, stock alliances, and other social relations now seek to convert cattle into land as a private exploitable resource, further tightening the noose of declining access to resources around the necks of their less wealthy neighbours. As the lineaments of an economy of shared resources and responsibilities become increasingly blurred, differentiation between rich and poor, landed and landless, employers and workers, grows, and the struggle within Maasai society over just what it means to be Maasai intensifies. Thus, whereas in Waller's analysis of the colonial period issues of class are implicit, Campbell's work makes their contemporary relevance explicit, adding a new dimension to the construction of ethnicity in a capitalist context.

Fratkin's paper focuses on the impact of the market in northern Kenya where land is still relatively abundant. In a valuable restudy of Spencer's work conducted in the 1960s, he is able to show how penetration of the market has radically transformed relations between Rendille camel herders and Samburu Maasai cattle herders in just a couple of decades. Spencer (1973) found that the widespread phenomena of Rendille becoming Samburu was a result of the low reproduction rate of camels combined with delayed marriage for men and low rates of polygyny in Rendille, compared with a much higher reproduction rate for cattle, earlier marriages, and higher polygyny rates in Samburu. Rendille were thus able to exchange daughters who, because of the lack of bridewealth, could not be married in their own society, for Samburu cattle. This also provided them with a means for entering the cattle economy and thereby 'becoming Maasai'. The intermediaries in this transfer process were the Ariaal, a people who shared aspects of both cultures and so provided a stepping stone for Rendille seeking to become Samburu. With increasing commoditization of cattle, however, Fratkin now sees relations between the two as a function of the market, with Rendille adopting the Maa language, not to become Maasai, but to participate in cattle and labour markets dominated by Maa-speakers. 'Being Maasai' for these outsiders, ironically, is now associated less with entering the transhumant pastoral economy than with participating in the settled spheres of urban markets and employment.

The terms of Maasai identity are thus clearly in flux today, although it is less clear what this means for the future construction of that identity. Even the fundamental identification of language with ethnicity is now in dispute. As Maasai struggle to reconcile modern development with an identity forged in the past, class is increasingly becoming the language of identity, and Maasai now find it difficult to reconcile sharpening internal differentiation with their communal ethos. 'Being Maasai' and the whole complex of institutions and values that entails, it seems, are in the midst of their third major transformation in as many centuries.

Eleven

Acceptees
& Aliens

Kikuyu Settlement
in Maasailand*

RICHARD WALLER

The dynamics of identity formation and change among the Maa-speakers, and of their relations with outsiders, have been re-evaluated in recent years. Emphasis has shifted away from the delineation of neat ethnic boundaries towards a concern with the ways in which such boundaries are first drawn and then maintained, adjusted or even dissolved; and it is in this context that the processes of community formation and change can best be examined. Formerly, the Maasai, in particular, were seen as the type of a self-consciously exclusive ethnic group rigidly devoted to a highly specialized form of subsistence which generated cohesion within the community and served to mark it off symbolically, economically and socially from others. They now appear as a prime example of adaptation and ethnic mutability, pursuing strategies of accumulation and survival within a regional economy which included a variety of local communities with different but interdependent modes of subsistence.[1]

Much of the impetus for re-evaluation has come from the study of the Maa-speakers during their expansive phase in the nineteenth century when boundaries between different Maa-speaking communities and between pastoralists, cultivators and hunters in the Rift Valley region were permeable, constantly shifting and subject to continuous redefinition. Individuals and groups moved between different communities and economies, altering their identities as they did so. Communities were able to absorb — and to shed — members easily and rapidly in response to changes in the availability of resources and in the demand for labour (Waller, 1985b).

With the establishment of colonial rule after 1900, the era of expansion came to an end. Communities which had previously had shared economic interests and, in part, a common ideology of growth were now being separated by divergent patterns of development and by different experiences under colonial rule. In the process, identities that had once

226

been complementary now came to symbolize norms and values that could be perceived as being alien or opposed (Galaty, 1982b). Identities also became more exclusive and, in some cases, bitterly contentious. Imprecisely drawn boundaries hardened and became policed borders that divided rather than united communities on either side. This tightening up was partly in response to colonial administrative policies and to the creation of legally defined and ethnically exclusive Reserves; but it was also the result of internal readjustments within African societies themselves. The triple impact of rinderpest, smallpox and intersectional conflicts in the early 1890s had temporarily destroyed the cattle economy. The social fabric which rested upon it was rent apart. Society and economy had thus to be rebuilt in a new and potentially hostile world. A heightened concern with identity was an essential part of the exercise, not only in order to erect barriers against colonial intrusion but also to arrive at an agreed and defensible definition of 'Maasainess', made necessary because so many Maasai had, at least temporarily, 'left pastoralism' to take refuge with surrounding populations of cultivators and hunters (Waller, 1985b and 1988).

Although the broad assumptions and detailed applications of colonial policy played an important role in shaping new frameworks of interaction and in determining the language of debate, much of the experience on which both the Maasai and their neighbours drew in their attempts to redefine the boundaries between them, and much of the idiom in which claims were couched and allowed or refused and identities expressed or rejected still derived from constructions of the pre-colonial past. That past, suitably interpreted, appeared to provide a basis for those who still wished to maintain and exploit older ties across the border: and there were many that did. Differently interpreted, however, it could also be used to legitimate new identities which looked inwards as well as outwards and it was these identities and their historical underpinnings that informed the models of 'tribe' with which colonial administrators worked and which were then taken up by later ethnographers and historians. Thus the apparently authentic and unchanging ethnic identities which scholars believed they had uncovered from the pre-colonial period and which they distinguished sharply from contemporary variations were in fact the products of internal conflict and debate in the much more recent past (Vail, 1989; Berntsen, 1980; Waller, 1984).

This chapter examines the development of a distinctive 'Maasai' identity during the colonial period by looking at changes in one of the most enduring and complex of the interethnic relationships which bound communities in the Rift Valley together: that between Maasai and Kikuyu. It focuses on the ambiguous and sometimes conflicting responses of the Maasai and the colonial administration to what was officially regarded as Kikuyu 'infiltration' into areas of Maasailand. The predicament of Kikuyu settlers in Maasailand, 'caught in the middle' between two developing ethnicities, 'Maasai' and 'Kikuyu', suggests how boundaries between the Maasai and their neighbours were drawn. And Maasai responses to infiltration reveal much about the way in which the meaning of 'Maasainess' was being defined.[2]

Complementary Expansion: The Frontier Past

During the nineteenth century, Maasai and Kikuyu had been on opposite sides of a shifting frontier of expansion and accumulation (Waller, 1985b). The close economic and social ties between the two societies were symbolized by the Maasai concept of *osotua*, a term for 'bond friendship' that expressed the idea that preferential exchanges between two partners created a kind of kinship transcending social boundaries. In an important sense, the period up to the 1890s was, for the small-scale societies of the Rift and its environs, the 'time of *osotua*' (Sobania, 1991). Interaction was most intense along the periphery. The Maasai sections involved were those whose patterns of movement took them closest to Kikuyuland — the Kaputiei and Keekonyokie in the south and the Purko in the north. In the frontier areas of Kikuyu settlement, in Kabete and Nyeri, the local economy emphasized stock-keeping and there was a high degree of ethnic mixing as households traded, raided, intermarried and took refuge with each other across the frontier.

Interaction was based on complementary economies and, in particular, on interlocking cycles of accumulation. Kikuyu household heads needed access to Maasai small stock in order to advance in elderhood and to increase the size of their family networks. The conversion of perishable foodstuffs into reproductive stock through trade with pastoralists was a means of turning the direct product of agricultural labour into an investment in domestic growth. Maasai households needed access to a reliable supply of vegetable foods to make up for any shortfall in the milk supply from their herds; and they might also require extra herding labour which could be obtained by taking in Kikuyu dependants. Service in a Maasai household, and the patronage that went with it, offered important advantages to ambitious Kikuyu. Learning the language and making contacts in Maasailand enabled a man later to establish himself as a trading entrepreneur and an intermediary on the frontier and, thus, to accumulate wealth and authority (Waller, 1985b; Marris and Somerset, 1971: Ch. 2).

For women too there were opportunities. Maasai wives controlled their households' food supplies and were responsible for conducting exchanges with outsiders. Kikuyu women acted as porters in the trade and sometimes emerged as entrepreneurs and investors in their own right. Where ethnic boundaries were fluid, women were important as intermediaries and as reproductive assets. Patterns of intermarriage both facilitated the reciprocal flow of resources and reflected the changing circumstances of the communities involved, with pastoralists gaining

Photo 11.1 Kikuyu Women Planting in a Frontier Area c. 1900. The murran *in the background are probably also Kikuyu, though they are wearing items of 'Maasai' dress.*

women in good times and losing them in bad (Waller, 1979; Clark, 1980; Spear, in this volume).[3]

Both Kikuyu and Maasai were expanding during the nineteenth century, in ways that were complementary rather than competitive. The process of Kikuyu expansion involved the acquisition of new forest land by syndicates (the *mbaris*) who then cleared it for cultivation and recruited others to help them extend and defend the pale of settlement. Membership of an *mbari* gave rights in the shared land and created a social bond. From this sprang the notions, central to the moral order, of the identification of land with kinship and of the social creativity and value of labour. The fact of expansion thus shaped both the social and the moral fabric of Kikuyuland (Berman and Lonsdale, 1992).

Expansion also shaped the Maasai — though in a slightly different way — by creating a central core of fully pastoral communities who controlled strategic water and grazing resources and who were united by a shared body of tradition which emphasized internal cohesion and the historical identity of the Maasai and an outer periphery of ex- or would-be pastoralists whose claim to a Maasai identity was increasingly contested as moral worth and community membership came to be identified with stock ownership and with pastoral values (Waller, 1979;

229

Galaty, 'Maasai Expansion', in this volume).[4] Expansion took place as a series of thrusts against other Maa-speaking peoples, such as Iloogolala and Laikipiak, which left the losers either absorbed by the victors or relegated to the periphery where they often took refuge with neighbouring peoples. In defeat, families were divided. Many of the Maa-speaking refugees in Kikuyuland had relatives among the Maasai. They capitalized on their marginality and their ties to act as brokers between communities across the frontier; and their presence added another strand to the web of relations linking Maasai and Kikuyu (Waller, 1985b).

Thus, by breaking up and reforming existing social groups and by drawing the boundaries of pastoralism more tightly, Maasai expansion provided a constant supply of detached people. As clients, warriors or wives these might be absorbed into new social formations on the Kikuyu frontier where a constant demand for labour and stock offered opportunities for personal advancement and accumulation.

Ultimately, 'food is friendship'. If one of the forces that animated frontier communities was the hope of profit, the other was the fear of famine (Ambler, 1988). In times of drought, or when cattle were lost to disease or raiders, Maasai could take refuge with their Kikuyu partners. In the 1890s, when disaster struck the Maasai, they flooded into Kikuyu, making use of existing ties or creating new ones by presenting themselves to wealthy Kikuyu household heads as clients or prospective affines. For many Maasai, this was the 'time of *enaashe*' ('thanks') during which they and their families were given help by Kikuyu and thus contracted what were regarded as debts that might be called in later — much as they had been, on a smaller scale, in the past. Another layer of obligation was added to what already bound the societies together. Other Maasai, especially isolated women and orphaned or abandoned children, were incorporated more permanently into Kikuyu households through marriage or adoption. They were, in a sense, lost to their Maasai communities; but they or their families might sometime return and demand their rights. Like the Maa-speaking refugees before them, they added another ambiguous element to the structure of interethnic relations (Waller, 1988).

The frontier past thus represented a series of claims, options, and identities which were not always compatible with each other and which came increasingly under scrutiny and strain in the colonial period as Maasai and Kikuyu moved apart. On the one hand, they provided the basis for future interaction. Ties of sentiment — *osotua* and *enaashe* — were strong and the dense network of relationships and obligations which joined families and communities was still largely in place.[5] On the other hand, the morality of the frontier was changing. Debts could be repudiated, relations terminated or placed on a different basis, and common interests denied. Identity was becoming a political issue and, with boundaries closing, migrants were placed at the mercy of their hosts. The fate of some of the Maasai refugees in the 1890s, sold as slaves rather than incorporated into lineages, was an early warning sign.[6] As the emphasis in interethnic relations shifted from inclusion to exclusion, marginality was rapidly becoming a liability rather than an asset and what had once been an open frontier of opportunity was now reduced to enclaves of insecurity. Those who continued to operate on the frontier were increasingly those who could not fit into, or had been extruded from, their home communities. They now had to create an identity and a living space for themselves that would somehow preserve their contacts with both worlds (Waller, 1984).[7]

A Magnet for Aliens: The Moral Economy of Adoption and Settlement

When the frontiers of Maasailand were effectively closed by the demarcation of reserve boundaries just before the First World War, there were already numbers of resident Kikuyu who regarded themselves as assimilated Maasai or 'adoptees' and were so regarded by the Maasai. Many of them had been with the Maasai on Laikipia and had been moved into the Masai Reserve with them. They were the product of the long tradition of intermarriage, patronage and trade contacts between Maasai and Kikuyu households sketched out above and their presence within Maasailand, like the periodic arrival of parties of Kikuyu traders, provided a visible link with the past.[8]

These Kikuyu migrants and settlers were usually individuals who had prior contacts with the Maasai and whose families had previously successfully straddled the frontier. Their absorption into Maasai communities remained a matter of public agreement between Kikuyu client and Maasai patron and it was expressed and regulated through the idiom of formal sponsorship and adoption. Formal adoption ensured that immigrants to Maasailand were fully integrated into the basic structures of Maasai society — by joining an age-set and becoming a member of a specific household and sub-clan — and that their previous kinship ties were transferred to the host community when the adoptee was symbolically reborn as a Maasai. These steps, and the degree of supervision and control that they implied, prevented the development of separate, non-Maasai enclaves within Maasailand and left the gateway to pastoralism firmly in the guardianship of sponsoring elders (Waller, 1979). It was on this measured and apparently 'traditional' procedure, later institutionalized by written contract and overseen by committees of local elders, that the colonial administration relied to distinguish between legitimate 'assimilees' or 'acceptees' and illegal 'aliens', even though adoption had probably always been somewhat less formal in practice and despite the fact that it was being tempered and adapted to cover new circumstances — by, for example, substituting for *enkiyela e mbere* (adoption of the spear) the less binding *enkiyela e nkurma* (adoption of the *shamba*).[9]

Migration of this kind still continued, driven both by pressures in Kikuyuland, which forced migrants out, and by the demand for labour and wives among the Maasai, which drew them in. For some Kikuyu, Maasailand was still a place of wealth and opportunity where pioneering and entrepreneurial skills could be profitably deployed (Marris and Somerset, 1971). Indeed, as land shortage and conflict mounted at home, it seemed more than ever inviting in its openness, emptiness and comparative lack of administrative regulation.[10] Maasailand was 'a magnet to alien natives' (*NDAR*, 1930), a place of refuge from a variety of colonial plagues: extortionate chiefs and lineage heads, labour recruitment and the burden of taxation (Kanogo, 1987; Furedi, 1989). For the Maasai, access to outside food supplies was still important, and becoming perhaps more so. With the exclusion of important dry-season grazing areas and water-points from the Reserve, the resource base of pastoralism contracted and Maasai grazing movements became more circumscribed. Some Maasai were beginning to establish semi-permanent bases in dry-season reserve areas like the Mau where they could obtain food from neighbouring Kikuyu settlers. Others were becoming *de facto* mixed farmers who kept stock but also had Kikuyu wives and dependants to cultivate plots near their homesteads.[11] Up to the 1940s, however, Maasai cultivation was still intermittent, except near Ngong where a small group who had returned from Kikuyu or who had education and work experience outside the Reserve had taken up small-holder production for the Nairobi market using Kikuyu wage-labour.[12] But the bulk of Kikuyu labour was still used for herding — not cultivation (MT/M/KE1, 17).

Between the wars, however, the flow of Kikuyu immigration into Maasailand increased and its character changed.[13] Older forms of assimilation were still common; but, in localities where agriculture was possible, distinct enclaves of Kikuyu settlement were growing up.[14] The immigrants who formed these settlements differed in important respects from previous 'adoptees'. While some still came first to work for Maasai households and then obtained separate cultivation plots, others negotiated more or less directly for land.[15] They had not necessarily had prior contact with their 'hosts'. Increasingly, would-be settlers arrived under the auspices of existing Kikuyu networks in the Reserve, in which 'assimilees' and Maasai/Kikuyu (*nusus*) played a key role, rather than being invited in as direct clients of the Maasai.[16] Indeed, Maasailand had not always been their original destination. Some were ex-squatters from white farms who had moved across the Reserve boundary onto the Mau when labour contracts were tightened up in the early 1930s (Kanogo, 1987).[17]

Whereas 'adoptees' continued to invest in a pastoral way of life and an identity as assimilated Maasai, these new immigrants were attempting to exploit what amounted to a new frontier of settlement outside Kikuyuland in ways rather similar to Kikuyu 'colonization' of the white farms in the Rift Valley and with the same intention of re-creating the form of the frontier *mbari* (Kanogo, 1987). Relations between these settlers and the Maasai were of a different order. They were not necessarily seeking adoption; nor did they wish to shift from a Kikuyu to a Maasai identity. Many of them brought families and stock with them or called them in later. Even though they made use of the idiom of patronage, kinship and protection[18] in order to obtain land and the right to remain in Maasailand, this was often re-interpreted, by both sides, to include a specifically contractual element in which the Kikuyu cultivator became, in effect, a share-cropper or, in some cases, apparently a tenant or squatter, rather than a protégé with wide but unspecified obligations and rights.[19]

Moreover, many of the new settlers believed that their rights of access rested ultimately on the essentially Kikuyu notion of pioneering which implied that those who cleared the land thereby enjoyed its use.[20] The Maasai saw things differently. Lacking a notion of specific proprietorship of the soil, they believed that, in principle, land was open to all Maasai and could be grazed freely by anyone, with the agreement of the section or neighbourhood within whose boundaries it lay. Use in itself, however, conferred no rights. Non-Maasai might be allowed to cultivate but had no rights of residence or part in the local community unless they obtained them through formal adoption.[21] The word often used to describe such people, *isinkan*, denoted their low status and lack of rights.[22]

The gap between Kikuyu and Maasai perceptions need not in itself have mattered. Relations on the frontier had always been ambiguous and, despite their apparent precariousness, alien agricultural enclaves had a long history in Maasailand (see Sutton, in this volume). They had always been part of the support network of pastoralism — 'plug[ging] the gaps in the Masai economy', as one DC put it (MT/A9) — and they acted both as refuges for the stockless and as staging points for assimilation, places where aspiring non-Maasai might learn to become Maasai (Waller, 1979). There are some indications that a similar process of accommodation and acculturation was at work on the new frontier. Cooperative relations developed. Kikuyu settlers passed themselves off as Maasai and married their daughters to Maasai elders; while their sons joined — or at least imitated — the *murran*.[23] Indeed, in some ways, spatially as well as economically and socially, the frontier remained the same. Networks flourished, accommodations were made and, if parts of Nyeri or Kabete had once resembled Maasailand, now parts of Maasailand were beginning to look like Kiambu. But the direction of flow and the respective values of agriculture and pastoralism had reversed themselves. Kikuyu had once laboured to bring Maasai stock home: now the reward was a Maasai registration certificate or a permit to reside away.[24]

Clients, Patrons and Administrators: Kikuyu Settlement and its Enemies

Yet times *had* changed. Two things now distinguished the new frontier from the old, dividing acceptees and aliens. One was the narrowing of obligation under pressure which made the reinterpretation of rights and obligations problematic. The other was the additional presence of a colonial administration in the Masai Reserve determined to enforce a policy of exclusion, based on supposedly ethnic criteria, which made the continued assertion of a contrary (Kikuyu) identity unacceptable.

To administrators, who tended to lump together economy, identity and place and to assign an appropriate label to each package of characteristics (Waller, 1984),[25] the presence of non-Maasai in the Masai Reserve was certainly anomalous and suspicious, and probably illegal. 'They have no colour of legal right to be here, steal land and then destroy it' (*NDHOR*, October 1946). Twenty years earlier immigrant Kikuyu had been 'the greatest thorn in the side of the Administration' (*NDAR*, 1926), responsible for much of the petty crime in the Reserve, and this remained the general opinion (*MPAR*, 1921, vol. 1; *MPHOR*, December 1946). Suspicion was partly justified. Some of the immigrants did receive stock stolen from adjacent farms, operate black market rings and peddle witchcraft. The imposition of colonial law created its own kinds of criminality. Since many Kikuyu in Maasailand were already living by definition beyond the law it is not surprising that some should have turned this to account.[26] However, the extreme reaction to infiltration, to the establishment of Kikuyu communities and, especially, to those of mixed descent suggests a deeper concern with (ethnic) purity in danger and an anxiety that sprang from the confusion of categories in the administrative mind.[27]

Official policy until 1940 was to exclude aliens from the Masai Reserve, or at least to keep them to an 'irreducible minimum' (*NDAR*, 1926), and to remove Kikuyu who had entered Maasailand without permission since the Maasai Move from Laikipia in 1912. Under the Outlying Districts Ordinance (1902), the Masai Reserve had been declared a Closed District to which entry was allowed only under permit and its restrictions were enforced against Kikuyu squatters.[28] In the 1940s, the district administration reluctantly accepted a degree of controlled 'interpenetration' which, in effect, widened eligibility and thus increased the number of registered acceptees without opening the Reserve.[29] This change came about largely as a result of pressures emanating from central government and from other provinces; but it also marked the realization that exclusion could not be made effective. Although the administration had the legal instruments to hand,[30] the practical difficulties of policing the border, checking credentials, issuing summonses and evicting 'illegals' in the face of widespread evasion and

Maasai connivance were insuperable.[31] In 1939, the Officer in Charge complained that: 'In spite of repeated action taken over the last twelve years, the Kikuyu persist in returning and continuing measures are necessary'; and ten years later, despite increased surveillance, detention and blacklisting, the situation had hardly changed.[32]

The execution of policy followed a familiar cycle. Until the late 1920s, direct action against Kikuyu settlers was relatively infrequent. Indeed, the provisions of the Outlying District Ordinance were aimed more at trespassers and itinerant traders than at established squatters — to keep people out rather than to evict those already in. As on the white farms, these were the golden years for Kikuyu migrants and pioneers. During the next decade, however, the screws progressively tightened — as they did all over Kenya. The rate of prosecutions rose sharply, and between 1936 and 1940 police sweeps followed by wholesale evictions and hut burnings were regular occurrences on the Mau and in Ngong.[33] By 1940, this tough policy had led to a confrontation between the Masai and Kikuyu district administrations and to intervention by both the Kikuyu Central Association (KCA) and the Secretariat. There was simply no room in Kikuyuland for squatters who had often migrated to the Rift decades before and who now had no effective land rights 'at home'. 'Repatriation' by the Masai administration created a crisis for their colleagues in Central Province. Understandably, the latter were as anxious to find an alternative solution as the former were determined to rid themselves of the squatter problem. The clash ended with neither side fully satisfied and the Masai administration remained highly suspicious of 'rather facile and ignorant agitation by certain officers in Central Province with an anti-Masai bias' (*NDHOR*, March 1946) which might lead to further attempts either to 'dump' surplus Kikuyu in Maasailand or demand more land for settlement schemes (*MPHOR*, December 1946).[34] The opening of Olenguruone in 1941 had reduced the pressure but did not solve the problem of Kikuyu infiltration.[35] Since mass evictions had now been ruled out, the Masai administration was obliged to fall back on a cumbersome process of screening and registration which merged into the last period of control and resettlement in Kenya in the early 1950s and which was to become all too familiar to some of the same squatters during the Emergency. Strict categories based on ethnic acceptability and length of residence were set out and tribunals of local Maasai elders appointed to judge the validity of each claim.[36]

Under pressure, the squatters used all the avenues into Maasailand which the long and complex history of relations between Kikuyu and Maa-speaking communities provided. They petitioned to be allowed to remain, offering to pay taxes at the (higher) Maasai rate and to conform to the prescribed identity.[37] They sought out protectors to 'give them a place to stay' (MT/M/DT8) or to 'write them on', i.e. to attest that they were legally employed (MT/M/KE25); and found sponsors willing to vouch for their Maasai credentials. Such credentials were easy to assume and difficult to disprove. There were so many different strands of obligation and versions of the past that, in so far as the administration had committed itself to investigating and validating degrees of 'Maasainess', the arguments of history and ethnicity could sometimes be turned against it. Claimants created or rediscovered appropriate pasts for themselves which they hoped might strike the right note with the local headman or the investigating committee. Gathatwa (see note 9) was, eventually, adjudged to be a Loitai war captive. Ernest Sokoiyan, whose real father had apparently been an early Kikuyu settler in Ngong, claimed to have been adopted by a local Maasai elder and to have taken his name.[38] Some, like Kinaiya, Kamuni and Isiah at Siyabei (see note 16), were 'returnees' whose stories were supported by others. Some of them claimed Laikipiak, Loosekelai or Loogolala ancestry which gave them a place in Maasai tradition and a reason for returning (MT/M/KA6; *ibid.*/P11, 14). None of these claims and pasts were inherently implausible; nor were they necessarily false — though some probably were. But this is to miss the point. They were not intended as 'real' life histories. They represented attempts on the part of the immigrants to accommodate themselves to what they understood to be the dominant concern of the colonial administration, to speak the prescribed language of ethnicity and tradition upon which their interrogators insisted and to make themselves acceptable to prospective neighbours. Separating the alien goats from the acceptable sheep through an ethnic 'means test' was, and is, primarily an outsiders' problem; and it is certain that neither the Maasai elders nor their protégés shared the colonial officers' certainty that degrees of 'Maasainess' could be precisely calibrated. For the Maasai, acceptability was situationally determined, as it always had been. 'Maasai is as Maasai does'; and if the face fitted then so did the life history.[39]

Nevertheless, in colonial Maasailand, it was outsiders who had the power to act on their own assumptions and understandings of what 'Maasai' was; and the penalties for 'getting it wrong' or getting caught were severe.[40] In the last resort, 'illegals' responded by escape and evasion. They entered on temporary permits and overstayed. They forged registration certificates and wrote in the names of elders on work permits. They refused to appear before tribunals; and, at the approach of a police patrol, they melted into the forests or crossed the district boundary, leaving huts, crops and sometimes families to be rounded up.[41]

Colonial legality did not always accord with the morality of the frontier. Inevitably, corruption flourished in a situation of such insecurity and uncertainty where behaviour which was by colonial definition criminal was viewed differently by local standards. Albeit distorted by the alarm and irritation of harassed and suspicious colonial officials who were engaged in the thankless task of policing and who were only partially aware of the undercurrents of intrigue in their areas,[42] a picture emerges of headmen and *boma* clerks who sometimes took bribes or extorted payments and of local bosses who built up private fiefdoms by 'fixing things' for squatters and migrant labourers.[43] Ngong was 'controlled', in this sense, by patrons like ex-chief ole Nakordo and Abdulla Kaurai, both local Kaputiei farmers and businessmen and members of the LNC, and others like Harry Nangurai and Thomas Mootian whose interests extended into smuggling and illegal timber cutting as well as 'protest politics'.[44] Keekonyokie chief ole Saitaka's fiefdom included much of the Kikuyu border area west of Ngong where he was accused of 'doing as he likes', trafficking in grazing and building permits and flooding Ngong with his own people and Kikuyu cultivators. His colleague ole Ngipeda, whose jurisdiction included the squatter centre of Nairage Ngare, an area of notoriously high political pressure on the Mau, was encouraging infiltration and 'establishing a feudal squatter system of his own'.[45] Private interests and conflicts, intensified by the arbitrariness of colonial law, thus informed the context in which identity was determined.

Constructions of Ethnicity: Land, Development and the Community

We have described the situation of the Kikuyu in colonial Maasailand in some detail, partly because of the way that it illustrates the strong elements of continuity with the pre-colonial past in Maasai–Kikuyu relations; but also to emphasize the fact that the definition or redefinition of community and the construction of ethnicity took place within a colonial state, as Iliffe's covering dictum that 'Europeans believed Africans belonged to tribes; Africans built tribes to belong to' reminds us (Iliffe, 1979: 324). Studies of ethnicity have often concentrated on the conscious efforts of the ambitious few to create constituencies for themselves to rule over or to act as spokesmen for, as though ethnic identity could be developed, altered and discarded and 'tradition' created by an act of intellectual will alone. Yet discourse about the community, its past and future, drew on the popular imagination and spoke to general anxieties. In parts of Maasailand 'belonging' was a serious matter — if not of life or death then at least of land and security.[46]

Here, as in Kikuyuland or on the Rift Valley farms, the struggle to belong, to keep an identity, turned on questions of public morality even as it was prosecuted in immoral ways and for private ends. Patrons and protégés both appealed to custom and complained of bad faith and deception. For the Maasai, the obligations of *enaashe* and *osotua* were strained to the limit: 'We did not mind when poor Kikuyu came and worked for us and got food in time of famine but now they come with families and herds of stock . . .' 'Guests' refused to leave when asked and kept returning in defiance of their hosts. Outraged clients believed that they had been deliberately enticed, casually discarded and chased without cause when they demanded their due. Both were right.[47]

Public morality was embedded in tradition — in this case, the tradition of expansion and interaction. The fact of nineteenth-century expansion was real enough; but, at a deeper level, both Maasai and Kikuyu traditions expressed an ideology of growth and movement in space and time which was moral in its inspiration and content. It dealt with both 'becoming' and 'being' — how community arose, how individuals became citizens, and what that citizenship involved. Public tradition was elaborated after the event and out of private memory to provide a vehicle for expounding values and for distinguishing between rival claims on the community. It was part of the community identity but, since it rested on a particular version of events, it could be challenged by other versions or reinterpreted to point a different moral (Sobania and Waller, n.d.; Sobania and Spencer, in this volume). During the colonial period, the past became a battleground in which differing versions of 'tradition' were put forward in support of competing views of the community in the present and the future (Berman and Lonsdale, 1992; Waller, 1984).

Across the border, different elements of the community were fighting each other over what it meant to be 'Kikuyu'. In Maasailand, the colonial administration was imposing its own definition of what it meant to be 'Maasai' and energetically trying to enlist Maasai support for it, using the image of 'the alien' both as a threat and as something against which 'Maasainess' could be measured. There were three sets of actors in search of a usable past: the Maasai, the colonial administration and the Kikuyu immigrants.[48] Each group had its own 'progressive traditionalists' (Iliffe, 1979: 329), codifying and restating tradition, whether absorbed in the cattle camp or the club, in order to establish some common ground of agreement or opposition, and, in effect, to determine what 'Maasainess' was.[49] But those who sought to do this had also to take public opinion into account for it was ultimately the audience that set the limits of the debate and which 'arbitrated' the claims to knowledge put forward.[50]

We may begin with the district administration since it was they who 'made all the running' (MT/A5) over the issue of Kikuyu infiltration and settlement and who sought to carry the Maasai with them. We have noted some of their concerns with categorization and crime; and we may now examine how they presented the issue publicly, both to the Maasai and to the colonial government. For the district administration, it was the moral responsibility of government and trusteeship that was fundamentally at issue. In acting against infiltrators and in the 'spirit of the Masai Treaty', they were defending the Maasai — a people whose traditional way of life, protected by solemn treaty, was threatened by land-hungry alien cultivators. Severe measures were necessary because of the growing magnitude of the problem, since aliens were cunning and the Maasai themselves often too 'supine' or unconcerned — or perhaps betrayed by the private greed of a few unrepresentative and corruptible elders and headmen — to defend themselves.[51] District commissioners continually reminded the Maasai that aliens were encroaching on and spoiling their land and drove the point home by asking whether they did, in fact, wish to lease or sell land outright to other peoples — which they did not.[52]

This was a shrewd line to take, for two reasons. In grounding their objections to infiltration in the absolute inviolability of Maasai boundaries under the provisions of the 1911 Agreement, they made it necessary for proponents of interpenetration or of reciprocal leasing either to grapple with the legal difficulties of overriding the Agreement or to secure the general agreement of the Maasai to boundary modifications which, in turn, would require a substantial *quid pro quo* from government.[53] By raising the spectre of land alienation at meetings, the district administration hit a very sore spot. The Maasai were far more concerned about threats to their land than about threats to their ethnic integrity (as envisioned from outside) and successive officers played on their concern to obtain general assent to their policy of exclusion and expulsion.[54] In 1904 and 1911-12, the Maasai had lost large areas of valuable grazing and several vital water-points which they had not succeeded in regaining, despite continual agitation. They were deeply suspicious, therefore, of anything which seemed likely to deprive them of more land or to infringe their control of what remained to them within the Reserve boundaries. In the early 1930s, serious drought, which highlighted the previous loss of valuable resources, and the hearings of the Kenya Land Commission, which raised the issue of boundary revisions and gave the Maasai an excellent opportunity to air their complaints, coincided with the increased influx of Kikuyu squatters. It was easy to join the issues of land shortage and alien infiltration and package them under an appeal to community solidarity and ethnic particularism.[55]

Yet official attitudes were neither quite so simple nor so homogeneous in practice. Initially, nomadic pastoralism had been viewed with suspicion and disfavour. Since pastoralists did not seem to use land productively and apparently contributed little to the colonial state, they neither required nor deserved extensive reserves. They were to be encouraged to settle and to take up agriculture, the next rung on the ladder of human evolution. Land alienation and the example of neighbouring peoples might provide the necessary 'encouragement'. This punitive attitude, however, was modified by one that was more protective. District administrators, in particular, tended to regard the archetypal pastoral Maasai as something of an endangered species, likely to 'die out peacefully of inanition' unless they could be induced to change. As nomads, 'they [could] not possibly become much more than interesting zoological specimens' (*NDAR*, 1929).[56]

Before 1930, however, development in Maasailand was more a matter of exhortation than action, and the pastoral economy stagnated (Waller, 1975). Much as Kikuyu immigration was deplored, it was acknowledged that many of the immigrants were productive agriculturalists whose habits might perhaps encourage change among their Maasai neighbours. Unchecked, however, they would turn 'the most fertile parts of the Province . . . [into] an annexe of the Kikuyu Reserve' and thus deny this option to the Maasai in the long term (*MPAR*, 1929 vol. 2). The view that valuable land was locked up in the Masai Reserve, and thus out of the hands of those who could make best use of it, remained strong even within the district administration and was reflected in the thinking of successive government commissions.[57] The crises of the early '30s hardened opinions and pointed a dilemma. The near collapse of the Maasai economy under the pressure of drought, disease and trade restriction, and the consequent reduction of tax revenue, forced a reassessment of policy in Maasailand. Even if only in order to force them to take a more effective part in supporting the colonial state, the Maasai would have to be developed (Waller, 1986). But would it be possible to fashion a 'new Maasai' way of life in the image of the old? Administrative opinion was split between those who envisaged a form of commercial or peasant pastoralism essentially dependent on markets among more 'advanced' peoples outside the Reserve and who viewed alien settlement inside the Reserve as almost a natural consequence of increased articulation, and those who urged the encouragement of Maasai agriculture as part of an ambitious plan to reshape the pastoral economy from within and who were determined that agricultural land, like grazing, should be retained for the exclusive use of Maasai mixed farmers (Waller, 1986). The issues of economic development, social change and land use were thus related (see further, Campbell, in this volume) and this in turn influenced policies towards alien settlement. It also raised the crucial question of what the essential elements of 'Maasainess' were and thus linked re-evaluations of identity to shifts in economy.

The inclusionists were mostly administrators with a wider view of Kenyan development and, especially, with a sense of impending crisis in over-populated reserves elsewhere.[58] They continued to argue that, since the last available reserves of high potential agricultural land lay virtually unused in Maasailand, controlled settlement should be sponsored as a natural safety-valve or outlet for surplus people. They believed that commercial pastoralism should be integrated into the development of the wider African market in Kenya; and that interpenetration would sufficiently safeguard Maasai identity.[59]

The exclusionists were predominantly local district officers concerned to prevent the Maasai — and what they appeared to symbolize — from being overwhelmed and marginalized by a tidal wave of alien immigration.[60] In keeping with the times, they also argued persuasively that valuable forest land was in danger of being destroyed by the same sort of wasteful and inefficient agriculture that was apparently ruining

Kikuyuland.[61] They tended to oppose central government policy in principle on the grounds that it devalued pastoralism,[62] and they believed that the particularistic Maasai way of life, as they saw it, was capable of careful adaptation and had a future of its own. The Maasai were 'not dying out but changing' (*NDHOR*, March 1946). The right sort of gradual development would widen economic horizons while still conserving the best parts of Maasai tradition.[63] In October 1936, the annual Maasai sports meeting at Narok included a propaganda display put on by the DC, Buxton, which dramatically illustrated the 'progressive traditionalism' of the administration. Three sections described 'Masai Pride' as the paladins of the nineteenth-century Rift Valley; 'Masai Misfortunes', chiding the Maasai for being slow to realize the opportunities of the *pax Britannica* and for allowing others to outstrip them while they took refuge in past glories from their present problems; and a 'Masai Future' in which their considerable natural assets might be used, by active participation in development schemes, 'to win, and hand on, greater glory for their tribe'. The display ended with a homily which epitomized the moral message of invented tradition: 'As the Masai today are rightly proud of their ancestors so must they see to it that their descendants have reason to be proud of them.'[64]

Maasai attitudes to the Kikuyu settlers are hard to pin down; but they were certainly ambivalent and divided. Fazan's assessment that there was little serious opposition to a degree of controlled interpenetration was probably accurate enough (*MPMIR*, April 1935). Yet their spokesmen were under pressure from the administration to deny their relationships with the Kikuyu. Accordingly, they expressed their public opposition to infiltration and, in private, continued to exercise discretion and patronage for the real benefits that they brought.[65] Administrators found the combination of ostensible cooperation with covert obstruction infuriating. In his handing-over notes, one Kajiado DC complained that while the LNC demanded the removal of aliens 'whenever you try to remove any individual . . . there is a storm of protest'.[66]

The benefits of patronage were not merely economic, in the form of labour service and 'bribes', as the administration construed the various kinds of reciprocities involved,[67] but also social and political — as they always had been. Clients and the daughters they offered as wives[68] enlarged an elder's household and gave him weight in the community. Purko Senior Chief Masikonte had 'his' Kikuyu at Rotian and so did many other chiefs and influential elders. As one elder put it: 'There was no Maasai camp without its Kikuyu. "That's my Kikuyu!" "That's mine!"' (MT/M/P42).[69] They increased the strength of the section in whose territory they were settled and supplied contacts with the outside world, necessary, for instance, to smuggle stock or to retain a stake in central politics.[70]

However, such was the double-edged nature of ethnicity, sponsoring Kikuyu settlement laid both individuals and sections open to charges of betraying Maasai interests and, even, of not being 'true' Maasai themselves. Given past history, there was often enough plausibility in this for it to be used in local feuds. Each faction tried to undermine the credibility of its opponents by implicitly questioning both their 'loyalty' and their commitment to Maasai values.[71] Politicization of identity became most acute where access to grazing and water was involved. On the Mau there was conflict over sectional boundaries between Purko, Damat and Keekonyokie and all three used the issue of Kikuyu settlement as a weapon — and also, by recruiting Kikuyu followers, as a resource. Similar conflicts were pursued over the Ngong Hills between Keekonyokie and Kaputiei and in the Kedong Valley between grazers and cultivators. Kikuyu settlers were merely pawns caught in the undergrowth of Maasai politics and, while on some occasions this made it easier to hide from the administration, on others, when the nightmares of district administrators coincided with the private feuds of Maasai elders, it left them exposed to retaliation and arrest.[72]

Defending Ethnicity: The Progressive Dilemma

If ethnicity was double-edged, it was also multi-layered. Setting the question of ethnicity within the context of local politics and colonial manipulation is helpful but it cannot entirely explain why, for instance, some of the most vocal advocates of exclusion were themselves patrons or of mixed background, or why headmen like Mariani ole Kirtela who were supporters of the 'acceptee'-dominated Masai Association chased aliens so relentlessly from the late 1930s.[73] Nor does such an exclusively instrumental view take into account the growing Maasai concern with, and distrust of, the spread of Kikuyu settlement.[74] To go further, we must consider other levels of discourse within the Maasai community and thus return to the question of Maasai identity.

In their attitudes to alien settlement, the Maasai were playing on colonial images and phobias to maintain their autonomy and to keep both Kikuyu migrants and administrators under control. They developed a formal ethnic identity not because they were in search of a community but because, as boundaries hardened under colonial definition, the loosely articulated community that they had could not deal effectively with outsiders without one. By confronting aliens Maasai were also finding a language for dealing with the effects of change and division amongst themselves. Appeals for solidarity against outsiders were meant for internal consumption as well as external show — even, or perhaps especially, when voiced by patrons who were bending rules to their own ends. Similarly, assertions about the historical and moral basis of inter-community relations, the language of reciprocity and obligation, when applied to recalcitrant clients and adoptees insisted that an overarching moral order still existed despite external challenges. Thus 'Maasai' might be what 'others' could not be. In this sense, aliens took the place of 'Dorobo' as 'the mirror in the forest', defining the community by posing its opposite.[75] It did not always work. Purko appealed to Damat as fellow-members of a wider Maasai community; Damat responded as one section dealing with another. Aliens, unable to become *echte* Maasai, formed their own communities and rejected the subordinate and insecure client status allotted to them in the Maasai world. Yet the concern with unity and community, with determining 'Maasainess' and denying non-Maasai laid the matrix within which a single definitive Maasai identity developed.[76] The Maasai 'became Maasai' partly to prevent others from doing so.

The dominant Maasai voice in the debate was that of the traditionalists, 'progressive' or otherwise, leading spokesmen of the stock-owning elite, like ole Galishu and ole Kirtela, whose wealth and influence gave them the confidence to speak for their community. But there were other voices, less patrician and less secure, also striving to be heard. They belonged to the marginal men, living precariously between Maasai and the outside world and seeking a place in both by attempting to reconcile being Maasai with being something else as well.[77] They had an organizational nucleus in the Masai Association (founded in 1930) and a platform provided by Maasai concern over land losses. The debate over development in Maasailand gave them the opportunity to argue that one did not need to be a subsistence pastoralist in order to be a full Maasai.

Their first efforts revolved around the Land Commission hearings at which they presented a petition on behalf of the Maasai in October 1932. The petition dealt with grievances over the Maasai Treaties and subsequent land disputes and included a demand for the return of the Laikipia Plateau from which the Maasai had been removed in 1912. It made its case by carefully reviewing the statements of previous government commissions and by 'plac[ing] on record glimpses of our status prior to the British advent as well as the characteristics and our origin as analysed by eminent Britishers from time to time'. This set the argument firmly within the public tradition of the Maasai Moves. It established the 'historical fact' of Maasai hegemony over, and 'beneficial use' of, the Rift Valley plains and the present causes of Maasai poverty in their loss of land and lack of appropriate development opportunities. But the petitioners also argued that agriculture had been, in effect, forced on them by the reduction of grazing and the restrictions on movement. They were now perforce becoming mixed pastoralists to survive and required guaranteed access to agricultural land. The petition appeared under the names of forty-six elders including most of the section headmen and chiefs and the age-set spokesmen but few of the more obvious 'marginals' who had inspired it. It was a first attempt to establish a consensus between different 'voices', to enlist the influential and to create a sense of identity which was consciously based on the traditional past yet aware of change and able to adapt to it.[78]

This last was timely, for in November the *East African Standard* printed extracts from the Chief Native Commissioner's Annual Report for 1931 under the headline: 'Degeneration of the Masai. Is the Tribe Heading Towards Extinction?' The report repeated the familiar official wisdom about the unwillingness of the Maasai to respond to new ideas or to adapt to new conditions and warned that they would be swamped by more vigorous and progressive immigrants. Maasai seemed synonomous with backwardness and decline. The Masai Association responded angrily to what they saw as 'the worst libel that has ever been published in respect of any living community' and had their recent petition circulated as a pamphlet in rebuttal of 'this wholesale and sweeping condemnation of the Masai Tribe'. In the preface, they argued that such statements merely damaged the credibility of government and showed how difficult a 'redemption' of the tribe would be under such 'unsympathetic' rulers. It became clear that staking out an identity would involve a more explicit advocacy of change and that this might bring the Association and its supporters into direct conflict with the administration.[79]

In 1934, when the Commission findings were released — and alien infiltration was increasing — the progressives moved a step further in a letter which announced that [sic] 'the time have now arrival when we have started taking interested in Agriculture. We means to work hard and want to cultivate as much land as is possible.' This time the letter was signed by leading figures in the Masai Association alone.[80] They had apparently been unable to carry the majority with them; but their struggle to escape from the exclusive 'pure pastoral' image and to assert a Maasai identity which was flexible and 'progressive' and which included, in Thomas Mootian's words, 'rearrangements [of] our old tribe customs . . . throw[ing] out the sheeps and cattles for cultivations of land' continued (quoted in King, 1971a: 132). Sadly, however, despite their obvious pride in the Maasai past, men like Mootian were too close to the alien 'other' to be acceptable spokesmen for the community at large.[81] In some ways, they shared the predicament of the Kikuyu squatters, caught between hardened economic and social boundaries. In 1939, Mootian, who had been settled at Olenguruone since 1934, was evicted to make way for the Kikuyu even though his mixed farming had been encouraged by the DC and he had 'take[n] carefully [to] the new fashion at presents' in building a modern house and taking up cultivation.[82]

By the late 1940s, the progressives had split. Some, like Mootian, followed the logic of their increasingly anti-colonial stance, remained with central politics and ended in detention during Mau Mau. As far as local ethnicity was concerned their voice was stilled. Others, however, like many of the Maasai teachers, found their way back into the community as 'progressive traditionalists'. Their voice was eventually heard in the District Councils, the local courts and the Maasai primary schools. They 'became Maasai' partly to instruct others in how to be so.[83]

The apparent difficulty of finding an alternative but still valid voice

Photo 11.2 Thomas Maitei ole Mootian
(based on photograph in King,
Kenneth J. and Salim, Ahmed I.,
Kenya Historical Biographies,
Nairobi, East African Publishing
House, 1971.)

suggests that, however open to debate Maasai identity might be, it
remained firmly grounded in a particular set of values which could not
easily be discarded or re-ordered. Thus tradition and its re-interpreters
alike acknowleged the age system with its particular sense of time and
maturation as the core of both personal and community identity (see
Spencer and Galaty, in this volume). On this point there was little
disagreement between the proponents of different versions of Maasainess, though there was much argument about how the system should
be maintained in practice.[84]

Concepts of wealth and achievement, however, did become an issue.
Maasai values were still based on a cattle standard. Control over stock
and its product was a mark of full adulthood for both men and women
and a measure of civic responsibility and virtue — even though the
fortunes of herding were unpredictable and there were always households
temporarily on the edge of insolvency (see Telelia, in this volume).
Taking up the 'new fashion' did not bring much tangible reward in
Maasai terms, and aspiring 'new Maasai' were put at a serious disadvan-
tage in their efforts to win acceptance for their views. Mission converts,
clerks and teachers had little but salary and civility to show for their

innovation, as they themselves were aware, and it seemed to their critics within the Maasai community that 'progress' was to be equated with poverty and, thus, with immaturity rather than with wealth and responsibility (King, 1971a and 1971b; Waller, 1986). Such people were becoming 'more like Kikuyu' than Maasai and, whatever their standing with the colonial administration as the inheritors of the New Earth and the proponents of a new Maasai identity, they could hardly speak with the authority of stock and family ownership.[85] It was not until much later, after a further period of drought and marginalization had dented the assurance of the stock-owning elite and when, with the encroachment of a free market, control of land itself was becoming a source of power and of somewhat uneasy and divisive wealth (see Campbell, in this volume), that they were freed from this constraint. In the 1970s, the call for a 'new Maasai' was being reluctantly listened to, even by those who deplored its need but recognized that, once again, it would be necessary to create an identity as a defence against powerful outsiders (who dealt in cash not clientage) and their political allies inside the community.[86]

Conclusion

It remains only to restate some of the wider themes embedded in our discussion. The first is the continuing importance of the frontier. Although the creation of a colonial state in Kenya changed the context in which the Maasai and their neighbours interacted, many of the older networks and linkages remained. People preferred to hold on to what was familiar rather than to embrace what was new. If some opportunities were now denied, others emerged or were simply redefined. Cross-border trade, for instance, became smuggling and 'black-marketeering'. The 'tribalism' of colonial officials, attempting to distinguish between the indistinguishable, threatened to split apart the old solidarities of the frontier, but their subjects knitted them together again and the frontier was never quite closed. Indeed, by the 1940s it seemed to be almost more open than ever — to 'infiltration', as migration and settlement had now been defined. Thus boundary maintenance and the redefinition of identity continued to move in counterpoint against the background of a regional economy that was still expanding, but in order to understand the harmony we need to know more about its shifting colonial context.[87]

Keeping the frontier open and maintaining ethnic interaction along it was not costless, however. The cost was paid, mostly by migrants and clients, in insecurity and moral outrage. The moral economy of the frontier changed and perhaps soured under two sets of pressures. One was the developing sense of ethnic exclusivity among Maasai which sharpened the bite of 'custom' and tradition and became a means by which clients could be more effectively dominated by their patrons. The rules of adoption, for instance, were simplified but adoption itself became looser, open to challenge and abuse and, therefore, less of a protection to the weak. The other pressure came from the imposition of colonial law. The state now defined what was criminal and in some circumstances ethnic identity could be a crime. Squatters in Maasailand were 'out of place' both as Kikuyu in the Masai Reserve and as cultivators in a pastoral area when these categories of residence and occupation were elaborated as an integral part of the reconstruction of ethnicity by Maasai and colonial administrators alike. Their plight thus illustrates two lines of investigation — the moral economy of marginality and the criminality of 'tribe' — which have yet to be fully explored in the historiography of colonial Africa.[88]

The third theme ties settlement, land use and identity together. Although the problems posed by Kikuyu settlers were presented by the colonial administration, and, under some pressure, by the Maasai chiefs also, in ethnic terms — as the infiltration of aliens and the creation of unwanted and exploitative 'bastard' (Maasai/Kikuyu) communities on the fringes of Maasailand — the underlying issue was that of land. Maasai identity was rooted in a sense of place, however mobile and extensive that might be,[89] and land, its use and control, runs as a subtext throughout Maasai history. During the nineteenth century, different Maa-speaking groups had struggled to gain control of the strategic grazing areas on which their herds — and therefore their pastoralism — depended. After 1900, it was the enormous extent of the area that the Maasai occupied and the way that they used or misused it that concerned white settlers and administrators (Sandford, 1919). Later it was the insufficiency of land available to maintain pastoralism that brought the Maasai into conflict with the Land Commission. Finally, it was fears of losing land that focused Maasai attention on immigrants. Access to land was bound up with identity: land use was even more so. The threat of a different kind of land use in Maasailand, with its implications for image and identity, was as important in influencing attitudes towards Kikuyu settlers as the fear of infiltration itself. The identification of Maasai with cattle ownership implied an equal identification with herding and thus with using land in a particular way. Pastoral land-use was seen in positive terms and contrasted with the (negative) use of land for growing crops. In the past, the opposition between herding and agriculture had perhaps provided one means of expressing the boundary between Maasai and alien, although it had always been a shifting and ambiguous one.[90] To a degree, squatter settlement reinforced this opposition. As grazers, Kikuyu clients might become members of the community: as farmers, by definition, they were not. Socially and economically, as well as geographically, they remained on the forest margins. But where do 'cultivating Maasai' and the positive image of modernization which some Maasai wished to adopt fit into this scheme? It is likely that dealing with such apparent anomalies within a Maasai cultural tradition had always exercised the community in the past (see Spear, 'Being Maasai', in this volume). Simple pre-colonial oppositions between pastoral centre and non- or semi-pastoral periphery in Maasailand which have shaped models of interaction in the past must then be reconsidered in the light of responses to Kikuyu settlement and of interpretations that consider land use and apportionment as central issues in colonial (and post-colonial) Kenya.

Gradually, an explicit ethnic identity, available for use by outsiders as well as by Maasai, began to emerge out of the interplay between a variety of ideas, not always mutually compatible, about what 'being Maasai' — and being non-Maasai — meant. For different people it might mean being pastoralists or being mixed farmers; remaining within the bounds of 'tradition' or escaping from the backwardness that 'tradition' seemed to imply; being part of a tight-drawn community or moving between different communities. The many strands of Maasainess is the last theme. To generate the variety of ideas that fed into the debate about identity required an equal variety of actors, both inside and outside the Maasai community. Kikuyu settlers and colonial administrators were as actively influential in shaping ideas of Maasainess as were Maasai themselves. They were not simply part of the context within which an autonomous development took place. Historians, too, are now part of this process as they engage in dialectic with the Maasai. Our conclusion has indicated new lines of general enquiry suggested by the Maasai case. Similarly, previous developments in colonial historiography have made it possible to frame the questions pursued here and thus to enter the debate and to contribute to the construction or re-creation of the Maasai in history.

Discourse about identity, as a means of communication, requires an audience which is composed of 'others' as well as members of the community itself (see Klumpp and Kratz, in this volume). These 'others' are not merely listeners but participants. In this debate, Kikuyu settlement was a central issue not just because it seemed to threaten the integrity of Maasailand but also because of the serious questions that immigrants, as ambiguous 'others', raised about alternative constructions of 'Maasainess'. Just as Maasai had always existed as part of a social and economic system which included non-Maasai, so 'Maasainess' could only develop and be redefined in a continuous debate with others. Were there no 'other', there could be no 'Maasai'.

Notes

* I am indebted to my co-editor and to other colleagues for comments on an earlier draft of this chapter; and, especially, to John Lonsdale for sharing with me his ideas in draft on Kikuyu civic morality and citizenship which have greatly stimulated my own thinking. Some references to files in the Kenya National Archives [KNA] are abbreviated as follows:
Kajiado District, *Annual Reports* [KDAR] (1930–1933) DC/KAJ 2/1/1
Masai Province, *Annual Reports* [MPAR] (1914–1939) 3 vols. PC/SP 1/2/1–2, DC/NRK 1/2/1.

Acceptees & Aliens

Masai Province, *Handing-Over Reports* [*MPHOR*] (1936–1946) PC/SP 2/1/1
Masai Province, *Monthly Intelligence Reports* [*MPMIR*] (1934–1937) PC/SP 3/1/1
Narok District, *Annual Reports* [*NDAR*] (1920–1941) DC/NRK 1/1/1–3
Narok District, *Handing-Over Reports* [*NDHOR*] (1946) DC/NRK 2/1/1

1. The prevailing orthodoxy is still that of Jacobs (1965) despite criticisms by, amongst others, Berntsen (1979a); Waller (1979); and Sobania (1980). See also the Introduction to this volume by Spear.
2. The development of Kikuyu ethnicity during the colonial period has been examined in detail by Berman and Lonsdale (1992).
3. It is possible, though we know too little about it, that the freedom of the frontier placed women in a position of relative autonomy and influence which was later eroded when the horizons of household and community narrowed during the colonial period — see J.Guyer, 'Household and Community in African Studies', *African Studies Review*, 24 (1981: 87–137); Cohen and Odhiambo (1989).
4. Both Berntsen (1980) and Waller (in Lamprey and Waller, 1990) have argued that the emphasis on a purely pastoral diet and ethos is both atypical and, probably, ephemeral, a result of increased pastoral specialization and conflict during the nineteenth century.
5. It was often difficult to separate 'Maasai' and 'Kikuyu' branches of a single kinship network on the frontier — *MPAR* (1922) vol. 1. Some of the flavour of this complexity is conveyed in KLC (1934a) *Evidence* I, especially e.g. pp. 227–235; M[aasai]T[ext]/K[ikuyu] 2 (texts of interviews are deposited in Cambridge and Nairobi and are accessed by a section and number code). In some circumstances it was still politically astute in Kikuyuland to claim kinship with important Maasai families, notably that of Mbatiany, the *laibon* — see e.g. notes in file 'Unsorted Misc.', Barlow Papers, University Library, Nairobi (I am grateful to Dr Berntsen for drawing my attention to these); *Harry Thuku: An Autobiography* (Nairobi, 1970: pp. 95–96).
6. Their repudiation was partly the result of strain in local economies unable to cope with the volume of famine refugees; but it was also an indication of shifts in the basis of wealth and authority, later accentuated by colonial rule, that threatened interethnic reciprocities (Waller, 1988).
7. Some of the returning Maasai/Kikuyu 'marginals', for example, found a home at the Africa Inland Mission settlement at Siyabei near Narok and a sense of community and identity in Christianity and through the political activities of the Masai Association (Waller, 1986; King, 1971b).
8. 'Memorandum on the [Northern] Masai', n.d. KNA: Native Affairs Dept.Mss, III, part II, 19/iii/48; Laikipia District, *Annual Report* [*AR*] (1909/10) KNA: DC/LKA 1/1; Dagoretti Sub-District, *AR* (1912/13) KNA: DC/KBU 1/4; *NDARs* (1920/21, 1930); Waller (1975).
9. Minute of DOs Meeting, June 1941, quoted in Officer in Charge, Masai Reserve [OIC Masai] to Chief Secretary [CS], 19 September 1941, and Minute of Joint Local Native Council Meeting, July 1941, quoted in same to same, 1 March 1945, both in KNA: MAA 2/1/7/2; Secretariat Circular 29, 5 July 1948, KNA: PC/NZA 2/1/106; notes on adoption and case file: R. vs Gathatwa, both in *Walker Papers*, Rhodes House, Oxford. One case suggests that intermarriage customs were changing in similar ways. When Paul Kinanjui wished to marry a Maasai girl in 1941, his prospective father-in-law, who had no sons, insisted that his son-in-law settle near him, 'be his son' and 'be a Masai in all respects'. In return, he was to be given land on retirement and was allowed to visit his [Kikuyu] kin — Station Master, Dagoretti [Kinanjui] to Commissioner of Police, 23 October 1952, KNA: PC/Ngong 1/1/16.
10. Not all land shortage was due to population pressure. The commonage was being steadily engrossed and some of the Kikuyu who were settling in Ngong, for instance, were herd-owners in search of grazing rather than squatters seeking farmland — 'Political Records to 1924' in *Ngong Political Record Book*, Part A, KNA: DC/KAJ 1/2/1; *MPHOR*, March 1936; minute by Chief Native Commissioner [CNC], 9 February 1940, on PC Central to CS, 29 January 1940, MAA 2/1/7/2; Ngong survey data, July 1948, in PC/Ngong 1/1/16.

Contestations & Redefinitions

11. MT/M[aasai]/KA12; *ibid.*/KE25; MT/A[dministrator]9. These shifts were very gradual, until the serious droughts of the early 1930s created near famine conditions in much of Maasailand and emphasized the need to secure reliable alternative food supplies — MT/M/KE7; *MPARs* (1914/15, 1918/19) vol. 2; *NDAR* (1920/21); *KDAR* (1930); *MPARs* (1931, 1934–35) vol. 2 and *idem* (1933–34) vol. 1; *MPMIR*, May 1935; MT/M/DT5; *ibid*/P37.
12. *MPARs* (1928-29, 1931) vol. 2; MT/M/KA16,20; *ibid.*/KL10. In 1928 the total area of Maasai cultivation at Ngong was estimated at 500 acres and the scale, if not the extent, remained small. Only three farms of over ten acres were recorded in 1948. Two belonged to early pioneers, Abdullah Kaurai and James Ngatia, who had 20 and 50 acres and employed four and three labourers respectively — Ngong survey data, *op. cit.*; MT/M/KA1, 19.
13. All colonial population statistics are difficult to interpret and figures for non-Maasai in Maasailand are no exception. Only officially registered aliens were enumerated and the categories under which they were entered in reports varied. Between 1920 and 1940, the alien population roughly doubled, according to the provincial annual reports; but the 1948 census figures, taken together with the numbers previously evicted (over 1,000 from Ngong in 1937, for instance), suggest that the increase was in fact much greater. By 1948, there were about 6,000 aliens residing in the Reserve. Around 1930, there had been perhaps c. 1,300 Kikuyu officially resident in the Masai Reserve, approximately the same number recorded for Kajiado District alone in the 1948 census — East African Statistical Dept., *African Population of Kenya Colony and Protectorate: Geographical and Tribal Studies* (Nairobi, 1950).
14. Apart from the gazetted townships of Ngong and Narok, where aliens might apply for residential or shop plots, and the mission at Siyabei, the main areas of Kikuyu settlement were on the south-eastern Mau (Il Melili and Nairage Ngare) around the Ngong Hills (Ololua, Kiserian) and on the slopes of Ol Doinyo Orok (Namanga) — *MPARs* (1924, 1928, 1939) vol. 2.
15. 'Political Records to 1924', *op. cit.*; *MPAR* (1928) vol. l.
16. *NDAR* (1926); OIC Masai to CS, 3 March 1945, *op.cit.*; *MPHOR*, December 1946; CNC to [?], 3 November 1952, PC/Ngong 1/1/16. Among the *'nusus'* accused of harbouring 'illegals' were the mission converts at Siyabei — 'Kikuyu camouflaged as Masai' (*NDAR*, 1925). In an earlier age, such men might have been regarded as patrons and entrepreneurs rather than as dubious characters — *MPAR* (1935) vol. l. For an example of how such networks operated, see the story of Kinaiya, Kamuni and Isiah, three 'returnees' from Kiambu in the late 1920s, recounted in MT/M/KE5.
17. Labour Officer, Nakuru to Principal Labour Inspector, Nairobi, 18 March 1935, PC/Ngong 1/1/44; *MPMIR*, March 1936; *MPARs* (1936–37) vol. 1; ag. PC Rift to OIC Masai, 5 August 1936, and DO Narok to DC Kiambu, 15 September 1936, KNA: DC/Ngong 1/1/22. More than 4,000 farm squatters allegedly settled on the Mau — Exeeutive Council memo., 2 March 1950, KNA: DC/NKU 4/1. The majority came from the adjacent white farm districts, especially Naivasha, between 1933 and 1935 — no doubt using contacts developed through the border markets where farm squatters exchanged produce with the local Maasai and, perhaps, also relying on obligations incurred when Maasai moved onto the farms to escape the 1933/34 drought. But the fact that some immigrants came from farms as far away as Ol Kalou, Subukia and even Rumuruti suggests the existence of a much wider squatter network — Furedi (1989: 43, 52, 64–65, 81); *MPAR* (1934) vol.1; Manager, Lesirko Ltd. [Ol Kalou] to OIC Masai, 7 September 1936, and Griffin [Ol Kalou] to same, 12 September 1936, DC/Ngong 1/1/22. Biographical details of Mau squatters from repatriation lists compiled in 1940 in files KNA: PC/RVP 6A/l/17/2 and MAA 2/1/7/2.
18. MT/M/DT5; *ibid.*/KE17, 21, 25. Informants noted the appeal to ties of *osotua* and *enaashe* as well as to kin and clan.
19. *MPAR* (1928) vol. 1; *NDAR* (1936), copy in *Buxton Papers*, Rhodes House. For an example of a Maasai squatter contract, see request by Francis Nguseo for permission

to bring in a Kikuyu *shamba* worker who preferred to be given a piece of land in lieu of wages — Ole Nguseo to OIC Masai, 3 April 1937, DC/Ngong 1/1/22. Petitions of this sort were common.

20. For the Kikuyu 'labour theory of value', see Berman and Lonsdale (1992). The expectations of Kikuyu squatters in Maasailand came out clearly at Olenguruone (Throup, 1987; Kanogo, 1987). Although the Olenguruone protesters based their claims primarily on their original right-holdings in Kiambu, they also argued that they had subsequently developed rights in Maasailand itself — Kanogo (1987: 109–111); Gaitho to Koinange, 15 October 1946, PC/RVP 6A/l/17/1. See also DO Olenguruone to DC Nakuru, 31 May 1947, *ibid.*, and minutes of meeting at CNC's office, 14 April 1947, DC/NKU 6/2. I am grateful to Dr Throup for allowing me access to his notes on the Olenguruone files in the KNA.

21. See e.g. statements in case file R. vs Gathatwa, *op.cit.* Maasai 'custom' as regards land rights was expressed in Council meetings and strongly endorsed by the local administration — Kajiado Local Native Council [LNC] Minutes, February 1935, DC/KAJ 5/1/3; *MPAR* (1937) vol. 3; *MPHOR*, December 1946.

22. The earliest citation of *osinka* (sing.) (Erhardt, 1857: 17) gives 'captive' or a name for 'Dorobo'. Broadly, the word means 'servant' or 'menial' — a Kisongo elder quoted in Johnston (1886: 407) uses it in the latter sense and so does a folk tale collected by Hollis (1905: 186, 292). It could also refer to a slave. Only in Johnston does it have a specifically agricultural context. By 1930, *osinka* was apparently being used in Kajiado as an alternative for *ol chekuti*, 'dependent herder' (presumably in the sense of 'labourer'); but it retained its earlier status reference in Narok — *NDAR* (1930, Appendix). It was precisely this status of hireling that the Olenguruone settlers, for example, were bitterly rejecting. In Kikuyu terms, they regarded themselves as *ahoi* not *ndungata*.

23. MT/M/DK3; *ibid.*/P42; *MPAR* (1921) vol.1; *NDAR*s (1926, 1928); Mathu to CS, 3 March 1945, MAA 2/1/7/2. Marriage ties often smoothed the way towards absorption. As Paul Kinanjui (see note 9) put it in his petition: 'I am no longer a Kikuyu as per agreement made between my parents, myself and the parents of my wife . . .' — Kinanjui to Commissioner of Police, 23 October 1952, *op. cit.*

24. Compare descriptions of the Kikuyu frontier around 1890 with one of the Ngong area half a century later — KLC, *Report*, Appendix I; memoranda and minutes of meeting, September 1937, encl. in OIC Masai to CS, 22 October 1937, PC/Ngong 1/2/7; *NDAR* (1930).

25. The DC Narok, noting that Maasai did not take to agriculture, stated bluntly that those who did have *shambas* were not pure Maasai (*NDAR*, 1939). Belief in the axiom: 'Maasai = pastoral' was widely shared by administrators and ethnographers alike — see Tidrick (1980).

26. *NDAR*s (1923, 1926, 1930–31). Maasai and Maasai/Kikuyu were also implicated in harbouring stolen stock; and the Mau, especially, like other relatively inaccessible border areas, became a node point in the regional geography of crime — see e.g. cases in file PC/RVP 6A/17/19; Furedi (1989: 65, 142–143).

27. OIC's remarks in notes of meeting, 7 March 1941, and in minutes of PCs Meeting, October 1941, MAA 2/1/7/2. The language used in discussion — 'undesirable alien', 'half-caste' — is suggestive and so is the assertion that the Maasai might degenerate or even disappear if 'mixing' took place — see e.g. *MPAR* (1921) vol. 1; Narok LNC Minutes, July 1940, DC/KAJ 2/1/11. The official account of Mau Mau explicitly equates 'Kikuyu' with 'criminal' in Maasailand — F.D. Corfield, *Historical Survey of the Origins and Growth of Mau Mau*, Cmd 1030 (London, 1960: 208–209). The text reference is to Mary Douglas's classic study of pollution — *Purity and Danger* (London, 1966).

28. Sandford (1919: 147–148, 55); *MPAR*s (1929–30) vol. 3; DC Kajiado to DC Kiambu, 4 October 1932, DC/KAJ 2/1/4.

29. PCs Meeting, October 1941, Minute 23, DC/Ngong 1/1/24; *MPHOR*, December 1946. For interpenetration policy, see 'Interpenetration Between Tribes: Précis for

PCs Meeting April 1941', Secretariat, 16 January 1941, *ibid.*; PCs Meeting, Minute 10, April 1941, and PC Nyanza circular to DCs, 29 April 1941, PC/NZA 2/1/70; CS circular to PCs: 'Statement of Government Interim Policy with Regard to Interpenetration and Infiltration in Native Land Units', 19 July 1945, and Secretariat Circular 29, July 1948, PC/NZA 2/1/106. The question of interpenetration was raised by the Land Commission (KLC, *Report*, sects.1477–81). Its recommendations regarding Kikuyu in Maasailand (*ibid.*, sects. 661–74) were accepted in principle by Thompson, the then OIC, and by his successor, Fazan; but not by their district commissioners or by later OICs — OIC Masai [Thompson] to CS, 14 May 1934, DC/Ngong 1/7/7; OIC [Fazan] to PC Central, 19 October 1935, and to DC Kiambu, 12 November 1935, DC/Ngong 1/1/22; *MPHOR*, March 1936, [Tomkinson to Vidal]; and OIC [Vidal] to CS, 28 March 1936, enclosing Fazan's letters, DC/Ngong 1/1/22.

30. Apart from the Outlying Districts Ordinance, squatters (and those who harboured them) were often prosecuted under the Native Authorities Ordinance (1912), a catch-all through which LNC resolutions and by-laws, Native Authority rules and orders, and Native Tribunal decisions could be enforced.

31. *NDARs* (1926, 1929); OIC Masai to CS, 8 February 1940, and headman Ole Kirtela to OIC, 17 and 24 July 1939, encl. in OIC to CS, 9 February 1940, MAA 2/1/7/2.

32. *MPAR* (1939) vol. l; Narok District, *Monthly Intelligence Report* [*MIR*], November 1940, PC/Ngong 1/1/1; DO Ngong to DC Kajiado, 31 March 1953, PC/Ngong 1/1/16.

33. *MPAR* (1924) vol. 3 and (1937) vol. 1; OIC Masai to PC Central, 29 October 1936, DC/Ngong 1/1/22; DC Narok, 'Report of the Removal of Kikuyu Living in the Narok District', n.d. [?Feb. 1940], and OIC Masai to CS, 1 March 1945, both in MAA 2/1/7/2. Judicial statistics in *MPARs passim*, vol. 3.

34. See correspondence in file MAA 2/1/7/2, especially PC Central to OIC Masai, 9 March 1940; same to CS, 12 April 1940, and Secretariat minutes thereon; Governor's draft despatch, 19 April 1940. There had been an earlier abortive intervention when mass repatriations first began and Throup may be correct in implying that the Masai administration was attempting in one last drive to remove all Kikuyu squatters before they were given a measure of protection under the proposed 'interpenetration' policy — see PC Central to OIC Masai, 26 October 1936, and reply, DC/Ngong 1/1/22; Throup (1987: 122).

35. *NDARs* (1940–41). Olenguruone was part of a large area of the south-west Mau forest which the government, after protracted negotiations with the Maasai, had purchased for Kikuyu settlement in 1939. The scheme was originally intended as part of a resettlement package to make the new squatter ordinance of 1937 more palatable to the Colonial Office; but it was cleverly appropriated by the Masai administration as a 'final solution' to their own infiltration problems — Native Courts Officer to CNC, 8 March 1950, DC/NKU 4/1; Kanogo (1987: 97, 107); notes of meeting, 26 April 1940, MAA 2/1/7/2; MP, *AR* (1941) MAA 2/3/41 (II).

36. OIC Masai to CS, 1 June 1945, and reply, 14 June 1945, minutes of joint LNC meeting, July 1945, all in MAA 2/1/7/2; CNC to [?], 3 November 1952, *op. cit.* Significantly, however, the administration was opposed to leaving the responsibility for checking aliens to the Maasai authorities alone — Minute of Meeting, 7 March 1941, MAA 2/1/7/2. For policy generally, see Throup (1987) and Berman (1990).

37. See e.g. the petition of Nganga wa Weru, May 1934, one of several in DC/Ngong 1/1/22.

38. R. vs Gathatwa file, *op. cit.* (I am indebted to P.H. Walker for explaining the background of this case to me); *NDHOR*, March 1946; Bhandari and Bhandari, Advocates to CNC, 17 and 22 October 1953, PC/Ngong 1/1/16. Sokoiyan's Maasai father, Nteiga, was himself an ex-refugee from Meru with an involved past (MT/M/KE11, 12). Sokoiyan's petition was refused at the time, possibly because both he and his putative father were 'politicals', members of the Masai Association, the KCA and KAU — precisely the sort of modern 'detribalized' Maasai whom the administration feared and distrusted.

39. This somewhat cynical point was made by informants on several occasions as they

reviewed the credentials of their neighbours — see the comments on 'Njau's' story (MT/M/KE1) by another prominent elder (*ibid./KE3*).
40. The case of Nganga wa Weru (note 37) was fairly typical. His petition was refused and he was sentenced to three months imprisonment for disobeying an expulsion order. On completion of sentence he again appealed, with the support of local elders, and the order was reversed. However, no compensation was offered for the loss of cultivation and property and Nganga was warned that he remained in Ngong on sufferance — OIC Masai circular letter 29 March 1935, DC/Ngong 1/1/22.
41. *MPMIR*, March 1936; headman Ole Kirtela to OIC Masai, 17 and 24 July 1939, *op. cit.*; DO Narok, *Safari Diary*, June 1938, DC/Ngong 1/1/27; DC Narok, 'Report of the Removal of Kikuyu', *op. cit.*
42. E.g. the DC Narok's comments on 'cross currents of political chicanery, exhibiting at times a distinct "agricultural" flavour . . .', *NDAR* (1941).
43. In 1951, for example, an illegal labour recruiting ring was uncovered in Ngong. About fifty Kamba family heads had been recruited by Maasai visiting Machakos to buy goats. They had been promised grazing land and cultivation plots in return for work. On discovery, the Kamba complained that they had been issued licences by the local headman or the district clerk for which they had been made to pay heavily. Neither the headman nor the clerk, both of whom were part of the educated Maasai farming community in Ngong, had the necessary authority to issue licences without approval by the local elders' committee — DC Kajiado to OIC Masai, 11 May 1951, and OIC Masai to DC Machakos, 18 May 1951, KNA: DC/MKS 15/1. See also, chief Kimiyu of Mukaa to DC Machakos, 18 January 1949 [fwd. to DC Kajiado], and reply by DC Kajiado, 9 February 1949, *ibid.*; Cowie to OIC Masai, 22 February 1937, DC/Ngong 1/1/22.
44. DO Ngong to DC Kajiado, 15 September 1953, DC/Ngong 1/1/9; MT/M/KA19; *KDAR* (1933), Kajiado District, *Handing-Over Report* [*HOR*], 1938, MAA 2/3/5; DO Ngong to PC Southern, 3 April 1954, PC/Ngong 1/1/16; King (1971a: 134).
45. Kajiado Chiefs to OIC Masai, 13 January 1936, and notes thereon by DC, PC/Ngong 1/1/44; DO Narok, *Safari Diary*, June 1936, DC/Ngong 1/1/27. Both may have been victims of local intrigues; but they, and chief ole Nakordo, were all under a cloud by the late 1930s. Ole Saitaka was allowed to retire and died in 1938; ole Ngipeda was suspended from duty in the same year and ole Nakordo resigned under pressure from both the DC and leading elders in 1939.
46. Iliffe (1979), especially Ch. 10; Vail (1989), especially Introduction and chapters by Ranger, Vail and White, and Papstein.
47. Elder's statement from Narok LNC debate on the exclusion of aliens, reported in *MPMIR*, February 1936; Narok LNC Minutes 4 and 13/40, DC/KAJ 2/1/11; *NDAR* (1940); PC Central to CS, 29 January 1940, and CNC's minute, MAA 2/1/7/2. The settlers' perceptions and complaints of 'hypocrisy' bear a close resemblance to those of the farm squatters — Kanogo (1987: 48–49, 62–68).
48. The search for a Kikuyu 'usable past' is beyond the scope of this chapter, but see Berman and Lonsdale (1990 and 1992).
49. Few histories or collections of traditions were produced in colonial Maasailand (in comparison with, for instance, Nyasaland, Buganda or parts of Tanganyika — Vail (1989: 152–173); Iliffe (1979: 336–337). Nonetheless, the impulse towards shaping and using the past was clearly present in petitions and in oral discourse — see, for example, memo. from 'Masai chiefs, headmen and elders', printed in KLC (1934a) *Evidence* II: 1,242–1,248; T.M. Mootian, 'The beginning of the Masai in their land and what they did there and how they lived together', typescript (seen by permission of the author). Late colonial publications, officially sponsored but drawing on earlier traditions, include: *Maisha ya Sameni ole Kivasis yaani Justin Lemenye* ['The Life of Justin'] (Nairobi, 1953); J.T. Mpaayei, *Inkuti Pukunot oolMaasai* ['Some Customs of the Maasai'] (Oxford, 1954); S.S. Sankan, *Intepen e Maasai* (Nairobi, 1979 (but from an ms. written c. 1960 and kindly shown to me by the author)).

50. For the notion of public scrutiny and the 'arbitration of knowledge', see Cohen and Odhiambo (1989) and also Feierman (1990).
51. *MPMIR*s, August 1937, January 1936; Narok District, *MIR*, November 1940, *op.cit*. The statement which best conveys the sense of moral crusade which often pervaded the debate comes, in fact, from one of the neighbouring settler district associations (who had their own interest in the matter because the Masai Reserve was a refuge for their absconding squatters). It combines 'breach of faith', Maasai Treaties, responsible trusteeship and the destruction of a noble race in a spirited call for the removal of Kikuyu from Maasailand — Njoro Association resolution, February 1936, fwd. in Ag. PC Rift to CS, 24 March 1936, DC/Ngong 1/1/22.
52. E.g. Kajiado LNC Minutes, March 1932 and July 1937, DC/KAJ 5/1/2 and 4; *NDAR*s (1930, 1939); 'Meeting of local Natives Nairage Ngare', note by OIC Masai, 28 October 1939, DC/KAJ 2/1/11. The sanctity of the Reserve became almost an article of faith in the eyes of some administrators — see e.g. irate correspondence between DC Kajiado [Buxton] and his colleague in Machakos in DC/MKS 1OB/5/1 and Wilson [settler, Machakos] to Fazan (personal), 26 November 1935, PC/Ngong 1/1/16 (complaining that it was a criminal offence for a Kamba to set foot on 'holy ground', i.e. the Masai Reserve).
53. For the difficulties raised by the 1911 Agreement, see Sandford (1919: 57); KLC, *Report*, sects. 664–7, 670–1. The exclusive interpretation was reluctantly endorsed by government after the Agreement had again been publicly confirmed by the Governor in 1939 and Maasai administrators continued to cite the Masai Treaties when refusing alien residence permits — CNC to CS, 23 April 1940, MAA 2/1/7/2; OIC Masai to DC Machakos, 2 July 1945, DC/MKS 15/1.
54. See e.g. the account of an LNC meeting in February 1940 attended by the CNC to ascertain Maasai opinion of the removal of Kikuyu from the Mau. The minute was forwarded to the Secretariat — Narok LNC Minute 13/40, DC/KAJ 2/1/11 and copy in file MAA 2/1/7/2. The administration always acted ostensibly on Maasai instructions — *MPMIR*, April 1936; OIC Masai to PC Central, 10 June 1936, *op. cit.*
55. See e.g. the heated exchanges over the management of the Mbagathi Forest in Kajiado LNC Minutes, 4 October 1931, DO/KAJ 5/1/2, and also *MPHOR*, March 1936; *NDAR* (1946). For Maasai land grievances and demands, see 'Masai Province: Secretary's Précis', memo. by Buxton, DC Kajiado, 15 January 1930, memo. from 'Masai chiefs, headmen and elders', all printed in KLC (1934a) *Evidence,* II:1175–88; 1242–8; 2227–30; minutes of meeting, 29 August 1932, and 'Masai General Meeting' to CS, 28 August 1934, both encl. in OIC Masai to CS, 29 August 1934, DC/Ngong 1/7/7. Explanations of the findings of the Land Commission convinced the Maasai that 'much of their land is to be taken away and given to Europeans and Kikuyu' — *MPMIR*, July 1934.
56. These attitudes are discussed in Waller (1975).
57. E.g. memo. by Deck [OIC Masai 1928–32], April 1933, printed in KLC (1934a) *Evidence*, II: 1263–4; *MPMIR*, April 1935; *Report of the Commission on Closer Union of the Dependencies in Eastern and Central Africa*, Cmd 3234 (London, 1929: 341–346); KLC (1934b) *Report*, sects. 661–74, 711 (Hemsted, one member of the KLC, had been OIC Masai 1913–23). The agricultural settlements produced large maize surpluses for local sale and barter — *NDAR* (1926); *MPAR* (1936) vol. 2.
58. Fazan was an influential example. He was essentially a central policy-maker rather than a field officer and by the time that he became OIC Masai in 1936 he had already had wide experience, especially of Kikuyu land problems, as a member of the committee on Native Land Tenure in Kikuyu, as author of an economic survey of Kikuyuland (1931) and as secretary to the Kenya Land Commission. His views are summarized in *MPHOR*, January 1936 [Fazan to Tomkinson].
59. As it evolved, official policy distinguished between 'interpenetration', which was good because immigrants were accepted by, and absorbed within, the host community and conformed to their customs; and 'infiltration', which was bad because it led to the creation of separate ethnic enclaves — see memo. by Lambert, January 1946, PC/NZA 2/1/106.

60. Buxton was an outspoken and hard-line exclusionist. He was a long-serving field officer (DC Narok 1923, 1935–37, DC Kajiado 1928–31, OIC Masai 1937–38) with considerable experience of, and commitment to, the Maasai and a notoriously idiosyncratic view of administration which probably blighted his chances of promotion. He was by no means a conservative, however, and his efforts to get the *murran* out to work on public projects sparked off the Rotian Riot in 1935. Anecdotes about his enthusiasms are many and, predictably, he made an impression on Margery Perham. His views can be found in, especially, *Report of the Agricultural Committee* (Nairobi, 1929) and *NDAR* (1936).

61. Kajiado District, *AR* (1942) KNA: PC/SP 1/5/3; *NDHOR*, October 1946; OIC Masai to CS, 1 March 1945, and 'Report of Removal of Kikuyu', MAA 2/1/7/2. For anti-erosion generally, see D.M. Anderson, 'Depression, Dust Bowl, Demography and Drought: The Colonial State and Soil Erosion in East Africa During the 1930s', *African Affairs*, 83 (1984: 321–343).

62. The DC Narok's [Dawson] comments on the Land Commission Report were succinct: 'Anyone but a market gardener decadent'(sects. 662–3) and 'Cabbages vs cattle again i.e. agriculture more important than stock' (sect. 711) — comments encl. in OIC Masai to CS, 29 August 1934, DC/Ngong 1/7/7.

63. See e.g. *NDAR* (1936) and Buxton to OIC Masai, 25 July 1936, both in *Buxton Papers*; 'Development Plan — Masai Extra Provincial District', draft encl. in OIC Masai to CS, 5 February 1945, PC/Ngong 1/1/37; *MPHOR*, December 1946. Apart from the strong emphasis on stock marketing and grazing and water improvement, development projects also included schemes to persuade Maasai cultivators to replace evicted Kikuyu in Nairage Ngare and Ngong — *MPMIR*s, October 1936, August 1937, and plans in Ngong Development (1937) file PC/Ngong 1/2/7. For administrative attitudes, see N. Farson, *Last Chance in Kenya* (London, 1949) Ch. 13.

64. Notes in *MPMIR*, October 1936. The clear sub-text was that, as once the Maasai had prospered by raiding their (agricultural) neighbours, now they might again dominate by outproducing them.

65. See e.g. Kajiado LNC Minutes, March 1932, DC/KAJ 5/1/2; extracts from LNC minutes quoted in OIC Masai to CS, 6 May 1936, DC/Ngong 1/1/22; notes of Governor's meeting with Maasai in *MPMIR*, September 1937. At the height of the Narok evictions in 1940, the small Kikuyu settlement at Olololunga was protected by local elders — Narok LNC Minute 21/40, DC/KAJ 2/1/11.

66. Kajiado District, *HOR*, September 1946, DC/KAJ 3/1. However, as another, more perceptive, officer realized, the Maasai were hostile to all attempts at outside interference with their affairs even though they were willing to 'please and flatter' and to make a show of acquiescence — *KDAR* (1931).

67. *NDAR* (1930); Narok District, *MIR*, November 1940, *op. cit.*

68. Bridewealth for wives acquired in this way was lower than for those imported directly from Kikuyuland where 'bridewealth inflation' was raging; and also involved fewer affinal obligations — *NDAR* (1928) and field notes.

69. MT/M/P37; *ibid.*/KE2. See also pp. 232–3, 235–6 and notes. Aspiring patrons were not always successful. Lekotet ole Partakulen was prosecuted by his own chief for attempting to bring in a 'horde of Kamba' — DC Kajiado to DC Machakos, DC/MKS 15/1.

70. Through the Masai Association, for example, which had many mixed Maasai/Kikuyu as members and attracted qualified support from influential Maasai spokesmen as well. The Association had links to the KCA and to African politics in Nairobi; and these contacts helped the 'Masai Chiefs' to draw up their submission to the KLC — see King (1971a).

71. E.g. some of the accusations made by his opponents against chief ole Saitaka — see p. 237 above and note 45; MT/M/KE2. In a discussion that hints at another feud, the Kajiado LNC, prompted by its Kaputiei members (themselves local patrons), refused the wish of an influential Matapato elder to settle Kikuyu clients in the Ngong area and minuted that no section could permit aliens to reside in the territory of another — Kajiado LNC Minutes 3–4/48, PC/Ngong 1/1/16.

72. The situation on the eastern Mau was especially tense. The small Damat section were under pressure from their numerically stronger neighbour, Keekonyokie, with whom they had a history of bad relations. Both sections accepted Kikuyu settlement in their areas. Keekonyokie included many 'returnees' and 'acceptees' who formed a nucleus of settlement at Nairage Ngare, and Damat had a similar nucleus at Melili. The major force on the Mau, however, were the Purko who had moved there in 1912 and who, in uneasy alliance with Keekonyokie, were now gradually displacing Damat from the areas above and east of Narok. It was their spokesman, ole Galishu, who put pressure on the weaker section to refuse Kikuyu settlers and demanded evictions — though the Damat 'did not discuss it or care as they were few'. The roots of this feud went back to the 1890s — *NDAR*s (1930, 1936); DO Narok, *Safari Diary*, June 1936, *op. cit.*; Lamprey and Waller (1990: 21–22); MT/M/KE21; *ibid.*/P37; *ibid.*/DT5; Waller (1988: 80). For a similar example of 'competitive adoption' and moral suasion in Trans-Mara, see Waller (1984: 280–283).

73. See e.g. Kajiado LNC Minutes, March 1932 and January 1936, DC/KAJ 5/1/2,3. 'Returnees' and former 'acceptees', like Kinaiya (note 16), also toed the line and called for the removal of Kikuyu settlers — 'Meeting of Local Natives Nairage Ngare', October 1939, DC/KAJ 2/1/11. Ole Kirtela was a member of the Masai Association who collaborated later on Sankan's book and eventually became a nationally known Maasai elder and traditional historian, i.e. a 'progressive traditionalist' — see interview printed in Hanley (1971: Appendix 1).

74. MT/A9. Warning against Kikuyu infiltration, ole Galishu used the simile of a tree which grows by supporting itself on others and then smothers them (MT/M/DT5). He was a fierce advocate of extreme measures against aliens (MT/M/P37) but, like Buxton, was prepared to press for rapid change to serve Maasai interests as he defined them. He had great prestige as a 'traditionalist' and bitter personal memories of colonial intervention in the Maasai Moves — *NDAR*s (1929, 1936, 1939).

75. For the language of obligation, see MTs cited throughout. In March 1932, speaking to an LNC resolution on Kikuyu in the Ngong area, ole Nakordo, the Kaputiei chief and local 'boss', stated that 'various Masai have made arrangements with their Kikuyu, and they ought to be called to show cause why their Kikuyu should not be expelled'. Doubtless, the irony was not lost on his fellow councillors — Kajiado LNC Minutes, *op. cit.* Reference in text to 'Mirror in the Forest' (Kenny, 1981).

76. These concerns were powerfully amplified in the 1950s and '60s and transmitted to a wider audience by 'modern' histories and ethnographies. Sankan's compilation of Maasai traditions and customs, for instance, is interlaced with calls for Maasai unity through an understanding of a shared and definitive past history and culture. The work of A.H. Jacobs has provided scholarly underpinning for an exclusionist and traditionalist interpretation of Maasai identity.

77. For some, it was important to reconcile Christian conversion, including its particular notions of what constituted civilization, with remaining Maasai. There were ingenious attempts to produce a Christianized 'tradition' and the female circumcision crisis at the Siyabei mission in 1930 should be seen in this context and not simply as an outgrowth of 'Kikuyu politics' — see MT/M/P27; *ibid.*/KE9; Mootian, 'The Beginning of the Masai'; King (1971b: 19–24).

78. 'Memorandum by Masai Chiefs, Headmen and Elders', printed in KLC (1934a) *Evidence*, II: 1221–30. The 'eminent Britishers' included Thomson, Baumann, Hinde and Merker.

79. *Memorandum Presented to the Committee of Enquiry on Land by the Masais at Ngong, 27th October 1932* (Nairobi, n.d. [1933?]) (copy seen by kind permission of Fr. F. Mol). The pamphlet reprints the newspaper and Native Affairs Dept reports. Anger at administration attitudes reached the point at which the Association could assert that the government had no interest in development at all and 'but one aim i.e. probably to exterminate the Masai population entirely'. This provoked a furious reaction and a summary of current development plans in response — 'Petition against proposals on Mau Forest in Masai land', 17 May 1951 (addressed to the Colonial Office) and note by OIC

Masai, PC/SP 6/3/1. See also MT/M/KE9; King (1971a: 135).

80. Olguyai ole Nanchiro, T.M. Mootian, A.G. Tameno, Kairrak ole Saitaka and A. Kaurai to OIC Masai, 1 October 1934, encl. in OIC to CS, 9 October 1934, DC/Ngong 1/7/7. Another letter, signed by most of the 1932 signatories, had been presented at a stormy meeting with the Colonial Secretary but was withdrawn after pressure and the other substituted — OIC to CS, 29 August and 3 September 1934, *ibid.*

81. Mootian's claims to speak for the Maasai were directly repudiated by the Narok LNC and the administration regarded him and his colleagues as troublemakers and not really Maasai at all — Narok LNC Minute 53/39, DC/KAJ 2/1/11; Narok District, *MIR*, May 1939, PC/Ngong 1/1/1; OIC Masai to CS, 15 May 1951, PC/SP 6/3/1.

82. Mootian to DC Narok, 18 April 1939, quoted in King (1971a: 132). Earlier correspondence involving Mootian suggests a background of private local land disputes — OIC Masai to DC Narok, 2 November 1934, and reply, 5 November 1934, and Mootian to CNC, 11 December 1934, all in DC/Ngong 1/7/7.

83. King (1971a: 132-136); transcript of interview with T.M. Mootian by K. King (kindly made available by Mootian). *Olturrur loolMaasai Oisumate* (OLO) [The Group of Educated Maasai] which emerged in local politics at the end of the War was a more cautiously cooperative and self-improvement oriented body which took pains to be 'Maasai' in its organization and outlook and distanced itself from both protest and the affairs of aliens — *MPHOR*, December 1946.

·84. In 1947, a plenary meeting of representatives of all sections to discuss modifications to the age-organization, to standardize it and also to reaffirm its significance was sponsored by the Kenya and Tanganyika Administrations with the enthusiastic support of both 'traditional elders' and 'modern Maasai' — *MPAR* (1947) PC/SP 1/2/3; Sankan (1979: 109-110).

85. Such views were still current in the early 1970s. The reference is to E. Huxley, *A New Earth* (London, 1960) which features a single Maasai, Revd Daudi Mokinyo, among the progressive elect. Mokinyo was one of a small group to take advantage of the African Land Development individual grazing and stock improvement scheme in Kajiado in the 1950s. His herd of 200 head, though respectable, did not compare with those of many of his unimproved neighbours and, despite his staunch advocacy of Maasai values, he had little influence at the time beyond his immediate group of Christian progressives — Huxley (1960: 161); *African Land Development in Kenya, 1946-62* (Nairobi, 1962: 77); MT/M/L3.

86. See, for example, the acrimonious and revealing public exchanges on the relationship between 'Maasai-ness' and development between the Maasai MPs for Kajiado District, John Keen and Stanley Oloitipitip.

87. For examples, see G. Kitching, *Land, Livestock and Leadership* (Nairobi, 1981) and D. Anderson and D. Throup, 'Africans and Agricultural Production in Colonial Kenya: The Myth of the War as a Watershed', *Journal of African History*, 26 (1985).

88. For one example, but in an urban context, see J. Penvenne, 'Here Everyone Walked With Fear', in F. Cooper (ed.), *The Struggle for the City* (London, 1984). I am particularly indebted to David Anderson for insights on these topics.

89. In traditions, Maasai territorial divisions and regional identifications suggest a strong sense of 'place' — see Waller (1979).

90. Myths of origin among Maasai and their neighbours suggest this symbolic opposition strongly, but this should not be confused with an enduring historical cleavage within the Maa-speakers — see Berntsen (1980) and Galaty, in this volume.

Twelve

Land as Ours,
Land as Mine

*Economic, Political & Ecological Marginalization
in Kajiado District**

DAVID J. CAMPBELL

Introduction

A fundamental characteristic of the Maasai economy is its concept of
land use. The patterns of ownership and use reflect a variety of social,
political and economic characteristics of their society and its interaction
with the environment. The land was traditionally seen as a communal
territory containing resources rather than as a *resource* which could be
appropriated by individuals. The use of the territory was governed by
social and political conventions designed to reduce the risks associated
with the unpredictable climate of the semi-arid environment.

Over the past century forces from beyond and within Maasai society
have altered the pattern of land use and land ownership such that fundamental aspects of the Maasai system have been changed. At the outset
of the colonial period the territory of the Maasai was curtailed by treaty
with the British. This together with subsequent losses of land to farming
and to wildlife uses have severely restricted the resources available. With
population growth, land pressure increased. Encouraged by government
policy and informed by the desire to protect their territory from
encroaching land uses, Maasai agreed to the demarcation of land units
to which individuals or groups held legal title. Continued demand for
land from both within and beyond Maasailand has finally resulted in
the concept of land as *territory* being replaced by that of individual
holdings.

The resulting land units are ecologically incapable of supporting the
dairy economy and a major social and economic transformation is
inevitable. Poorer Maasai are selling their land and in the absence of
alternative economic opportunity are joining the rapidly increasing class
of the ecologically, economically, and politically marginalized already
deprived of their land-based economy elsewhere in Kenya.

The contemporary situation faced by the majority of Maasai is

258

markedly different from that which existed prior to colonization. While many values and traditions are still known and held, the basis of the economy, the concept of land as *territory*, has been transformed such that the survival of their herding system is in jeopardy. This situation is but the current point in a process of change in rural society as it adapts to the opportunities and constraints of the emerging national economic, social, and political systems.

The existing circumstances in Kajiado District reflect both local and national responses to land shortage. Locally herders find a lack of grazing resources while national elites in their search to acquire more land are now looking to expand into the 'marginal' rangelands. This chapter will focus on the experience of Kajiado District because, while it is unique in many ways, it reflects the outcome of forces which will affect developments throughout the arid and semi-arid lands of Kenya. It will address the question of whether groups, such as the Maasai, can maintain their characteristic economic and social institutions within a national economic context which promotes individual gain at the expense of the well-being of the majority.

Evolution of Contemporary Land Use Patterns

Kajiado District is part of the wide area of land that was controlled by the pastoral Maasai prior to the colonization of Kenya by the British. The area supported large livestock herds and abundant wildlife. These activities have been added to by the influx of large numbers of farmers who cultivate on the slopes of the hills and around the swamps of the District. As the wetter lands have been put under crops and set aside within national parks so the herders have seen the quality of their grazing lands decline. Further, as the farming population has grown so a shortage of arable land has developed. A consequence is that today the resources available are insufficient to meet the needs of a rapidly growing population.

The Pre-Colonial Period

Prior to the arrival of the British the area that is now Kajiado District was dominated by the Maasai. Livestock formed the basis of their economic and social system and the fundamental goal of the society was to maintain their herds within an unpredictable physical environment in which recurrent drought and disease threatened their subsistence. Critical to this was access to and control over sufficient grazing and water resources (Western and Dunne, 1979). During the wet seasons they were dispersed across wide areas where water and pasture were available but during the dry seasons and droughts they congregated around those areas which afforded secure supplies of water and grass, such as the slopes of the hills and the swamp margins.

The territory was divided into regions associated with specific Maasai sections (Kituyi, 1990), but during years of poor rainfall cross-section movement of herds was practised on a reciprocal basis. The land was thus communally owned; it was Maasai *territory*, while the herds were owned by individual families. Maintaining sufficient numbers of livestock rather than access to land was the basic objective of the production system. There was little pressure on resources as the *murran* were able to assure access to sufficient water and grazing to support the herds.

In the period immediately prior to colonization their military and economic power diminished due to the effects of smallpox and cholera on the population and of rinderpest and contagious bovine pleuro-pneumonia on their livestock. As the British administration alienated land for European settlement and demarcated areas as Native Reserves, Maasai were unable to support their fierce military reputation with effective resistance. The British were able to alienate lands from the Maasai by act of treaty. This alienation of productive rangeland represented the first in a long sequence of events by which Maasai have been deprived of the better-watered margins of the rangelands.

The Colonial Period
The immediate impact was that the Maasai were restricted to the lands set aside as the Masai Reserve under the Treaties of 1904 and 1912 (Sandford, 1919). The Reserve included the area which today comprises Kajiado and Narok Districts. At the time it was designated it was considered adequate to meet the needs of the Maasai whose numbers had been recently reduced by epidemics and drought. This might have been the case initially, but by the early 1930s the District Commissioner of Kajiado District reported that Maasai had more cattle than at any time in their history (Kenya, 1932). The impact of land alienation became evident as Maasai had lost some of the best grazing land, land which had been particularly valuable in times of drought.

The awareness of the administration that the Maasai had restored their herds coincided with concern about the perceived environmental problems of overgrazing and soil erosion. That such environmental degradation was a direct result of irrational and intentional efforts to increase herd sizes to demonstrate wealth became a fundamental assumption of administration policy towards the pastoral people which has continued to the present day. It generated a series of policies to promote environmental management through stimulating sales of 'superfluous' stock.[1]

To Maasai, however, the question of livestock numbers was more complex. Livestock had several roles within the Maasai system. The most important was to provide subsistence. Given the frequency of drought and disease, Maasai attempted to increase their herds in good years to protect against the anticipated losses in bad years.

This objective did not weaken with the imposition of the colonial economy; rather it became reinforced. The restriction of the grazing lands to those of the Reserve might have forced Maasai to consider limiting livestock numbers by increasing sales and turning to purchasing crops as an alternative source of subsistence. The pricing policies of the government precluded this, however. Maasai were willing to sell animals when a competitive price was offered (Kenya, 1936), but in the late 1920s and early 1930s the price of livestock dropped relative to that of food crops (Kitching, 1980) and thus Maasai were encouraged to emphasize their traditional sources of subsistence rather than develop alternatives through the sale of stock.

The need to maintain stock numbers under these circumstances was made more important by the recurrence of drought during the period.[2] While the administration saw environmental problems emerging as a direct consequence of the irrational build-up of herd sizes by Maasai, from the Maasai perspective any pressure on resources was a direct consequence of the limitation of their grazing lands by the creation of the Reserves and of the progressive loss of lands in the Reserve to cultivation.

The expansion of cultivation during this period resulted principally from the impact of the alienation of land from Kikuyu for European settlement. Maasai extensive land use systems were disrupted and the land available to graze livestock was significantly reduced. In consequence, crops replaced livestock as the major source of income and wealth and, as the population increased within a restricted area, land acquired a value which was unknown in the pre-colonial period (Kitching, 1980). As land became scarce so people looked for alternative locations to cultivate and many Kikuyu farmers migrated to the better-watered locations in adjacent areas. In the Masai Reserve the focus of such migration was initially the Mau Escarpment, the Ngong Hills and later the slopes of Mount Kilimanjaro and Ol Doinyo Orok near Namanga.

The occupation of these lands by farmers led to recurrent conflicts with Maasai over stock thefts and grazing rights, particularly during droughts when Maasai drove their animals into the farmers' fields (Kenya, 1929, 1930, 1935). Maasai quickly saw the dangers of losing some of their best grazing lands to cultivation, and as early as 1927 there was mention in official reports of the possibility of restricting the immigration of Kikuyu and Kamba farmers to the District (Kenya, 1927).

Thus, in the years prior to the outbreak of World War Two, Maasai were adapting to the restructuring of their resource base by the creation of the Masai Reserve and trying to re-establish their herds within the constraints of recurrent drought. The colonial economy offered little opportunity for diversification of their activities beyond subsistence herding, and in fact restricted existing trade with farming people by devaluing livestock relative to food crops. Attempts to increase sales through government channels were stymied by the refusal of the government to pay competitive prices. There were also indications of problems with the immigration of farmers to the Reserve, problems which were to become increasingly severe as the numbers of immigrants increased, resulting in cultivation of the most productive of the Maasai grazing lands.

Kikuyu and Kamba farmers continued to move into the District during the war and the government continued to be concerned with their effects on soil erosion and forest clearance. Maasai were more concerned with the loss of grazing land, particularly during the drought years, when they found that many of their traditional drought-retreat areas had become occupied by farmers. Legal procedures to limit cultivation were implemented in 1947 and 1951, though their success was limited by the fact that many immigrant farmers were relatives of Maasai by marriage and were thus permitted to settle in the area by custom (Kenya 1946, 1947, 1951; see also Waller, this volume).

The degree of conflict was drastically reduced when thousands of Kikuyu farmers were expelled from the Ngong and Loitokitok areas in 1952 and 1953 following the declaration of the Emergency in 1952. The area under crops did not pose a problem again until immigration of farmers redeveloped in the years just prior to independence, although those who continued to farm were pressuring the government to grant them legal title to the land.

While the threat to Maasai resources from cultivation was reduced during the 1950s, a second land use began to compete with the Maasai for grazing and water. Preservation of wildlife had long been a concern of the colonial administration and areas of Kajiado District had been included in the Southern Game Reserve as early as 1910 (Casebeer, 1975). The passing of the National Parks Ordinance in 1945 began a process whereby specific areas were set aside exclusively for the use of wildlife as National Parks. Other areas were incorporated as National Reserves in which wildlife was protected but other land uses were permitted at the discretion of local councils. Maasai had to adjust to the creation of the Nairobi and Tsavo National Parks and the Amboseli Reserve. These areas enclosed water and pasture resources which had formerly been used as dry-season areas by Maasai. The effect of their inclusion in the parks became evident during the drought of 1953 when Maasai suffered heavy losses (Kenya, 1953).

Government policy towards the Maasai continued to be dominated by related efforts to increase sales of livestock and to reduce the incidence of overgrazing. The concern with overgrazing as a major focus of development efforts is surprising in that the District reports indicate that overgrazing was strongly correlated with drought and that in intervening years the land was not overstocked. The coincidence of policy reviews, drought and environmental decline,[3] combined with the administration's lack of understanding of the rationale of the Maasai economy, probably explains much of the emphasis on destocking and rangeland management which culminated in the policies proposed by the Swynnerton Plan (Kenya, 1954). Further, the District Reports make it clear that sales of livestock would have been higher but for the disruption of the cattle market by the policies designed to contain the Emergency (Kenya, 1953). In the event, the success of government development efforts in this period was negligible, as the vast majority of herders opposed them (Jahnke, 1978).

Among the policies enacted was the beginning of a process of adjudication of parts of Maasai territory into individual ranches (IRs). The first IR was demarcated in 1954 and operated under the strict supervision of the veterinary department. This ranch proved to be a success. By 1958 four others had formed and the government was seeking more applicants (Kenya, 1958). The IRs were to be created on land which had better rainfall than the majority of the District, such as that near Loitokitok and to the south-east of Ngong where water was also available from the Ngong pipeline. The granting of these lands to individuals reduced the quality of the communal resource base and raised the possibility of select individuals benefiting at the expense of the majority.

This period saw the beginnings of many changes in Maasai society which were to alter the basis of their social and economic system (Kituyi, 1990). The establishment of the IRs marked the first time that Maasai had begun to move away from the traditional values which saw cattle as the basis of production towards a view of land, no longer as Maasai *territory*, but as the basic resource for individual advancement. The transition from cattle to land as the basis of wealth had occurred in central Kenya in the 1930s (Kitching, 1980), but it was only in the late 1950s that Maasai began to follow suit, and then only under considerable pressure from the government. While the government saw land ownership as a primary means of assuring that land degradation would be reduced they were concerned that 'while some Maasai genuinely wish to establish an individual ranch and improve their stock, others merely wish to jump on the bandwagon and grab land as a speculation' (Kenya, 1959:19).

By the late 1950s Maasai were in a position of relative wealth and security, but a number of processes which would ultimately combine to change the whole structure of land use in the District had been set in motion. The designation of the Parks and Reserves and the beginning of adjudication of land to individual farmers and herders threatened to exclude from Maasai territory those areas which had the greatest natural productivity and which represented the most secure of the grazing and water resources.

This became clear during the drought years of 1960–61 when losses of livestock were very high. The only place to retain grazing was the Kisongo section around Mount Kilimanjaro. Kisongo, continuing the practice of sharing the resources of Maasai territory, opened their pastures to other Maasai sections, and found themselves in difficulty as a result (Kenya, 1961). This area, to which so many Maasai retreated, was one of the locations which had been so attractive to cultivators and the potential consequences of the loss of such lands from the herders' resource base were evident during this period.

Post-Independence

In the period from the outbreak of World War Two to the end of the British administration the pattern of land use in Kajiado District was influenced by a number of social, political, economic and environmental forces. Maasai had responded to these in ways which had permitted them to maintain their basic social and economic institutions and their concept of land as *territory*. Following independence, a number of processes which had been latent in the colonial period began to impinge on the better-watered hillslopes and swamp margins. These included population growth among the Maasai, immigration of farmers, and the extension of the area enclosed in National Parks. While any one of these alone may not have had a detrimental impact in the short term, their synergistic effect has resulted in a contemporary situation in which the people of the District are increasingly unable to meet their subsistence needs under existing land use systems.

Kenyan government policy for the District has maintained the colonial focus upon means for promoting a herding strategy which would be less destructive to the enviroment, supporting wildlife management, and encouraging cultivation. The major instrument to promote management of resources was to provide Maasai legal title to the land, on either an individual or a group basis. The experience with IRs had demonstrated that they could not support the whole population and, while they continued to be demarcated, the strategy for the majority of Maasai was to create group ranches (GRs) (Ayuko, 1981; Olang, 1982).

It was the original intention of the administration that each GR would be based on traditional grazing areas and would enclose resources sufficient to meet the demand both in the wet and in the dry season (Fallon, 1962; Jacobs, 1963; Davis, 1971; Hedlund, 1971). In practice, while the ranches have been able to meet people's needs in years of adequate rainfall, in bad years movement beyond the ranch boundaries has been needed (Halderman, 1972; Campbell, 1984). Thus the concept of land as *territory* remained critical.

The objective was that the ranches would use their titles as collateral to secure loans which would permit investment in infrastructure such as dips and boreholes and thus raise productivity. With greater infrastructural investment, regular sales of livestock would follow (Meadows and White, 1979), thus reducing the potential for overgrazing. There is a consensus that the government's goals were only partially achieved (Hedlund, 1971; Von Kaufman, 1976; Helland, 1978; Evangelou, 1984). In general the Maasai responded positively to the promotion of GRs, not so much because they supported the government's view that the ranches would enable improved resource management, but rather because they saw in the legal title to the land a means of protection from the intrusion of farmers from outside the District.

The immigration of farmers which had caused problems to the Maasai in the years prior to the Emergency was forcibly reduced during that period and great population pressure built up in central Kenya. After independence people were again able to relocate freely and migrations to arable areas outside of the overcrowded highlands ensued. Such migration was rapid in the late 1960s and its focus was the foothills of Mount Kilimanjaro and the Ngong Hills (Campbell, 1981). Some of the areas in which farmers settled were IRs whose owners had subdivided them to accommodate the demand. In such areas the administration's fears that adjudication was really land speculation were realized. Other farmers settled around swamps such as Namalok and Kimana. Cultivation of these areas has proved a success, with vegetables produced at Kimana being exported by air to Europe.

This process represents an ongoing spread down the ecological gradient of the adjustments of land rights and use involving the replacement of livestock by crops as the basis of production and ownership of cattle by land as the objective of accumulation. These changes had occurred in the 1930s among the Kikuyu, and as farming spread into Kajiado District, so the opportunities associated with individual title to land became available to those Maasai who could gain access to land. For the majority who belonged to GRs, however, the traditional view of land as a communal territory continued to be held until much later.

The change in land use from herding to farming in these better-watered locations added to the losses of grazing and water resources incurred when Tsavo and Nairobi and later Amboseli National Parks were gazetted. The drought of 1972–76 demonstrated the impact of these land use changes on the population (Campbell, 1979a, 1984) but the long-term implications were such that, even in the absence of drought, pressure on resources began to reach critical levels by the 1980s (Campbell, 1986). The drought also showed the continued strength of traditional Maasai strategies for coping with its effects, based on a variety of social, economic, political, and environmental resources (Campbell, 1984). In a recent study of the Maasai response to the 1984 drought, however, the traditional strategies are seen as being rapidly disrupted by changes in the socio-economic conditions prevailing in the district (Campbell, forthcoming; Grandin *et al.*, 1989).

The experience of the drought in the 1970s forced many Maasai to re-evaluate the basis of their economy. Older people maintained more traditional ideas but many younger Maasai were assessing alternative occupations and herding strategies. Some began to farm plots on the GRs and there was discussion of the need to subdivide the GRs to supply land for the increasing population (Campbell, 1979b).

The major impetus for subdivision came from the sons of those who had initially obtained membership of the GRs. By the mid-1970s many of these young men were of legal age yet not eligible to be members of ranches in their own right. Many found themselves as owners of livestock but without legal rights to the land on which to graze them (Ole Pasha, 1986). The growth of population and the restriction of lands available to the herders had created a land shortage which forced the majority of Maasai for the first time to recognize land rather than cattle as the fundamental resource of the economy.

The government's response to the growing realization by Maasai that subdivision of GRs might be necessary was supportive. In 1981 a policy encouraging subdivision was enacted and politicians and administrators in Kajiado District became very vocal in calling for subdivision of GRs. In turn this became the major agenda for discussion in nearly all GR committee meetings in the district (Ole Pasha, 1986: 5). By the end of 1984, twenty-nine of fifty-one GRs had either been subdivided or had passed resolutions to subdivide. Proximity to urban centres, availability of cultivable land, and long experience with group ranching are features of those ranches which were the first to subdivide while those that remain intact are located in the drier areas of the district.

The move towards subdivision is seen by its supporters as a means for self-advancement. The success of the original IR owners, who represent the wealthy class in the District, supports this. However, those people received on average 2,000 acres while the current process of subdivision would give each rancher an average of only 250 acres (Ole Pasha,1986). Given the unequal distribution of livestock among GR members the nature of subdivision is critical. If it were to give an equal share to all then the stock-wealthy would have insufficient pasture. Such a situation might lead them to purchase access to pasture from the stock-poor or it might be that the wealthy buy out the poor. This would be most probable during a drought as the poor tend to lose a greater share of their herds than the wealthy in such conditions (Campbell, 1979a), and would thus have an incentive to sell their land.

An alternative for the poor might be to replace herding with farming or other more intensive activities if the resources on their land would support it (Campbell, 1985; Ole Pasha, 1986). The resource base of the District offers a variety of opportunities for economic development. The wildlife sector (Western and Thresher, 1973; Western, 1982), farming, and a diversified livestock industry (Campbell, 1981) are some of the potential activities which have not been seen by policy makers as offering opportunities for the majority. Both Campbell (1981, 1985) and Ole Pasha (1986) were looking at the potential of developing the economy of Kajiado District in ways which would allow a larger population to be supported at higher levels of income. They argued that, in the absence of such alternatives, continuation of existing trends and policies could only result in the extinction of the herding system and its replacement by a form of production whose survival would, in all likelihood, depend upon exogenous support during recurrent periods of environmental stress.

Such analyses correctly recognized that, in the absence of more aggressive policies to diversify the rangeland economy, the majority of Maasai would be forced off the land through a process of marginalization. Their discussion of the impact of the subdivision of the GRs is, however, limited in that they focused only on the implications for the local population. It is, in fact, becoming evident that the economic opportunities that they indicated might support a larger local population, such as income from wildlife and livestock-based industries, are being coveted by local and national elites. The economy of Maasailand is being transformed by government policies defined through collusion between these elites.

The motive behind government policy is not merely that of seeking a way to resolve the problem of population pressure in Kajiado District. The realization that areas which have long been defined as economically 'marginal' have substantial revenue-earning potential has contributed to the motivation of national elites to legislate policies facilitating the subdivision of the GRs. The resulting IRs will not be able to support the existing subsistence dairy economy and the majority of Maasai may be forced to sell their IRs. The demand for such land is not wanting. Shrewd politicians and wealthy elites will take the opportunity to buy the IRs as a means of gaining access to the income from wildlife-related activity and beef ranching. It has been predicted that by the first decade of the next century Kenya will be a net importer of beef and thus the potential returns to beef production in areas now under subsistence dairy production are great.

Such opportunities are also recognized by local Maasai who have themselves profited from past allocations of IRs. For example, families in the Loitokitok area who were the first to be allocated IRs and became wealthy by subdividing them and selling the land to immigrant farmers are now strong supporters of the political initiative to break up the GRs as they are in a position to purchase land.

A second local group is also interested in purchasing land in the existing GR areas but for different motives. Maasai 'nationalism' is increasingly evident in areas such as the Mau Escarpment and in the Loitokitok area. Recent parliamentary election campaigns provided evidence of this. Cultivators have recently been forcibly removed from the Mau by Maasai and in the Loitokitok area some are preparing to purchase lands from the divided GRs to prevent a small number of landowners coming to dominate the area.

Such local opposition to the implications of the break-up of the GRs is confronted not only by the political alliance between local wealthy people and national elites but also by energetic national and international groups lobbying on behalf of the national parks and reserves. The existing land uses on the GRs allow for wildlife dispersal beyond the boundaries of the parks and reserves. Landowners are rewarded with revenues generated by wildlife-viewing activity by the Ministry of

Tourism and Wildlife (MTW). The MTW is concerned, however, that, with the subdivision of the GRs, the IRs may be fenced. Fences would interfere with the wet-season dispersal of the wildlife and possibly undermine the viability of the parks and reserves.

A number of options are available to the MTW as it seeks to preserve the wildlife resource. The first is to require the creation of a 'buffer zone' between the parks and the IR areas. From the Maasai perspective this solution has a number of problems. Who will own the buffer zone? Will the Maasai be compensated for the land included in the zone? Who will get the wildlife revenues generated in the zone? Can the MTW be trusted to maintain agreements over the long term? In the recent past agreements over boreholes and distribution of Wildlife Utilization Fees in the Amboseli area have been abrogated and there is much distrust on the part of the Maasai of any MTW initiative, such as the 'buffer zone' concept.

To avoid this the MTW is contemplating increasing the revenues paid to individual landowners in the dispersal areas on condition that they do not fence their land or otherwise restrict access to wildlife. This objective would be best achieved were the land owned by a small number of people owning large tracts. It is in such a situation that an alliance appears likely between the MTW, and its supportive international wildlife lobby, and the political/economic elites who seek to own the land and acquire the income from wildlife-based tourism and from beef ranching. Such an alliance would be extremely powerful and would likely subdue any attempts by Maasai to maintain their already slender hold on the lands demarcated to them by the British as the Masai Reserve.

For the majority of Maasai currently living on GRs, their subdivision will lead to a loss of ecological and economic viability. The economic, political and ecological marginalization of Kenya's poor, already accomplished in areas of higher agricultural potential, is being extended down the ecological gradient into the rangelands (Bernard *et al.*, 1989). The political and economic elites who have conspired to prevent the development of policies which would have expanded the economic potential of these areas for the majority of their inhabitants now seek to acquire these areas for alternative land uses which will yield significant wealth for the few.[4]

The response among Maasai to this situation is not homogeneous. There are different views among members of IRs and GRs and between different areas. The area being subdivided around Ngong is close enough to Nairobi to offer prospects of profit from land sales to the majority of owners. In the Loitokitok area the potential for an urban land market does not exist. Here at least three groups are actively seeking to purchase land as the GRs are broken up. Two represent Maasai from the area and the third consists of land speculators from outside the District. The latter are linked to the political process which is favouring the creation of land units which will support the wildlife industry and promote beef production. One of the Maasai groups has identical objectives. These are Maasai whose families benefited from the original distribution of IRs and they see the current situation as a second opportunity to benefit from land speculation.

The second Maasai group has a very different perspective. It consists of Maasai who can afford to purchase land but whose stated purpose in doing so is to maintain the land in Maasai ownership. They view the other Maasai group as not holding to Maasai values, as not representing the interests of the Maasai community. Rather, they are seen as being in collusion with national elites whose appeal is to a 'Kenyan' rather than a 'traditional group' identity, where being 'Kenyan' means forsaking values associated with the well-being of the majority to aggressively promote that of individuals.[5]

The experience of the Kajiado Maasai must be seen as a discouraging precursor to that of other pastoral groups in Kenya. The pressure is evident in Narok District and in northern Kenya where a few wealthy stockowners already dominate the livestock production system. The relentless acquisition of land resources by the economic elite continues, creating production systems which condemn the existing inhabitants to the life of poverty already experienced by the majority elsewhere in Kenya.

Conclusion

Maasai have long been viewed as people of cattle, whose culture and economy were closely bound to their dairy based pastoral subsistence system. Such an identity was plausible while grazing and water resources were held in common and access was controlled by the Maasai community. From the onset of the colonial period to the present, policies have been implemented which have come to undermine the assumption of land as a common resource. Increasingly land has come to be individually owned and the cattle economy which depended on access to pasture and water has had to adjust to differential control of resources. While cattle may still represent the core of being Maasai, it is access to land upon which to graze them that now defines participation in cattle raising. Further, for many Maasai, control of land is seen as a means of acquiring wealth, not in cattle, but in the monetary economy.

This recent tendency for Maasai to invest in land reflects a national pattern established during the colonial period. Nationwide, the land available for purchase in areas of high agricultural potential is limited and landed elites have been inexorably moving down the ecological gradient (Bernard *et al.*, 1989). Areas which in the past were deliberately neglected and defined as marginal are now being redefined as economically viable. The rangelands have acquired economic potential and facilitative policies, previously denied to the 'marginal' rangelands, are being enacted.

The availability of land in the rangeland areas will be seized upon by the landowning elites who have seen the opportunities for land acquisition dwindle elsewhere in Kenya. The limited economic potential afforded to subsistence dairy pastoralism within the colonial and independent economy is not seen to inhibit land purchasers as more remunerative alternative forms of land use become possible once land tenure is redefined to large individually-managed ranches. Such alternatives include beef ranching and wildlife-related activities both of which have great revenue-generating potential within the present structure of the national economy.

It is in this context that opportunistic elements, both national and local elites, have seized upon conflict arising from population–land pressure on GRs in Kajiado District to pursue aggressively a policy of breaking up of the GRs into small individually-owned units. The anticipated acceleration of land sales will permit the accumulation of large, individually-managed units which will support more remunerative activities. These interventions are consistent with a view that the long-term objective of development policy for Maasai areas has been to replace the dairy-based, largely subsistence economy with other land uses which offer greater economic returns, namely beef ranching and wildlife-related activities.

For the majority of Maasai the future is bleak. Local groups are beginning to examine the options available on the small, recently created IRs but their ecological constraints preclude most agricultural activities. Land sales will be widespread but there are few alternative occupations available in the area and migration to cities or to other, even drier areas is a likely outcome. Neither holds great hope for the future.

The cultural identification of Maasai with cattle is no longer universal. As the pattern of land ownership changes from communal to individual, so the opportunities for and the degree of participation in the livestock economy and in the national monetary economy have become differentiated. The distribution of wealth is in flux. Some Maasai have become wealthy, in land, cattle, and/or cash while others are being marginalized as landless and herdless. Maasai culture is being reformed in response to both internal and external factors as land replaces cattle as the means of acquiring wealth within the increasingly diversified monetary economy.

As in the past, Maasai are responding to the opportunities and constraints arising from changing political, economic, and environmental circumstances. In this process there will be winners and losers and questions arise as to who they will be. What are the class, gender, and age implications of change? What are the environmental consequences? How will the social and political structures which underpinned the traditional, largely subsistence Maasai dairy economy adapt to altered circumstances? Will the Maasai survive as a distinct cultural entity or will the notion of 'being Maasai' merely come to refer to a person's ancestry and adherence to certain traditions, such as circumcision and age-sets, while their existential identity represents their status within a more generic concept of 'being Kenyan'? The transfer of the definition of wealth from cattle to land has profound implications. Identity and ethnicity are being redefined for Maasai and the outcome is uncertain.

Notes

* The research on which this is based was funded by a post-doctoral fellowship from The Rockefeller Foundation.

1. Throughout the colonial period the administration complained that Maasai were unwilling to sell their animals because they had an irrational proclivity to accumulate stock, but even in official reports there is recurrent reference to the fact that when a competitive price was offered sales would occur (Kenya, 1936, 1947, 1950, 1953, 1954). Meadows and White (1979) and Evangelou (1984) discuss the issues related to the sales of livestock in Kajiado District.
2. Heavy losses of livestock due to the effects of drought are reported in the Annual Reports for the District for 1929, 1933 and 1935 (Kenya, 1929, 1933, 1935).
3. The problem of overgrazing was frequently identified during the colonial period as the major constraint to livestock development and a wide variety of strategies — enforced sales, grazing schemes, group ranches etc. were evolved to deal with it. Close examination of the historical record suggests that overgrazing was more a recurrent problem consequent upon drought than a continuous constraint to the development of the livestock industry. The Annual Reports of Kajiado District speak of overgrazing as a problem after or during droughts and in a number of years when good range conditions prevailed specific attention was drawn by the District Commissioner to the fact that no overgrazing existed or that it was limited to areas of livestock concentration (Kenya, 1938, 1948, 1951, 1954). It may have been more appropriate in the context of the conditions in which the livestock economy was developing to have identified drought rather than overstocking as the constraint. A further factor concerning the importance given to overgrazing as the basic issue may have been the coincidence of drought (during which overgrazing may have occurred as the carrying capacity would have been suddenly reduced) and major reviews of development. The Carter Commission (Great Britain, 1934), the post-World War Two period, the Swynnerton Plan (Kenya, 1954) and the move to independence around 1960 all coincided with years of drought and major livestock losses. Within the prevailing Maasai economy such losses were anticipated and strategies had been evolved to accommodate them. However, to policy makers the situation appeared irrational and in need of change; Maasai economy was viewed as a destructive rather than as a viable production system upon which a more commercial system could be developed.
4. Recent concerns with the determinism of many studies written within the broad dependency paradigm have led to a revisionist perspective which examines the degree to which African societies resisted incorporation within the colonial state and thus mediated colonial objectives. The fact that Maasai have been able to maintain so much of their 'Maasainess', to keep intact their economic and social institutions, to recent times might lead to the conclusion that they resisted intrusion more successfully than other societies, such as the Kikuyu.

   While the basic concept that local people made history within the structure of colonialism is valid, the conclusion that the cohesion of Maasai culture provided a firmer base for resistance to colonial intrusion than groups like the Kikuyu can be questioned. An alternative explanation might lie in the fact that the colonial and post-colonial elites were geographically selective in their penetration of rural society, moving into areas of higher ecological potential before those of lower potential (Bernard *et al.*, 1989). This would have led to the agriculturally productive highlands being occupied before the rangelands.

The process of penetration has continued from colonial days to the present but its spatial impact was not temporally coincident throughout Kenya. That Kikuyu lived in the areas first settled by the colonialists and that Maasai lands were of little initial interest may have more explanatory value than notions of the relative ability of these groups to resist. The economic and political structures behind land acquisition have remained powerful to the present and they continue to undermine rural socio-economic systems when and where the elites choose to accumulate land. The continued power of the elites to apply structural forces to dominate local groups should not be underestimated in revisionist analyses.

5. This definition of 'becoming Kenyan' is similar to that of Kituyi (1990:1–2): 'The process of becoming Kenyan has two aspects. First is the structural integration by which physical integration is accompanied by a process where local political organs are crushed or subordinated to institutions serving the national political authority; economic institutions are increasingly appended to those operating in the national economy . . . The other aspect of becoming Kenyan is an adaptational integration by which adaptive strategies and career patterns among the Maasai draw upon resources in the national economy; individuals increasingly identify constraints and resources beyond the confines of their traditional economy.'

Thirteen

Maa-Speakers of the Northern Desert

Recent Developments in Ariaal & Rendille Identity[1]

ELLIOT FRATKIN

Recent developments among Ariaal and Rendille pastoralists of northern Kenya illustrate the continuing influence of Maasai culture on surrounding peoples. This chapter discusses the spread of the Maa language among Rendille in the contemporary context of pastoral sedentarization and market integration.

The Ariaal, along with Samburu and Elmolo of Lake Turkana, are the most northerly of Maa-speaking peoples. Numbering between 7,000 and 9,000 people, Ariaal herd camels, cattle, goats and sheep between Mount Marsabit and the Ndoto Mountains in Marsabit District, north-central Kenya. The Ariaal form a cultural bridge between Samburu cattle pastoralists (pop. 70,000) and Rendille camel pastoralists (pop. 15,000), and speak both Samburu (a dialect of Maa) and Rendille (a Cushitic language related to Somali).

Paul Spencer (1973) first described the Ariaal as a product of the larger Samburu–Rendille alliance, which was based on the non-competitiveness of their herding environment, their mutual defence against common Turkana and Boran enemies, and, most importantly, the outmigration of Rendille men and women into Samburu society via Ariaal. Spencer proposed that Rendille outmigration was a result of demographic pressures where their human population grew at a faster rater than their camel herds and where their rules of inheritance (by primogeniture) impoverished second and third sons. Poorer Rendille men joined Ariaal settlements near the highlands to take up cattle and small stock production, while women from the essentially monogamous Rendille married more polygynous Samburu and Ariaal men as second wives.

Since Spencer's research in the late 1950s, the Rendille and Ariaal have undergone substantial change in residence and economy. They, as other northern Kenyan pastoralists, have experienced political disruptions following Kenyan independence in 1963, including the *shifta* civil war in the 1960s, devastating droughts in the 1970s and 1980s, the

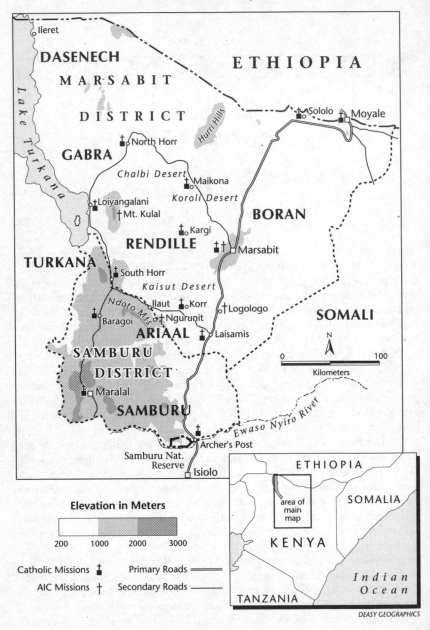

DEASY GEOGRAPHICS

Map 13.1 Northern Kenya: Location of Ariaal and Rendille

growth of permanent towns around Christian missions distributing famine-relief foods, and, most recently, the arrival of large-scale international development projects including UNESCO-Integrated Project in Arid Lands. Attracted to growing towns by physical security and mechanized wells for their livestock, Ariaal and Rendille have benefited from new opportunities in wage labour, commercial entrepreneurship, and access to schools and health care. Since the 1970s, nearly one-half of Rendille and Ariaal have settled in or near the towns of Korr, Kargi, Ngurunit and Laisamis (Fratkin, 1991; O'Leary, 1990).

Where the Ariaal have a long history of bilingualism in Samburu and Rendille, few Rendille could speak Samburu until very recently. Heine (1976a) found in 1975 only 11 per cent of Rendille men who were fluent in Samburu, compared to 74 per cent of Ariaal men who were fluent in both Samburu and Rendille. By 1989, however, bilingualism had grown to 91 per cent of Ariaal men and 27 per cent of Rendille men, with nearly one-half of Rendille men under 25 years old speaking Samburu. This last figure represents a two and one-half increase in bilingualism among Rendille, a population that was virtually monolingual fifteen years ago.

It is interesting to ponder why the Rendille have increased their ability to speak Maa in this period of economic transition and social transformation. The ability of Rendille to speak Samburu no longer appears based on immigration into Ariaal society. As this study will show, Ariaal are increasingly marrying among themselves (rather than taking wives from Samburu or Rendille), and, while Rendille men have not slowed down their migration to Ariaal, they have not increased it. This explanation of increasing bilingualism among Rendille focuses on economic change and national integration.

During the period of Spencer's research (1957–1962), Samburu and Rendille were only marginally integrated in the market economy, and immigration and assimilation into Samburu cattle-keeping society provided one of the few economic alternatives for poorer Rendille. Since the 1970s, however, Rendille and Ariaal have increasing settled near towns and have integrated more fully in the market economy, increasing their commerce in livestock and participation in wage-labour jobs such as construction or as watchmen. Importantly, Rendille have increased their ownership and marketing of cattle (despite poorer herding conditions) without migrating to Ariaal or Samburu (O'Leary, 1990; Roth, 1990).

Two immediate questions are (1) is the spread of Maa related to cattle ownership, and (2) if so, how does this process unfold in the contemporary context of national identity formation, cultural pluralism, and economic transformation?

This paper analyses the process of cultural assimilation through the use of multivariate regressions. A first regression locates the degree to which cattle ownership among Rendille is affected by bilingualism, changes in marriage preference, age of speaker, education levels, and experience in wage labour; a second regression looks at how bilingualism is affected by wage labour, cattle ownership, and educational levels.

The analysis will show that bilingualism among Rendille is associated not only with increased ownership and marketing of cattle (as expected), but also with the degree of formal education and experience with wage labour. The Maa language is continuing to expand, as in the past, by combinations of economic, political, and cultural forces, but it is spreading in new ways in the context of sedentarization, urbanization, and market integration.

The Ariaal and Rendille Communities

The Ariaal are a population of about 7,000 who live in patrilineally based communities along the eastern base of the Ndoto Mountains and the western side of Marsabit Mountain in Marsabit District, Kenya. Occupying an ecological interface between the highland Samburu and lowland Rendille and utilizing their kinship ties to the larger groups to graze their animals, Ariaal raise both cattle (which need highland water and grazing) and camels (which thrive in the hot lowlands) as well as small stock of goats and sheep to provide milk, meat, and animals for trade (Fratkin, 1986, 1991).

Not quite a separate society, Ariaal are a particular social formation, distinguished from Samburu by their bilingualism, camel-keeping, and following certain Rendille customs in settlement organization and rituals affecting livestock, and from Rendille by their bilingualism, cattle-keeping, and their inclusion in Samburu descent groups and age-set rituals.

Ariaal share many cultural features with the Rendille including large lowland settlements (often over thirty houses of five people each) as well as practising rituals associated with camel production including *sorio* and *almhodo* (Schlee, 1989). However, Ariaal clans, which constitute the core of residential settlements, are affiliated with the Samburu rather than the Rendille descent system, particularly with Lorokushu, Longieli, Lukumai, Masala, and the composite Turia descent sections. Ariaal age-set ceremonies follow the Samburu rather than Rendille ritual cycle, including the performance of five ritual ox-slaughters (*mugit*) over the fourteen-year period between age-set initiations (Spencer, 1973: 89–93). While Rendille also follow a fourteen-year age-set cycle (and indeed Samburu and Maasai may have borrowed this system from them (Beaman, 1981)), their ritual structure is quite distinct from Samburu. Ariaal are not permitted to attend the large *gaalgulamme* ceremony following Rendille age-set initiation which defines Rendille inclusion and identity (Schlee, 1989: 9).

In appearance, language, and social identity, Ariaal see themselves as Samburu and part of the Maa-speaking community; yet they also retain strong ties of descent and marriage with Rendille. Their identity can be as problematic to Ariaal as to outsiders. Kitoip Lenkiribe, an Ariaal elder from Lewogoso Lukumai clan settlement, said in 1985,

'We're something in between Samburu and Rendille. We are not something altogether different; we are really both things together. We live in Rendille country, keep camels, and follow camel rituals of *sorio* and *almhodo*. Although we stay away from the *gaalgulamme* [Rendille age-set initiation ritual] as we don't think the Rendille want us there, we do send our camels there to be blessed. Our houses are Rendille, and we speak both languages. Yet we also keep cattle, we follow the Samburu *mugit* [age-set rites], and speak the Samburu language. If I was in Nairobi and someone asked me who I was, I would say Samburu. But when I'm in Maralel [the capital of Samburu District], they call me "filthy Rendille", and when I'm in Korr [a Rendille settlement] they call me Ariaal. In fact Lewogoso Lukumai [a Samburu clan] and Tubsha [a Rendille clan] are brothers — we came from the same people a long time ago. The younger brothers of Rendille families [i.e. those without camel inheritances] came towards Samburu, or Samburu came down into the lowlands to keep camels; they are now the same people who live in the same country.'

Rendille are a more defined and cohesive group than Ariaal, or, as Schlee (1989:50) points out, a 'society easy to leave, difficult to join'. A small population of about 15,000 (the 1979 census figure of 21,794 includes Ariaal) residing in the arid lowlands between Lake Turkana and Mount Marsabit, Rendille have until recently subsisted exclusively on the milk of their camel herds and meat and trade from their small stock. Rendille are organized into two moieties (*Belesi Bahai* and *Belesi Berri*) composed of nine patrilineal clans. As among Ariaal, Rendille settlements are large and occupied mainly by sub-clan agnates and their families, forming essentially exogamous local descent groups.

Rendille were formerly more nomadic and occupied a much larger area than their present concentration in the Kaisut Desert. Sobania (1988b) determined that, in the early twentieth century, Rendille grazed their camels and small stock from the north-east shores of Lake Turkana south to the Uaso Nyiro River, a herding environment ten times greater than today. Rendille lost lands as Boran and Turkana pastoralists expanded south and east, and the British administration imposed 'tribal boundaries' to restrict movements in the Northern Frontier District. After Kenyan independence, Rendille faced political insecurity during the *shifta* war of the 1960s, repeated famines in the 1970s and 1980s, and the influx of western missions and international relief efforts, which led to the settling of Rendille around towns (Fratkin, 1991).

Market Integration of Rendille and Ariaal

Ariaal and Rendille are essentially subsistence pastoralists, living on the milk, meat, and blood products of their herds while selling annual offtakes of 5–7 per cent of the cattle and 10–20 per cent of their small

Photo 13.1 *Ariaal Camels*

Photo 13.2 *Rendille at Korr Catholic Church*

stock, primarily to purchase grains during dry seasons when milk supplies are low (IPAL, 1984: 387). Ariaal have been able to sell more animals than Rendille because they have larger herds of cattle and small stock and because they rely on the camel rather than cattle for milk.

Rendille are newcomers to the livestock market, having had until recently both poor marketing facilities and insufficient surpluses of cattle and small stock to sell; the camel market is almost non-existent and Rendille are reluctant to sell them owing to their low reproductive rates and their importance as milk producers and transport animals. Recently Rendille have increased their cattle herds, primarily to generate cash income through trade as well as for bridewealth payments (Roth, 1990; O'Leary, 1990).

Under colonial rule, market conditions were poor in Marsabit District and only gradually improved, as the new government continued its neglect of the pastoral regions, emphasizing programmes in crop rather than pastoral livestock production. The *shifta* political disturbance where northern Kenyan Moslems attempted to secede (after responding to a British mandated plebiscite that they wished to join Somalia) inhibited widespread marketing in Marsabit District until the end of the 1960s, while the droughts of 1973 and 1982–84 led to a glut of animals on the market as pastoralists tried to sell their undernourished animals in exchange for grains (O'Leary, 1990).

The nomadic settlement pattern of Rendille declined during the famines of the 1970s and 1980s as western missions engaged in famine-relief work. The Catholic Diocese of Marsabit established missions in the Rendille area at Korr, Kargi, and Laisamis and the Protestant African Inland Church concentrated on Ariaal communities at Ngurunit, Logologo, and Marsabit town. Many Rendille families settled around these towns in search of food, security, health care, and education. While some of these households retained their livestock, herding them in distant camps, many became permanent dependants on mission aid.

In 1976 the UNESCO–IPAL project was established in Marsabit District, initially as an ecological research station run by Europeans on Mount Kulal monitoring environmental degradation. By the early 1980s IPAL had grown into a major development agency headed by Kenyans and funded by West Germany with stations in Marsabit, Korr, and Ngurunit. Concerned that much of the environmental decline and 'desertification' in Africa was the product of human mismanagement, IPAL initiated programmes to increase pastoral livestock sales as a means to cull herds and reduce overgrazing. These efforts dovetailed neatly with government efforts to promote livestock marketing in the pastoral regions, and IPAL and goverment ministries in Marsabit worked together to construct roads, mechanize wells, distribute veterinary medicines, and hold livestock auctions. IPAL trucks transported livestock to markets in Nanyuki and Nairobi, and they sent mobile shops selling foods and household goods on camel-back to nomadic communities to

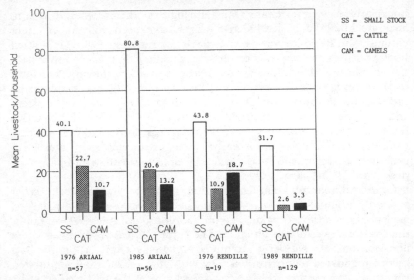

Fig. 13.1 Livestock Ownership in Ariaal and Rendille

further encourage the nomads to sell livestock. By 1986, however, the IPAL project ground to a halt, suffering from both its own internal inertia and poor relations with Rendille and Ariaal who accused IPAL of corruption and making promises IPAL could not keep (Fratkin, 1991).

Despite their failings, IPAL did increase marketing opportunities for the Rendille and Ariaal. Their trucks transported livestock to Isiolo at fees lower than the local shopkeepers charged, they held periodic auctions at Korr and Ngurunit, and, importantly, they introduced wages to over thirty Rendille and Ariaal as herders, watchmen, and assistants. IPAL had hoped that by introducing wages Rendille would develop a greater appetite for western goods and increase their livestock sales; they sadly discovered, however, that their Ariaal and Rendille employees used most of their wages to purchase livestock sold at the IPAL auctions! (Fratkin, 1991: 104).

Changes in Household Economy

Both the Ariaal and Rendille went through large changes in household economy following the sedentarization of the late 1970s. Figures 13.1 to 13.4 compare relative differences in livestock ownership, livestock sales, and levels of education and wage-labour participation for Ariaal and Rendille in both 1976 and 1985 (for the Ariaal) and 1989 (for the Rendille).

Figure 13.1 shows the relative equivalence of Ariaal and Rendille livestock holdings in 1976, before widespread sedentarization, when both societies averaged over 40 small stock per household and over 10 large stock, although Rendille had larger camel herds and Ariaal larger cattle herds. By 1989, however, Rendille had greatly reduced livestock holdings, with 31.7 small stock per household and less than 5 large stock per household. This drastic decline resulted from severe restrictions in their grazing lands, loss of stock during the 1982–84 drought, and their sedentarization around the missions.

In contrast to the Rendille figures, Ariaal livestock increased dramatically after the drought, to 80.8 small stock, 20.6 cattle, and 13.2 camels per household. The decline in cattle ownership was a result of high mortalities during the drought, while increases in small stock reflect both their faster recovery rate and the Ariaal strategy of building up small stock to trade for cattle. These average household holdings, however, do not show the wide degree of heterogeneity and polarization among Ariaal and Rendille households, or the high degree of impoverishment that resulted after the Ethiopian Famine of 1984 (Fratkin and Roth, 1990).

Despite their reduction in total herd size, Rendille increased participation in the cash market, selling 3.5 small stock and 0.2 cattle per house annually (for an average price of KSh230 (US$14.30) and 1,000 shillings (US$62.50) respectively in 1989, compared to no livestock sales in 1976. Ariaal sales for the two periods remained the same for small stock (3.7 per household), but showed a large increase in cattle sales (from 0.2 to 1.2 per household) as shown in Figure 13.2 below.

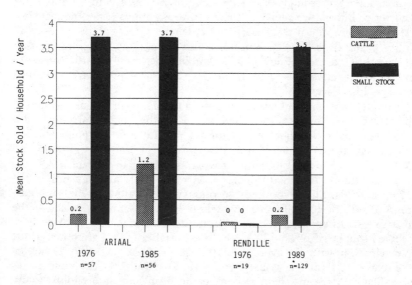

Fig. 13.2 Livestock Sales in Ariaal and Rendille

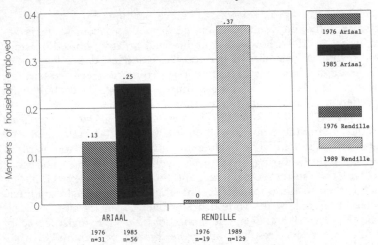

Fig. 13.3 Wage Labour: Mean Individuals Employed per Household

Opportunities for wage labour have increased dramatically in the past fifteen years. As among Samburu and Maasai, Rendille and Ariaal men gain employment in the military, police, or Game Department. More adults have found employment as construction workers at the missions or as herders and watchmen with the UNESCO-IPAL. Younger Rendille, particularly members of the unmarried *murran* age-grade, have increasingly taken jobs as watchmen in Nairobi and other centres to the south as have warriors from Samburu (Sperling, 1987a). Although the rate of wage employment is very low compared even to other pastoralists like the Samburu and Maasai, it is significant that the level of wage employment has doubled in Ariaal from 0.13 to 0.25 persons per household and from 0 to 0.37 members per Rendille household, as seen in Figure 13.3.

Finally, recent sedentarization around mission centres has resulted in increased social services for Ariaal and Rendille, particularly in health care and primary school education. The Marsabit Catholic Diocese developed primary schools and dispensaries in Laisamis, Illaut, and Marsabit town in the 1960s and at Korr and Kargi in the late 1970s; the African Inland Mission at Logologo, Mount Kulal, and Ngurunit in the 1960s and 70s. The government secondary school at Marsabit is increasingly absorbing Rendille primary school leavers. Figure 13.4 shows the distribution of educated members of households in Ariaal and Rendille, where it can be seen Rendille have a much higher, although more recent, participation with an average of 0.75 household members in school compared to 0.33 for Ariaal. Roth (1991) found that the majority of Rendille children in school at Korr came from poor households, many from blacksmith families.

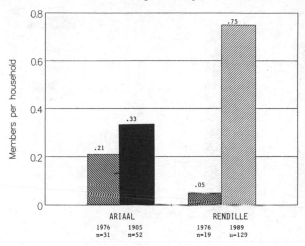

Fig. 13.4 Education: Mean Individuals Schooled per Household

The Dynamics of Assimilation

Sedentarization and the increase in livestock marketing have altered Spencer's original model of Rendille immigrating into Samburu via Ariaal. While some Rendille continue to migrate to Ariaal, town residence and new opportunities in wage labour, education, and livestock commerce provide economic alternatives and diminish the necessity of Rendille migrating to Ariaal to take up cattle pastoralism.

We can locate changes in the Ariaal–Rendille relationship by measuring changes in several variables that have occurred between 1976 and 1989: (1) migration of Rendille men into Ariaal; (2) marriage preferences among Rendille and Ariaal men; (3) polygyny rates in Ariaal and Rendille; and (4) comparative levels of bilingualism.

1. *Migration*: Immigration of Rendille into Ariaal remained virtually unchanged; Rendille immigrants represented 22.8 per cent of male stockowners residing in Ariaal settlements in 1976 and 21.4 per cent in 1985, as shown in Figure 13.5. Many Rendille immigrants to Ariaal are poor brothers of women married to Ariaal men attempting to build up small stock or cattle herds in the highland areas. The stable number of immigrants to Ariaal shows that immigration remains a strong option for poor Rendille, confirming an important component of Spencer's model.

2. *Marriage Preference*: There has been an increase in marriage preference by Ariaal men for Ariaal women rather than wives from Rendille or Samburu in the past 15 years. Figure 13.6 shows the increase in the proportion of wives from Ariaal settlements from 36 per cent in 1976 to 47 per cent in 1985, while the Rendille rate of marrying Ariaal women has remained the same, measured at 19 per cent in 1976 and 17 per cent in 1989.

283

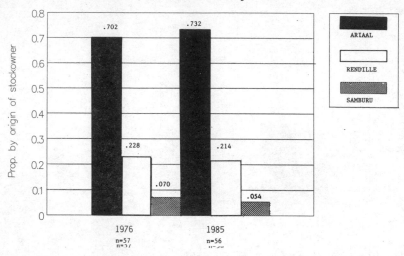

Fig. 13.5 *Immigration into Ariaal*

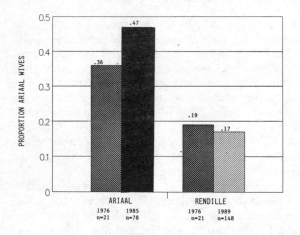

Fig. 13.6 *Marriage Preference: Proportion of Ariaal Wives*

3. *Polygyny*: Ariaal showed an increase in polygyny rates from 1.28 in 1976 to 1.39 in 1985, the Rendille remained unchanged from 1.11 in 1976 to 1.15 in 1989, as shown in Figure 13.7.

This increase in polygyny by Ariaal men is characterized by a higher rate for members of the *Kishili* age-set (initiated in 1963–64 and released as elders in 1976–78) than for older age-sets, and is probably associated with the higher cattle ownership of this generation than their seniors (because cattle reproduce at a faster rate than camels, a man with twenty cattle can generate brideprice of eight large animals within ten years

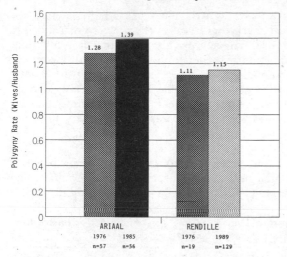

Fig. 13.7 Polygyny Rates in Ariaal and Rendille

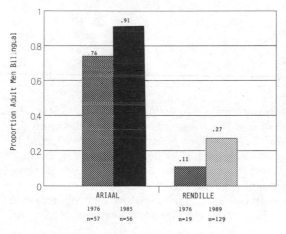

Fig. 13.8 Bilingualism in Maa and Rendille

while a man with twenty camels may never generate that surplus in his lifetime). It was expected that Rendille polygyny would also increase with cattle ownership, but it did not.

4. *Bilingualism*: Of these four variables, the bilingualism rate has changed the most in the past fifteen years, without corresponding changes in marriage preference, emigration, or polygyny. Bilingualism in Maa and Rendille among surveyed adult Ariaal men increased from 74 per cent in 1976 to 91 per cent in 1985; for Rendille men it increased from 11 per cent to 27 per cent by 1989, as shown in Figure 13.8.

These data show a process where Ariaal are consolidating themselves as distinct social entities, marrying amongst themselves and with less intermarriage with Rendille. The surveys also show that Rendille (like Ariaal) are increasing their cattle ownership to generate cash income to buy food and other commodities; they are also increasing their wage employment and education levels. Rendille have not immigrated or assimilated into Ariaal in greater numbers, they are simply raising more cattle. However, Rendille have increased their ability to speak Samburu, with over 50 per cent of men under thirty years old bilingual in Samburu and Rendille.

A logistic regression was performed to seek correlations between cattle production, bilingualism, wage labour, education levels, marriage preference, age, and period (1976 vs 1989) in both Ariaal and Rendille.

Table 13.1 *Results of Regression Analysis of Cattle Ownership: Effects on Bilingualism, Marriage Preference, Age, Period, Education and Wage Labour*

VARIABLE	COEFFICIENT	STD ERROR	|T|	P
Constant	−0.947	0.129	7.332	>.001
Bilingualism	+0.227	0.047	4.848	>.001
Education	−1.154	0.542	2.127	.034
Wage Labour	+0.009	0.054	0.167	.867
Period (1989)	−0.194	0.053	3.655	>.001
Age	+0.364	0.161	2.267	*0.024
Marriage Preference	+0.044	0.050	0.880	.380
			$R^2 = 0.183$	

The regression shows that cattle ownership among both Rendille and Ariaal is correlated to age (the younger the age-set, the more the cattle ownership in proportion to other types of stock owned) and to language (the more cattle owned, the higher the degree of bilingualism); there is no correlation of cattle ownership to marriage preference, wage labour, or levels of education.

A second regression searched for correlations between bilingualism (rather than cattle ownership) and wage labour, educational levels, and cattle ownership.

This regression shows that bilingualism is strongly correlated with wage labour, education, and cattle ownership, which appear to be mutually independent. All of these factors have increased for the Rendille and Ariaal since 1976.

Discussion

Spencer's model of assimilation of Rendille into Ariaal and Samburu is based on both ecological and demographic principles that postulate that the Rendille human population outstrips its camel herd reproduction, leading to the outmigration of Rendille men to take up cattle production

Table 13.2 *Logistic Linear Analysis of Probability of Head of Household Being Bilingual (adjusted for effects of period and ethnic affiliation)*

MODEL	DEGREES OF FREEDOM	LIKELIHOOD RATIO χ^2	PROBABILITY
Bilingual*Wage* Cattle*School	201	943.63	
Model with Main Effects			
Bilingual + wage + cattle + school	802	1058.62	n.s.
Bilingual + wage + cattle [– school]	804	1283.54	>.001
Bilingual + wage + school [– cattle]	803	1079.15	>.001
Bilingual + school + cattle [– wage]	804	1326.81	>.001

among the Samburu and Ariaal. Where this model reflected conditions during Spencer's fieldwork in the late 1950s, the events of recent years, including the constriction of Rendille camel grazing lands and their sedentarization around permanent mission stations, has led to a decline in Rendille nomadic camel pastoralism. Simultaneously Rendille have increased their raising and marketing of cattle. Poor Rendille have not increased their immigration into Samburu or Ariaal, but have chosen to live in the growing mission towns or larger urban areas where they can seek wage labour, engage in livestock markets, and send their children to school. While Ariaal have not settled to the same degree as Rendille, they have also increasingly entered the wage economy and are beginning to send their children to primary and secondary schools.

The question remains why, in the absence of recruitment into Ariaal society, have Rendille increased their bilingualism in the Maa language? There is no single answer to this; the logistic regressions show that bilingualism in Maa among Rendille is multi-causal, related independently to cattle ownership, wage labour, formal education, and age of speaker.

The mechanism for acquiring the Maa language seems to work in different ways for different sectors of the Rendille and Ariaal populations. Increased cattle ownership implies changes in labour and herding regimens, where Rendille adolescents and *murran* spend time in highland cattle camps among Ariaal and Samburu herders, learning Maa in that context. This culture contact re-occurs in later life as adult men sell livestock in local markets attended by other Maa-speakers. In this respect the spread of Maa *is* related to cattle specialization and the livestock market.

Photo 13.3 Ariaal Killing Ox at Wedding Ceremony

There are, however, other factors not associated with the pastoral economy which influence bilingualism. Wage labour has led to increased contact with Maa-speakers at several levels. For uneducated Rendille or Ariaal, the opportunities for wage-earning are few and confined mainly to low-skill jobs such as watchmen in towns to the south. Maasai, Samburu, and Rendille have a reputation as brave and reliable guards, and there are scores of Rendille warriors in Nairobi working as watchmen. Seeking each other out in these foreign contexts, Rendille youth learn to speak with more numerous Samburu and Maasai in their language. A similar mechanism operates for Rendille in the army, police, or Game Department where they often work with other Samburu and Maasai.

Other wage jobs closer to home also encourage bilingualism. Rendille men may find work in construction around the missions or as paid herders for development and government projects such as UNESCO-IPAL. It is often Maa-speaking Samburu from Marsabit or Maralel towns who are in supervisory positions as foremen in these jobs owing to their longer histories of work and education. Learning Maa provides an important qualification for promotion in these occupations.

Formal education represents a final influence to learn Maa, particularly in district-wide secondary schools where Maa-speakers may outnumber Rendille-speakers both as teachers and students. This situation continues as educated Rendille gain wage work with local or national government offices which employ Maasai and Samburu, particularly in senior positions. Although secondary school students and government employees will usually speak Swahili or English, those from Rendille, Samburu, and Maasai backgrounds will talk to each other in Maa if possible.

Rendille are becoming bilingual, but they are not becoming Ariaal. They have not increased immigration into Ariaal; they have not increased their marriage to Ariaal or Samburu spouses; and they have not abandoned Rendille customs and social organization for a Samburu or Ariaal identity. Rendille have tenaciously held on to their culture despite changes in their economy and nomadic way of life, and are vociferously demanding a political and economic place of their own in Kenyan society.

It is in the wider context of national integration that Rendille are speaking Maa. Maa is an important language of the marketplace, both for the sale of livestock and labour. Bilingual Rendille are not the same people as bilingual Ariaal, although both raise cattle as well as camels and small stock. They follow different customs and have different senses of themselves and their social identity. The spread of Maasai culture, or at least the Maa language, is not a question simply of economic specialization raising cattle. Speaking Maa by Rendille and Ariaal is a by-product of market integration involving livestock entrepreneurship, wage labour, formal education and political participation. In north-central Kenya these activities continue to be influenced by Maa-speakers.

Notes

1. Data used in this study were collected from 56 Ariaal and 19 Rendille households in 1976, 57 Ariaal households re-surveyed in 1985, and 129 Rendille households surveyed by Eric Abella Roth at Korr in 1989. I am grateful to the Office of the President, Republic of Kenya, for their permission to conduct research, and the Institute of African Studies, University of Nairobi, for their cooperation in this study. I thank Larian and Anna Marie Aliyaro, Patrick Ngolei, and Lugi Lengesen of Korr, Marsabit District, Kenya, for their assistance in the fieldwork, Anne V. Buchanan and James W. Wood for their assistance with the statistical analyses, and Patricia Draper, Patricia L. Johnson, Martha Nathan, Thomas Spear, and Richard Waller for their comments on this manuscript. I am grateful to Eric Abella Roth for the generous sharing of his data collected in 1989, and his ongoing collaboration and friendship. Funding for this research was provided by the Social Science Research Council (USA), the National Geographic Society, and the Pennsylvania State University.

PART FIVE

Conclusions

RICHARD WALLER

At the beginning of this century, S.L.Hinde, one of the first administrative officers among the Kenya Maasai, published a book entitled
The Last of the Masai (Hinde and Hinde, 1901). His counterpart in
Tanganyika, Moritz Merker, concluded the first serious ethnography of
the Maasai with similarly gloomy views (Merker, 1910: 351):

> The process of settlement . . . will probably be accomplished slowly, but with
> appalling sacrifices of human life and by the destruction of the tribe as such.
> A small section, who are now richest in stock, may . . . continue to live as
> nomads, or the poorest, by way of agriculture, may become nomadic again and
> graze their herds in enforced peacefulness. But even these will then have ceased
> to be Masai, for a Masai with a shepherd's staff and pipe is a Masai no longer.

Hinde's and Merker's dismal prophecies have been echoed in many
subsequent accounts, and now, almost a century later, Hinde's title itself
has been revived on the cover of yet another glossy book for tourists
(Amin and Willetts, 1990). While Hinde and Merker believed that the
Maasai would be swallowed up by agriculture and inter-breeding, later
writers have blamed sedentarization, education and the encroachment of
capitalism for their impending, but regrettable, demise.

Why this predisposition always to see the Maasai — and, indeed,
'real pastoralists' generally — as a dying breed? Partly, no doubt, it
stems from a mixture of romantic nostalgia and fashionable guilt, but
it also suggests that western observers have always had a far more
rigid attachment to the outward trappings of 'tribe' than the 'tribesmen'
themselves. Few have questioned whether the Maasai, whose passing
they deplore, are not simply one particular manifestation of a general,
enduring but highly mutable and varied identity which they happen to
observe on the point of its apparently becoming something else. Maasai
themselves were clearly more optimistic about their future, as Merker
himself continued (Merker, 1910: 351):

Conclusions

In the face of such expectations for the future, it affects one almost painfully when one hears how firmly the Masai believe in the restoration of their might . . .

There is, then, a problem of perception ('ours' rather than 'theirs') in trying to understand how different Maasai identities may have been constructed (and by whom) and how they might be defined, re-ordered and maintained over time, over a wide area and in different economic, social, and political contexts. The fact that the definitions and processes involved in being and becoming Maasai are constantly changing explains why 'Maasainess' is such a slippery concept. Our contributors have approached this by explaining, from a variety of different perspectives, how people became Maasai and what it has meant at different times and places to be Maasai. They have not, on the whole, attempted a particular definition of Maasai. In the Conclusion we return to four major themes from the Introduction, as a way of showing how our case studies complement each other, placing them in the wider context of ethnicity and suggesting areas for further debate.

Our first theme is that of the relationship between Maasai and pastoralism. Almost any picture of the Maasai inevitably has a backdrop of stock or herding, and this outsider's impression is still shared in essence by many Maasai. Being Maasai has meant, historically, 'being under cattle' (Galaty, 1982a). Telelia's world is comfortably bounded by stock, and the critical points in her life have involved losing, exchanging or gaining animals. She looks back on the achievement of building up a herd with her husband, and this is what gives her life its structure and meaning. Relations both within the Maasai community itself and between Maasai and non-Maasai have been, and still to a large extent are, mediated through stock. Yet a 'modern Maasai' might well be a wheat farmer, and the Trans-Mara has become one of the main maize-producing areas of western Kenya. Are these Maasai, then, still Maasai? They believe so. One needs to ask what, exactly, has changed and what has not — and why.

One starting point is to look at resource allocation. Ethnicity has always been a way of controlling or regulating access to the resources crucial to survival. Until quite recently, the critical resources have been stock, the labour to herd it, and the grazing and water on which both animals and people depend. The '*Iloikop* Wars' in the nineteenth century, as well as those between Maasai and other pastoral peoples, were fought partly to determine who would be able to continue pastoralism and who would not, and their courses were shaped by the strategic map of water-points and dry-season pastures in the Rift Valley. When the Laikipiak lost their stock and grazing, as Sobania argues, they also lost their identity. More generally, all 'frontier' Maasai, in Galaty's phrase, were 'disenfranchised' when they were forced onto the margins of Maasailand and, in making a different use of resources, 'became'

Conclusions

something else. However, as Sutton and Spear remind us in different ways, the 'pure pastoral' tradition has not been the only one in Maasailand nor, in the long term, has it necessarily been the dominant mode. Here our unavoidably foreshortened perspective, focusing on the last two centuries, has distorted the picture. Maasai farmers like the Arusha have a place in the past as well as the present, and it is possible that further investigation will enlarge their role once the historiographical blinkers have been removed. Moreover, even though in the relatively recent past the dominant ethos, implicit in Spencer's chapter, has been shaped and managed by the wealthy stock-owning elite, this has probably always been the creed of a dominant minority, a point to which we will return. Restricted, rather than equal, access has been characteristic of many pastoral peoples, and this is revealed starkly in times of crisis when the rich, better able to endure loss, survive, and the poor die or move out. Indeed, the equation between stock wealth and 'Maasainess' has only been maintained by the expedient of defining stockless Maasai out of the community. Some of them become the 'other', whether as 'Dorobo' or as 'wastrels' (Spencer, 1988), against which moral virtue and material success can then be measured.

Recently, however, a new stage in the 'evolution' of the Maasai has begun. Again, it is marked by shifts in the balance of resources, in this case away from pastoral subsistence as wealthy Maasai elders convert cattle holdings into privately owned land and into the capital resources required for large-scale market production. Differentiation, always present, is becoming more formalized as large camps in which labour is shared shrink to smaller kin-based units where extra labour is acquired through wage and contract. Investment in social relations based on stock and marriage networks is being replaced by private cash investment in, for instance, education. School and outside work are changing notions of time and maturity (Kituyi, 1990). The 'other' is now becoming 'us', to borrow a phrase from Berntsen's (1980) discussion of the Maasai/*Iloikop* dichotomy.

There are a number of reasons why a shift from stock to land has taken place. Waller emphasizes the effect of incorporation within a colonial state which was preoccupied with defining and adjudicating exclusive rights in land. Fratkin has examined the effects of recent sedentarization and the development of a commercial economy in northern Kenya in establishing new criteria of access based on physical proximity to markets and to famine relief (Fratkin, 1991). Where you are may now be as important as who you are. Campbell's is perhaps the most direct statement of modern change and his chapter appropriately concludes the case studies. From his perspective, the alien periphery has now invaded the Maasai centre, thus reversing Galaty's model of expansion and perhaps confirming the fears expressed by Maasai during the colonial period. Outsiders now effectively control much of the resources of Maasailand by virtue of having superior access to the state, which is now far more interventionist than before. Through joint business ventures with Maasai and the mechanisms of an externally-imposed land market, they have title to large tracts of land. As grazing land is being turned to agricultural use, the mixed pastoralism which was characteristic of frontier areas like Loitokitok and Ngong has now spread widely to include some group ranches as well as privately-owned estates.

One should not, however, see these changes as representing a complete break with the past, or exaggerate their effect. There may be a thread of continuity here. Access to land, in the form of pasture and water-points, and not merely stock, has always underpinned pastoralism. Even if the nature of wealth is changing from one based on milking herds, the indirect product of land, to one based on cultivation and beef ranching, a direct product, the importance of control over scarce resources remains. New constructions of Maasai identity are finding ways of disengaging land and stock while preserving, or perhaps regaining, privileged access to both. Inevitably, however, as the community re-orients itself, it will have to shed its weakest members, just as it has done under pressure in the past. Some of these, in turn, may find new identities as well as new niches.

Another important area in which there is continuity is in the framework of relations between Maasai and others. As the Introduction and several of the chapters have made clear, Maasai have always existed within a regional context that has included non-Maasai and non-pastoralists. This is our second theme. Relations with outsiders are essential in two senses. Non-Maasai are central to any definition of being Maasai. Becoming Maasai is, for some, a process of ceasing to be non-Maasai, and the non-Maasai 'other' has often been critical in defining — negatively — what Maasai is. At the same time, the different but complementary modes of subsistence that others represent have supported Maasai pastoralism by supplying needs and offering refuges across economic and ethnic boundaries. It is the apparent contradiction, explored throughout this book, between a strong sense of ethnic exclusivity among Maasai themselves and a fluid pattern of exchange and assimilation among small-scale communities of pastoralists, farmers and hunter-gatherers that gives coherence to the regional system as a whole and supports the identities of its constituent parts. Difference, sharply drawn and strongly maintained, facilitates interdependence between peoples exploiting different ecological niches.

The regional focus remains, even though it is increasingly diffused through the expansion of the modern state which claims to incorporate or transcend older solidarities. However, despite successive attempts to split these apart and to re-align communities separately with a new colonial or later national centre, regional spheres survive. Kinship may cross ethnic boundaries but it does not yet encompass the state. National marketing has not entirely supplanted local and regional exchange.

Conclusions

While the social and economic logic of regional spheres remains compelling, the place of Maasai within the system is assured.

Within the region, frontiers retain their practical and symbolic importance, even though they have shifted in space — most strikingly where urban and agricultural development has encroached on the plains. The frontier still acts as a focal point of interaction as well as a boundary, where different communities and ethnicities rub up against and shade into one another. The morality of frontier life may be a matter of dispute, but its values and personalities remain strikingly constant below the surface, and Maasailand remains a land of investment and promise for determined or lucky outsiders.

The regional system does more than set the framework for interaction and negotiation. It also creates and preserves ecological and social niches in which communities and ethnicities may take root. Not all of these niches are necessarily occupied at any one time. Within the present structure of the Rift Valley region are traces of older ethnicities, some of which are discussed by Sutton and Lamphear. Il Kiriman, a cattle-keeping Rendille group with close relations to the Laikipiak, is an example of an earlier Ariaal-like development, now defunct (Spencer, 1973; Schlee, 1989). Elmolo, a 'Dorobo' fishing community on Lake Turkana, and Il Gira, Turkana acculturating to Samburu, still exist (Sobania, 1988a; Hjort, 1981). Each has formed in the interstices between larger and seemingly more viable groups through a process of social and economic logic and represents another possible variation. Not all have survived, or will continue, as independent entities but, as we shall argue later, 'failed' identities are as important to the understanding of the development of ethnicity as apparently successful ones.

Much of the earlier work on Maasai ethnicity grew out of interactive models rooted in the historical study of regional interdependence (Berntsen, 1976; Waller, 1985a). Such models have the important advantage of being inherently dynamic and of being capable of expressing the fluidity of small-scale society, but, as Spear indicates in the Introduction, they are essentially instrumental in their approach to identity as they explore the mechanisms of exchange and survival, and, since they often assume that ethnic form follows economic function, they also tend to be deterministic (Lovejoy and Baier, 1975; Waller, 1985a; Ambler, 1988). They do not deal with 'core concepts', the intangible sets of values and ideas which shape the community's view of itself and the world, or in what one might call the 'moral economy of being'. Thus, while they can help to explain why change in identity occurs and, perhaps, why identities emerge and disappear, they cannot fully reveal how each community constructs its own ethnicity and what that means to its members.

To go further, we must look at Maasai ethnicity from several different perspectives at once and track it through a long span of time. One way of doing this is to focus on the community. Our third theme, then,

Conclusions

constructing the community, brings us to the central thread of the book: the nature of Maasai ethnicity and how this has been conceived of at different times. Africanists are now more sensitive to the somewhat Protean nature of ethnicity, its ability to adapt itself over time in response to changing needs and circumstances and to present itself in and through different media. Our contributors have the advantage of working with an ethnicity which is both specific and self-consciously distinctive, but, at the same time, mutable and generalized over several economic modes. Indeed, it is the very persistence and variety of 'Maasainess' that makes it such an important example of ethnicity.

The creative tension within Maasai between exclusive and inclusive definitions has provided much of the dynamic of community growth as it has allowed Maasai to draw human resources from the outside while still retaining their cohesive sense of self. The distinctiveness of Maasai has never prevented others from being accepted into the community, but acculturation and socialization within an all-encompassing age-system has usually been strong enough to prevent 'Maasainess' from seeping away in the process. The emergence of Turkana to the west was, as Lamphear demonstrates, a rather similar process. Both might be contrasted with the Ngoni far to the south where little is left but the ethnic label and a glorious expansionary past, now upheld largely by those whom the Ngoni originally absorbed but who, in turn, absorbed them (Vail, 1981).

Yet one might still ask precisely what it is that is unequivocally Maasai. All the disciplines represented here address this question in some way, for each deals with a different version of community. Community exists at varying levels of inclusiveness. Vossen's genetic tree of language offers perhaps the widest definition of Maasai: all those who speak Maa. A Maasai community in this sense has been in existence for a very long time. The archaeological record provides evidence of an alternative form of community based not on language but, apparently, on mode of subsistence. The pastoral tradition also has an ancient pedigree, if not a demonstrably continuous existence as 'Maasai pastoralism'. Here, the bounds of language and economy are not coterminous. History offers yet another view of community, emerging from shared experiences which have been consciously shaped and given a teleological structure. Even if the Maasai are not quite like the Yoruba, whose 'truest ethnography may well be history' (Peel, 1989: 213), the way that their history is represented, by Galaty for example, gives valuable insights into what Maasai themselves understand as being the essence of community. In this sense, the recalled past is both a descriptive and an operational model of 'Maasainess' (Caws, 1974). But showing that notional communities of language, subsistence and experience, however they may be related, exist in the ethnic niches mentioned above is obviously not sufficient. How have real communities — of Maasai, Samburu, Arusha and the like — been constructed at particular historical junctures and how have they changed their shape or even 'disappeared' like the Laikipiak?

Benedict Anderson (1983) has pointed out that communities have first to be imagined before they can be realized. This observation, on which recent work on the African state has drawn (Lonsdale, 1986), is a useful starting point for our discussion of the construction of identity, even though Anderson's communities were built on literacy and spread through the printed word. Maa-speakers have, until quite recently, been pre-literate and even now the vernacular press has a limited impact. But there are other, rich, languages of imagination available to the non-literate. Dress is one such. The Maasai silhouette is a mark of distinctiveness and, as Klumpp and Kratz would argue, beads talk. Oral tradition is another. Maasai traditions of the nineteenth century convey a strong sense of community through a richly imagined past (Berntsen, 1979a; Waller, 1979). They are structured in such a way as to express both inclusion and exclusion, and they debate the question of who is (or was) a Maasai, and who is not and why. Since traditions may at any time be reformulated to reflect the changing self-image and specific concerns of the audience, they also offer an entry into a community which ostensibly they portray as closed. Kin and clan deal with related kinds of historical imagination and their importance is attested in myths of origin. If kinship is a language of obligation, clanship is a way of expressing the structure of community over time. Like kinship, clans are often fictive but they likewise convey an essential truth about the nature of a given community and its relations with others. Clan structures enable the community to recall concisely how it came into existence and how it emerged from older communities now 'disappeared'. In a sense, clans are a form of oral tradition expressed in nomenclature, cattle brands and, sometimes, ritual. They may also provide a way of saving options within the repertoire of identities, so acting as a kind of retrieval system. The clearest examples of this at present, however, come from non-Maa-speaking peoples. Il Kiriman, mentioned above, now appears as a clan in Rendille (Schlee, 1989). Lamphear has argued that clan names and histories among the Jie of north-east Uganda describe how the present community emerged as a result of the fusion of disparate elements, each of which is separately recalled as a clan (Lamphear, 1976, 1983). Similarly, the clan structure of the Dasenech, north of Lake Turkana, shows the incorporation of 'Samburu' and 'Rendille' as well as of a fishing group akin to El Molo. Their ceremonies make use of a ranking system among the constituent clans, based on their notional order of 'arrival', in order to recall how the present community was 'made', and the ethnic ties which the different clans represent are related to a regional trade network in which exchange both creates and is structured by kinship (Sobania, 1980, 1991).

It is clear, then, that communities can be imagined without recourse to print or a written language. However, Maasai now live in an increas-

ingly literate world. They have been able to draw on the new resource
of literacy in at least two ways. Maasai have seized the opportunity of
print to fix and standardize both history and language and to use this
as a measure of 'Maasainess', much as others have done before them
(Peel, 1989). New generations of Maasai will be able to 'read' the community much as their forebears 'imagined' it — though much of the
creative imprecision of the past will be lost, perhaps to be replaced by the
kind of open political and cultural debate which took place recently at
the first Maasai Conference in Tanzania (Galaty, personal communication). Maasai have also been able to make use of what is written about
them by outsiders — notably by the authors of the glossy coffee-table
books with which the Introduction started. These fix images of 'the
Maasai' in the imagination of others and, in so far as they influence the
way in which outsiders see and react to the Maasai, they have an impact
on the community itself. From early in the colonial period, if not before,
Maasai attempted to turn outsiders' perceptions of them to their own
advantage. By conforming in some degree to stereotype, they were
able to distance themselves from intrusion and to retain the initiative in
encounters. This remains the case and, indeed, as the external elements
of 'Maasainess' — the ochre, the beads, the cattle and the landscape —
become more simplified and instantly 'recognizable', the distance
increases. As the Maasai become more and more accessible through
picture and print, their apparently distinctive 'identity' becomes a
protective but illusory image, like the smile of the Cheshire Cat, behind
which the community continues to re-imagine itself in ways which may
not be in accord with its outer form of contrived ethnicity.

Constructing the community inevitably poses the question of whose
construction is accepted for what, or perhaps which, community. While
African historians and anthropologists have become far more aware of
how communities may be differentiated or stratified according to age,
gender and wealth, they have not usually applied these insights directly
to the question of ethnicity itself. Perhaps because studies of ethnicity
in Africa have often been part of the political sociology of 'tribalism' and
'national development', ethnic identities have been viewed as shallowly-
rooted defensive or offensive constructs created through and for participation in local or national politics, with the emphasis placed on the
demarcation and maintenance of external boundaries and on the means
of mobilization within a homogeneous society (Gulliver, 1969; Tonkin,
McDonald and Chapman, 1989). Such an approach focuses on conflict
and debate between rather than within communities and tends to assume
that only one identity emerges at a time rather than several simultaneously. In so far as multiple identities are apparent, they are thought
to be fractured or incomplete representations of a single reality. Implicit
in several of our chapters, however, is the notion that being Maasai
might have different meanings for different parts of the community, that
there might be alternative and possibly conflicting notions of identity

within one community, with incompatibilities accommodated through 'gaps' in the ideological structure, and that some assertions of identity might come to be widely accepted — and others not.

'Maasainess' might be both perceived and articulated from a number of different points of view within the community. Studies of gender in Maasai society have tended to conclude that, while Maasai women have significant spheres of autonomy, they are essentially subordinated to a male view of the culture of pastoralism, even though their presence and participation may be crucial to its conceptualization. Women like Telelia, for example, seem on the whole to acquiesce in and uphold the dominant view of the community (Galaty, 1979; Llewelyn-Davies, 1979 and 1981; Spencer, 1988). Other studies have suggested that women's roles have been curtailed or devalued recently as a result of the impact of colonialism and capitalist development (Talle, 1988; Kipuri, 1989). Yet there are indications not only that women have an independent voice in certain contexts but also that their understanding of what being Maasai entails might be different from that of men. Llewelyn-Davies (1981: 353) makes the interesting comment, in a discussion of Maasai concepts of nature/culture, that women are, indeed less "cultural", less "Maasai" than men'. What does this imply for a study of ethnicity? It is, after all, Kratz's 'Dorobo' *women* who proclaim their difference openly through dress and Hodgson (n.d.) reports that some Maasai women in Tanzania have even begun to assert the value of agriculture in opposition to their husbands' 'outmoded' attachment to stock. These comments, however, apparently came from poorer families and this should remind us that variations in wealth, and in other measures of status, are likely to cross-cut gendered perceptions of identity just as they do other areas (Little, 1987; Ensminger, 1987). Even so, these expressions, supported by Cambell's and Fratkin's observations, suggest that pressure for change in the content of identity may come from below, and that women may be the innovators here. What is at present an assertion of difference might in time become accepted as the norm.

Ethnicity, then, might well be gendered. It might also vary with social age, at least in the extent to which particular aspects of being Maasai are emphasized at different stages in the maturation process. For instance, although the *murran* are clearly marginal to the ordered and normative life of the cattle camps, they exemplify a particular set of Maasai ideals which, as Spencer's careful analysis reveals, is complementary as well as apparently opposed to that of elders, which the *murran* will in time become. As they do so, the altruism and solidarity which are the essence of *murran*hood are qualified, though never entirely replaced, by the 'selfishness' and individualism of elderhood, thus expressing, while separating in time and maturity, the two sides of Maasai: public cooperation and private competition (Llewelyn-Davies, 1981; Spencer, 1988).

However, although it is the *murran* in their finery who symbolize 'Maasai' to outsiders, it is the much less eye-catching elders, Llewelyn-

Davies' 'patriarchs', the controllers of property, who dominate the community, and whose view, emphasizing the careful accumulation of private property in stock and dependants and the *gravitas* of individual and collective authority, is implicitly accepted as 'the Maasai way'. As in Baraguyu, it is elders rather than *murran* who are socially 'potent' and, in a sense, 'becoming Maasai' has inevitably meant 'becoming elders' (Beidelman, 1980). Nonetheless, this view, like that of 'women's place', has a certain deliberate timelessness. There are indications that the balance of voices by age is also subject to change over time. *Murran*, like women, have seen their position eroded since the beginning of this century. In the past, their sphere was both more autonomous and more central to Maasai survival and expansion. This is reflected in the fact that much of the historical tradition of the pre-colonial period, as detailed for instance in the chapters by Galaty, Lamphear and Sobania, represents a *murran*'s-eye view of the world, even though it is mediated through the voice of elders (Berntsen, 1979a; Waller, 1979).

An uncritical acceptance of an adult male view is unfortunately common in much of the literature on African ethnicity, even though it is challenged by studies of gender and maturation. It is all the more so in pastoral societies because the still pervasive influence of the myth of egalitarianism helps to legitimate a simple unitary and homogeneous view of society. Although its economic reality can be questioned, the egalitarian ideology remains powerful and appealing, partly because its critics have tended to focus their attention on how practical inequality in wealth and influence is managed within an ostensible commitment to equality; but more importantly perhaps because less influential and wealthy elders do seem, like women, to subscribe to the myth. It is difficult to dismiss the premise of equality, like 'tribalism', as merely a piece of 'false consciousness' (Mafeje, 1971). It might be better to see it as an expression of the hegemony of a stock-owning elite and thus as an integral part of *their* construction of 'Maasainess' — which is elegantly set out in Galaty's model of synthesis through symbolic opposition discussed in the Introduction. It is not, however, the only possible construction and it will be interesting to see how Galaty's triangular opposition of pastoralists, hunters and farmers is reformulated to cope with the increasing impoverishment of many stock owners and the emergence of class differentiation in pastoral societies (Galaty, 1981).

Maasai identity has been defined by the successful. Indeed, 'Maasainess' may be a projection of that success. But that does not mean that we can ignore the possibility that other views exist and that some of these might come to the surface in future. There may be not a permanent hierarchy of identities, ranging from dominant to suppressed, but instead a wide repertoire from which the community may choose under changing circumstances. This comment gains force when it is considered in conjunction with an important article on the formation of 'tribe' in western Kenya (Lonsdale, 1977). Lonsdale discusses how some forms of primarily economic identity 'succeeded' and others 'failed' in pre-colonial times. Success led to the creation of ethnicities, such as that of the Gusii, which, initially almost experimental, have since acquired a misleading aura of solidity and permanence. Failures have been expunged from the record, in a kind of 'genealogical amnesia', or simply treated as deviant. This book has explored not only 'Maasai' but also, importantly here, 'Ariaal' and 'Arusha' as alternative but equally valid expressions of 'Maasainess'. One might also include 'Turkana' as a non-Maa example of the same phenomenon. These have all been successful identities. By contrast, 'Sirikwa' ultimately failed as an identity of itself but survived within the repertoire of the Kalenjin, while now defunct *Iloikop* groups have variously been obliterated or regarded as historical aberrations. However, one age's aberration is another's norm. 'Pure pastoralism' which, despite its evident decline, is still largely accepted as the ideal for being Maasai, is, in fact, a relatively modern development (though it may also have existed in the Neolithic) and it may well become, in time, just another vanished identity (Lamprey and Waller, 1990; Marshall, 1990).

We have argued that there are at least two main forms of ethnicity in play: one, with many variants, constructed *by* the Maasai, the other constructed *for* them. How, if at all, do they relate to each other? One answer may lie in the question of survival, our final theme. 'Since the beginning', when the first Maasai climbed up the Escarpment to escape from a drought, the community has been attuned to survival. It is often with crisis and response in mind that scholars, like other outsiders, now approach the Maasai. However, we can only analyse crises presented to us in recent memory and not those of the more remote past, such as the expansion of 'zebu power', described by Lamphear, or the eclipse of the Sirikwa. Two apparently opposed options seem always to have been open: drawing the bounds of the community tightly against outside pressures and, at the same time, insisting on an exclusive and rigorous definition of Maasai; or shifting modes of subsistence and crossing boundaries when crisis strikes, and then regrouping to re-establish the community when better times return. Tradition offers support for both strategies and it is clear that they are not so much opposed as complementary.

The emergence of Maasai has involved a long process of becoming in which ethnic identity has been continuously re-examined and refor-mulated. Our contributors have suggested different stages of transforma-tion, from 'pre-Maasai' to 'modern Maasai'. In the last two stages, from the late nineteenth century to the present day, Maasai have shifted between the two options. In the aftermath of war and disaster, the community turned inwards and attempted to re-create itself in the image of a partly remembered and partly imagined past. During the first half of the present century, this set up contradictions, both within the com-munity and between it and outsiders, as the ideal of the community came to be increasingly at odds with the reality of its colonial experience and also with the aspirations of at least some of its members. More recently, especially in the last twenty years, the community has looked outwards again. Survival now seems to lie in adaptation and in fashioning an identity flexible enough to encompass the variety of modern experience and to make use of modern resources. Yet this presents a dilemma as well as an opportunity — for modernization has two apparently contradictory faces.

One of the most obvious resources available is development aid tied to the capitalist sector of the national economy. In order to enter the world of development, however, Maasai must accept the 'modernization' of their economy and the invasion of their world by outsiders. This is certainly within the tradition of adaptation for survival. Entering the market, going to school or moving to town are merely new forms of boundary crossing, though the boundaries here may be internal boundaries of class as well as external ones of language and ethnicity. The new *Iloikop* are likely to come from the growing rural proletariat composed of former or marginal pastoralists (Hedlund, 1979). However, this kind of differentiation conflicts with the other image of the Maasai as egalitarian 'traditionalists' living in a reassuringly timeless ethnographic present, the reverse aspect of their incorporation. One requirement of survival on Western terms is that 'natives' should be 'disappearing' or failing to survive in their own world. The 'Disappearing World' also has its resources and opportunities, but it exacts a price by appropriating Maasai and others as objects of aesthetic and moral appreciation by the West (Saitoti, 1986). Thus the two options reappear in a new guise. In order to retain access to critical resources and to function effectively within the context of the modern state, the Maasai must create an image of themselves as 'progressive' citizens, but, to qualify as the modern equivalent of the 'noble savage', they must acquiesce in the external construction of themselves as ethnographic artefacts and, therefore, choose the more 'traditionalist' and exclusive option. In conforming to this construction of themselves, they will survive in the imagination of others. In rejecting it, they may survive in their own. However, shifting identities, juxtaposing internal and external constructions and thus apparently ceasing to 'be', while continuing to 'become' Maasai — the paradox with which this Conclusion began — satisfy the requirements and allow them to survive in both worlds.

The dilemma faced by the Maasai is neither new nor unusual; nor is the solution. The conscious creation and manipulation of an image appropriate for external consumption is a common line of defence for colonized or subordinated communities. Dorward shows how the Tiv, for example, regularly 'changed' to conform to their administrators' ideas of who they were and how their society 'worked' (Dorward, 1974). Leach goes further in stating that 'traditional societies' are always 'products of the ethnographer's imagination', a point convincingly demonstrated by Wilmsen with regard to the Kalahari 'Bushmen' (Leach, 1989: 38; Wilmsen, 1989). What Leach is arguing here is that 'tribal' society is as much subject to change as any other and that outside observers are an integral part of the process. This observation applies as much to ethnic identity as it does to socio-economic structure, in so far as the two can be separated. It not only rescues communities from the limbo of the ethnographic present but also confronts us with the fact that observers are also actors in the social field, partly because they make demands of the society and partly because, in what Peel (1989: 199) aptly calls the 'cultural work' of building ethnicity, some of the material as well as some of the scaffolding is derived from outsiders' images of what that ethnicity should be.

The point of our argument has been that ethnicity need not be strictly defined. Our contributors have demonstrated that 'Maasainess' consists of a wide range of identities deployed across a shifting and complex social field which includes non-Maa-speakers as well as Maa-speakers. Each of the four themes addressed here, the relationships between Maasai and pastoralism and between Maasai and non-Maasai, the construction of communities and the means of survival, has illustrated different aspects of this complexity and emphasized the importance of process in understanding Maasai identity. Ethnicity is best seen as the joint product of all these identities, both active and latent. Communities 'make up the rules as they go along', as Sahlins (1985: 26) puts it, and there is nothing which is 'authentically Maasai' in some absolute sense. Approaching ethnicity in this way enables us to examine its specific historical and social dynamic and also to avoid being caught in a false dichotomy between 'primordial' and 'instrumental' views. The fact that ethnic identity is fashioned — not given — does not, however, rob it of its evocative power; it is the very means of survival. Each of the authors and disciplines represented here has focused on a particular dimension of ethnicity and it is the interplay between them that has been essential to our understanding of the whole social field — past, present and future — in which people 'become' Maasai in an endless process of transformation.

Bibliography

Adamson, Joy. 1967. *Peoples of Kenya*. New York, Harcourt, Brace and World.
Almagor, Uri. 1979. 'Raiders and Elders: A Confrontation of Generations among the Dassanetch' in Fukui, K. and Turton, D. (eds), *Warfare among East African Herders*: 119–145. Osaka, National Museum of Ethnology.
Ambler, Charles H. 1988. *Kenyan Communities in the Age of Imperialism*. New Haven, Yale University Press.
Ambrose, Stanley H. 1982. 'Archaeology and Linguistic Reconstructions of History in East Africa' in Ehret, C. and Posnansky, M. (eds), *The Archaeological and Linguistic Reconstruction of East African History*: 104–157. Berkeley, California University Press.
—— 1984. 'The Introduction of Pastoral Adaptations to the Highlands of East Africa' in Clark, J.D. and Brandt, S. (eds), *From Hunters to Farmers*: 212–239. Berkeley, California University Press.
Amin, Mohamed and Willetts, D. 1987. *The Last of the Maasai*. Nairobi, Westlands Sundries.
Anacleti, A.O. 1977. 'Serengeti: Its People and their Environment'. *Tanzania Notes and Records*, 81/82: 23–34.
Anderson, Benedict. 1983. *Imagined Communities*. London, Verso.
Anderson, David M. 1981. 'Some Thoughts on the Nineteenth-Century History of the Il Chamus of Baringo District'. Institute of African Studies, Paper no. 149.
—— 1988. 'Cultivating Pastoralists: Ecology and Economy among the Il Chamus of Baringo, 1840–1980' in Johnson, D. and Anderson, D.M. (eds), *The Ecology of Survival*: 241–260. Boulder, Westview University Press.
—— 1989. 'Agriculture and Irrigation Technology at Lake Baringo in the Nineteenth Century'. *Azania*, 24: 84–97.
Anderson, Perry. 1974. 'The Nomadic Mode of Production' in *Passages from Antiquity to Feudalism*: 217–228. New York, New Left Books.
Andreski, Stanislav. 1954. *Military Organization and Society*: 103. Berkeley, California University Press.
Arhem, Kaj. 1985. *Pastoral Man in the Garden of Eden*. Uppsala, Research Reports in Cultural Anthropology.
Avanchers, Leon des. 1859. 'Esquise Géographique des Pays Oromo ou Galla, des Pays Soomali, et de la Côte Orientale d'Afrique'. *Bulletin de la Société de Géographie*, 17: 153–170.
Aylmer, L. 1911. 'The Country Between the Juba River and Lake Rudolf'. *The Geographical Journal*, 38: 289–296.
Ayuko, L.J. 1981. 'Organization, Structures and Ranches in Kenya'. ODI Pastoral Network Paper 11b.
Barth, Frederick. 1969. *Ethnic Groups and Boundaries*. Boston, Little Brown.
Baumann, Oscar. 1894. *Durch Masailand zür Nilquelle*. Berlin, D. Reimer.
Baxandall, Michael. 1972. *Painting and Experience in Fifteenth-Century Italy*. Oxford, Oxford University Press.
—— 1985. *Patterns of Intention: On the Historical Explanation of Pictures*. New Haven, Yale University Press.
Baxter, P.T.W. 1979. 'Boran Age-Sets and Warfare' in Fukui, K. and Turton, D. (eds),

Bibliography

Warfare among East African Herders: 69–95. Osaka, National Museum of Ethnology.

Baxter, P.T.W. and Almagor, U. (eds). 1978. *Age, Generation and Time*. London, Christopher Hurst.

Beaman, A.W. 1981. 'The Rendille Age-set System in Ethnographic Context'. Ph.D. thesis, Boston University.

Beech, Mervyn. 1911. *The Suk*. Oxford, Clarendon.

Beidelman, T.O. 1960. 'The Baraguyu'. *Tanganyika Notes and Records*, 55: 245–278.

—— 1961. 'Beer Drinking and Cattle Theft in Ukaguru: Intertribal Relations in a Tanganyika Chiefdom'. *American Anthropologist*, 63: 534–549.

—— 1980. 'Women and Men in Two East African Societies' in Karp, I. and Bird, C. (eds), *Explorations in African Systems of Thought*. Bloomington, Indiana University Press.

Bentley, G. Carter. 1987. 'Ethnicity and Practice'. *Comparative Studies in Society and History*, 29: 24–55.

Berman, Bruce. 1990. *Control and Crisis in Colonial Kenya*. London, James Currey.

Berman, Bruce and Lonsdale, John. 1990. 'Louis Leakey's Mau Mau: A Study in the Politics of Knowledge'. *History and Anthropology*, 5: 1–62.

—— 1992. *Unhappy Valley*. London, James Currey.

Bernard, F.E., Campbell, D.J. and Thom, D.J. 1989. 'Carrying Capacity of the Eastern Ecological Gradient of Kenya'. *National Geographic Research*, 5: 399–421.

Berntsen, John L. 1976. 'The Maasai and their Neighbors: Variables of Interaction'. *African Economic History*, 2: 1–11.

—— 1977. *Maasai and Iloikop: Ritual Experts and their Followers*. Madison, Wi., African Studies Program.

—— 1979a. 'Pastoralism, Raiding, and Prophets: Maasailand in the Nineteenth Century'. Ph.D. thesis, Wisconsin.

—— 1979b. 'Maasai Age-Sets and Prophetic Leadership, 1850–1912'. *Africa*, 49: 134–146.

—— 1979c. 'Economic Variations among Maa-Speaking Peoples' in Ogot, B.A. (ed.), *Ecology and History in East Africa (Hadith 7)*: 108–127. Nairobi, Kenya Literature Bureau.

—— 1980. 'The Enemy is Us: Eponymy in the Historiography of the Maasai'. *History in Africa*, 7: 1–21.

Bianco, Barbara. n.d. 'Women and Things: Pokot Motherhood as Political Destiny'. Unpublished paper.

Blackburn, Roderic. 1971. 'Honey in Okiek Personality, Culture and Society'. Ph.D. thesis, Michigan State.

—— 1974. 'The Okiek and their History'. *Azania*, 9: 139–157.

—— 1976. 'Okiek History' in Ogot, B.A. (ed.), *Kenya Before 1900*: 53–83. Nairobi, East African Publishing House.

—— 1978. 'The Okiek and their Neighbors: The Ecological Distinctions'. Unpublished paper, African Studies Association.

—— 1982. 'In the Land of Milk and Honey: Okiek Adaptations to their Forests and Neighbors' in Leacock, E. and Lee, R. (eds), *Politics and History in Band Societies*: 283–305. Cambridge, Cambridge University Press.

Bonte, Pierre. 1974. 'Études sur les Sociétés de Pasteurs Nomades: 2. Organisation économique et sociale des pasteurs d'Afrique de l'Est'. *Cahier du CERM*, 110: 1–95.

—— 1975. 'Cattle for God: An Attempt at a Marxist Analysis of the Religion of East African Herdsmen'. *Social Compass*, 22: 381–396.

—— 1977. 'Non-Stratified Social Formations among Pastoral Nomads' in Friedman, J. and Rowlands, F. (eds), *The Evolution of Social Systems*: 173–200. London, Duckworth.

—— 1981. 'Marxist Theory and Anthropological Analysis' in Kahn, J. and Llobera, J. (eds), *Anthropology of Pre-Capitalist Societies*: 22–56. London, Macmillan.

Bonte, Pierre and Galaty, John (eds). 1991. *Herders, Warriors and Traders: The Political Economy of African Pastoralism*. Boulder, Westview.

Bower, J.R. and Nelson, C.M. 1978. 'Early Pottery and Pastoral Cultures of the Central Rift Valley, Kenya'. *Man*, 13: 554–556.

Bibliography

Campbell, David J. 1979a. 'Response to Drought in Kenya Maasailand: Pastoralists and Farmers in the Loitokitok Area, Kajiado District'. Discussion Paper 267, Institute for Development Studies, Nairobi.

—— 1979b. 'Development or Decline? Resources, Land Use, and Population Growth in Kajiado District'. Working Paper 352, Institute for Development Studies, Nairobi.

—— 1981. 'Land Use Competition at the Margins of the Rangelands: An Issue in Development Strategies for Semi-arid Areas' in Norcliffe, G. and Pinfold, T. (eds), *Planning African Development*. London, Croom Helm.

—— 1984. 'Response to Drought among Farmers and Herders in Southern Kajiado District, Kenya'. *Human Ecology*, 12: 35–64.

—— 1985. 'A Regional Approach to Population–Resource Imbalance in Rural Africa: A Case Study of Kajiado District, Kenya'. *Papers and Proceedings of the Applied Geography Conferences*, 8: 320–332.

—— 1986. 'The Prospect for Desertification in Kajiado District, Kenya'. *The Geographical Journal*, 152: 44–55.

—— Forthcoming. 'The Impact of Development upon Strategies for Coping with Drought among the Maasai of Kajiado District, Kenya'. *Proceedings of the Colloquium on Pastoral Economies in Africa and Long Term Responses to Drought*. University of Aberdeen, African Studies Group.

Casebeer, R L. 1975. 'Summaries of Statistics and Regulations Pertaining to Wildlife, Parks, and Reserves in Kenya'. Project Working Document 8, UNDP/FAO Wildlife Management Project, Nairobi.

Cavendish, H.S.H. 1898. 'Through Somaliland and Around the South of Lake Rudolf'. *The Geographical Journal*, 11.

Caws, P. 1974. 'Operational, Representational and Explanatory Models'. *American Anthropologist*, 76.

Chang, Cynthia. 1982. 'Nomads without Cattle: East African Foragers in Historical Perspective' in Leacock, E. and Lee, R.B. (eds), *Politics and History in Band Societies*: 269–282. New York, Cambridge University Press.

Chanler, William A. 1896. *Through Jungle and Desert*. London, Macmillan.

Chaundy, G.H. 1931. 'A Short Account of the West Suk Tribe'. Unpublished paper, Kenya National Archives (HOR/886).

Clark, Carolyn. 1980. 'Land and Food, Women and Power in Nineteenth-Century Kikuyu'. *Africa*, 50: 357–370.

Cohen, David William and Atieno Odhiambo, E.S. 1989. *Siaya*. London, James Currey.

Cohen, R. 1978. 'Ethnicity: Problem and Focus in Anthropology'. *Annual Review of Anthropology*, 7: 379–403.

Comaroff, J.L. 1987. 'Of Totemism and Ethnicity: Consciousness, Practice and Signs of Inequality'. *Ethnos*, 3/4: 301–323.

Cory, Hans. 1948. 'Tribal Structure of the Arusha Tribe of Tanganyika'. Unpublished paper, Hans Cory Papers, University of Dar es Salaam.

David, Nicholas. 1982a. 'The BIEA Southern Sudan Expedition of 1979' in Mack, J. and Robertshaw, P. (eds), *Culture History in the Southern Sudan*: 49–140. Nairobi, British Institute in Eastern Africa.

—— 1982b. 'Prehistory and Historical Linguistics in Central Africa' in Ehret, C., and Posnansky, M. (eds), *The Archaeological and Linguistic Reconstruction of African History*: 78–95. Berkeley, California University Press.

Davis, R.K. 1971. 'Some Issues in the Evolution, Operation and Organization of Group Ranches in Kenya'. *East African Journal of Rural Development*, 4: 22–33.

Dimmendaal, J.G. 1990. 'Language Death and the Case of Kore (Lamu)'. Unpublished paper, International Symposium on Language Death in East Africa, Bad Homburg, Germany.

Dorward, David C. 1974. 'Ethnography and Administration: A Study of Anglo-Tiv "Working Misunderstanding"'. *Journal of African History*, 15.

Dundas, Charles. 1924. *Kilimanjaro and Its People*. London, H.F. and G. Whitherby.

Bibliography

Dundas, K.R. 1910. 'Notes on the Tribes Inhabiting the Baringo District, East African Protectorate'. *Journal of the Royal Anthropological Institute*, 40: 49–71.

—— n.d. 'Notes on Tribes in the Kikuyu District (Kiambu)'. Kenya National Archives, NADMs, II Part I, 19/ii/11.

Dunne, T. 1977. 'Intensity and Control of Soil Erosion in Kajiado District'. Project Working Document 12, UNDP/FAO Wildlife Management Project, Nairobi.

Durkheim, Émile. 1912. *The Elementary Forms of the Religious Life*. London, George Allen & Unwin.

Edgerton, R. 1971. *The Individual in Cultural Adaptation*. Berkeley, California University Press.

Ehret, Christopher. 1971. *Southern Nilotic History*. Evanston, Northwestern University Press.

—— 1974a. *Ethiopians and East Africans*. Nairobi, East African Publishing House.

—— 1974b. 'Some Thoughts on the Early History of the Nile-Congo Watershed'. *Ufahamu*, 5: 85–112.

—— 1974c. 'Cushites and the Highland and Plains Nilotes to AD 1800' in Ogot, B.A. (ed.), *Zamani*: 150–169. Nairobi, Longman.

—— 1980. *The Historical Reconstruction of Southern Cushitic Phonology and Vocabulary*. Berlin, D. Reimer.

—— 1982. 'Population Movement and Culture Contact in the Southern Sudan, c. 3000 BC to AD 1000' in Mack, J. and Robertshaw, P. (eds), *Culture History in the Southern Sudan*: 19–48. Nairobi, British Institute in Eastern Africa.

Eliot, Charles. 1905. 'Introduction' in Hollis, A.C., *The Masai*: xi–xxviii. Oxford, Clarendon.

Emley, E.D. 1927. 'The Turkana of Kolosia District'. *Journal of the Royal Anthropological Institute*, 57: 160–199.

Ensminger, J. 1987. 'Economic and Political Differentiation among Galole Orma Women'. *Ethnos*, 52.

Epstein, H. 1971. *The Origins of the Domestic Animals of Africa*, 2 vols. New York, Africana.

Erhardt, James J. 1857. *Vocabulary of the Enguduk Iloigob as Spoken by the Masai-tribes in East Africa*. Ludwigsburg and Wurtemburg, F. Riehm.

Evangelou, Phyllo. 1984. *Livestock Development in Kenya's Maasailand*. Boulder, Westview.

Evans-Pritchard, E.E. 1940. *The Nuer*. Oxford, Clarendon.

Fallon, Leland E. 1962. 'Masai Range Resources: Kajiado District'. Unpublished paper, USAID.

Farler, J.P. 1882. 'Native Routes in East Africa from Pangani to the Masai Country and the Victoria Nyanza'. *Proceedings of the Royal Geographical Society*, 4: 730–742.

Feierman, Steven. 1990. *Peasant Intellectuals*. Madison, Wisconsin University Press.

Fischer, G.A. 1882–83. 'Bericht über die im Auftrage der Geographischen Gesellschaft in Hamburg unternommene Reise in das Masai-Land'. *Mitteilungen der Geographischer Gesellschaft in Hamburg*: 36–99.

Flatt, Donald. 1980. *Man and Deity in an African Society*. Dubuque, Iowa, Lutheran Church in America.

Foner, N. 1984. *Ages in Conflict: A Cross-Cultural Perspective on Inequality between Old and Young*. New York, Columbia University Press.

Fosbrooke, H.A. 1948. 'An Administrative Survey of the Masai Social System'. *Tanganyika Notes and Records*, 26: 1–50.

—— 1956. 'The Masai Age-Group System as a Guide to Tribal Chronology'. *African Studies*, 15: 188–206.

Fratkin, Elliot. 1979. 'A Comparison of the Role of Prophets in Samburu and Maasai Warfare' in Fukui, K. and Turton, D. (eds), *Warfare among East African Herders*: 53–67. Osaka, National Museum of Ethnology.

—— 1986. 'Stability and Resilience in East African Pastoralism: The Rendille and the Ariaal of Northern Kenya'. *Human Ecology*, 145: 269–286.

—— 1987a. 'Age-sets, Households, and the Organization of Pastoral Production: The Ariaal, Samburu, and Rendille of Northern Kenya'. *Research in Economic Anthropology*, 8: 295–314.

Bibliography

—— 1987b. 'The Organization of Labor and Production among the Ariaal Rendille, Nomadic Pastoralists of Northern Kenya'. Ph.D. thesis, Catholic University.

—— 1989a. 'Two Lives for the Ariaal'. *Natural History*: 39-49.

—— 1989b. 'Household Variation and Gender Inequality in Ariaal, Rendille Pastoral Production'. *American Anthropologist*, 91: 45-55.

—— 1991. *Surviving Drought and Development: Ariaal Pastoralists of Northern Kenya*. Boulder, Westview.

Fratkin, E. and Roth, E.A. 1990. 'Drought and Economic Differentiation among Ariaal Pastoralists of Kenya'. *Human Ecology*, 18/4: 385-402.

Frontera, Ann. 1978. *Persistence and Change*. Waltham, Crossroads.

Fukui, Katsuyoshi and Turton, David. 1979. 'Introduction' in Fukui, K. and Turton, D. (eds), *Warfare Among East African Herders*: 1-13. Osaka, National Museum of Ethnology.

Furedi, Frank. 1989. *The Mau Mau War in Perspective*. London, James Currey.

Galaty, John. 1977a. 'In the Pastoral Image: The Dialectic of Maasai Identity'. Ph.D. thesis, Chicago.

—— 1977b. 'East African Hunters: "So-Calling" Some Historical Myths'. Unpublished paper, American Anthropological Association.

—— 1979. 'Pollution and Pastoral Antipraxis: The Issue of Maasai Inequality'. *American Ethnologist*, 6: 803-816.

—— 1980. 'The Maasai Group Ranch: Politics and Development in an African Pastoral Society' in Salzman, P. (ed.), *When Nomads Settle*. New York, Praeger.

—— 1981. 'Land and Livestock among Kenyan Maasai' in Galaty, J. and Salzman, P.C. (eds), *Change and Development in Nomadic and Pastoral Societies*: 68-88. Leiden, Brill.

—— 1982a. 'Being "Maasai": Being "People of Cattle"; Ethnic Shifters in East Africa'. *American Ethnologist*, 9: 1-20.

—— 1982b. 'Maasai Pastoral Ideology and Change' in Salzman, P.C. (ed.), *Contemporary Nomadic and Pastoral Peoples: Africa and Latin America*. Williamsburg, Va., College of William and Mary.

—— 1985. 'Ainesse Cyclicite et Rites dans l'Organisation des Ages Maasai' in Abeles, M. and Collard, C. (eds), *Age, Pouvoir et Société en Afrique Noire*: 287-316. Paris, Éditions Karthala.

—— 1986. 'East African Hunters and Pastoralists in a Regional Perspective: An Ethnoanthropological Approach'. *SUGIA, Sprache und Geschichte in Afrika*, 7/1: 105-131.

—— 1987. 'Form and Interaction of East African Strategies of Dominance and Aggression' in McGuiness, D. (ed.), *Dominance, Aggression and War*: 223-249. New York, Paragon.

—— 1988. 'Pastoral and Agro-Pastoral Migration in Tanzania: Factors of Economy, Ecology and Demography in Cultural Perspective' in Bennett, J.W. and Bowen, J.R. (eds), *Production and Autonomy*: 163-183. Lanham, Md, University Press of America.

—— n.d. 'Models and Metaphors: On the Semiotics of Maasai Segmentary Systems' in Holy, L. and Stuchlik, M. (eds), *The Structure of Folk Models*: 63-92. London, Academic.

—— 1991. 'Pastoral Orbits and Deadly Jousts: Factors in the Maasai Expansion' in Bonte, P. and Galaty, J. (eds), *Herders, Warriors and Traders*. Boulder, Westview.

Gold, A. 1981. 'The Nandi in Transition: Background to the Nandi Resistance to the British, 1895-1906'. *Kenya Historical Review*, 8.

Gramley, R. 1975. 'Meat-Feasting Sites and Cattle Brands: Patterns of Rock-Shelter Utilization in East Africa'. *Azania*, 10: 107-121.

Grandin, B.E., de Leeuw, P.N. and Lembuya, P. 1989. 'Drought, Resource Redistribution, and Mobility in Two Maasai Group Ranches, Southeastern Kajiado District' in Downing, T.E., Gitu, K.W. and Kamau, D.M. (eds), *Coping with Drought in Kenya*. Boulder, Lynne Reinner.

Gray, Robert. 1963. *The Sonjo of Tanganyika*. London, Oxford University Press.

Great Britain. 1934. *Report of the Kenya Land Commission*. London, HMSO.

Greenberg, Joseph H. 1963. *The Languages of Africa*. The Hague, Mouton.

Gregory, J.W. 1896. *The Great Rift Valley*. London, J. Murray.

Grum, A. n.d. 'The Rendille Calendar'. Unpublished paper.

Bibliography

Gulliver, Pamela and Gulliver, P.H. 1953. *The Central Nilo-Hamites*. London, International African Institute.

Gulliver, Philip H. 1957a. 'A History of Relations between the Arusha and Masai' in *Conference Papers of the EAISR*, Kampala.

—— 1957b. 'Report on Land and Population in the Arusha Chiefdom'. Unpublished paper, Hans Cory Papers, Dar es Salaam.

—— 1958. 'Turkana Age Organization'. *American Anthropologist*, 60: 900–922.

—— 1961a. 'Land Shortage, Social Change, and Social Conflict in East Africa'. *Journal of Conflict Resolution*, 5: 16–26.

—— 1961b. 'The Population of the Arusha Chiefdom: A High Density Area in East Africa'. *Human Problems in East-Central Africa*, 28: 1–21.

—— 1961c. 'Structural Dichotomy and Jural Processes among the Arusha of Northern Tanganyika'. *Africa*, 31: 19–35.

—— 1963. *Social Control in an African Society*. London, Routledge and Kegan Paul.

—— 1965a. 'The Arusha: Economic and Social Change' in Bohannan, P. and Dalton, G. (eds), *Markets in Africa*: 250–284. New York, Natural History Library.

—— 1965b. 'The Arusha Family' in Gray, R.E. and Gulliver, P.H. (eds), *The Family Estate in Africa*: 197–229. London, Routledge and Kegan Paul.

—— 1969. 'The Conservative Commitment in Northern Tanzania: The Arusha and Masai' in Gulliver, P.H. (ed.), *Tradition and Transition in East Africa*: 223–242. London, Routledge and Kegan Paul.

—— 1976. 'Opposing Streams and the Gerontocratic Ladder: Two Models of Age Organization in East Africa'. *Man*, 11: 153–175.

Halderman, J.M. 1972. 'Analysis of Continued Nomadism on the Kaputiei Maasai Group Ranches: Social and Ecological Factors'. Discussion Paper 152, Institute for Development Studies, Nairobi.

Hamilton, Claude. 1965. 'A Scrapbook of Masai History: A Tale of "Old Unhappy, Far-off Things and Battles Long Ago", and a Blend of Fact and Fiction'. Unpublished mss, Nairobi University Library.

Hancock, I. 1970. 'Patriotism and Neo-Traditionalism in Buganda: the Kabaka Yekka ("The King Alone") Movement, 1961–1962'. *Journal of African History*, 11: 419–434.

Hanley, G. 1971. *Warriors and Strangers*. London, Hamilton.

Harms, Robert. 1979. 'Oral Tradition and Ethnicity'. *Journal of Interdisciplinary History*, 12: 61–85.

Hay, Margaret Jean, 1975. 'Local Trade and Ethnicity in Western Kenya'. *African Economic History Review*, 2: 7–11.

Hedlund, Hans G.B. 1971. 'The Impact of Group Ranches on Pastoral Society'. IDS Staff Paper 100, Institute for Development Studies, Nairobi.

—— 1979. 'Contradictions in the Peripheralization of a Pastoral Society: the Maasai'. *Review of African Political Economy*, 15/16: 15–34.

Heine, B. 1975. 'Language Typology and Convergence Areas in Africa'. *Linguistics*, 144: 27–47.

—— 1976a. 'Notes on the Rendille Language (Kenya)'. *Afrika und Übersee*, 59: 176–223.

—— 1976b. *A Typology of African Languages*. Berlin, D. Reimer.

Heine, B. and Vossen, R. 1975–76. 'Zür Stellung der Ongamo-Sprache (Kilmandsharo)'. *Afrika und Übersee*, 59: 81–105.

—— 1979. 'The Kore of Lamu: A Contribution to Maa Dialectology'. *Afrika und Übersèe*, 62: 272–288.

—— Forthcoming. *Maa Historical Reconstructions*.

Heine, B., Rottland, F. and Vossen, R., 1979. 'Proto-Baz: Some Aspects of Early Nilotic-Cushitic Contacts'. *SUGIA , Sprache und Geschichte in Afrika*, 1: 75–91.

Heine, B., Schadeberg, Th. D. and Wolff, E. (eds). 1981. *Die Sprachen Afrikas*. Hamburg, Buske.

Helland, J. 1978. 'An Anthropologist's View of Group Ranch Development'. Course Notes, International Livestock Centre for Africa, Nairobi.

Herbich, Ingrid. 1987. 'Learning Patterns, Pottery Interaction, and Ceramic Style among

Bibliography

—— 1989. 'Luo Pots' in Barbour, J. and Wandibba, S. (eds), *Kenya Pots and Potters*: 27–40. Nairobi, Oxford University Press.

Hinde, H. and Hinde, S.L. 1901. *The Last of the Maasai*. London, Heinemann.

Hjort, A. 1981. 'Ethnic Transformation, Dependency and Change: The IlGira Samburu of Northern Kenya' in Galaty, J. and Salzman, P.C. (eds), *Change and Development in Nomadic and Pastoral Societies*. Leiden, Brill.

Hobley, C.W. 1902. *Eastern Uganda*. Journal of the Royal Anthropological Association, Occasional Paper, No. 1.

—— 1910; reprinted 1971. *Ethnology of the A-Kamba and Other East African Tribes*. London, Cambridge University Press.

Hodder, Ian. 1978. 'The Maintenance of Group Identities in the Baringo District, Western Kenya' in Green, D. *et al.* (eds), *Social Organization and Settlement*: 47–58. British Archaeological Reports, International Series, No. 47.

—— 1982. *Symbols in Action*. Cambridge, Cambridge University Press.

Hodgson, D. n.d. 'Gender and Social Transformation Among the Kisongo Maasai of Tanzania'. Unpublished paper.

Höhnel, L. von. 1894. *Discovery of Lakes Rudolf and Stefanie*, 2 vols. London, Longmans, Green and Co.

Hollis, A.C. 1905; reprinted 1970. *The Masai: Their Language and Folklore*. Oxford, Clarendon.

Huntingford, G.W.B. 1929. 'Modern Hunters: Some Account of the Kamelilo-Kapchepkendi Dorobo (Okiek) of Kenya Colony'. *Journal of the Royal Anthropological Institute*, 59: 333–376.

—— 1931. 'Free Hunters, Serf Tribes, and Submerged Classes in East Africa'. *Man*, 31: 262–266.

—— 1953. *The Southern Nilo-Hamites*. London, International African Institute.

Hurskainen, Ari. 1984. *Cattle and Culture: The Structure of Pastoral Parakuyo Society*. Helsinki, Finnish Oriental Society.

Huxley, Elspeth. 1956. *White Man's Country: Lord Delamere and the Making of Kenya*. London, Chatto and Windus.

Iliffe, John. 1979. *A Modern History of Tanganyika*. London, Cambridge University Press.

IPAL. 1984. 'Integrated Resource Assessment and Management Plan for Western Marsabit District, Northern Kenya'. IPAL Technical Report A-6. Nairobi, UNESCO Integrated Project in Arid Lands.

Jacobs, Alan. 1963. 'The Pastoral Masai of Kenya: A Report of Anthropological Field Research'. Unpublished paper, Ministry of Overseas Development, London.

—— 1965. 'The Traditional Political Organization of the Pastoral Masai'. Unpublished D.Phil. thesis, Oxford.

—— 1968a. 'A Chronology of the Pastoral Masai' in Ogot, B.A. (ed.), *Hadith 1*: 10–31. Nairobi, East African Publishing House.

—— 1968b. 'The Irrigation Agricultural Masai of Pagasi: A Case Study of Maasai–Sonjo Acculturation'. *Makerere Institute of Social Research Social Science Research Conference Papers, C: Sociology*.

—— 1972. 'The Discovery and Oral History of Narosura'. *Azania*, 7: 79–87.

—— 1975. 'Maasai Pastoralism in Historical Perspective' in Monod, T. (ed.), *Pastoralism in Tropical Africa*: 406–425. Oxford, International African Institute.

—— 1978. 'Development in Tanzania Maasailand: The Perspective of Twenty Years, 1957–1977'. Washington, USAID.

—— 1979. 'Maasai Intertribal Relations; Belligerent Herdsmen or Peaceable Pastoralists?' in Fukui, K. and Turton, D. (eds), *Warfare among East African Herders*: 33–52. Osaka, National Museum of Ethnology.

Jahnke, H.E. 1978. 'An Historical Review of Range Development in Kenya'. Course Notes, International Livestock Centre for Africa, Nairobi.

Johnson, Douglas H. 1982. 'Tribal Boundaries and Border Wars: Nuer-Dinka Relations in the Sobat and Zaraf Valleys, c. 1860–1976'. *Journal of African History*, 23: 183–203.

Bibliography

Johnston, H.H. 1886. *The Kilima-Njaro Expedition.* London, Kegan, Paul, Trench.

Kanogo, Tabitha. 1987. *Squatters and the Roots of Mau Mau.* London, James Currey.

Kaufman, R. von. 1976. 'The Development of the Range Land Areas' in Meyer, J., Maitha, J.K. and Senga, W.M. (eds), *Agricultural Development in Kenya.* Nairobi, Oxford University Press.

Kenny, Michael G. 1981. 'Mirror in the Forest: Dorobo Hunter-Gatherers as an Image of the Other.' *Africa*, 51: 477-496.

Kenya. 1927-1961. *Kajiado District: Annual Reports.*

—— 1926-53. *Narok District: Records.*

Kenya Land Commission (KLC). 1934a. *Evidence and Memoranda*, 3 vols. London, HMSO.

—— 1934b. *Report*, Cmd 4556. London, HMSO.

King, K.J. 1971a. 'The Maasai and the Protest Phenomenon, 1900-1960'. *Journal of African History*, 12: 117-137.

—— 1971b. 'Malonket ole Sempele' in King, K. and Salim, A. (eds), *Kenya Historical Biographies*: 1-28. Nairobi, East African Publishing House.

Kipuri, Naomi N. Ole. 1983. *Oral Literature of the Maasai.* Nairobi, Heinemann.

—— 1989. 'Maasai Women in Transition: Class and Gender in the Transformation of a Pastoral Society'. Ph.D. thesis, Temple University.

Kitching, Gavin. 1980. *Class and Economic Change in Kenya.* New Haven, Yale University Press.

Kituyi, Mukhisa. 1990. *Becoming Kenyans: Socio-Economic Transformation of the Pastoral Maasai.* Nairobi, ACTS Press.

Kjekshus, H. 1977. *Ecology Control and Economic Development in East African History.* London, Heinemann.

Klumpp, Donna. 1981. 'Women Artists as Innovators and Conservators of Tradition in Kenya'. Unpublished paper, African Studies Association.

—— 1987. 'Maasai Art and Society: Age and Sex, Time and Space, Cash and Cattle'. Ph.D. thesis, Columbia.

—— 1989. 'Ethnic Identity and Color Coding: The Maasai Center and Periphery'. Unpublished paper, Eighth Triennial Symposium on African Art, Washington.

Knowles, J.N. and Collett, D.P. 1989. 'Nature as Myth, Symbol and Action: Notes Towards a Historical Understanding of Development and Conservation in Kenyan Maasailand'. *Africa*, 59: 433-460.

Köhler, O. 1955. *Geschichte der Erforschung der Nilotischen Sprachen.* Berlin, D. Reimer.

Koponen, Juhani. 1988. *People and Production in Late Precolonial Tanzania.* Helsinki, Finnish Society for Development Studies.

Kopytoff, Igor (ed.). 1987. *The African Frontier.* Bloomington, Indiana University Press.

Krapf, J. Ludwig. 1854. *Voeabulary of the Engutuk Eloikob.* Tübingen, Fues.

—— 1858. *Reisen in Ostafrika*, 2 vols., Stuttgart Kornthal.

—— 1860. *Travels, Researches and Missionary Labours during Eighteen Years Residence in Eastern Africa.* Boston, Ticknor and Fields/London, Trübner and Co.

Kratz, Corinne. 1980. 'Are the Okiek really Maasai? or Kipsigis? or Kikuyu?' *Cahiers d'Etudes Africaines*, 79: 355-368.

—— n.d. 'Okiek Livestock and Agriculture'. Unpublished paper.

—— 1986. 'Ethnic Interaction, Economic Diversification and Language Use'. *SUGIA, Sprache und Geschichte in Afrika*, 7/2: 189-226.

—— 1987. 'Chords of Tradition, Lens of Analogy: Iconic Signs in Okiek Ceremonies'. *Journal of Ritual Studies*, 1: 75-97.

—— 1988a. 'Okiek Ornaments of Transition and Transformation'. *Kenya Past and Present*, 20: 21-26.

—— 1988b. 'Emotional Power and Significant Movement: Womanly Transformation through Okiek Initiation'. Ph.D. thesis, Texas.

—— 1990a. 'Persuasive Suggestions and Reassuring Promises: Emergent Parallelism and Dialogic Encouragement in Song'. *Journal of American Folklore*, 103: 42-67.

—— 1990b. 'Sexual Solidarity and the Secrets of Sight and Sound: Shifting Gender Relations and their Ceremonial Constitution'. *American Ethnologist*, 17: 31-51.

Bibliography

—— In press a. 'Amusement and Absolution: Transforming Narratives During Confession of Social Debts'. *American Anthropologist.*

—— In press b. ' "We've Always Done it Like This . . . Except for a Few Details": "Tradition" and "Innovation" in Okiek Ceremonies'. *Comparative Studies in Society and History.*

Kroeber, A.L. 1957. *Style and Civilizations.* Ithaca, Cornell University Press.

Labov, William. 1973. *Sociolinguistic Patterns.* Philadelphia, Pennsylvania University Press.

Lamphear, John. 1976. *The Traditional History of the Jie of Uganda.* Oxford, Clarendon.

—— 1983. 'Some Thoughts on the Interpretation of Oral Traditions Among the Central Paranilotes' in Vossen, R. and Beckhaus-Gerst, M. (eds), *Nilotic Studies,* Pt. I, Berlin.

—— 1986. 'The Persistence of Hunting and Gathering in a "Pastoral World" '. *SUGIA, Sprache und Geschichte in Afrika,* 7/2: 227–265.

—— 1988. 'The People of the Grey Bull: The Origin and Expansion of the Turkana'. *Journal of African History,* 29: 27–39.

—— 1989a. 'Historical Dimensions of Dual Organization: The Generation–Class System of the Jie and the Turkana' in Maybury-Lewis, D. and Almagor, U. (eds), *The Attraction of Opposites: Thought and Society in the Dualistic Mode*: 235–254. Ann Arbor, Michigan University Press.

—— 1989b. 'The Rise and Fall of the Turkana *Ngimurok*'. Unpublished paper, London, Conference on Seers, Prophets and Diviners.

—— 1991. *The Scattering Time: Turkana Responses to the Imposition of Colonial Rule.* Oxford, Oxford University Press.

Lamprey, R. and Waller, R.D. 1990. 'The Loita-Mara Region in Historical Times: Patterns of Subsistence, Settlement and Ecological Change' in Robertshaw, P. (ed.), *Early Pastoralists of South-western Kenya*: 16–35. Nairobi, British Institute in Eastern Africa.

Langlin, T. 1980. 'Environment, Political Culture and National Orientations: A Comparison of Settled and Pastoral Masai' in Paden, J.N. (ed.), *Values, Identities and National Integration*: 91–103. Evanston, Northwestern University Press.

Larick, R. 1986. 'Iron Smelting and Interethnic Conflict among Precolonial Maa-speaking Pastoralists of North-Central Kenya'. *African Archaeological Review,* 4: 165–176.

Lawren, William L. 1968. 'Maasai and Kikuyu: An Historical Analysis of Cultural Transmission'. *Journal of African History,* 4: 571–583.

Leach, Edmund. 1954. *Political Systems of Highland Burma.* London, G. Bell.

—— 1989. 'Tribal Ethnography: Past, Present, Future' in Tonkin, E. *et al.* (eds), *History and Ethnicity.* ASA monograph. London, Routledge.

Lemenye, Justin. 1953. *Maisha ya Sameni ole Kivasis yaani Justin Lemenye.* Nairobi, Eagle Press.

—— (Trans. H.A. Fosbrooke). 1955–56. 'The Life of Justin: An African Autobiography'. *Tanganyika Notes and Records,* 41: 30–56, 42: 19–29.

LeRoy, Alexandre. 1893. *Au Kilima Ndjaro.* Paris, Savard and Derangeon.

Levine, Robert A. and Sangree, Walter H. 1962. 'The Diffusion of Age-Group Organization in East Africa'. *Africa,* 32: 97–110.

Leys, N. 1924. *Kenya.* London, Hogarth.

Lienhardt, Godfrey. 1961. *Divinity and Experience.* Oxford, Oxford University Press.

Little, Peter D. 1985. 'Social Differentiation and Pastoralist Sedentarization in Northern Kenya'. *Africa,* 55: 243–261.

—— 1987. 'Woman as Ol Payian (Elder): The Status of Women among the Il Chamus (Njemps) of Kenya'. *Ethnos,* 52: 81–102.

—— 1992. *The Elusive Granary: Herder, Farmer, and State in Northern Kenya.* Cambridge, Cambridge University Press.

Llewelyn-Davies, M. 1979. 'Two Contexts of Solidarity among Pastoral Maasai' in Caplan, P. and Bujra, J.M. (eds), *Women United, Women Divided*: 206–237. Bloomington, Indiana University Press.

—— 1981. 'Women, Warriors and Patriarchs' in Ortner, S. and Whitehead, H. (eds), *Sexual Meanings*: 330–358. Cambridge, Cambridge University Press.

Bibliography

Lonsdale, John. 1977. 'When Did the Gusii (or any other group) Become a "Tribe"?' *Kenya Historical Review*, 5: 123–133.

—— 1986. 'Political Accountability in African History' in Chabal, P. (ed.), *Political Domination in Africa*. Cambridge, Cambridge University Press.

Lovejoy , P. and Baier, S. 1975. 'The Desert-Side Economy of the Central Sudan'. *International Journal of African Historical Studies*, 8.

Low, D.A. 1963. 'The Northern Interior, 1840–1844' in Oliver, R. and Mathew, G. (eds), *History of East Africa*, vol. 1. London, Oxford University Press.

—— 1965. 'British East Africa: The Establishment of British Rule, 1895–1912' in Harlow, V. and Chilver, E.M. (eds), *History of East Africa*, Vol. 2: 1–56. Oxford, Clarendon.

Luanda, N.N. 1986. 'European Commercial Farming and its Impact on the Meru and Arusha Peoples of Tanzania, 1920–1955'. Ph.D. thesis, Cambridge.

Mack, John. 1982. 'Material Culture and Ethnic Identity in the Southeastern Sudan' in Mack, J. and Robertshaw, P. (eds), *Culture History in the Southern Sudan*: 111–130. Nairobi, British Institute in Eastern Africa.

Mafeje, A. 1971. 'The Ideology of Tribalism'. *Journal of Modern African Studies*, 9: 253–261.

Marris, Peter and Somerset, Anthony. 1971. *African Businessmen*. London, EA Publishing House.

Marshall, Fiona B. 1986. 'Aspects of the Advent of Pastoral Economies in East Africa'. Ph.D. thesis, Berkeley.

—— 1990. 'Cattle Herds and Caprine Flocks' in Robertshaw, P. (ed.), *Early Pastoralists of South-western Kenya*: 205–260. Nairobi, British Institute in Eastern Africa.

Meadows, S.J. and White, J.M. 1979. 'Structure of the Herd and Determinants of Offtake Rates in Kajiado District in Kenya, 1962–1977'. ODI Pastoral Network Paper 7d.

Merker, M. 1910. *Die Masai*. Berlin, D. Reimer.

Mol, F. 1978. *Maa: A Dictionary of the Maasai Language and Folklore (English–Maasai)*. Nairobi, Marketing and Publishing.

Mpaayei, J.T. 1954. *Inkuti Pukunot oolMaasai*. Oxford University Press.

Muller, Harold K. 1989. *Changing Generations: Dynamics of Generation and Age-Sets in Southeastern Sudan (Toposa) and Northwestern Kenya (Turkana)*. Saarbrucken, Verlag Breitenbach.

Murdock, George P. 1959. *Africa: Its Peoples and their Culture History*. New York, McGraw-Hill.

Muriuki, G. 1971. 'Chronology of the Kikuyu'. *Hadith 3*: 16–27.

—— 1976. *A History of the Kikuyu, 1500–1900*. Nairobi, Oxford University Press.

New, Charles. 1873. *Life, Wanderings and Labours in Eastern Africa*. London, Hodder and Stoughton.

Nimmo, J.R. 1948. 'Handing Over Notes, Lokitaung'. Unpublished paper, Kenya National Archives.

Norton-Griffiths, M. 1977. 'Aspects of Climate in Kajaido District'. Project Working Document 13, UNDP/FAO Kenya Wildlife Management Project, Nairobi.

Ochieng, W.R. 1975. *An Outline History of the Rift Valley of Kenya up to AD 1900*. Nairobi, East African Literature Bureau.

Ogot, B.A. 1967. *History of the Southern Luo*. Nairobi, East African Publishing House.

—— 1968. 'The Role of the Pastoralist and the Agriculturalist in African History: The Case of East Africa' in Ranger, T.O. (ed.), *Emerging Themes of African History*: 125–133. Nairobi, East African Publishing House.

Ogot, B.A. and Kieran, J.A. (eds). 1968. *Zamani*. Nairobi, East African Publishing House.

Olang, M. 1982. 'Organizations and Procedures in Group Ranch Development in Kenya'. ODI Pastoral Network Paper 13c.

O'Leary, M.F. 1990. 'Drought and Change amongst Northern Kenya Nomadic Pastoralists: The Case of the Rendille and Gabra' in Palsson, G. (ed.), *From Water to World-Making*: 151–174. Uppsala, Scandinavian Institute of African Studies.

Ole Pasha, I. 1986. 'Evolution of Individuation of Group Ranches in Maasailand'. Unpublished paper, Workshop on Range Development and Research in Kenya.

Bibliography

Oliver, R. 1983. 'The Nilotic Contribution to Bantu Africa' in Vossen, R. and Bechaus-Gerst, M. (eds), *Nilotic Studies*, Vol. 2: 357-374. Berlin, D. Reimer.

Organization of African Unity. 1973. *The Distribution of Tsetse Flies in Africa, 1973*. Nairobi, Interafrican Bureau of Animal Resources.

Peel, J. 1989. 'The Cultural Work of Yoruba Ethnogenesis' in Tonkin, E., *et al.* (eds), *History and Ethnicity*. (ASA monograph). London, Routledge.

Peirce, C.S. (C. Hartshorne and P. Weiss, eds). 1931-1958. *Collected Papers*. Cambridge, Harvard University Press.

Phillipson, D.W. 1977. *The Later Prehistory of Eastern and Southern Africa*. New York, Africana.

Pratt, D.J. and Gwyne, M.D. 1977. *Rangeland Management and Ecology in East Africa*. London, Hodder and Stoughton.

Rebmann, J. 1849-50. 'Narrative of a Journey to Madjame in Jagga'. *Church Missionary Intelligencer*, 1: 272-6, 302-12.

Rennie, A.K. 1984. 'Ideology and State Formation: Political and Commercial Ideologies among the South-Eastern Shona' in Salim, A.I. (ed.), *State Formation in Eastern Africa*: 162-194. Nairobi, Heinemann.

Rigby, Peter. 1985. *Persistent Pastoralists*. London, Zed.

—— 1987. 'Class Formation among East African Pastoralists: Maasai of Tanzania and Kenya' in Gailey, C. and Patterson, T. (eds), *Power Relations and State Formation*. Washington, American Anthropological Association.

Robertshaw, Peter 1986. 'Engaruka Revisited: The Excavations of 1982'. *Azania*, 21.

—— 1989. 'The Development of Pastoralism in East Africa' in Clutton-Brock, J. (ed.), *The Walking Larder*: 207-214. London, Unwin and Hyman.

—— (ed.). 1990. *Early Pastoralists of South-western Kenya*. Nairobi, British Institute in Eastern Africa.

Robertshaw, Peter and Collett, David. 1983a. 'A New Framework for the Study of Early Pastoral Communities in East Africa'. *Journal of African History*, 24: 289-301.

—— 1983b. 'The Identification of Pastoral Peoples in the Archaeological Record'. *World Archaeology*, 15: 67-78.

Robinson, Paul W. 1985. 'Gabbra Nomadic Pastoralism in Nineteenth and Twentieth-Century Northern Kenya: Strategies for Survival in a Marginal Environment.' Ph.D. thesis, Northwestern.

Roe, Peter. 1980. 'Art and Residence among the Shipibo Indians of Peru: A Study in Microacculturation'. *American Anthropologist*, 82: 42-71.

Rosen, D.M. 1968. 'Preliminary Report of Research among the Mukogodo, Laikipiak District'. Unpublished paper, Institute for Development Studies, Nairobi.

Roth, E.A. 1990. 'Modelling Household Decision-Making: Livestock Marketing in Kenya'. *Human Ecology*, 18/4: 385-402.

—— 1991. 'Education, Tradition and Household Labor among Rendille Pastoralists of Northern Kenya'. *Human Organization*, 50: 136-141.

Sahlins, Marshall. 1961. 'The Segmentary Lineage: An Organization of Predatory Expansion'. *American Anthropologist*, 63: 322-345.

—— 1981. *Historical Metaphors and Mythical Realities*. Ann Arbor, Michigan University Press.

—— 1985. *Islands of History*. Chicago, Chicago University Press.

Said, Edward. 1979. *Orientalism*. New York, Vintage.

Saitoti, T. 1986. *The Worlds of a Maasai Warrior*. Berkeley, California University Press.

Sakata, Hiromi. 1987. 'Hazara Women in Afghanistan: Innovators and Preservers of a Musical Tradition' in Koskoff, E. (ed.), *Women and Music in Cross-Cultural Perspective*. New York, Greenwood.

Sandford, G.R. 1919. *An Administrative and Political History of the Masai Reserve*. London, Waterlow.

Sankan, S.S. 1971. *The Maasai*. Nairobi, East African Literature Bureau.

—— 1979. *Intepen e Maasai*. Nairobi, Kenya Literature Bureau.

Sassoon, H. 1966. 'Engaruka: Excavations during 1964'. *Azania*, 1: 79-99.

Bibliography

Schlee, Gunther. 1985. 'Interethnic Clan Identities among Cushitic-Speaking Pastoralists'. *Africa*, 55: 17–38.
—— 1989. *Identities on the Move*. Manchester, Manchester University Press.
Sherzer, Joel and Sherzer, Dina. 1976. 'Mormaknamaloe: The Cuna Mola' in Young, P. and Howe, J. (eds), *Ritual and Symbol in Native Central America*: 23–42. Eugene, Oregon Anthropological Papers.
Sieber, Roy. 1973. 'Approaches to Non-Western Art' in d'Azevedo, W. (ed.), *The Traditional Artist in African Societies*: 425–434. Bloomington, Indiana University Press.
Sindiga, I. 1986. 'Population and Development in Maasailand, Kenya'. Ph.D. thesis, Syracuse.
Smith, A. Donaldson. 1897. *Through Unknown African Countries*. London, Edward Arnold.
Sobania, Neal. 1979. *A Background History to the Mount Kulal Region of Northern Kenya*. Nairobi, UNESCO.
—— 1980. 'The Historical Tradition of the Peoples of the Eastern Lake Turkana Basin, c. 1840–1925'. Ph.D. thesis, London (SOAS).
—— 1988a. 'Fishermen Herders: Subsistence, Survival and Cultural Change in Northern Kenya'. *Journal of African History*, 29: 41–56.
—— 1988b. 'Pastoralist Migration and Colonial Policy: A Case Study from Northern Kenya' in Johnson, D. and Anderson, D. (eds), *The Ecology of Survival*: 219–239. Boulder, Westview.
—— 1991. 'Feasts, Famines and Friends: Nineteenth-Century Exchange and Ethnicity in the Eastern Lake Turkana Regional System' in Bonte, P. and Galaty, J. (eds), *Herders, Warriors, and Traders*. Boulder, Westview
—— In press. *Man, Millet and Milk: Shifting Ethnicity in Pre-Colonial Kenya*.
Sobania, Neal and Waller, Richard. n.d. 'Oral History and the End of Time', unpublished paper.
Spear, Thomas. 1978. *The Kaya Complex*. Nairobi, Kenya Literature Bureau.
—— 1981. *Kenya's Past*. London, Longman.
—— 1989. 'The Ideology of Production and the Production of Ideology: The Arusha and Meru Peoples of Northeastern Tanzania'. Unpublished paper, Walter Rodney Seminar, Boston University.
Spear, Thomas and Nurse, Derek. 1985. *The Swahili*. Philadelphia, Pennsylvania University Press.
—— In press. 'Maasai Farmers: The Evolution of Arusha Agriculture'. *International Journal of African Historical Studies*.
Spencer, Paul. 1965. *The Samburu*. London, Routledge and Kegan Paul.
—— 1973. *Nomads in Alliance*. London, Oxford University Press.
—— 1976. 'Opposing Streams and the Gerontocratic Ladder: Two Models of Age Organization in East Africa'. *Man*, 11: 153–175.
—— 1978. 'The Jie Generation Paradox' in Baxter, P.T.W. and Almagor, U. (eds), *Age, Generation and Time*: 131–149. London, Christopher Hurst.
—— 1984. 'Pastoralists and the Ghost of Capitalism'. *Production Pastorale et Société*, 15: 61–76.
—— 1988. *The Maasai of Matapato: A Study of Rituals of Rebellion*. Manchester, Manchester University Press.
—— 1989. 'The Maasai Double-Helix and the Theory of Dilemmas' in Maybury-Lewis, D. & Almagor, U. (eds), *The Attraction of Opposites*: 297–320. Ann Arbor, Michigan University Press.
—— 1992. 'Automythology and the Reconstruction of Aging' in Okely, J. and Callaway, H. (eds), *Anthropology and Autobiography*. ASA monograph 29. London, Routledge.
—— n.d. 'Models of the Maasai', draft ms.
Sperling, L. 1987a. 'Wage Employment among Samburu Pastoralists of North Central Kenya'. *Research in Economic Anthropology*, 9: 167–190.
—— 1987b. 'Food Acquisition during the African Drought of 1983–84: A Study of Kenyan Herders'. *Disasters*, 11: 263–272.
Stigand, C.H. 1910. *To Abyssinia Through an Unknown Land*. London, J.B. Lippincott.

Bibliography

—— 1913. *The Land of Zinj*. London, Constable.

Strathern, Marilyn. 1981. 'Culture in a Net Bag: The Manufacture of a Subdiscipline in Anthropology'. *Man*, 16: 665–688.

Sutton, J.E.G. 1970 (reprinted 1975). 'Some Reflections on the Early History of Western Kenya' in Ogot, B.A. (ed.), *Hadith 2*: 17–29. Nairobi, East African Publishing House.

—— 1973. *Archaeology of the Western Highlands of Kenya*. Nairobi, British Institute in Eastern Africa.

—— 1976. 'The Kalenjin' in Ogot, B.A. (ed.), *Kenya Before 1900*. Nairobi, East African Publishing House.

—— 1978. 'Engaruka and its Waters'. *Azania*, 13: 37–70.

—— 1984. 'Irrigation and Soil Conservation in African Economic History'. *Journal of African History*, 25: 25–41.

—— 1986. 'The Irrigation and Manuring of the Engaruka Field System'. *Azania*, 21: 27–51.

—— 1987. 'Hyrax Hill and the Sirikwa'. *Azania*, 22: 1–36.

—— 1989. 'Towards a History of Cultivating the Fields'. *Azania*, 24: 98–112.

—— 1990. *A Thousand Years of East Africa*. Nairobi, British Institute in Eastern Africa.

Talle, Aud. 1988. *Women at a Loss: Changes in Maasai Pastoralism and their Effects on Gender Relations*. Stockholm, Studies in Social Anthropology.

Thomson, Joseph. 1885; reprinted 1968. *Through Masailand*. London, Sampson Low, Marston, Searle and Rivington.

Throup, David W. 1987. *Economic and Social Origins of Mau Mau*. London, James Currey.

Tidrick, K. 1980. 'The Masai and their Masters: A Psychological Study of District Administration'. *African Studies Review*, 23: 15–31.

Tignor, R.L. 1972. 'The Maasai Warriors: Pattern Maintenance and Violence in Colonial Kenya'. *Journal of African History*, 12: 271–290.

Tomikawa, Morimichi. 1979. 'The Migrations and Inter-Tribal Relations of the Pastoral Datoga' in Fukui, K. and Turton, D. (eds), *Warfare among East African Herders*: 15–31. Osaka, National Museum of Ethnology.

Tonkin, E., McDonald, M., and Chapman, M. (eds). 1989. *History and Ethnicity*. (ASA monograph). London, Routledge.

Tornay, Serge. 1980. 'Generational Age-Systems and Chronology'. Unpublished paper, Seminar on the Archaeology and Ethnohistory of the Southern Sudan and Adjacent Areas, London.

Turpin, C.A. 1948. 'The Occupation of the Turkwel River Area by the Karamojong Tribe'. *Uganda Journal*, 12.

Turton, David. 1979a. 'War, Peace and Mursi Identity' in Fukui, K. and Turton, D. (eds), *Warfare Among East African Herders*: 179–210. Osaka, National Museum of Ethnology.

—— 1979b. 'A Journey Made Them: Territorial Segmentation and Ethnic Identity among the Mursi' in Holy, L. (ed.), *Segmentary Lineage Systems Reconsidered*: 119–143. Belfast, Department of Social Anthropology.

—— 1991. 'Movement, Warfare and Ethnicity in the Lower Omo Valley' in Bonte, P. and Galaty, J. (eds), *Warriors, Herders, and Traders*: 145–169. Boulder, Westview.

Vail, LeRoy. 1981. 'The Making of the "Dead North": A Study of Ngoni Rule in Northern Malawi, 1855–1907' in Peires, J. (ed.), *Before and After Shaka*. Grahamstown, Rhodes University, Institute of Social and Economic Research.

—— (ed.) 1989. *The Creation of Tribalism in Southern Africa*. London, James Currey.

Vossen, Rainer. 1977. 'Eine wortgeographische Untersuchung zür Territorialgeschichte der Maa-sprechenden Bevölkerung Ostafrikas'. M.A. thesis, Köln.

—— 1978. 'Linguistic Evidence Regarding the Territorial History of the Maa-Speaking Peoples: Some Preliminary Remarks'. *Kenya Historical Review*, 6: 34–52.

—— 1980. 'Grundzüge der Territorialgeschichte der Maa-sprechenden Bevölkerung Ostafrikas'. *Paideuma*, 26: 93–121.

—— 1981. 'The Classification of Eastern Nilotic and its significance for Ethnohistory' in Schadeberg, Th.C. and Bender, M.L. (eds), *Nilo-Saharan*: 41–57. Dordrecht, Foris.

—— 1982. *The Eastern Nilotes: Linguistic and Historical Reconstructions*. Berlin, D. Reimer.

Bibliography

—— 1983. 'Comparative Eastern Nilotic' in Bender, M.L. (ed.), *Nilo-Saharan Language Studies*: 177–207. East Lansing, Michigan State University Press.

—— 1988. *Towards a Comparative Study of the Maa Dialects of Kenya and Tanzania*. Hamburg, Buske.

Vossen, R. and Heine, B. 1989. 'The Historical Reconstruction of Proto-Ongamo-Maa: Phonology and Vocabulary' in Bender, M.L. (ed.), *Topics in Nilo-Saharan Languages*: 181–217. Hamburg, Buske.

Wakefield, T., 1870. 'Routes of Native Caravans from the Coast to the Interior of East Africa'. *Journal of the Royal Geographical Society*, 40: 303–338.

Waller, Richard. 1975. 'Uneconomic Growth: The Maasai Stock Economy, 1919–1929'. Unpublished paper.

—— 1976. 'The Maasai and the British, 1895–1905: The Origins of an Alliance'. *Journal of African History*, 17: 529–553.

—— 1979. 'The Lords of East Africa: The Maasai in the mid-Nineteenth Century, c. 1840–1885'. Ph.D. thesis, Cambridge.

—— 1984. 'Interaction and Identity on the Periphery: The Trans-Mara Maasai'. *International Journal of African Historical Studies*, 17, 2: 243–284.

—— 1985a. 'Ecology, Migration, and Expansion in East Africa'. *African Affairs*, 84: 347–370.

—— 1985b. 'Economic and Social Relations in the Central Rift Valley: The Maa-Speakers and their Neighbours in the Nineteenth Century' in Ogot, B.A. (ed.), *Kenya in the Nineteenth Century* 83–151. Nairobi, Bookwise.

—— 1986. 'Research on Maasai History'. Unpublished ESRC Report.

—— 1988. '*Emutai*: Crisis and Response in Maasailand, 1883–1902' in Johnson, D. and Anderson, D.M. (eds), *Ecology of Survival*: 73–113. Boulder, Westview.

—— 1990. 'Tsetse Fly in Western Narok, Kenya'. *Journal of African History*, 31: 81–101.

Walter, B. 1970. *Territorial Expansion of the Nandi of Kenya, 1500–1905*. Athens, Ohio University Center for International Studies.

Weatherby, John M. 1967. 'Nineteenth-Century Wars in Western Kenya'. *Azania*, 2: 133–144.

Webster, J.B. *et al.* 1973. *The Iteso During the Asonya*. Nairobi, East African Publishing House.

Weiner, Annette. 1976. *Women of Value, Men of Renown*. Austin, Texas.

Western, D. 1982. 'Amboseli National Park: Enlisting Landowners to Conserve Migratory Wildlife'. *Ambio*, 11: 302–308.

—— 1983. *A Wildlife Guide and a Natural History of Amboseli*. Nairobi, General Printers.

Western, D. and Dunne, T. 1979. 'Environmental Aspects of Settlement Site Decisions among Pastoral Maasai'. *Human Ecology*, 7: 75–98.

Western, D. and Thresher, P. 1973. 'Development Plans for Amboseli: Mainly the Wildlife Viewing Activity in the Ecosystem'. Unpublished paper.

Wiessner, Polly. 1984. 'Reconsidering the Behavioural Basis for Style: A Case Study among the Kalahari San'. *Journal of Anthropological Archaeology*, 3: 190–234.

Willoughby, J.C. 1889. *East Africa and its Big Game*. London, Longmans, Green.

Wilmsen, E. 1989. *Land Filled with Flies*. Chicago, Chicago University Press.

Wilson, G.McL. 1952. 'The Tatoga of Tanganyika'. *Tanganyika Notes and Records*, 33.

Wilson, J.G. c. 1969. 'Preliminary Observations on the Oropom People of Karamoja'. Unpublished typescript, Moroto.

Winter, C. 1977. 'Maasai Shield Patterns: A Documentary Source for Political History' in Mohlig, W., Rottland, F. and Heine, B. (eds), *Zür Sprachgeschichte und Ethnohistorie in Ostafrika*: 324–347. Berlin, D. Reimer.

Zwanenberg, Roger van. 1976. 'Dorobo Hunting and Gathering: A Way of Life or a Mode of Production?' *African Economic History*, 2: 12–24.

Zwanenberg, Roger van, with King, Anne. 1975. *An Economic History of Kenya and Uganda, 1800–1970*. Nairobi, East African Literature Bureau.

Index

Index

Index

Index